Western Economies in Transition:

Structural Change and Adjustment Policies in Industrial Countries

Also of Interest

World Economic Development: 1979 and Beyond, Herman Kahn

Hudson Institute Studies on the Prospects for Mankind

Western Economies in Transition: Structural Change and Adjustment Policies in Industrial Countries
edited by Irving Leveson and Jimmy W. Wheeler

The major economic changes that have occurred in the United States, Europe, and Japan during the past decade have created strong pressures for governments to devise viable policy responses. Contributors to this book examine these changes—shifts in demand, patterns of competition, technology, raw material and energy prices, and productivity, to name only a few—and consider the reasons for them, solutions to the problems they generate, and prospects for the future. The book grew out of a conference, "Outlook and Policy for Industrial Structure Change in OECD Countries," organized by Hudson Institute for the U.S. Departments of State, Commerce, and Labor in January 1979.

Irving Leveson is director of economic studies at Hudson Institute. Prior to joining Hudson in 1974, Dr. Leveson worked with the National Bureau of Economic Research, the Rand Corporation, and the New York City Department of City Planning. Jimmy W. Wheeler, an economist at Hudson Institute, previously was assistant professor of economics at Florida International University and also taught at Rutgers University and the University of Missouri.

Western Economies in Transition:

Structural Change and Adjustment Policies in Industrial Countries

edited by Irving Leveson
and Jimmy W. Wheeler

with the editorial assistance
of Ernest Schneider

Westview Press • Boulder, Colorado

Croom Helm • London, England

Hudson Institute Studies on the Prospects for Mankind

This book is based on papers and proceedings of "Outlook and Policy for Industrial Structural Change in OECD Countries," a conference conducted by the Hudson Institute, January 25-26, 1979. The project was funded by the Departments of State, Commerce, and Labor under Contract No. 1722-820109. Views and conclusions contained in this study should not be interpreted as representing the official opinion or policy of the U.S. government.

Published in 1980 in the United States of America by
Westview Press, Inc.
5500 Central Avenue
Boulder, Colorado 80301
Frederick A. Praeger, Publisher

Published in 1980 in Great Britain by
Croom Helm Ltd.
2-10 St John's Road
London SW 11

Library of Congress Catalog Card No.: 79-16548
ISBN (U.S.): 0-89158-589-3
ISBN (U.K.): 0-7099-0213-1

Printed and bound in the United States of America

Contents

Preface

This project is one of a number done by academic and other research institutions for the Department of State, as part of its external research program. This particular project was also supported by the Departments of Commerce and Labor. External research projects are designed to supplement the research capabilities of State and provide independent expert views to policy officers and analysts on key questions with important policy implications.

The idea for this study, to determine the outlook for the industrial structures of the OECD countries in the face of slower economic growth, shifts from industrial to service-oriented economies, and increasing LDC output, was proposed by the State Department's Bureau of European Affairs. The work statement for the project was developed by a department working group chaired by Warren H. Reynolds of this office on the basis of a draft prepared by Stanley Black, former special assistant to Richard N. Cooper, undersecretary of state for economic affairs. This working group, subsequently expanded to include representatives from the Departments of Commerce, Labor, and Treasury and the Agency for International Development, undertook the overall monitoring of the project.

The Office of External Research plans and manages this program for drawing on the independent expertise of the private research community. Queries about the program or comments on this study may be addressed to:

E. Raymond Platig
Director, Office of External Research
Bureau of Intelligence and Research
Department of State
Washington, D.C. 20520

Irving Leveson
Jimmy W. Wheeler

Acknowledgments

The editors wish to express their thanks to the authors and discussants for an outstanding job of dealing with difficult material under tight constraints, and to thank the interagency working group for its guidance and the Departments of State, Commerce, and Labor for funding the effort. The authors wish especially to thank Warren H. Reynolds of the State Department's Office of External Research, who monitored the project. The project benefited from excellent contributions from many people: Ernest Schneider helped to extract insights from the discussion and in general editing of the book. Maryellen Pitcairn assisted in numerous ways in filling in gaps and trouble-shooting. Kathryn Finch produced the charts, Annie Small provided administrative and secretarial assistance, Stephanie Tyler prepared most of the tables, and Dorothy Worfolk did the principal typing of the manuscript. To all of these we are grateful. Throughout this effort it has been a pleasure to work with the staff of Westview Press: Lynne Rienner, Miriam Gilbert, Lynn Lloyd, and Brad Kava.

I. L.
J.W.W.

Contributors

Irving Leveson: director of economic studies, Hudson Institute.
Jimmy W. Wheeler: economist, Hudson Institute.

Robert E. Baldwin: professor of economics, University of Wisconsin, Madison.
Edward M. Bernstein: president, EMB (Ltd.) Research Economists.
James H. Cassing: assistant professor of economics and member of the graduate faculty, University of Pittsburgh.
Sidney Golt: consultant; advisor on trade policy, International Chamber of Commerce (formerly deputy secretary, Department of Trade and Industry, United Kingdom).
H. Peter Gray: professor of economics, Douglass College, Rutgers University.
Robert G. Hawkins: professor of economics and chairman, International Business Department, Graduate School of Business Administration, New York University.
Robert D. Hormats: senior deputy assistant secretary of state for economic and business affairs.
Anne O. Krueger: professor of economics, University of Minnesota, and senior research associate, National Bureau of Economic Research.
Maurice Lengellé: principal administrator, Directorate for Agriculture and Food, Organization for Economic Co-operation and Development.
Angus Maddison: professor of economic sociology, University of Gronigen, Netherlands.
Selma Mushkin: director, Public Services Laboratory, Georgetown University.
M. Ishaq Nadiri: professor of economics, New York University, and research associate, National Bureau of Economic Research.

Larry D. Neal: professor of economics, and director, Center for West European Studies, University of Illinois.

Richard R. Nelson: professor of economics, Yale University.

Kazuo Nukazawa: deputy director, Economic Cooperation Department, Keidanren (Federation of Economic Organizations), Tokyo, Japan.

Emilio Pagoulatos: associate professor, Food and Resource Economics Department, University of Florida.

Victoria Curzon Price: associate professor, Graduate Institute of European Studies, and faculty member, Centre for Education in International Management, University of Geneva, Switzerland.

Thomas A. Pugel: assistant professor of economics and international business, Graduate School of Business Administration, New York University.

Julian L. Simon: professor of economics and marketing, University of Illinois.

Robert Sorensen: associate professor of economics, University of Missouri–St. Louis.

Paul A. Wachtel: associate professor, Graduate School of Business Administration, New York University.

J. Fred Weston: professor of business economics and finance, Graduate School of Management, University of California–Los Angeles.

Part 1
Overview and Context

1

The Policy Context

Robert D. Hormats

There could not be a better time to discuss structural change in the OECD countries.

We can look back with some satisfaction at economic developments in the OECD countries since the Bonn Economic Summit in July 1978. The United States fulfilled its Summit commitment to implement an antiinflation program and energy programs to reduce oil imports below what they otherwise would have been. Germany fulfilled its commitment to take stimulative measures of up to one percent of gross national product (GNP) and, as a result, could achieve 4 percent growth during 1979. Overall, we expect that, due to the convergence of growth rates in the industrial countries and the effects of exchange rate changes, the pattern of current account balances should be more sustainable in the near future. We expect that the U.S. current account deficit will be reduced by one-half or more in 1979 and that we will also see reductions in the persistent surpluses of Germany and Japan. This should contribute to a lessening of the volatility in foreign exchange markets that we witnessed prior to November 1, 1978.

Behind the talk of growth rates and current account balances, there is a sense that the OECD countries face some profound economic challenges. Fundamental structural changes in our economies will be necessary if many of the OECD economies are to continue stable internal growth and to engage in productive economic exchange with the more dynamic economies such as Japan and the rapidly industrializing developing countries.

But there is stubborn resistance to needed structural changes. In many developed countries growth is not vigorous enough to increase employment significantly. In some countries antiinflation measures have led to growing unemployment. In such circumstances adjustment to new employment patterns becomes more difficult because new jobs are not created rapidly enough to absorb unemployed workers. Workers

3

in declining industries strongly resist adjustment, preferring to hang on to the job they have rather than take their chances on being picked up by an expanding industry. In this way, cyclical problems contribute to structural difficulties.

Having achieved a certain measure of prosperity in the 1970s, our citizens now have a stronger desire to preserve what they have. They are less willing to take risks; less willing to accept the burden of adjustment even to those changes which would increase general economic welfare in the long run. This aversion to risk is often reinforced by those unions which draw their membership from a narrow field. Unions in the OECD countries that cover a wide variety of activities tend to be less rigid in protecting jobs in particular sectors.

Finally the pace of change, in terms of patterns of trade among countries, patterns of production within countries, and the introduction, of new technology, has increased rapidly in recent years. The needed social and economic adjustments are not keeping up.

The bulk of economic dislocation results from productivity improvements, competition, and industrial consolidation within our countries. We live with these changes because we understand that they lead to growth, improved consumer welfare, and lower rates of inflation. It is somehow harder to reconcile ourselves to the more visible dislocations caused by foreign competition even though the beneficial effects are the same.

Looking over the agenda for this conference, I can see that various dimensions of the structural problems bedeviling the OECD economies will be covered. Three persistent structural problems deserve the most attention: inflation, which in 1978 averaged about 7 percent for OECD countries; unemployment, particularly among youth and minority groups, which continues to remain very high by historical standards; and private investment, which is sluggish in most countries. These problems are, of course, interrelated: low investment leads to a low growth rate in output and in productive capacity, with the consequence that unemployment and inflation will be higher than otherwise would be the case. With greater international equilibrium likely in 1979, we have the opportunity to devote more attention to these important structural problems.

The seemingly intractable problem of inflation has emerged in this country and in many countries of Western Europe as the dominant economic issue. The standard prescription, and often the right prescription, is tighter monetary and fiscal policy. But too often we ignore many of the causes of inflation which are built into our economies through legislation and regulation—through specific decisions in such areas as environmental protection, health and safety regulations, minimum wages, agricultural policy, and import restrictions. There are, from time to time, entirely appropriate reasons to take actions which also have the effect of contributing to inflation. But too often the inflationary impact of individual measures is not given sufficient weight compared to the possible benefits which might be attained. And too often rigidities caused by past actions have become embedded in our systems, and those who have a vested interest in them prevent their removal. There is no question that failure to allow needed structural change, for example, by protecting a dying industry, is an important cause of inflation.

But inflation is not only a result of resistance to structural change; it is also a cause of that resistance. The persistant inflation of recent years has undoubtedly had a depressing effect on capital investment. By postwar standards, the recovery of investment in the United States since the trough of the recession in 1975 has been weak and slow. Furthermore, investment as a percent of GNP is lower in the United States than in any other major advanced industrial country. Many factors have been cited as causes: lack of confidence in the ability of our economy to grow at an adequate rate, uncertainty about the cost and availability of energy, and the effect of burdensome regulations. Real factors such as low capacity utilization rates and low after-tax rates of return on investment are probably just as important as, if not more important, than the psychological factors.

The corollary of lagging investment is lagging productivity. The rate of growth of labor productivity has been sinking since the mid-1960s. One explanation offered is that employment has shifted out of manufacturing to the service industries. Another is that governments have not been sufficiently supportive of research and development (R&D) needed to increase technical progress and thus labor productivity. In the United States, real federal expenditures on research and development have declined since the mid-1960s. Other analysts cite antitrust, patent, and other regulations as creating an unattractive climate for investment in technology. Still others decry what they consider to be excessive U.S. emphasis on defense-related R&D at the expense of the development of new production processes which result directly in higher productivity and competitiveness. These questions are critical to continued U.S. export competitiveness which today rests on a comparative advantage in technology-intensive products. They are also important to the other industrial democracies whose growth has been spurred by U.S. technological advances.

Slow growth is obviously a cause as well as an effect of lagging investment and slowing industrial innovation. Slow growth and resultant excess capacity discourage firms, particularly those which have heavily committed their resources to present production processes, from undertaking the capital costs required to switch to new technologies. This is a major explanation for the failure of many firms to replace the energy-intensive capital stock made obsolete by the sharp increase in oil prices, even though some of this equipment now lies idle. Slow growth also forces many firms and governments to curtail their research and development efforts. We thus have a vicious circle; the absence of capital investment and technological advance ensures that we will continue to have slow growth in the future.

The third critical structural problem which must be addressed is unemployment of low-skilled workers. In this country, these people tend to be young, between the ages of 15 and 24, and they tend to be black or belong to other disadvantaged groups. The unemployment rate for minority teenagers continues to be a frightening number—close to 35 percent as opposed to a rate of 3.5 percent for white adult males. Throughout the OECD area, unemployment rates for the young average three times overall unemployment rates. Behind these cold statistics is a real threat to social cohesion in the industrial democracies as we create a large group of people who feel that they have no stake in the existing society.

We need a fresh look at government regulations to determine whether the benefits of taxes on employment, policies to assure equitable wage levels and fringe benefits, and policies to increase job security outweigh their costs in terms of reduced employment opportunities. We need more creative approaches to the problem of encouraging the unskilled worker to acquire those skills for which there is greater demand. We need to ask whether our educational systems are developing the kind of people who have the skills and adaptability to operate in a modern industrial economy. Labor mobility is a problem in much of Europe but less so in the United States. Our educational system, however, may be weaker in developing the specific skills needed in today's economy.

A particularly troublesome manifestation of the failure of the OECD countries to address adequately the problems of structural change is the persistence of protectionist pressures. We face a serious challenge in the form of a small number of developing countries (Mexico, Brazil, Taiwan, South Korea, Malaysia, Singapore, and the Crown Colony of Hong Kong) which have in this decade been increasing their exports of manufactured goods to the United States and to Europe at annual rates between 30 and 50 percent. The exports have largely been concentrated in certain categories, including textiles, footwear, and consumer electronics, but many of these countries are now moving into capital-intensive sectors such as steel and autos.

Countries in Western Europe are particularly sensitive to this issue. They are uncertain about their ability to compete with the United States in future growth sectors such as computers and aircraft. They already face intensive competition from what they call the "supercompetitive" developing countries in labor-intensive goods and are concerned that these developing countries will exacerbate present overcapacity in traditional capital-intensive industries (including steel, paper, and chemicals). These concerns underlie the strong European position in the Geneva trade negotiations in favor of legitimatizing selective action against imports from certain countries.

The OECD countries can meet this challenge either through appropriate adjustment or by increasing protectionism. Governments have found it hard to resist protectionist measures even in the knowledge that they reduce productivity, increase inflation, and reduce the ability of other countries to buy their exports. While the U.S. record relative to that of other OECD countries is good, we have nevertheless taken some restrictive measures in textiles, electronics, and shoes.

The Bonn Summit participants, nevertheless, came down clearly on the side of adjustment, by endorsing the guidelines on "positive adjustment" drawn up in the OECD. The positive adjustment approach is based, to the extent possible, on market forces to encourage the movement of capital and labor to their most productive uses. In those infrequent cases where protective actions can be justified, the actions are to be temporary, progressively reduced, and linked to plans to phase out obsolete capacity. Emphasis is placed on positive measures such as training and improved labor mobility in order to facilitate adjustment to shifting demands, technological progress, and changing patterns of trade. Adjustment will result in dislocations, which those specific groups affected will understandably resist. Failure to adjust, however, is to waste the opportunities which appropriate adjustment and trade expansion create. The export sector is the most dynamic sector in our economy, and our fastest growing markets include the very countries which are perceived as "supercompetitive." We should look upon the success of these countries as an opportunity rather than as a threat.

The OECD countries must adjust to changes in the world economy or face a continuous decline in their economic strength and ability to exercise global leadership. International cooperation in the management of these problems becomes increasingly important as the health of our domestic economies becomes more and more dependent on the world economy. Economic summits and meetings under the auspices of the OECD, the GATT, and the UN are important opportunities to strengthen this international cooperation.

Adjustment to change requires effective leadership by governments. One of the challenges is *for governments to be candid and persuasive in communicating to their citizens the elements of trade-offs between conflicting social and economic objectives.* Economic growth, increased equity, a cleaner environment, and lower rates of inflation are objectives with which most of us can identify, but these objectives are not automatically compatible. Increased benefits for some groups require sacrifices by others. These sacrifices are less tolerable when the size of the pie is growing slowly or not at all. They can be more tolerable when governments communicate to their constituents the need to set priorities and the long-term consequences of failure to do so.

Another challenge facing OECD governments is to *convince their societies that social and economic policies are fair;* that sacrifices are fairly apportioned and that benefits are going to those who need them the most. Inflation does not apportion sacrifice fairly; neither does protectionism.

A final challenge is for governments to *resist strong temptations to shift sacrifices to other societies through government intervention* at the border or elsewhere. This undermines the essential cooperation between societies needed today to solve our problems.

2
Structural Change and Policy: An Overview of the Papers and Commentary

Irving Leveson
and Jimmy W. Wheeler

Major Policy Perspectives

Industrial countries have always experienced enormous economic changes, but the variations since 1973 have seemed to be especially great. Coming after a long period of relative stability, the nature of those changes and the responses to them appear to be markedly different from the past. The evolution of the world economy and the clustering of serious shocks and economic shifts during the early 1970s have interacted in a very complex fashion. This complexity has dramatically increased the risks inherent in medium and longer term decision making of both a public and private nature. In this environment more than ever, designing policies requires an understanding of the underlying forces, the ways in which they will play themselves out, and the appropriateness of various means of adapting to them. The challenges facing policymakers and the interrelationships of the problems are clearly presented by Robert Hormats in the opening paper.

Of the plethora of large changes underway in the world economy, several are emphasized by conference participants as in some sense overriding:

1. The apparent decline in growth rates of the OECD countries and its proximate causes: investment trends, technical advance, demographic change, etc.;
2. Sectoral and industrial shifts, especially the shift from manufacturing to services; and
3. The changing organization of global production and trade: (a) among OECD countries; (b) in terms of industrial organization and state participation; (c) between OECD countries and less developed countries; and (d) as a result of the evolution of commercial policies, including both tariff and nontariff barriers.

Policy views expressed by participants reflect a variety of perceptions about the seriousness of adjustment problems and the weight to be given to their uneven impact on individuals, population groups, industries, and firms. Beliefs in the ability of market forces to produce socially desirable outcomes in the absence of intervention influenced thinking about policy, but those who urge reliance on market forces do not do so on purely theoretical grounds. Extensive concerns are voiced about the effectiveness of various forms of intervention, contradictory inter-actions, and contravention of market adjustment processes. These concerns are based on empirical studies and significant examples of counterproductive behavior. Discussions therefore range widely, including analyses of the workings of the market economy, assessments of the state of knowledge and of relevant research findings, evaluations of historical forces within and among countries, and experiences with specific policies and actions.

There is frequent recognition of the changing importance of social goals such as the increased desire for job security. Yet with few exceptions, the speakers and discussants express strong doubts about the benefits to be derived from movements toward greater intervention into the natural processes of market adjustment. This does not preclude disagreement about many of the specific elements of the discussion. Among those explicitly presenting strong arguments against increased intervention are Golt, Krueger, Curzon Price, and Pagoulatos and Sorenson. The outstanding exception is Gray who explicitly emphasizes the distribution of income and employment and the alienation of disadvantaged ethnic groups in his judgments about choice of policy direction. Nevertheless, in recommending policy responses, Gray emphasizes subsidies rather than restrictions on imports or expanded social spending.

There is convincing evidence, discussed by Krueger and others, that imports have had far less of an impact on domestic employment in OECD countries than is often alleged. Moreover, serious questions are raised about whether policies should be specifically directed at aiding areas, industries, firms, or individuals affected by imports or whether effects of imports even could be isolated from other sources of change (Krueger, Curzon Price, Golt, Cassing). Many programs now exist which ease hardships associated with economic dislocation regardless of source. Programs independent of the source of the change do not lend themselves as easily to ad hoc special interest uses. They more easily can be prevented from excessively raising costs to the public and reducing incentives to respond to new conditions.

There is a remarkable divergence of views concerning the definition of structural change. Indeed, change often was deemed structural based on some perception of its importance or of the difficulty of adjusting to it. For example, Maddison does not consider the growth of service industries as much a structural change as a long term trend. Similarly, Nukazawa minimizes the problem of adjusting to the growth of textile imports because it had been going on for such a long time. In fact, Maddison emphasizes that *concern* about structural problems is cyclical.

Several attributes of change contributed to its classification as structural:

1. Magnitude,
2. Speed,
3. Effect on the economy's responsiveness to stimuli,
4. Likelihood of automatic reversal, and
5. Predictability.

Although these elements may be used to characterize changes, they do not define structural change. An interesting definition was provided by Bernstein, who considered as structural any changes which could not be dealt with by monetary and fiscal policy.

Views of the importance of structural change differ in ways which can be accounted for only partly by the varying definitions. Nelson, for example, treats the growth of regulation to protect the environment as a policy decision, involving the deliberate choice of slower growth to achieve greater welfare than reflected in gross national product. While he clearly notes that the costs proved to be far higher than most people had expected, the imposition of those costs is not treated as a structural change, as it is in most other discussions.

Economic Growth

Since World War II the global economy has experienced a period of unprecedented growth and economic change. Output grew close to 5 percent per year, while growth in the volume of international trade approached 9 percent per year. Both the industrial and the developing countries participated in this global expansion. This steady growth terminated in 1974 with the most severe international recession since the 1930s. Developing countries as a whole, even excluding OPEC, experienced a smaller growth decline than did the industrial countries. Recovery from this recession has been halting and incomplete in Western Europe and Japan; while in the United States, after an apparent

one time downward shift in productivity, economic growth progressed,
but at a cost of extraordinarily high inflation.

Many factors contributed to the aberrant conditions of the mid-1970s,
and conference participants were concerned about the relative importance of secular (structural) declines in growth rates and temporary
cyclical forces. A relatively broad consensus emerged that for the OECD
countries as a whole, the present economic slowdown represents a
macroeconomic, cyclical problem to a greater degree than it reflects
structural shifts. Yet a number of important structural changes have
modified growth patterns and are expected to continue to do so.
Structural changes were seen as relatively more important in the United
States.

Productivity Growth

In an important sense productivity growth (increase in product per
unit of labor and other resources) is at the heart of improvement in the
human condition. Productivity growth implies rising real wages and
living standards as traditionally defined. The rapid, perhaps exceptionally rapid, productivity growth of the postwar period can be attributed
to many factors. In addition to high investment rates, movement of labor
off farms, and rising education, Nelson emphasizes:

1. *Initial conditions:* physical losses during World War II,
    economic stagnation during the 1930s, perception of large unmet
    needs of private and public goods, extreme capital shortages, and
    a large stock of technical advance not yet embodied in the
    production system.
2. *Governments* were willing to pursue *policies* more conducive to
    economic growth or, perhaps more importantly, avoid mistakes
    that had been made in the past.
3. *Research and development (R&D)* spending rose rapidly in all
    OECD countries during the rapid growth era as compared to
    previous periods.

Although all the sources of growth are strong complements of each
other, Nelson stresses that "only a very small fraction of the productivity
increase could have been achieved without technical advance" (p. 68).

Nelson finds strong similarities among countries in the industrial
pattern of improvements in efficiency:

1. "Rapid productivity growth in agriculture, in the face of price-
    inelastic demands, freed-up labor which moved into manufac-

turing where initial productivity levels were higher" (p. 79).
2. Growth of productivity in manufacturing as well as in public utilities and transport, on the average, was quite rapid.
3. Services and construction exhibited low rates of productivity advance in most countries.
4. Within both services and manufacturing, important subsector productivity growth differences existed.
5. "Interindustry productivity growth patterns not only were similar across the different OECD countries, they also tended to persist over time" (p. 81).

Intercountry, intersectoral, and interindustry differences shed light on the reasons for productivity change. Nelson finds that there is a strong negative correlation between initial productivity levels and productivity growth rates in OECD countries during the period since World War II. Maddison finds some convergence in productivity levels among sectors in the major countries: this is a result which is dominated by observations from a small number of countries.

There is a clear break in the trend of production and productivity in the OECD countries after 1973. Nadiri points out that Nelson does not really explain why this occurred. Wachtel cites Kendrick's calculations which imply that nearly half of the decline in the U.S. rate of productivity growth between 1966-73 and 1973-77 is attributable to the recession. Nadiri asks, unacceptingly, if the explanation is cyclical, is it not true that "all governments have to do is clean house, put the right fiscal and monetary policies in place, and productivity will take care of itself" (p. 100)? He notes the possibility that because of slower technological growth or other factors, the sharp slowdown of growth in the United States may account for part of the poor economic performance of other OECD countries. Nadiri also suggests that, while in the past it was taken for granted that energy would go to industry, we may increasingly see industry going to energy, and to understand this kind of impact it is necessary to look beyond the borders of the OECD countries.

Factors cited by various authors as responsible for the decline in productivity growth include:

1. Slower growth of capital per worker as a result of cyclical expansion and/or declines in demand.
2. Reductions in research and development activities, particularly cuts in government-sponsored and military and aerospace research.

3. Reductions in R&D and investment as a result of higher energy prices, environmental and safety regulations, and other changes in the social and regulatory climate that reflect changes in social values.
4. The high inflation, high business risk, and slow growth environment, which has significantly shortened the time horizon for both R&D and investment and discouraged pursuit of long term, large scale, or high risk projects.
5. Rapid increases in the percentage of the workforce accounted for by the young and by often less experienced female workers.
6. A possible decline in the importance of major innovations.
7. The longer term shift of employment out of manufacturing into lower productivity sectors.
8. Real political demands reflected in policies that involve "increased transfer payments and public provision of certain goods and services, and other legislation that has better shielded individual and family living standards from the pull and push of market forces. But one consequence is high tax rates which may well damp incentives to work and invest. Another possible consequence is that it may now be much harder to shift labor from activities where demand is declining to activities where demand is increasing" (p. 91.)

Capital Formation

Investment is the active element in the growth process; it provides productive tools for labor, embodies technical advance, and represents a key element of aggregate demand. At the same time investment is dependent upon continued growth since much of it builds additional productive capacity to satisfy future demand.

Several of the participants attribute part of the sluggishness of capital investment to inflation: high and variable inflation rates reduce investment in a wide variety of ways; market signals are distorted as prices of individual goods reflect inflationary pressures in varying degrees; long term commitments become more risky, higher interest rates increase the relative cost of long term versus short term projects and raise immediate cash flow requirements; taxes are often applied to "illusory profits"; and distorted financial signals obscure the true financial condition of corporations to both capital markets and a firm's own management.

Many elements of the current inflation are built into the economy. Therefore the standard prescription of tighter monetary and fiscal policy has greater difficulty in reducing inflation rates without high costs in terms of losses in real economic activity and high unemployment. In addition, an even more restrictive macropolicy than concerns about antiinflation generate has frequently been required by serious international imbalances. Indeed, several participants argue that restrictive and uncertain macroeconomic policies have been a major element preventing effective economic recovery.

Pugel notes that "the increase in the relative price of energy may inhibit capital formation to the extent that energy is a complement to capital in the production process" (p. 214). Further, to the extent that investment in energy-saving equipment is cost reducing rather than output increasing, in a medium-term growth sense the quality of investment has declined; until the economy is fully adjusted to higher energy prices, there is less growth per investment dollar.

Both Nelson and Pugel consider the effects of environmental laws on the cost and allocation of new investment. The impact is not so much a reduction in investment as a diversion to a "nonproductive" form in the traditional sense. Price suggests that there may not have been serious environmental cost increases or delays in the aggregate for most European countries (Germany is noted as having some cost increases but this is not analyzed in detail). Nevertheless, evidence from the United States suggests that such legislation can divert significant amounts of investment away from output-increasing forms.

Curzon Price, in analyzing the capital formation issue, concludes that for most major OECD countries, the investment problem has been largely a cyclical phenomenon. There is substantial agreement that cyclical forces were especially important outside the United States in accounting for reduced capital formation and, more generally, for sluggish economic growth since 1973. After looking at data through 1978, Curzon Price further observes that rates of investment were not as depressed as often stated, a point also made by several others. She therefore focuses on the question of why some nations continue to have high rates of capital formation without achieving commensurate rates of economic growth.

Curzon Price categorizes countries into three groups—the "stern stabilizers" (especially Germany and Switzerland), the "generous accommodators" (Italy, the United Kingdom), and the others (especially France) which differ in the ability of their social framework to accept structural change. The generous accommodators differ in four respects:

1. A tendency to try to spend their way out of a crisis.
2. Layoff terms and other labor provisions which impede adjustment.
3. A large government share of investment and of the growth of investment, with questionable payoff as well as a crowding-out of

private investment.

4. Government discretionary authority as to how public funds will be used, and the inevitability of the use of that authority in increasingly ad hoc and firm-specific ways.

The resistance to adjustment is not seen as new; what are new are the forms which that resistance takes. Public investment activities lower the "quality of investment" through less effective allocation, while ad hoc methods of adjustment assistance interfere with market processes and are seen as highly counterproductive. Both Wachtel and Pugel see Curzon Price's work as "catalytic," stimulating increasing discussion, but requiring further quantification and analysis of alternative interpretations. Charles Seton (Federal Reserve) urged greater consideration of the role of external demand in accounting for some of the intercountry differences.*

Population and Economic Growth

Simon and Neil examine the evidence on the relationship between population growth and economic growth and present preliminary findings of an attempt to develop a neoclassical model of the interrelationships between demographic and economic change. The authors take issue with the proposition that the general effect of increases in population is to reduce real incomes through diminishing returns, and indicate that "the data suggest that in more developed countries . . . population growth does not hinder economic growth" (pp. 107-108). Simon and Neil go on to argue that there are strong beneficial effects of population growth on productivity growth. If that were the case, then population growth would be especially important in accounting for the high rates of growth of GNP in industrialized countries in the postwar period and for the recent slowdown. Moreover, the authors support open immigration policies because of the perceived economic advantages of a large population. The formal and general discussions of the Simon and Neil paper take sharp issue with the evidence on the relationship between population growth and economic growth. Although forces operate in both directions, no clear cut, aggregate impact has been established. Moreover, there are substantial methodological questions about the evidence which is presented.

---

*Sentences in past tense indicate comments made at the conference not included in the prepared papers and discussion. First names and affiliations are included for individuals not on the program.

Mushkin emphasizes the importance of technology, stating "it is irrational to assume that additional production will be achieved through new ideas and advances in knowledge, just because there are more people," and "it is the automaticity of the concept of growth, tied to long-run population movements, to which I take strong exception" (pp. 135 and 136). While Maddison observes "you cannot make judgments about the impact of population on growth or welfare simply by juxtaposing densities or growth rates with corresponding levels of real income" (p. 137).

Simon and Neil develop their model by combining estimates of the effects of individual relationships based on various special studies, rather than by estimation of a complete model. The cornerstone of their analysis is a chart on the relationship between productivity and industry size, comparing the United States and the United Kingdom, which reflects what is referred to as "Verdoorn's Law." Leveson pointed out that the very large effects of population size which are drawn from this information are inconsistent with the absence of clear-cut evidence on country size effects on productivity growth in intercountry comparisons. Nelson noted that the apparent relationship may reflect what might be termed "Salter's Law," in which those industries which increase productivity most rapidly also lower prices relative to other industries, and therefore achieve the greatest expansion of size. Moreover, Pugel pointed out that in comparing the relative size of industries in the United States and the United Kingdom, the authors may be simply observing international specialization.

None of the participants addressed the question of guest labor policies. These clearly have been important in increasing the stability of labor-importing countries, and have served as an alternative to further permanent increases in immigration.

Prospects for Growth

Maddison projects a long run rate of productivity growth of 3.5 percent per year in the advanced capitalist nations. In discussion he indicated that he expected growth rates in the coming decades to return to patterns more like those experienced in developed nations during the period 1950-70, a period which abstracts from the more recent cyclical influences. In coming to this conclusion he emphasized that the rate of investment was still quite high and further opportunities exist to catch up on the United States. He expressed greater reservations about the United States, however.

Nelson takes the more widely accepted position that industrial countries have entered an era in which economic growth will be substantially slower than earlier.

> It is probably not feasible to attain again the pace of productivity growth
> achieved over the 1955-70 period . . . not so much in any physical limits to
> growth, but rather in the social limits to growth that we have built into our
> laws and institutions. In a sense the OECD societies have chosen to slow
> the pace of economic progress traditionally defined and measured, and
> tried to redirect the pattern of economic progress to one that better respects
> a variety of non-market values. At the same time they have attempted to
> better shield individuals and families from the vicissitudes of economic
> change. . . . It well may be that the OECD societies in their moves to protect
> other values have hindered the ability of their economies to achieve more
> conventional kinds of productivity growth to a greater extent than they
> bargained (pp. 92-93).

Nelson raises the further possibility that trend and cycle elements may
be linked, such that a protracted recession changes behavior and
expectations to also lower the subsequent trend. Curzon Price takes issue
with the suggestion that a trend-cycle interaction might exist beyond
what is normally experienced in deep or protracted cyclical downturns.
This suggestion runs counter to the picture of strong recovery which is
painted by Bernstein.

Bernstein sees industrial countries as going through a period of
adjustment, and by and large successfully adjusting to the special
problems of the 1970s. While no specific growth projections are
presented, his position represents a middle ground between the
optimism of Maddison and Nelson's suggestions that the cumulative
negative effects of the recession and slower growth trend may be more
serious than they seem. Bernstein foresees continuing international
adjustment problems as a result of low consumption levels in relation to
income in Japan, intensified international competition, differential
inflation rates, and continuing exchange rate fluctuations. However, in
subsequent discussion, Bernstein strongly rejected the suggestion that
the workings of the Eurodollar market will cause a serious disruption to
the international payments system.

Sectoral and Industrial Shifts

Shifting patterns of employment among sectors represent perhaps the
most pervasive structural change experienced by OECD countries along
with economic growth. Maddison finds the long-term evolution of
employment patterns to be quite regular. Services steadily increase in
share, agriculture decreases, and industry at first rises in share gradually,
levels out and then declines in a shallow bell pattern. Lengellé questions

whether the growth in the service sector's share of employment will continue to be so rapid since, with simple extrapolation, it appears as though it will reach 100 percent by the end of the century.

In Maddison's view:

> Ultimately, the direction and pace of structural change depends on seven factors. The three most important are probably:
>   1. the rate of growth of aggregate real income per head
>   2. the hierarchy of consumer tastes
>   3. the rate and direction of technical progress
> Also significant are:
>   4. the share and pattern of government consumption
>   5. the rate of investment
>   6. the share of foreign trade
>   7. the rate of depletion of material resources. (p. 42)

Both Maddison and Nelson emphasize the importance of rising income on patterns of demand. Expenditure patterns over time have evolved in a rather regular and predictable fashion. The importance of necessities declines and discretionary spending expands. Private consumption patterns have been fairly regular and predictable. But Maddison cautions that major elements of demand, particularly government and investment spending, can differ a great deal among countries and can vary significantly over time. Hence, "one must beware of propounding general laws about the evolution of expenditure patterns" (p. 50).

Output patterns also change in consistent fashion, with employment and expenditure trends. The share of agricultural output fell considerably between 1950 and 1976, the share of industrial output stayed more or less constant, while the share of service output increased markedly, dominating industrial output in virtually all of the countries investigated.

Among the "advanced capitalist countries" the initial level of development influenced output shares for industry. For the less advanced industrial countries in 1950, the share of industrial output in gross domestic product (GDP) significantly increased by 1976, while the more advanced industrial countries experienced rough constancy or moderate declines in the industrial share by 1976. While output patterns behaved similarly in direction to employment patterns, the percentage reduction in manufacturing output is not as large as the change in manufacturing employment.

Prices and productivity also tended to change systematically over time. During the period 1950-76, agricultural and industrial prices increased at roughly the same rate, while prices in the service sector rose more rapidly. Conversely, productivity growth in services has consistently been slower than in industry, and productivity growth in agriculture generally exceeded that in industry in most advanced countries. Aggregate productivity growth, as well as for each of the sectors, was significantly higher after 1950 than over the period from 1870 to 1950.

Lengellé confirms that the trend of structural changes in the OECD countries has proceeded through the recent economic cycle with only minimal modification. Contrary to agriculture and industry, the service sector was relatively unaffected by the economic slump. From a limited sample of countries, Lengellé also finds that from 1973 to 1976, more jobs were offered to females in service activities than to males. Further, more female jobs were created in services than were lost in agriculture and industry while, for males, more jobs were lost in agriculture and industry than were created in services over the same time span.

Herman Kahn (Hudson Institute) commented that it is useful to make a distinction between tertiary and quarternary services. The quarternary sector includes activities usually carried out for their own sake. They are community, social, and personal services as distinct from services which facilitate primary or secondary sector activities. Quarternary employment can be expected to grow especially rapidly, and the postindustrial society will be largely quarternary.

Several structural implications of the behavior of the service sector are of interest. Lengellé emphasizes that the service sector appears to be a partial check to cyclical unemployment in western economies. Nelson notes that the unevenness of technical progress across sectors and industries was of particular importance to the growth process. He raises concerns that industries growing rapidly in output may no longer be industries which are growing rapidly in productivity and have high price elasticities. If industries with good productivity growth are less able to expand through price and income effects, the result could be serious for productivity growth in the economy as a whole. Leveson maintains that the for-profit service industries in the United States have been entering a new era of high, although often unmeasured, productivity growth. He pointed out in discussion that measurement problems tend to result in overstatement of price changes and understatement of output changes, so that price elasticities appear low. As a result, productivity growth and price elasticities may in fact be high in services, as with leading sectors of the past.

Leveson questioned statements by Maddison and Nelson recommending government efforts to redirect R&D activities toward service industries. He maintained that the private market was clearly considering opportunities in all industries in deciding how much to invest in developing computers, for example. It will be more important to revise regulations which protect markets where new technology is rapidly making traditional distinctions obsolete, as in finance, so that government intervention does not impede the incentives which exist.

Changing Organization of Global Production and Trade

A number of important changes have occurred in the organization of production and trade. These are the result of (1) increased internationalization of production through multinational enterprise, (2) growth in the share of international exchange in total economic activity, (3) increased involvement of governments in the production and trade decisions in capitalist nations, (4) rapid growth of developing countries, and (5) changes in domestic and commercial policy.

Industry Concentration and International Trade and Investment

The organization of industry, in terms of ownership and control, is one important aspect of industrial structures. Policies in this area are frequently referred to as competition policies or, in the United States, as antitrust policies. Policy and research concerning industrial organization is biased to the extent that it ignores international aspects of industrial activity. Weston demonstrates that perhaps the most fundamental measuring device used by antitrust administrators, the concentration ratio, requires major revision to take account of international trade, and that when viewed in terms of international markets, many apparently concentrated industries are highly competitive.

Weston maintains that, while high profits in relation to concentration are taken as a fundamental signal of market distortion and inefficiency, the evidence is not generally supportive. Although older, rather simplistic, studies found a relationship between concentration and profits, more sophisticated and recent studies generally find a small and frequently insignificant relationship. One study cited found that profits tend to be related to size of firm, regardless of the degree of concentration in the industry.

Empirical evidence concerning the relationship between concentration and innovation is somewhat ambiguous. In the United States, most research and development is undertaken by the 400 to 500 largest companies having 5,000 or more employees. Five industry groups consistently account for nearly three-quarters of all privately financed research and development: chemical and allied products, electrical equipment and communication, motor vehicles and transportation equipment, machinery, and aircraft and missiles. Nevertheless, formal statistical analyses rarely find more than a weak positive relationship between research and development intensity and industrial concentration. There is some suggestion that the relationship is not constant; research and development activity and size may be related positively up to some critical level, depending on the industry, and then level off or decline.

Weston maintains that the evidence concerning the relationship between concentration and inflation is less ambiguous. In his view theoretical analysis suggests that there should be no relationship, and the available empirical evidence demonstrates that concentrated industries have actually shown better price performance during the recent inflation than have other segments of the economy.

Also of particular importance is the question of how international trade and investment influences conditions of competition in domestic markets. Pagoulatos and Sorensen find that existing evidence supports the position that "import competition can improve pricing and allocative performance in domestic markets. . . . [And] the multinational company [via direct investment] may be a source of rivalry and competition in domestic markets that could not come from international trade" (pp. 312, 314). A number of important caveats exist, particularly with reference to operations of the multinational corporation, but, in general, domestic competition increases as international interaction rises.

Hawkins sees a need for much more attention to the effects of international competition and foreign direct investment on domestic industrial structure before we can be fully satisfied with this conclusion. Hawkins further emphasizes the potential impact of an industry's competitiveness on its participation in international trade. In this regard the evidence is less clear. On the import side Pagoulatos and Sorensen find both theoretical and empirical support for the idea that increased concentration is likely to yield a higher level of imports in the industry. On the export side, theory is inconclusive, but the empirical evidence suggests that a "limited degree of market power may aid export performance" (p. 318).

On balance, Pagoulatos and Sorensen find the evidence ambiguous but slightly in favor of the view that trade both leads to and results from more competitive industrial structures. Hence, "competition policies should rather be based upon their domestic merit. Mergers essential to the achievement of genuine economies of scale or to the rationalization of fragmented industries should rightly be encouraged. At the same time, authorities should not fear to promote and preserve competitively structured industries where possible" (p. 319).

Weston emphasizes that it is imperative to include the existing degree of international competition in the process of evaluating domestic competition for policy purposes. If an industry is highly concentrated in the domestic market because of technical conditions such as economies of scale, capital intensity, and size of the market, while at the same time it is constrained in its pricing decisions by international competition, the justification for divestiture or other policies to reduce concentration is seriously diminished.

Firms engaged in export activity or direct investment in foreign markets tend to be larger firms in more concentrated industries. It is unclear how the act of exporting or undertaking foreign investment will influence the home country's industrial organization. Wheeler noted that such activity may be associated with an increase in concentration of the domestic market, but it is unlikely to be a causal factor in such an increase in concentration; both are likely to reflect opportunities for increases in productivity or cost reduction due to modernization, major capital investment, or path-breaking innovation.

Increased Competitiveness of Third World Exports

One of the most politically sensitive structural changes facing OECD countries is the growing importance of manufactured exports from developing countries. Several questions about the growth of LDC exports are of primary importance. First, is it indeed a real problem? If it is a real problem, how serious is it? Are specific policies required? Hormats clearly states the perceived problem as follows:

> We face a serious challenge in the form of a small number of developing countries (Mexico, Brazil, Taiwan, South Korea, Malaysia, Singapore, and the Crown Colony of Hong Kong) which have in this decade been increasing their exports of manufactured goods to the United States and to Europe at annual rates between 30 and 50 percent. The exports have largely been concentrated in certain categories, including textiles, footwear, and consumer electronics, but many of these countries are now moving into capital-intensive sectors such as steel and autos (pp. 6-7).

Further, it is feared that a whole tier of developing countries is reaching a stage of industrialization where they too can begin to export vigorously.

Within the OECD countries the industries most affected have tended to be those employing a disproportionate share of low-skilled workers.

Gray is specifically concerned that, due to a number of socio-political barriers, the market for low-skilled labor does not clear properly and special trade related policies may be required.

Krueger takes a quite different position:

> In the process of economic growth there will be individuals adversely affected, both because of changes in demand, technology, capital, and real wages, and because of regional differences in the impact of growth and change. While imports may intensify (or offset) these dislocations for some parties, it is extremely difficult to pinpoint any sector or subsector as being one where imports have caused major structural changes which otherwise would have been entirely avoided (pp. 238-240).

She goes on to note that: "When focus is upon LDC exports alone, there can be little question that the effects must have been confined to relatively small subsectors" (p. 240).

Krueger's strong conclusions as to the minimal role of imports in reducing the demand for labor in the United States may appear startling, and it is worth pausing to consider how the analysis should be interpreted. First, it should be noted that the data apply only to manufacturing industries and do not include losses in shipping and other areas. The data go through 1976 and do not indicate whether recent changes have been larger. Calculations are carried out at the two-digit level of industry classification and to some extent also at the four-digit level. Baldwin suggests that data which will become available for five-digit industries may reflect greater impacts. Furthermore, effects may well be concentrated in high cost geographic areas of importing countries and in certain years and firms, as Krueger clearly recognizes.

Herman Kahn pointed out that foreign competition may take away growth and that it may represent a large proportion of the market in a particular commodity, as occurred with magnetic tapes, tape recorders, and transistor radios.

Particularly important may be the possibility that imports have not had a large effect because we have prevented their growth where the impacts might be great, through devices such as quotas and voluntary restraint. Moreover, the figures only describe what has happened in the past and do not indicate what may be poised to happen. In addition, the data reflect only imports of goods and exclude the perception by domestic firms that entry of foreign firms into domestic production is part of the extent of foreign competition. Baldwin emphasizes Krueger's point that the association is statistical and does not prove causality, although he agrees substantially with the conclusion.

Krueger's position that competition in manufacturers from less developed countries has not produced large losses in U.S. employment is not contradicted by these points. However, it is not possible to leap to the conclusion that foreign competition from all sources will not cause more significant structural adjustment pressures in all industries in the future. Nevertheless, Krueger's point that the impacts have been greatly exaggerated is well taken. For example, she indicates that import competition is only one of many reasons that firms lost employment, and foreign competition is often conveniently blamed for these other problems. The ease with which false impressions are formed is illustrated by the fact that the U.S. has exported more steel to less developed countries than it has imported, when the steel content of exports of manufactures to those countries is taken into account.

In discussion, Harry Gilman (Department of Labor) asked about the effects of import competition on marginal firms and losses of specific human capital. Krueger responded that she was concentrating here on the size of the job loss rather than the cost of adjustment. Michael Aho (Department of Labor) stressed that the problem is that there are winners and losers even though there are gains for the nation as a whole. Krueger sees little need to distinguish between adjustments due to internal and external forces and little ability to distinguish them from each other.

Looking toward the future, Krueger divides the issues important for projecting manufactured export expansion from developing countries into three categories: those issues which are relevant to export levels from *current* major LDC exporters, those affecting growth in OECD countries, and those relating to the possible emergence of *new* major LDC exporters.

During the process of growth, a country begins losing comparative advantage in low value-added items. Krueger notes that: "A sizeable proportion of the expansion of textile exports from LDCs was offset by reduced exports from Japan. . . . This same sort of internal adjustment is beginning to take place in Korea, Taiwan, and other successful exporting countries, and will inevitably be repeated whenever an exporter is successful" (p. 241).

Expansion of the size of the market for new exporters of these items will merely come as a substitution for exports from current major exporters as current exporters lose competitiveness in labor-intensive commodities. This will mean "no more impetus to structural change in the OECD countries than there has been in the past" (p. 242). In fact, in the discussion, Krueger suggested that, while there are many uncertainties about the effect of imports in causing structural change in OECD countries, "it has probably already peaked."

Critical elements to the growth of manufacturing exports from all developing countries include the degree of openness to imports in OECD countries, the extent to which internal markets of the "super exporters" are opened up to import competition, and the degree to which these same countries shift away from exports of labor-intensive commodities. With reference to the latter point, Krueger notes that Korea is shifting and has plans to shift much more into high value-added products, while Taiwan has already shown considerable adaptation.

Krueger is very eclectic about the rate of growth of OECD countries, making no projections but emphasizing the importance of growth in affecting structural change:

> To the extent that growth rates for these countries [OECD] remain similar to their levels of the past decade and a half, there is little basis for believing that the pressures of structural adjustment will be any more severe than they have been in the past. . . . The problem would be more severe, however, if the growth rate of OECD countries slowed significantly. For, when growth slows down, any shifts in the labor force and in the composition of output are effected with increased difficulty, as profitable alternatives to existing activities become harder to find (p. 242).

In order to assess the possible emergence of new "super exporters" among the developing countries, Krueger argues that an important distinction exists "between relatively slow-growth countries whose living standards and wage levels are already in the medium income range—such as the oil-exporting countries of the Middle East, Venezuela, and Argentina—and the low-wage countries such as India and Indonesia" (pp. 242-243). In the first group, high wages will preclude specialization in labor-intensive products. In the resource-rich countries, export promotion policies will likely move them into direct competition with the middle income countries. It is more likely, however, "that the comparative advantage of those countries would lie in industries using their abundant raw materials—as petrochemicals in the case of the Middle East countries and products produced with animal materials, for example, in Argentina and Uruguay" (p. 243). A further consideration is that most of the countries in this tier "are by and large not heavily populated, and, relative to the size of the international market, it is unlikely that their exports would either be sufficiently alike or large enough in volume to result in observable dislocations in OECD countries" (p. 243). Therefore any potential pressure from structural change in OECD countries must come from low wage, heavily populated areas, most importantly China and South and Southeast

Asia. She argues that even in these countries potential export growth is frequently overestimated.

A critical implication of this discussion is that the development of policies will have to focus much more closely on what is expected to happen in the future than what has already occurred in the past and that a wider range of evidence and broad-based reasoning will be essential in the process.

Industrial and Commercial Policy

Industrial policy has typically referred to actions which are taken to deal with internal economic problems such as subsidies to firms, while commercial policy has dealt with tariffs and other measures directed toward international trade. With the growth of non-tariff barriers and domestic policies with strong international implications, these distinctions are increasingly blurred.

Pagoulatos and Sorensen review a wide range of policies and the evidence on the impacts of these policies. They conclude that industrial policies tend to be self-defeating and contradictory. New and detailed forms of protectionist measures have become important even in the United States, and there are a surprisingly large number of policies directed toward other goals (such as stimulating investment and subsidizing R&D) that represent a disguised form of protectionism.

The spectrum of actions that can loosely be called industrial policy include:

1. *Antitrust or Competition Policy*—whose goals usually are the promotion of competition and the control of restrictive business practices.
2. *Technological Policy*—whose purpose is to promote research and development activity in the nation.
3. *Regional Policy*—whose aim is to reduce regional imbalance in the allocation of economic activity.
4. *Adjustment Policy*—whose goal is to facilitate the adjustment of industrial structure to changes dictated by demand and technological forces or foreign competition (p. 305).
5. *Direct government involvement in decisionmaking and/or ownership of industry*—traditional motives were usually associated with national defense, unquestioned public goods, and regulation of industries with characteristics of public goods. More recent motives are frequently associated with high-risk, large-scale activities such as nonconventional energy sources, and regulation of somewhat risky

innovative processes such as pharmaceuticals, or a desire to support failing industries.

6. *Environmental policy, health and safety regulations, and other policies aimed at improving non-economic aspects of lifestyles*—whose primary aim is to shift resources into the production of, in some sense, more socially desirable products.

7. *Other social policy*—increasingly detailed social legislation which strongly influences the pace and pattern of change in industrial structures although the goals are often attempts to insulate individuals from the vicissitudes of market forces.

Gray notes that "clearly, what have been viewed as domestic policy issues can no longer be analyzed and legislated in a purely domestic framework. Implications of economic policies for the international competitiveness of industries must also be analyzed" (p. 300).

The interaction of policies that are aimed at quite narrow and specific domestic or international objectives frequently produce side effects, or for that matter direct effects, that are in conflict with other policy objectives. Price describes in detail the restrictive manpower policies, subsidies, and other industrial policies in Western Europe to which Wachtel comments, "To an American, her descriptions . . . are a source of relief. One can relax with the knowledge that things are much worse elsewhere" (p. 216). Golt's remarks about how far goverment intervention with market forces has gone in England are equally disconcerting. While the British government's role is greater than most others, there is an increasing march toward what has been called "the new protectionism."

Gray's discussion of labor markets provides a good example of conflicting policy objectives. Public policy increasingly has been focused on labor adjustments in low-skilled categories, yet it is in just these categories where government policy has created some of the strongest distortions to market incentives. Structural change is inevitable, and low productivity employment will experience the brunt of the adjustment process as new employment opportunities, industries, and activities emerge. Gray was particularly concerned that, due to our policy/institutional matrix, OECD countries will experience a "long-lasting excess supply of low-skilled labor at the going wage" (p. 361). If in fact such a phenomenon is important to specific OECD countries, for whatever reasons (population bulge in certain age groups, excessive overbuilding in certain industries, structural slowing down of overall economic growth rates, shifting domestic demand patterns, or rapid growth in import competition), serious concern must be given to an appropriate policy response. Gray suggests special subsidies to employers of low-skilled labor. In response to Gray's policy recommendations, both Gold and Cassing observe that the desire to provide continued employment opportunities for the low-skilled worker must not detract us from the longer run goals of economic efficiency and continued growth. Nevertheless if, as Gray suggests, government policy contributes to particular adjustment problems, the low-skilled labor market requires special attention.

Golt suggests that the extent of government involvement in industrial affairs has gone so far, so rapidly, and takes on methods that vary so substantially from country to country, that it is virtually impossible to understand the side effects and interactions of these policies, much less the direct effects. Policies taken by the government in pursuit of this enlarged role often are not primarily, nor are they intended to be, protectionist, but nevertheless they have such an effect. There has also been increasing use of administrative and judicial processes in the name of "fairness" of trade, especially in the United States. He quotes Harry Johnson concerning the new forms of protectionist policies:

> The new techniques of mercantilist policy, for their part, reflect recognition of two facts. One is that the protective tariff of traditional mercantilist philosophy is a very crude and blunt instrument for favoring domestic industry, by comparison with the techniques now available. . . . The second fact is that in the modern world of industries based on high technology and hence subject to important economies of scale and diminishing cost, as overhead research-and-development investment is spread over a larger volume of output, protection of domestic producers in the domestic national market is no longer adequate or efficient. To be efficient, protection must extend to the export market (p. 339).

Recent practices closely reflect the French concept of "organized liberalization," "organized free trade," and "managed trade expansion" and completely contravene the Anglo-American trade philosophy of the early 1960s and indeed the entire spirit of the GATT.

Golt points to the Multifibres Arrangement and the Long Term Cotton Textiles Agreement (LTA), its predecessor, as perfect models of the type of policy system that will emerge under an organized liberalization concept.

> In its original form, the LTA could be defended, with some degree of conviction, as seeking to provide an orderly and progressive mechanism for abolishing existing import restrictions, and as a way of buying time during which a new equilibrium of the world's industrial pattern could establish itself. . . . This is not how things turned out. . . . At the end of sixteen years of the system, it is still restrictive—indeed, more so than

before, since its latest renegotiation has apparently proved to be a weapon at hand for retaining and solidifying protection, and in some respects for extending it (p. 341).

Not only has the policy framework become permanent but in terms of the original goals, adjustment of the textile industry, it has proved generally ineffective.

It is at least arguable that these changes [in the textile industries] have been brought about to a far greater extent by changes in technology and fashion than because of the effect of the arrangements, and it would be difficult to substantiate a claim that the restrictions, as they have operated, have made a significant contribution to the total well-being of the restricting countries, and probably equally difficult to demonstrate more than a marginal effect on the geographical pattern of development of textile industries throughout the world (p. 342).

Concern about the effectiveness of barriers in achieving their stated goals is voiced with respect to both industrial and commercial policy by many of the participants of the conference. Nukazawa provides several examples of how protective barriers in Japan had induced higher value added production by Japan's trading partners which permitted them to jump the import barrier.

Recent trade policy actions and the Tokyo Round of trade negotiations intensify the blurring of distinctions among forms of policy, and increase policy interdependence within and among countries. We have seen a "continuous weakening of respect for the fabric, and especially the procedures, of the GATT . . . [during] the current decade" (p. 340). Three sections of the current negotiations are particularly relevant in terms of providing an indication of future policy trends: those dealing with subsidies, safeguards, and public procurement practices.

With subsidies there was never any possibility of agreement concerning definition or classification. To have reached an agreement would have been a significant contribution to the GATT. The actions taken to date however tend

to modify substantially the attitude and emphasis of the text of the general agreement itself. The text of the GATT is studiously neutral. . . . The MTN [Multilateral Trade Negotiations] agreements are much more elaborate. . . . They aim at establishing rather stronger machinery of consultation and, perhaps, of surveillance. At the same time, however, they go much further than does the GATT towards explicitly accepting the legitimacy and appropriateness of the use of subsidies. They "recognize" that subsidies in general are used by governments "to promote important objectives of national policy," and that subsidies other than export subsidies are "widely used as important instruments for the promotion of social and economic objectives of national policy"; and they say specifically that it is not intended "to restrict the right of signatories to use such subsidies" (p. 348; the internal quotes in this passage refer to the *Framework of Understanding* produced at the GATT in July 1978).

With regard to safeguards it remains to be seen if the resulting agreement "will significantly limit the range and extent of the variety of protectionist practices of this kind—which include voluntary export restraints and orderly marketing arrangements" (p. 349). Indeed it may be feared by some of the smaller exporting countries that "by sanctioning 'selectivity,' the new agreement may simply make resort to safeguard measures the normal and natural response to any sizeable increase in competition from imports, especially from new entrants into a particular sector, and to any sustained domestic pressure for protection" (p. 349).

The one area where serious advance seems possible to Golt is public procurement. Even here he observes special problems that may erode the fabric of the GATT by weakening its multinational character. The Tokyo Round of trade negotiations plays a curiously asymmetric role in the current political environment. Failure of the GATT would be very serious indeed, but successful conclusions of the negotiations appear to have little or no positive impact on real actions of governments, in Golt's view. Indeed, Nukazawa argues that perhaps the greatest advantage of the Tokyo Round has been that it exists and can be used to counter domestic protectionist forces. "If the MTN were to drag on for a half a century or more, it would prove to be a boon for international trade" (p. 353).

The most recent formulation of policy adopted at the multilateral level appeared in the 1978 OECD Communique after the Ministerial Meetings, frequently referred to as the "Criteria Communique" due to its focus on establishing criteria for "more positive adjustment policies." Golt finds a disconcerting risk embedded within the position expounded.

> The paper itself . . . seems to envisage a substantial residuum of government intervention in and direction of the adjustment process. But there is not inconsiderable danger that the phrase "more positive adjustment policies" itself, to which the authors of the OECD paper have sought to give content based heavily on general measures designed to reduce rigidities, increase factor mobility, and put emphasis on long-term objectives reflecting market considerations, may lend itself only too easily to those who wish for more government intervention rather than less,

more specific and more detailed measures rather than more general ones, and activity calculated to produce more visible and quicker short-term results rather than quieter, slower, more fundamental but less politically advantageous action (p. 351).

Even in areas where industrial and commercial policies are designed with no obvious side effects, peculiar things can happen. Pagoulatos and Sorensen discuss one of the more widespread forms of nontariff barriers under negotiation in the current GATT negotiations: government procurement policies. "There is little doubt that this form of government intervention, with the possible exception of cases involving public health or national security, represents a deliberate import restriction" (p. 320). Their analysis and prepared comments deal almost completely with trade diversion aspects. However, one of Weston's case studies concerns the rather peculiar internal problems which have developed, largely due to government procurement practices, within the heavy electrical equipment industry. Heavy electrical equipment is primarily used in the electricity generation industry which is largely government controlled or owned in most countries. Because of extensive "buy domestic" policies, every country has a heavy electrical equipment manufacturing industry, and this has resulted in enormous excess capacity, particularly in Western Europe.

Wheeler noted that if the GATT negotiations alter government procurement policies in a major fashion and the respective governments obey both the letter and the spirit of this change, we are likely to see a whole new area of demands for support, protection, and adjustment assistance, due to "unfair" competition of these "protected" industries.

Weston works through five case studies of the interaction of domestic policies and international competition. If one can make one primary generalization from these five case studies it is that the policy complex produces quite different results in each industry. This is not surprising in view of the ad hoc basis on which many such policies are introduced. In general, industrial policies are a politically expedient solution to a perceived problem at one point in time which become embedded as permanent policy. The recent increased use of self-liquidating policies by the U.S. government reflects at least a partial recognition of some of these problems.

Curzon Price noted that there are really two definitions of industrial policy:

Industrial policy in its broad sense can be defined as any policy to promote or to prevent structural change. Industrial policy in its narrow sense, in its new and disturbing sense, is any government measure of a microeconomic or discretionary type to prevent or promote structural change. What is new is the discretionary and firm-specific element in industrial policy.

Furthermore, in commenting on the Pagoulatos and Sorensen paper, Curzon Price points out that "industrial strategy" and industrial planning, which bring together firms under the auspices of the government to discuss medium-term plans, exclude the foreign producer, and have consistently gone hand-in-hand with increased protectionism.

In discussing these issues, Weston asked, if industrial policies are self defeating, "how do you explain Japan?" Leveson suggested that industrial policy in Japan was being used in a deliberate attempt to allocate capital in the same way as the private market, only faster, in order to promote growth rather than support lagging sectors as in the West. Government support was going where productivity was increasing fastest rather than falling behind. Curzon Price added that, except for Germany and to some extent France, European policy has been characterized mainly by attempts to prevent rather than promote structural change. Weston responded that Japanese policy has concentrated on developing industries which had a large export potential, coupled with absolute prohibitions against imports for a long period while those industries were developing. He suggested that the growth need not reflect an inherently more efficient industry in Japan, given the large economies of scale, benefits of coordinating production decisions among industries, and other forms of government assistance.

Curzon Price explained in discussion that the purpose of the EEC steel plan was primarily "adjustment resistance" rather than "adjustment assistance" or a rationalization of the industry. She also pointed out the role of import competition in requiring domestic steel and other industries to adopt new technologies. Golt stressed that while a country may obtain gains for a short time from a protective policy of this kind, in the end what it is doing is destroying both the international trading order and its domestic trading order because of the process of retaliation that is set in motion. Unstated and perhaps implicit in the discussion was the possibility that only Japan could have employed such great protectionism without strong retaliation, and there were various suggestions that it may not be able to do so in the future.

Much of the debate over adjustment policies centers on their impact on competition. Pagoulatos and Sorensen maintain that free trade is the best method of achieving competition, and cite substantial evidence on this point. Curzon Price expresses serious concern over attempts by some countries to promote cartelization. Sorensen points out that governments are consistently more lenient in antitrust policy in countries which have a significant proportion of their gross national product accounted for by foreign trade.

Weston takes a somewhat different position, suggesting that the appropriate way to judge competition is by considering the number of major suppliers in the world in relation to the size of world markets. When that is done many industries are seen as far less concentrated than they appear to be when considering only individual countries. He further emphasizes possibilities for large benefits with rising firm size. Pagoulatos and Sorensen indicate that the available evidence suggests efficiency advantages of rising firm size up to a point, but that beyond some level the disadvantages of decreased competition dominate and rise with further concentration of industry. Baldwin questions whether it can be assumed that concentration is consistent with competition, in view of the leadership role in price, output, and investment which is observed. The implication is that competition cannot be assumed based on world market shares without regard to the domestic policies which restrict foreign competition.

Conceptual and Strategic Issues in Developing Policy Responses

The increased volume of protectionist actions are seen by several participants as a perplexing and potentially disastrous trend. Why have they occurred and what options are available? Cassing argues that it is first necessary to "identify the net losers from import competition and the extent of their losses . . . [then] explain how vested interests can secure and maintain policies which underwrite a suboptimal distribution of resources" (p. 394). Indeed, this argument is valid for all forms of requests for special support or aid, not just for protectionist demands.

Since the extent of protectionism in different industries in part reflects how much individuals stand to gain from the policies, Leveson suggested that the strength of intervention might be analyzed by applying Marshall's four principals, as Friedman has done for trade union behavior. For example, agriculture and minerals might have more extensive protectionism because they are imperfect substitutes for other commodities and, as intermediate products, account for less than one hundred percent of final output. This approach could explain the lack of conformity of primary industries with Cassing's expectations based on supply elasticities.

Cassing finds four groups adversely affected by any pressure on industries to adjust to foreign competition (or for that matter to any other source): (1) owners of truly mobile factors, (2) owners of industry-specific factors, (3) communities where the impacted factors represent a substantial share of the local economy, and (4) union leadership in the impacted industries. The interests of each of these groups and their associates are not identical. Yet they do form coalitions, and the process of coalition formation favors groups formed to support protection and other industrial policies over pressure groups to resist such action. In an important sense, it is one function of government to serve as the pressure group for the more pervasive impacts of trade on economic and social well-being. In the United States, spokesmen for the administration have tended to serve this role. Cassing concludes that:

> it is therefore entirely appropriate that alternatives to protectionism . . . obviously and certainly ameliorate the losses incurred as a result of the market's unfettered operation. That is, it must be made more attractive to adjust than not to adjust. . . . The task, of course, lies in designing the mechanism whereby relative unanimity for structural adjustment and against protection is secured (pp. 399-400).

Cassing attributes much of the adjustment resistance to the apparent failure of insurance markets. For owners of nonhuman capital, insurance can be acquired by diversification of assets. Diversification of human capital through purchase markets is not legal, and through skills is not practical.

> Consequently, the burden of structural change is apt to fall more heavily on a group that really has little opportunity to spread risk. . . . To some extent, the same argument applies to trade-impacted communities as a whole. Policy intervention, however, is justified only if private insurance markets have indeed failed *and* if government policy can succeed where private actions cannot (p. 397).

Cassing emphasizes that merely compensating the adjusting factors will not reduce pressures for protectionism. This results because those entities most affected by structural change are the inframarginal factors that do not adjust and have to write down their capital values. In an important sense, we are in a "second best" world. "The alternative to a compensation policy, however, is *not* 'free trade': it is protectionism. The objective becomes not unconstrained maximization of real national income, but rather enactment of a coherent adjustment policy for which the real cost is less than that of protectionism (no adjustment) through international commercial policy" (p. 400).

From this perspective, what then are the characteristics of a policy instrument targeted at adjustment problems? Cassing designed *desiderata* of an adjustment policy instrument which includes four "reasonable" requirements and is based on the assumption that "policy should aim at motivating acceptance of efficient structural change and compensating for market failure" (p. 400).

1. *Adjustment.* An appropriate policy instrument should encourage factor reallocation in the *right direction* over a *finite time* horizon. . . . In particular, the policy must undermine resistance to adjustment by ameliorating the perceived capital losses, risks, and adjustment costs imposed upon factor owners and communities. . . .
2. *Efficiency.* The policy instrument should be efficient in two senses. First, among instruments which impart equivalent impact, the appropriate choice is the least real cost instrument. . . . Second, the overall adjustment-enhancing policy should spread the burdens of adjustment—in particular, the costs of migration—so that all factor marginal costs of relocating are equal. . . .
3. *Focus.* The policy mechanism should achieve desired goals with minimal side effects. In the present case, these side effects are both national and international. It does little good to diffuse protectionism at home if the enacted policy fosters protection abroad. . . . Similarly, a policy which ameliorates losses of trade-impacted individuals at the expense of imposing great loss on another group of individuals is not acceptable.
4. *Viability.* The policy mechanism must be politically palatable. This suggests that the policy must both appeal to the electorate—perhaps achieving some norm of equity—and effectively diffuse protectionist pressure (pp. 400, 402).

Cassing uses his *desiderata* to evaluate the recently popular policy of bilaterally negotiated export restraining agreements, and a number of proposed policy options: safeguards, adjustment assistance to workers, firms, and communities; certain measures to insure economic security; and encouragement to R&D; with some discussion of antidumping charges and countervailing duties. He concludes from his assessment that

> Alternatives to protectionism must diffuse protectionist pressure by spreading the risks and gains associated with structural change. This strongly recommends a government policy of generous severance pay and regional development aid. Self-liquidating safeguards are a second-best alternative. Temporary protection, however, artificially underwrites capital values and so must be supplemented with a policy which discourages future investment in human or nonhuman capital in the protected sector.
> Still, many questions remain. In the absence of further research, manpower training and encouragement of R&D cannot be recommended.

Perhaps more important is the issue of moral hazard surrounding general severance pay schemes. It is not obvious that government intervention can succeed where private institutions fail (pp. 421-422).

Although agreeing with the basic argument presented by Cassing, Nukazawa suggests that a strategy for developing alternatives to protectionism should be extended in two directions: first, it "should include middle-term and long-term suggestions in addition to the immediate palliatives he discusses," and second, the strategy should be stratified into "a perception level (facts and figures), a value level (cultural and priority differences), and an interest level (who benefits?)" (p. 426).

Cassing takes the view that:

> even if markets are efficient, the political process affords an effective opportunity for some sectors to resist structural change. . . . Thus, the problem has a "second best" flavor—that is, a search for relatively efficient adjustment policies which are, above all, politically viable alternatives to protectionism. Our focus is structural change induced by changing patterns of international comparative advantage. If there are grounds for intervention, however, there is no reason to tie efficient policy to international trade issues alone (p. 404).

This final point was reiterated many times throughout the conference, perhaps most strongly by Krueger. There is no reason to select changes in international competitiveness out of the myriad of sources of pressure for structural change as particularly deserving of assistance. If industries, individuals, or communities deserve assistance based on some criteria of adjustment cost, the source of pressure for that adjustment is largely irrelevant.

Additional efforts to develop principles for policy formulation clearly would be worthwhile. This will probably require much more detailed attention to the full set of policies and programs which exist, whether aimed at trade dislocations or other sources of change. Important elements in development of strategies for responding to economic change include analysis of the conditions of introduction of existing policies, the ways assistance is targeted, a realistic assessment of benefits and costs, and the consideration of principles for effectively responding to the many practical situations which arise.

Part 2
Economic Growth and Structural Change: Issues and Prospects

Economic Growth and Structural Change in the Advanced Countries[1]

Angus Maddison

Structuralist Analysis

There is a recurrent tendency, when actual economic growth falls significantly below potential, for structural problems to be rediscovered or reemphasized. Concern with structural problems is, in fact, a cyclical phenomenon. It has been given considerable stress in the middle and late 1970s, "structuralist" arguments justifying a 6 percent unemployment rate were advanced in the United States in the late 1950s and early 1960s, and structural explanations of interwar British and European problems were often given great weight.[2] One reason for this is quite simply that macroeconomic weakness impacts unevenly in different sectors of the economy, some industries and regions suffering more from unemployment and bankruptcy than others. Structural problems do worsen in times of slack demand, and there is a myopic but natural tendency to assume that the cause is structural rather than macroeconomic. A second reason for this recurrent advocacy is that in periods of weak demand which may be due very largely to deliberate fiscal and monetary policy, governments can usually be pressured into structural activism to mitigate the social consequences of their macropolicy. Often such "structural" actions conflict flagrantly with the stated macropolicy intentions, but this does not worry politicians or lobbyists who are used to policy muddle. Such structural actions may also be supported by those who would normally advocate more expansionary macropolicy, but who, seeing that common sense has been temporarily overwhelmed by central bankers' rhetoric, are willing to settle for second or third best solutions.

My own feeling is that the major new problems of the 1970s are of a macroeconomic or socioeconomic character. The new structural problems have been the sharp rise in the relative cost of energy and some changes in the operation of labor markets, but these have been a good deal less disturbing than the acceleration of inflation and the move to a new international currency regime.

My general position is not that structural change is unimportant in capitalist development. On the contrary, technical progress and changing demand require constant structural change which raises serious problems for both displaced workers and bankrupt businessmen. I would argue only that structural change is nothing new and that most structural problems dissolve in conditions of full employment.

This paper deals with structural change in five different dimensions— employment, expenditure, output, productivity, and prices. These are all interrelated, and it is difficult to interpret or forecast one aspect of change without looking at all the others.

Ultimately, the direction and pace of structural change depends on seven factors. The three most important are probably:

    1. the rate of growth of aggregate real income per head
    2. the hierarchy of consumer tastes
    3. the rate and direction of technical progress

Also significant are:

    4. the share and pattern of government consumption
    5. the rate of investment
    6. the share of foreign trade
    7. the rate of depletion of natural resources

I have tried to take account of the first six below—interpreting developments over the past century and forecasting what is likely in the future.

Employment Patterns

The policy concern with structural change is mainly with employment opportunity. Figure 3.1 shows employment patterns plotted against real income levels for sixteen countries over a period of a century (the scatter diagram is based on readings for 1870, 1950, 1960, 1970, and 1976 from Tables 3.1 and 3.2). During this time, average per capita income (measured in 1970 U.S. prices) of these countries rose about sevenfold, the proportion of employment in agriculture fell from 49 to 8 percent, industrial employment rose from 28 to 36 percent of the total, and service employment rose from 24 to 56 percent.

Over the long term, the proportion of people in services has clearly

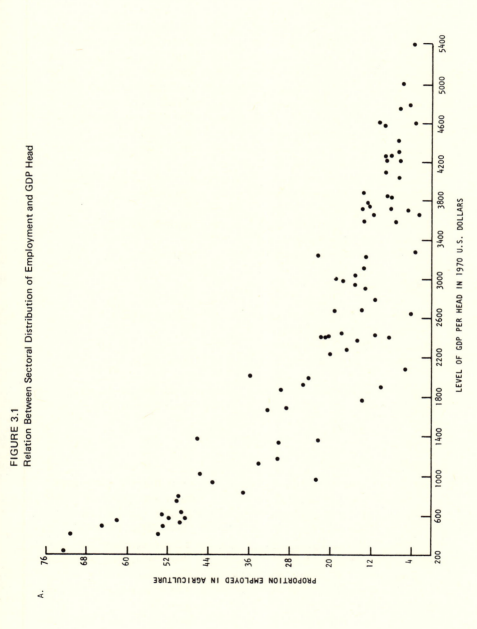

FIGURE 3.1
Relation Between Sectoral Distribution of Employment and GDP Head

44

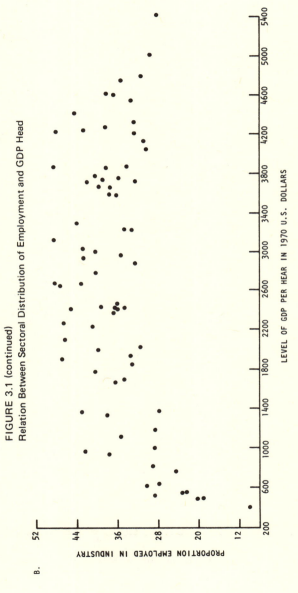

FIGURE 3.1 (continued)
Relation Between Sectoral Distribution of Employment and GDP Head

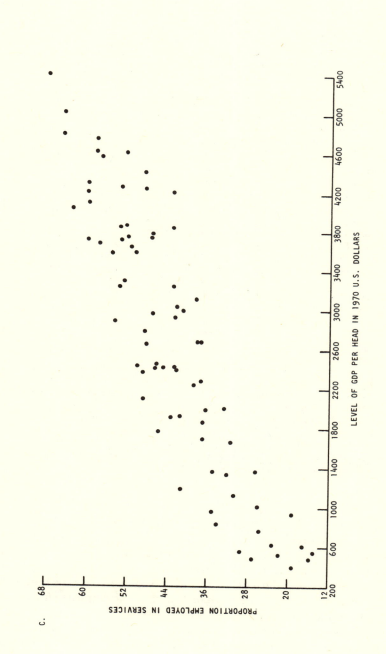

TABLE 3.1

Gross Domestic Product Per Head of Population (1970
U.S. Dollars Per Head)

	1870	1950	1960	1970	1976
Australia	1340	2363	2799	3840	4301
Austria	491	1132	1992	3000	3771
Belgium	939	1901	2411	3713	4615
Canada	619	2401	2892	4042	5014
Denmark	572	1923	2445	3642	4102
Finland	402	1374	2015	3226	3871
France	627	1693	2418	3732	4602
Germany	535	1374	2667	3859	4414
Italy	556	1016	1673	2666	3026
Japan	248	567	1181	2967	3752
Netherlands	830	1773	2434	3589	4203
Norway	489	1866	2408	3584	4563
Sweden	416	2234	2924	4263	4752
Switzerland	786	2262	3110	4220	4241
U.K.	972	2095	2641	3287	3671
U.S.A.	774	3223	3720	4789	5412
Average	662	1825	2483	3651	4269

Source: This table is a revised version of figures
appearing in Angus Maddison, "Phases of Capitalist Devel-
opment," Banca Nazionale del Lavoro Quarterly Review,
No. 121 (June 1977), pp. 103-137. The conversion of
figures into U.S. 1970 prices is based on I.B. Kravis,
A. Heston and R. Summers, International Comparisons of
Real Product and Purchasing Power (Baltimore: Johns
Hopkins University Press, 1978).

moved upward, with a range in 1976 from 42 percent in Italy to 68
percent in the United States. Services have been the predominant sector
in most of the countries for the whole postwar period, and it is
anachronistic to describe these countries as industrial societies. The
movement away from agriculture is also very evident over the long run,
with a range in 1976 from less than 3 percent of employment in the
United Kingdom to 15 percent in Italy.

For industry, the situation is more difficult to interpret, but
supplementing the scatter diagram with curves drawn for individual

TABLE 3.2
Structure of Employment (Percentage Share: I = Agriculture, II = Industry, III = Services)

	1870			1950			1960			1970			1976		
	I (%)	II (%)	III (%)	I (%)	II (%)	III (%)	I (%)	II (%)	III (%)	I (%)	II (%)	III (%)	I (%)	II (%)	III (%)
Australia	30.0	38.0	32.0	14.6	36.5	48.9	11.2	40.4	48.4	8.1	38.2	53.6	6.4	32.8	60.8
Austria	65.0	19.2	15.8	34.0	35.4	30.6	24.2	39.7	36.1	18.8	40.3	40.9	12.4	40.1	47.5
Belgium	43.0	37.6	19.4	10.1	46.8	43.1	8.4	45.3	46.3	4.6	42.1	53.3	3.4	38.1	58.5
Canada	53.0	30.0	17.0	21.8	36.0	42.2	13.1	32.5	54.4	6.4	30.6	63.0	5.9	29.5	64.6
Denmark	51.7[a]	n.a.	n.a.	25.1	33.3	41.6	17.8	36.1	46.1	11.3	37.1	51.7	9.2	30.9	59.9
Finland	71.2[a]	9.7	19.1	46.0	27.7	26.3	35.8	31.4	32.8	22.3	34.8	43.0	13.6	34.1	52.3
France	49.2	27.8	23.0	28.3	34.9	36.8	21.4	36.2	42.4	13.9	38.5	47.6	10.6	37.0	52.4
Germany	49.5	28.7	21.8	22.2	43.0	34.8	13.8	48.2	38.0	8.5	48.4	43.1	6.9	44.2	48.9
Italy	62.0[b]	23.0	15.0	45.4	28.6	26.0	32.2	36.3	31.5	19.1	43.0	37.9	15.2	42.7	42.1
Japan	72.6[b]	n.a.	n.a.	48.3	22.6	29.1	30.2	28.5	41.3	17.4	35.7	46.9	12.2	35.8	52.0
Netherlands	37.0	29.0	34.0	13.9	40.2	45.9	11.1	39.1	49.8	7.0	37.7	55.3	6.4	32.9	60.7
Norway	53.0[c]	20.0	27.0	29.8	33.2	37.0	20.9	34.5	44.7	13.5	36.1	50.4	9.4	33.1	57.5
Sweden	53.9[c]	n.a.	n.a.	20.3	40.8	38.9	14.9	42.6	42.5	8.1	38.4	53.5	6.2	35.4	58.3
Switzerland	49.8	n.a.	n.a.	16.5	46.4	37.1	13.2	48.4	38.4	8.6	48.1	43.4	8.6	43.0	48.4
U.K.	22.7	42.3	35.0	5.1	46.5	48.4	4.1	47.8	48.1	3.2	44.1	52.7	2.7	39.4	57.9
U.S.A.	50.0	24.4	25.6	13.0	33.3	53.7	8.0	32.3	59.7	4.2	31.1	64.7	3.7	28.2	68.1
Average	48.8[d]	27.5[d]	23.7[d]	24.7	36.6	38.7	17.5	38.7	43.8	10.9	39.0	50.1	8.3	36.1	55.6

Source: P. Bairoch and Associates, The Working Population and Its Structure (Brussels: Universite Libre de Bruxelles, 1968); Organization for Economic Co-operation and Development, Labour Force Statistics, various issues; International Labor Organization, Yearbooks, and national sources. Agriculture includes agriculture, forestry and fishing; industry includes mining, manufacturing, electricity, gas and water, and construction. Services is a residual including all other economic activity, private and governmental (including military).

[a] 1880

[b] 1872

[c] assumes that half of the living-in rural domestic workers were engaged in agriculture

[d] excludes Denmark, Japan, Sweden and Switzerland

countries over time, it appears that the movement in the proportion of employment in industry has had a shallow bell shape, rising gradually, flattening out, then declining. The average proportion employed in industry in 1976 was 36 percent as compared with 39 percent in 1970. In 1976, industrial employment ranged from 28 percent in the United States to 44 percent in Germany. In the 1970s, the industrial share of employment dropped in virtually all of these countries, and in half of them, the absolute level of industrial employment has been falling for a decade or more. In Austria, Belgium, Germany, the Netherlands, Sweden, Switzerland, and the United Kingdom the peak absolute level of industrial employment occurred in the mid-1960s.

Although the decline in the industrial share of employment predates the 1974-75 recession and subsequent inadequate recovery, the abruptness of the decline in the 1970s has a cyclical element in it, because demand for services (particularly when, as here, government services are included) holds up better than demand for industrial products in a recession, and the propensity of the service sector to hoard labor in times of faltering demand is greater than that in industry.

Expenditure Patterns

As per capita income increases, people change their spending priorities. At low levels of income, spending on necessities like food absorbs a very high proportion of consumer budgets. At higher levels there is more room for fantasy, the relative importance of necessities fades, and a much wider range of choice is available. Another important fact is the increasing desire for leisure as income rises. In the first century of economic growth, up to about 1860, working hours increased, but since then the working year has been cut by half. Consumer demand has a powerful influence on the direction of inventive activity and leads to creation of new products as well as cost reductions for old products. But as science is not omnicompetent, technical progress is easier in some directions than others, so consumer demand is influenced by the menu of technical possibilities. Demand patterns have also been influenced by the rapid growth of collective (government financed) consumption, by the rate of investment, the pressure of advertising, and the opportunities for international trade.

Table 3.3 presents a sample of the range of expenditure patterns experienced over the past two centuries at different income levels. In England in 1688, food, drink, and clothing absorbed over 62 percent of net expenditure, and in the impoverished Japan of 1952, 46.1 percent,

TABLE 3.3
Expenditure Patterns on Net Domestic Product
(Percentage Share at Current Prices)

	England & Wales 1688	Japan 1952	Japan 1976	Netherlands 1976	USA 1976
Food and Drink	41.9%	35.7%	20.9%	14.9%	12.5%
Clothing	20.5	10.4	6.3	5.7	5.2
Other Private Consumption	28.2	20.2	37.3	42.5	56.1
Total Private Consumption	90.6	66.3	64.5	63.1	73.8
Government Consumption	4.7	11.5	12.4	20.2	21.4
Net Capital Formation	3.3	21.1	22.2	13.0	5.2
Exports	10.0	13.5	15.6	60.0	9.4
Imports	8.7	12.4	14.7	56.3	9.9
Net Domestic Product	100.0	100.0	100.0	100.0	100.0

Source: P. Deane and W.A. Cole, British Economic Growth 1688-1959 (Cambridge: At the University Press, 1964), p. 2, and Organization for Economic Co-operation and Development, National Accounts of OECD Countries, 1950 - 1968 and 1976 editions.

whereas these "necessities" accounted for only 17 7 percent of U.S. expenditure in 1976, which in total was about twenty times as high as that in the United Kingdom in 1688, and eight times the 1952 Japanese level. In fact, necessities have not declined as much as one might expect, but it should be noted that the 1976 "necessities" contain a large convenience element of packing and processing which was absent from the seventeenth-century English basket. Other things worth noting in the table are: the increased importance of government spending in 1976, the United States being a moderate government spender by advanced OECD standards, and Japan being a minimal spender; the increase in investment spending, Japan having the highest investment rate in

OECD countries, and the United States the lowest; and the big variations in the importance of international trade—in the Netherlands, the share is one of the highest, in the United States, it is one of the lowest. It should be noted, however, that even in a country like the Netherlands, a sizeable part of output is not tradeable internationally (e.g., construction, government services, some components of private consumption).

It is clear that economic growth brings major changes in expenditure patterns. People do not simply spend more on the same things. Some of the changes in private consumption patterns have been rather regular and predictable. For the postwar period, consumption patterns in the United States, the lead country, have provided a good rough guide to likely developments in European consumption at the same income level. However, technical innovation can bring unforeseen changes, and national patterns vary because of differences in habit and income distribution. Other major elements in demand such as government and investment can vary a good deal among countries and may be reversed over time. Japan, for instance, had a much higher share of government expenditure in the 1930s than it has had since World War II. The steady increase in investment rates during the 1950s and 1960s in most countries seems unlikely to continue in the future. One must beware of propounding general laws about the evolution of expenditure patterns.

Output Patterns

It is not difficult to make inferences of a fairly aggregative kind about the likely structure of output, once we know the structure of employment and demand. Table 3.4 shows the pattern of output at current prices in 1950 and 1976 in twelve of the advanced OECD countries. In 1976, service output predominated over industrial output in all of the countries except Germany, whereas in 1950 there were four cases where industrial output was bigger than that in services. In all cases, agricultural output has fallen considerably as a share of the total. The 1976 share of agricultural output may appear rather low in Table 3.4, in relation to the share of expenditure on food and drink in Table 3.3; however, we have already noted that a fair proportion of modern food and drink consumption consists of industrial value added.

The output structure of countries at the same level of income and demand can vary within a fairly wide range because of differences in international competition and their propensity to international trade. This is obviously a point of major importance, which we will only touch upon here. We note simply that most of the trade of these advanced capitalist countries is with each other, and that they have an export

TABLE 3.4
Percentage Distribution of Gross Domestic Product at Current Prices

	1950			1976		
	Agriculture	Industry	Services	Agriculture	Industry	Services
Austria	17.8%	49.6%	32.6%	5.1%	44.1%	50.8%
Denmark	21.0	36.0	43.0	7.2	37.7	55.1
Finland	25.9	40.3	33.8	11.5	42.5	46.0
France	14.7	47.3	38.0	5.2	41.7	53.1
Germany	10.4	49.8	39.8	2.9	49.4	47.7
Italy	25.3	33.3	41.4	8.2	44.6	47.2
Japan	25.7	29.7	44.6	5.5[a]	44.5[a]	50.0[a]
Netherlands	14.2	39.8	46.0	4.7[a]	41.2[a]	54.1[a]
Norway	15.1	31.7	53.2	6.5	38.1	55.4
Sweden	10.7	43.3	46.0	5.0	39.9	55.1
UK	5.8	45.5	48.7	2.9	41.2	55.9
USA	7.0	38.8	54.2	2.9	33.4	63.7
Average	16.1%	40.4%	43.4%	5.6%	41.5%	52.9%

Source: Organization for Economic Co-operation and Development, National Accounts of OECD Countries, Paris, 1950 – 1968, and 1976 editions.

[a] 1974 figure

surplus with the rest of the world in manufactures and services and a deficit in primary products. The export surplus in manufactures has declined somewhat over the postwar period as a share of GDP, but this has not been a major cause of "deindustrialization."[3] The whole of manufactured imports from developing countries in 1976 was about 0.8 percent of the GDP of OECD countries.

Changes in Price Structure

There have been substantial and rather systematic changes in relative prices in the course of economic growth (see Table 3.5). Over the period 1950 to 1976, prices of agricultural and industrial products have generally risen more slowly than those of services. Productivity growth has been faster in commodity production than in services, but people employed in services have generally managed to raise their incomes as fast as those employed in commodity production. This has forced up the

TABLE 3.5
Rise in Prices by Sector: 1950 - 76
(annual average compound growth rates)

	Agriculture	Industry	Services
Austria	3.8 %	4.6 %	8.0 %
Denmark	4.3	5.2	6.3
Finland	7.7	6.8	8.2
France	4.9	4.4	7.3
Germany	2.7	3.3	5.3
Italy	4.5	5.5	7.1
Norway	5.6	5.8	4.8
Sweden	5.4	4.7	5.9
UK	4.0	6.0	6.9
USA	1.9	2.7	3.8
Average	4.5 %	4.9 %	6.4 %

Source: Organization for Economic Co-operation and Development, National Accounts of OECD Countries Paris, 1950 - 1968, and 1976 editions.

[a]1974 figure

price of services, which has been all the easier because of the relative lack of foreign competition in the service sector.

Productivity Changes by Sector

Perhaps the most interesting aspect of structural change has been the rather systematic variation in productivity performance between different sectors, which throws some light on the character of technical change. Table 3.6 shows the growth of output per person by sector for the postwar period for the countries where rough estimates are feasible. Productivity performance in the service sector has been a good deal slower in every case than in commodity production, and productivity in agriculture has grown faster than in industry in most countries.

Table 3.7 shows productivity growth by sector for the eight decades 1870 to 1950. In this period the overall pace of productivity growth was much slower, and this was true of growth in each sector. Again we find

TABLE 3.6
Growth of Output Per Person by Sector and Economy Wide:
1950-1976 (annual average compound growth rates)

	Agriculture	Industry	Services	GDP
Austria	6.0%	5.2%	2.9%	5.1%
Denmark	3.7	3.6	1.6	2.8
Finland	5.6	4.1	1.9	4.3
France	4.7	5.0	2.8	4.4
Germany	5.8	5.4	2.9	4.7
Italy	5.6	4.3	1.8	4.2
Japan	6.2	8.3	4.0	7.2
Netherlands	4.8	5.3	2.0	3.4
Norway	4.3	3.7	2.3	3.4
Sweden	4.6	3.9	1.6	2.8
U.K.	4.0	2.6	1.3	2.3
U.S.A.	5.1	2.8	1.4	1.8
Average	5.0 %	4.5 %	2.2 %	3.9 %

Source: Angus Maddison, "Long Run Dynamics of Productivity Growth," Banca Nazionale del Lavoro Quarterly Review, No. 128 (March 1979).

TABLE 3.7
Growth of Output Per Person by Sector and Economy Wide:
1870-1950 (annual average compound growth rates)

	Agriculture	Industry	Services	GDP
Germany[a]	0.2%	1.3%	0.7%	1.2%
Italy	0.5	1.4	0.6	0.9
Japan[b]	0.7	1.7	0.5	1.1
U.K.	1.4	1.2	0.2	0.8
Average	0.7 %	1.4 %	0.5 %	1.0 %

Source: Angus Maddison, "Long Run Dynamics of Productivity Growth." Banca Nazionale del Lavoro Quarterly Review, No. 128 (March 1979).

[a] 1871-1950

[b] 1906-1950

service productivity growing more slowly than industrial productivity, but agricultural productivity performance was by no means as bright in this earlier period as it has been since the second world war.

The higher productivity growth of these economies since the war has been due to a complexity of causes, with major significance attaching to the increased level of demand, and the much higher levels of investment. The great acceleration of productivity growth in agriculture has been due in large degree to the "pull" effect of high demand elsewhere in the economy, which provided an outlet for underemployed rural labor. In earlier decades of slower (below potential) growth, agriculture was a depository of hoarded labor. Now that the labor surplus has been so largely disgorged, it is perhaps unlikely that agricultural productivity will continue to outperform that of industry (though in terms of productivity levels, agriculture is still a lagging sector).

It is interesting to compare levels as well as the growth of productivity. This is done in Table 3.8, which compares productivity levels in 1950 and 1976 (measured in the prices of each of these years). The most striking change in the table is the reduction in the spread of productivity between sectors, with particularly marked reduction in the relative standing of the service sector.

In interpreting the relative productivity standing of different sectors it should be remembered that price structures differ between countries, and that the type of labor input varies between sectors in a somewhat systematic way. In the first place, about half of those employed in services are females, whereas only about a quarter of industrial employment is female, and about a third of that in agriculture (see Table 3.9). A second point worth noticing is that the average education level of people in services is higher than in the other two sectors. A third point is that working hours differ between sectors. In the United States, working hours are clearly lower in services than in agriculture or industry.[4] The same seems true of Denmark and the United Kingdom, but not of the other EEC countries.[5]

The Outlook

Having thus completed, on a rather aggregative and simplistic level, the analysis and review of past structural change, one is led (particularly in a conference of the Hudson Institute) to speculate on future trends.

A fundamental consideration is, of course, the likely rate of growth of total output. I have elsewhere indicated reasons for thinking that future growth will generally be slower than that experienced from 1950 to 1970.[6] My own analysis suggests that productivity (output per man-hour) growth potential of these countries is likely to be around 3.5 percent a year provided there is not a big fall in the rate of investment. In all these countries the labor force is expected to increase over the period 1975 to 1990 but the average increase in labor input may well be negligible, if economic policy and events of the past few years are any guide (see Table 3.10). Fear of inflation has led to restrictive macroeconomic demand management combined with labor market policies which have generally restricted the growth of labor supply. If this policy mix continues it seems quite likely that the work year will be generally shortened. If by 1990 it were shortened to 1500 hours per person a year (a 33.3 hour working week with seven weeks off for vacation, public holidays, etc.), then there would be no increase in labor input on average for these countries, and output growth would be more or less synonymous with productivity growth; i.e., GDP and output per man-hour would grow on average at about 3.5 percent a year in these

TABLE 3.8
Level of Output Per Man 1950 and 1976 (Gross Domestic Product per man--at current prices--in year specified = 100)

	1950			1976		
	Agriculture	Industry	Services	Agriculture	Industry	Services
Austria	52	140	107	41	110	107
Denmark	84	108	103	78	122	92
Finland	56	146	129	85	125	88
France	52	136	103	49	113	101
Germany	47	115	115	42	112	98
Italy	56	116	159	54	104[a]	112[a]
Japan	49	81	199	36[a]	126[a]	104[a]
Netherlands	103	99	100	90[a]	112[a]	93[a]
Norway	51	96	144	69	115	96
Sweden	53	106	118	81	113	95
UK	113	98	101	107	105	97
USA	54	117	101	78	118	94
Average	64	113	123	68	115	98

Source: Organization for Economic Cooperation and Development, National Accounts of OECD Countries, Paris, 1950-1968, and 1976 editions, and Labor Force Statistics, various editions. In some cases supplementary national sources were used.

[a] 1970

TABLE 3.9
Female Share of Employment in 1976
(Percent)

	Agriculture (%)	Industry (%)	Services (%)
Austria	46.4 %	25.4[a] %	47.2[a] %
Denmark	27.2	23.2[a]	51.9[a]
Finland	41.8	29.2[a]	60.3[a]
France	30.5	22.5[a]	48.2[a]
Germany	52.5	25.1[a]	47.9[a]
Italy	33.1	20.2[a]	35.0[a]
Japan	49.1	28.8[a]	40.3[a]
Netherlands	13.4[b]	12.3[b]	35.9[b]
Norway	32.1	18.1[a]	51.2[a]
Sweden	25.2	22.1[a]	57.1[a]
UK	19.7	24.1[a]	50.3[a]
USA	17.5	23.2[a]	48.0[a]
Average	32.4 %	22.9 %	47.8 %

Source: Organization for Economic Co-operation and Development, Demographic Statistics, and Labour Force Statistics.

[a] 1975

[b] 1971

countries to 1990, instead of the 4.9 percent per annum GDP and 4.4 percent per annum productivity growth experienced from 1950 to 1970. Even on this relatively modest hypothesis, 1990 output would be two-thirds higher than in 1975, and output per head would go up by more than half.

As far as expenditure structures are concerned, it seems likely that the investment share may decline modestly, and that the government share will be fairly stable, leaving a slight increase in the share of private consumption. Since the scope for further trade liberalization is not great within such a scenario, I would not expect much change in the ratio of trade to output. In terms of output structures (see Table 3.4), I would

TABLE 3.10
Estimates of 1990 Productivity and Output Levels

	1975 Level of GDP per Man Hour (1970 US Dollars)	Assumed Rate of Growth of GDP per Man Hour 1975-90 (b) (annual average compound growth rate)	Projected Level of GDP per Man Hour 1990 Derived from Cols. 1 & 2 (1970 US Dollars)	Estimate of 1990 Level of Total Hours Worked (million hours)	1990 GDP Derived from Columns 3 and 4 (million 1970 US Dollars)	1990 Population (millions)	1990 GDP per Head Derived from Cols. 5 and 6 (1970 US Dollars)
Australia	5.74	2.6%	8.44	11,806	99,643	15,622	6,378
Austria	4.80	4.2	8.89	5,384	47,864	7,520	6,365
Belgium	6.68	3.3	10.87	6,511	70,775	10,037	7,051
Canada	6.46	2.7	9.63	19,172	184,626	28,086	6,574
Denmark	4.85	3.3	7.90	4,055	32,035	5,259	6,091
Finland	4.55	4.0	8.20	3,563	29,217	4,918	5,941
France	5.44	3.7	9.38	36,395	341,385	55,113	6,194
Germany	5.91[a]	4.4	11.28	40,289	454,460	58,202	7,808
Italy	5.17[a]	4.0	8.60	34,723	298,618	59,082	5,054
Japan	3.69	5.2	7.90	87,441	690,784	127,863	5,403
Netherlands	6.41[a]	3.3	9.77	8,296	81,052	14,191	5,712
Norway	6.03	3.6	10.25	2,930	30,033	3,479	8,633
Sweden	6.13	3.3	9.98	6,786	67,724	8,353	8,108
Switzerland	4.97[a]	3.0	7.30	4,647	33,923	6,333	5,357
UK	4.50	2.7	6.71	41,006	275,150	56,562	4,865
USA	7.31	2.5	10.59	168,714	1,786,681	243,513	7,337

Source: Columns 1, 2, and 4 same as Table 3.6. Column 6 from Organization for Economic Co-operation and Development, Demographic Trends: Their Economic and Social Implications (Paris, 1979) Columns 3, 5 and 7 from the above.

[a] 1977

[b] Assumed rate is average of 1950-70 rate and the 2.5 percent achieved by the USA in 1950-1970.

expect the average situation in this group of countries in 1990 to be something like that in the United States in 1976, i.e., a negligible proportion devoted to agriculture, a third to industry, and over 60 percent to services.

I do not see much reason to expect the pattern of change in relative prices and productivity to diverge much over the next decade or so from the patterns exhibited in Tables 3.5 and 3.7, but I expect productivity growth rates to falter somewhat and the rate of price increase to accelerate.

Given such trends and the projected level of real GDP per head, one can get some idea of the likely pattern of employment in 1990. The average level of GDP per head in 1990 is projected (Table 3.10) at $6,429 for this group, an advance of about 50 percent on the 1976 level (the last year represented on the scatter diagram in Figure 3.1). Thus the average level of 1990 per capita income falls beyond the range illustrated on the right hand side of the scatter diagram, with assumed 1990 income levels ranging from $4,865 in the United Kingdom to $8,633 in Norway. Individual country situations will vary a good deal, but it seems probable that agricultural employment will average less than 5 percent of total employment, and service employment about two-thirds, with less than 30 percent of the labor force in industrial employment.

As the total increase in the labor force will be rather modest in most countries, such a scenario will mean further absolute reductions in industrial employment in several cases. There have already been such absolute reductions in Austria, Belgium, Germany, the Netherlands, Sweden, Switzerland, and the United Kingdom where the peak level was reached during the 1960s. The problem of adjusting to such change is therefore not new, and should not be a major cause for social concern, given the fact that service employment is generally more pleasant and provides more equal opportunity for both sexes. Nevertheless, problems of deindustrialization have given major cause for concern particularly in the United Kingdom, which is often wrongly assumed to have been unique in this respect. There are also dangers that efforts to preserve a certain level of industrial employment, because of sector fetishism à la Kaldor, will be inimical to both growth and welfare.[7]

Notes

1. This paper is rather aggregative. A more detailed treatment for postwar Europe can be found in United Nations, Economic Commission for Europe, *Structure and Change in European Industry*, New York, 1977. However,

international comparisons of a historical character are difficult to make with any degree of reliability, once one goes beyond the traditional three-sector approach developed by Colin Clark and Simon Kuznets.

2. For the 1970s type of argument, see Organization for Economic Co-operation and Development, *Structural Determinants of Employment and Unemployment*, Paris, 1977; the U.S. structural debate in the early 1960s is summarized in A. M. Okun, "Conflicting National Goals," in E. Ginzberg, *Jobs for Americans* (Englewood Cliffs, N.J.: Prentice Hall, 1976), pp. 67-71; a classic structuralist interpretation of interwar European problems is I. Svennilson, *Growth and Stagnation of the European Economy* (Geneva: United Nations, Economic Commission for Europe, 1954).

3. In 1976 the trade in manufactures of what GATT calls "industrial countries" (i.e., our "advanced capitalist" countries) was as follows (in billion dollars):

	Imports	Exports
From each other	287	287
From developing	35	128
Other	11	40

See R. Blackhurst, N. Marian, and J. Tumlir, *Adjustment, Trade and Growth in Developed and Developing Countries* (Geneva: General Agreement on Tariffs and Trade, September 1978). In 1976, the GDP of OECD countries was about $4.4 trillion.

4. See U.S. Department of Labor, Bureau of Labor Statistics, *Handbook of Labor Statistics*, Bulletin 1966, 1977, p. 137, and E. F. Denison, *Accounting for United States Economic Growth 1929-1969* (Washington, D.C.: Brookings Institution, 1974), p. 182.

5. See *Labour Force Sample Survey 1975* (Luxembourg: Eurostat, 1976), p. 106.

6. See Angus Maddison, in "Productivity Trends in Continental Western Europe 1950-90," *The Future of Productivity* (Washington: National Center for Productivity and Quality of Working Life, Winter 1977), p. 108. See also, idem, "Long Run Dynamics of Productivity Growth," *Banca Nazional del Lavoro Quarterly Review*, No. 128, March 1979.

7. British concern with this issue is amply explored in Frank Blackaby, ed., *Deindustrialisation* (London: Heinemann for National Institute of Economic and Social Research, 1979). There is also an interesting and highly disaggregated study of British postwar trends in employment and productivity in R. Wragg and J. Robertson, *Postwar Trends in Employment, Productivity, Output, Labour Costs and Prices by Industry in the United Kingdom*, Research Paper No. 3 (London: Department of Employment, June 1978). From 1954 to 1973 there was a decline in output in sixteen out of eighty-two British manufacturing industries, and a decline in employment in fifty-two of them. In services, where productivity rose much more slowly than in manufacturing, output fell in six out of twenty-two branches, and employment in eight out of twenty-two.

Commentary

Maurice Lengellé

I shall limit myself to two observations concerning the measurement of productivity and the comparison of productivity among the three economic sectors.

When you look at the charts compiled by Professor Maddison and try to project into the future—for instance, if you project the constant rate of growth of the employment share in the service sector to 2000—you will each more than 100 percent. It is hard to accept the idea that in 2000, more than 100 percent of employment will be in the service sector. The question I pose is whether there will be a kind of reversal of employment trends in the service sector. Productivity growth is most important to the answer.

I have two remarks on this point. The first concerns the methodology used to measure productivity in the service sector. As has already been observed by many economists, Professor Maddison notes that productivity growth in the service sector is much lower than in the two other sectors. His calculations are based on the national accounts. However, in some OECD countries the link between production and the labor force in the service sector is based on an assumption that productivity growth is low in that sector. Take France, for example. Our national planning administration has very sophisticated models within which the labor force for the service sector is derived from the forecast for production under the assumption of a declining growth rate of productivity. Of course, when you divide production by the labor force in such countries, what do you obtain? Low productivity for the service sector. This question has been addressed in the national planning in France and also at the OECD.

About ten years ago I was appointed by the OECD Secretariat to attempt measurement of production and productivity in about thirty groups of the service sector: banking, insurance, theaters, cinemas, hotels, restaurants, laundries, and also in some very strange activities like gambling casinos, auction rooms, church services, funeral services, and so forth. After looking into these fields and attempting to define production—deflating returns by prices, establishing a list of physical units, and also trying to produce a kind of utility measure for services—I made some progress comparable to that in the manufacturing industry. The results of my work and that of Victor Fuchs, who organized an important OECD symposium on the future of technology in the service sector, show an emergence of new technology in the service sector and a concomitant increase in productivity.[1]

The gap between results obtained by direct measurement of productivity and indirect measurement, as carried out for national accounts, may be attributed to two main factors. The first is the difficulty in taking into account the quality of services within national accounts. For instance, when you measure productivity in a hospital, will you divide the number of beds by the number of nurses? Will you consider the delay in caring for diseases? Will you take a lower rate of mortality into account? These questions show the difficulties involved in measuring the quality of services. This is a real problem that has not been very well studied.

The second reason why a gap exists between the results obtained by different measures of productivity is that a higher proportion of services provided by the tertiary sector—that is to say the service sector—merges into two other sectors in the form of services rendered by the agriculture and manufacturing industries. If you have more accountants, the productivity of accountants diminishes; but, thanks to better management in the two other sectors, the real productivity of accountants is probably growing. The work of Edward Denison, and an OECD study called *The Residual Factor*, shows that the unexplained component of economic growth (the residual factor) contains a high proportion of services—for instance education—which are provided by the tertiary sector and transferred to tangible goods-producing sectors.[2]

My second observation deals with Maddison's discussion of productivity growth among the sectors. Productivity growth in the three sectors has developed in successive waves. The decreasing spread of productivity among the three sectors is a recent event. Before World War II, gains in productivity were largely limited to manufacturing. Alan Fisher, Colin Clark, and Jean Fourastié tried to show that the service sector experienced flattening productivity growth during that period; they suggested that adjustment occurred by the movement of workers from tangible goods production to the service sector.[3] In the 1950s and 1960s, a boom occurred in agricultural productivity, thanks to two factors—substitution of capital for labor, and new technology (hybrid plants and improved animals with low feed conversion ratios). It is only during the last decade that productivity growth in the service sector has emerged, thanks to many factors: strong demand from both the government and consumers, increasing competition, economies of scale (hotels are a good example), better training of employees, mechanization, new technology (communication satellites are a good example), and better management and advertising. The question of measuring production and productivity is critical to understanding and forecasting employment trends. We simply do not know when the curve representing employment in the service sector will turn around and what kind of impact this will have on employment as a whole.

Notes

1. Organization for Economic Co-operation and Development, *Problems of Manpower in the Service Sector* (Paris: 1967).
2. Organization for Economic Co-operation and Development, *The Residual Factor and Economic Progress* (Paris: 1965).
3. Alan G. B. Fisher, *The Clash of Progress and Security* (London: MacMillan, 1935); Colin Clark, *Economic Progress and Social Security* (London: MacMillan, 1947); and Jean Fourastié, *Le Grand Espoir du XXeme Siècle* (Paris: 1948).

Commentary

Richard R. Nelson

Like many scholars in this field, I have been using Angus Maddison's data for many years. I also have been quite sympathetic with his earlier analyses of the sources of rapid postwar growth, and with his more current commentary on the slowdown. His present paper provides us with a fascinating set of tables. I enjoyed going over them and figuring out whether they were consonant with other things that I know about.

Maddison's focus is on the changing composition of employment and the forces behind it. Maddison has looked at two kinds of forces. One set of forces relates to changing patterns of demand for different types of goods and services as incomes grow in general, and as prices change among different classes of goods and services. The other set relates to differential productivity growth rates.

Considering demand side factors first, I would like to flag an interesting question. In terms of the composition of employment changes in an economy that is experiencing significant differences in productivity growth rates among different economic sectors, it matters considerably whether demands for particular products are elastic or inelastic. An intriguing thing that seems to have been happening recently—at least in the late 1960s and into the early 1970s—is that the demand for products of the sectors where productivity has been growing most rapidly—agriculture and various manufacturing industries—has been inelastic; meanwhile demand for services, one of the broadly defined sectors where productivity has been growing very slowly, also seems to be inelastic. Thus, resources are being drawn out of rapid productivity growth sectors into a less rapid growth sector. This is not inevitable; my conjecture is that in the earlier years of very rapid growth we were operating with regimes in which demand for the more rapid productivity growth sectors were much more elastic. I wonder why. Is something different now? If so, what?

Maddison sometimes talks about demand side forces as if demands were largely privately generated. But changes in the pattern of demand cannot be so simply modelled. In virtually all of the OECD countries, there have been significant increases in the magnitude of overall government expenditures. The shift into the services and away from manufacturing seems to be in considerable part a consequence of the growth of government expenditures and the pattern that this growth has taken. This has been disguised in countries like the United States, and earlier in Britain, by very large defense budgets, which were hardware manufacturing oriented. During recent years, if you identify increases in government expenditures in goods and services and try to trace where they have gone, you will find that the recipients are sectors like education and health—the service sectors. This phenomenon will be examined critically from a policy point of view in my paper.

The other side of Maddison's explanation relates to the striking differences in productivity growth rates across different sectors and different industries. If he had had more space and more time, I am certain he would have thrown in the caveat that measurement of output in service sectors is notoriously difficult. Too often we are measuring outputs in terms of inputs. I suspect that part of the differential productivity growth that we perceive is a measurement problem, but Angus Maddison and I would agree that a real phenomenon exists as well. It is hard to look at barbershopping or education and see much in the way of productivity growth over the last ten years—or one hundred years—even if one goes behind the raw data. Several studies have probed this, but not too effectively. I think it is a real phenomenon.

Let us assume that current patterns of demand shift continue for a period of time and, as a result, an increasing fraction of society's resources are involved in sectors where productivity growth is relatively slow. An important consequence of this is that, even if we returned to the pace of productivity growth, sector by sector, that occurred during the 1950s and early 1960s, in the macroeconomy as a whole, average productivity growth would be lower. The question then becomes, why has productivity growth been so slow in these particular sectors? There is a proximate answer that one can give. If you trace direct and indirect research and development expenditures (maybe over the last fifteen or twenty years) as a proxy variable for inventive input, you will find that slow productivity growth industries and sectors tend to be associated with smaller volumes of research and development expenditure.

One is tempted by the hypothesis that the shifts in the allocation of resources ought to be calling for significant changes in the composition and allocation of research and development resources. There are a host of interesting questions. Are allocation mechanisms with respect to research and development resources sensitive to these kinds of changes in demand patterns? Are they sensitive enough? What would happen in the service sectors which have experienced low productivity growth in the past, and have had low levels of research and development input, if they had significantly more R&D? One could entertain the hypothesis that inventive inputs in these sectors have been so low simply because it is very hard to do the job, in the sense that the industries and technologies underlying them differ significantly in the extent to which they are amenable to the types of activities that humankind has evolved over the last hundred years or so to enhance productivity. Or one could be more optimistic.

Maddison's data vividly depict societies where resources have increasingly shifted into service sectors. A good portion of these are public service sectors, but a number of private service sectors are involved as well. Measured productivity growth in these sectors has been quite slow compared with measured productivity growth in manufacturing and, more recently at least, in agriculture. Given this changed pattern of resources, gains to society from lifting productivity growth in these sectors would be quite high—much higher than before. Do we know how to do it?

4
Technical Advance and Productivity Growth: Retrospect, Prospect, and Policy Issues

Richard R. Nelson

Introduction

In the middle of the 1960s a number of books were written proposing that the Western market-oriented economies had solved the problem of simultaneously achieving rapid productivity growth, low levels of unemployment, and acceptable rates of inflation.[1] Self-congratulation has a way of foreshadowing trouble. I presume that the central questions of this conference are: What went wrong? How can we make things right again?

The recent economic malaise has been marked by a wide variety of symptoms: slow productivity growth, high unemployment rates, rapid inflation, and balance of payments stress. Obviously, the various features are strongly connected and any analysis of one cannot avoid some discussion of the others. The central focus of this essay is on productivity growth, and its most important proximate source— technical advance. But the analysis inevitably will bring other aspects of the current economic malaise into the picture.

This essay will examine the rapid growth experience of the 1950s and 1960s and the break in trend that occurred during the early 1970s, interpret and explain the productivity growth slowdown in a manner that provides some illumination of prospects for the future, and sketch out some of the major policy problems that must be faced and resolved if productivity growth rates are to recover. But before this discussion, it is necessary to describe the key processes and institutions involved in productivity growth.

Sources of Productivity Growth

This section will first consider the role of technical advance and other factors as sources of productivity growth and, second, look behind the scenes to consider the factors that influence the pace and pattern of technical advance. The purpose is to lay the groundwork for subsequent analysis of what has been happening.

"Accounting" for Growth

By economic growth I mean continuing increase over time in the value of goods and services produced per capita. There are a number of technical problems with the use of per capita GNP as the basic measure of growth, and deeper questions about the relationship between growth so defined and the human condition. However, it is apparent that most citizens in the OECD countries place high value on rising living standards conventionally defined, which, to be achieved widely, require growth of GNP per capita. The fall since the early 1970s in the rate of economic growth is widely regarded as a threat to hopes of continuing increases in living standards.

A large number of factors enter into growth of GNP per capita. Change over time in the fraction of population in the work force, the employment rate, and average hours worked per week or per year obviously are very important. But over the long run, growth has been largely the consequence of increase in product per hour worked. The focus here is on the sources of productivity growth in this sense.

During the 1950s and 1960s a considerable body of research was directed toward trying to assess how much of the growth of measured GNP per man-hour could be attributed to technical advance, and how much to other factors such as growth of capital per worker, increase in average educational attainments of the work force, changing age, sex, and experience composition of workers, and shifting allocation of resources among industries. Virtually without exception these studies concluded that only a very small fraction of the productivity increase could have been achieved without technical advance. These studies have been summarized and popularized in a number of places; therefore there is no point in reviewing them here.[2]

There is a point, however, in discussing two aspects of the productivity growth process that tend to be repressed in many reports. First, the sources of growth tend to interact as strong complements. Second, there are very great differences among sectors and industries in rates of measured productivity growth and technical advance. Understanding these aspects is essential to understanding what has been happening to productivity growth and why.

While many discussions of productivity growth implicitly treat the sources as in some sense independent and additive, clearly this is not so. In particular, technical advance and investment in physical capital are strongly complementary. Technical advance keeps the rate of return on capital high and investment attractive; at the same time new capital brings new technology into the production process. Moreover, in many industries much of inventive and innovative activity (often counted as research and development but sometimes not) is intimately associated with designing, building, and learning from new capital equipment. Similarly there are strong interactions among rising educational attainments and technical advance as sources of productivity growth. The rise of educational attainments among the working population has provided the scientists, engineers, and skilled flexible workers, who have contributed to technical progress. Conversely, it is the profitability of R&D and of the activities associated with technical progress in general which has made the market for scientists and engineers, and enhanced the desirability to employers of well-educated and flexible workers more generally.

In many countries the shift of resources, particularly labor, from low to high productivity industries—particularly from agriculture to manufacturing—has been an important source of growth of GNP per worker (average productivity). This source of growth also is connected with the pace and pattern of technical change that we have experienced. The uneven levels of productivity across sectors and industries is a reflection of the fact that past technical change has proceeded much more rapidly in some sectors than in others.

This fact, the unevenness of technical progress across sectors and industries, warrants careful attention. By conventional measures, productivity growth and technical advance have occurred much more rapidly in the chemical process industries than in house building, in air transport than in local transport, in manufacturing than in service industries. Table 4.1, reprinted from a study by Terleckyj, displays Kendrick's figures for U.S. productivity growth. Data from other countries suggest a similar pattern. There is good reason, therefore, not to think about an "overall" rate of productivity growth or technical progress at all, but rather to recognize that productivity growth occurs at significantly different rates in different economic activities. The consequences have been important. They have included major changes in relative prices, with the products of industries experiencing low productivity growth rising in price relative to those where productivity growth has been rapid.

Where price elasticities of demand in the rapid productivity growth sectors have been high, resources have moved into these sectors and out of low productivity growth sectors. Where price elasticities of demand for the products of the industries experiencing rapid productivity

TABLE 4.1
Productivity Growth and Research & Development

	Productivity Growth Rate Average, 1948-66	R&D Conducted Industry as % of Value Added, 1958	R&D Embodied in Purchased Goods as % of Value Added, 1958
Air transportation	8.0%	0%	3.1%
Coal mining	5.2	0	.4
Railroads	5.2	0	.3
Chemicals	4.9	8.6	2.6
Electric & Gas utilities	4.9	.1	.6
Textiles	4.0	.4	2.2
Rubber products	3.9	1.5	2.6
Communication utilities	3.8	.4	1.7
Electrical machinery	3.7	17.5	5.2
Lumber products	3.5	.2	.4
Farming	3.3	.5	.7
Oil and gas extraction	3.2	.2	.2
Transportation equipment & ordnance	3.2	25.5	7.6
Foods	3.0	.5	.7
Petroleum refining	3.0	4.5	1.2
Furniture	2.9	.2	.5
Instruments	2.9	7.8	4.3
Printing and publishing	2.7	0	.4
Machinery, excluding electric	2.6	6.2	2.0
Nonmetal mining	2.6	0	.5
Paper	2.5	.9	.6
Wholesale trade	2.5	0	.2
Metal mining	2.4	0	.6
Retail trade	2.4	0	.2
Stone, clay & glass products	2.4	.9	.6
Beverages	2.2	.3	.7
Apparel	1.9	.1	.3
Fabricated metal products	1.9	1.2	1.0
Leather products	1.7	.2	.3
Primary metal products	1.6	1.0	.8
Contract construction	1.5	0	.9
Tobacco products	1.1	0	.3
Water transportation	0.5	0	.4

Sources: Taken from Tables 1 and 2 of Nestor E. Terleckyj, Effects of R&D on the Productivity Growth of Industries: An Exploratory Study (Washington,D.C.: National Planning Association, 1974).

growth have been low the result has been the movement of resources out of those sectors. Symmetrically, sectors experiencing low productivity growth but with high price elasticities of demand have lost resources; low productivity growth sectors with low price elasticities of demand have drawn in resources.

Shifts in the allocation of labor across sectors, obscured in the macroeconomic accounts of growth, have been essential aspects of the overall growth process. These shifts have been facilitated where labor held flexible industry and job attachments, and investment rates were high, permitting rapid change in capital allocation across industries. Here again one recognizes the complementarity of the sources of growth. And one recognizes, as well, why growth is often a painful process which, while generating gains on the average, doles out losses to workers and capital in declining industries. And one comes to recognize a tension between the objective of rapid growth and the objective of income and job security, a tension that has become increasingly salient over the past decade. In almost all of the OECD countries, programs to protect incomes and sometimes jobs from the hurly-burly of growth have become increasingly important and strong.

Factors Generating and Molding Technical Progress

What lies behind the technical advance that has been achieved, molding its pace and uneven pattern? What are the key inputs, and the institutional structures guiding their allocation and influencing their effectiveness?

Considerable empirical research has supported the proposition that research and development activity is an important proximate source of technical progress. As indicated in Table 4.1, by and large the rapid productivity growth sectors and industries either are big R&D spenders (like chemicals) or purchase equipment from big R&D spenders (like air transport).

With the exceptions of R&D concerned with national security, space exploration, atomic energy, agriculture, and some areas of medicine, most of the applied research and development in the OECD countries is undertaken and financed by private business firms. Private industrial R&D is allocated quite unevenly across economic sectors and industries. It is this uneven allocation which lies behind the uneven pattern of technical advance we have experienced. How can one explain the allocation of private R&D spending? Scholars of technical advance have studied the role of two classes of factors—demand or payoff factors determining the returns from R&D if successful, and cost or feasibility factors influencing the resources that must be put into an R&D effort to have a reasonable chance of success.

The role of demand or payoff factors in influencing technical advance is very well documented. Changes in an industry's output level, prices of products or inputs, and regulatory requirements all have been shown to influence the amount and kind of research and development found worthwhile by those responsible for directing those activities. For example, growth of one industry relative to another is associated with a shift in the allocation of R&D effort of machinery makers toward equipment relevant to the expanding industry. A rise in the price of one input relative to another is associated with a shift of R&D attention to efforts designed to save on the more costly factor. Recently, the new regimes of regulation clearly have pulled private R&D attention to trying to meet the new requirements.

Understanding of factors influencing the cost or technical feasibility of different kinds of technical advance, and the effect of these factors on the allocation of R&D, is not as strong as understanding of demand factors. Most of the industries where technical advance has been rapid have been able to exploit the knowledge of strong fields of science in guiding the evolution of their technologies. Some of these industries' technologies are closely linked to certain academic fields of scientific inquiry—chemical products and electronics industries, for example. But in these industries and in others, there has been a strong and successful effort by industry and government to support the sciences relevant to the technologies.

Allocating industrial R&D according to what firms regard as profitable leads to considerable sensitivity of R&D on the one hand to individual and social wants as expressed in the marketplace or regulatory regimes, and on the other hand to the cost and feasibility of different kinds of endeavors. However, such an allocation mechanism working alone may lead to neglect of certain kinds of advances of major social value, and to the development of certain technologies of limited value which carry high social costs. There are two basic reasons. First, different kinds of R&D projects and different institutional settings involve different degrees to which a firm paying for R&D can capture the benefits. For example, where imitation is cheap and easy, a demand for certain product improvements may not generate much R&D; on the other hand, where the returns to a new design are well protected either by a patent, by market power, or by a long technical lead, the links between product demand and incentives for R&D are much stronger. Second, R&D incentives tend to be warped when certain important dimensions of product benefit or cost are not priced by the market, or not regulated. If pollution is not taxed or regulated, pollution costs will not be judged in the profit calculations regarding new technologies to be developed.

However, in for-profit firms funding their own R&D efforts, attending market incentives are far from the full story about R&D allocation. A nontrivial fraction of R&D is conducted by governmental or not-for-profit private institutions or is subsidized in one way or another. A variety of nonmarket mechanisms conflict with or add to the incentives and constraints directing R&D allocation.

Unlike applied research and development which in most OECD countries is largely undertaken by business firms, basic research is largely undertaken in universities, not-for-profit research institutions, and to some extent in government laboratories, and is largely financed by government. Governments support and sometimes undertake applied R&D in areas relating to public or quasi-public wants. The bulk of such funds go into R&D activities relating to defense, atomic energy, and space. Government funds for R&D on nondefense public sector needs have always been much more limited than funds for defense, but in recent years these funds have risen significantly, particularly in the United States. Governments traditionally also have supported R&D on health and agriculture, usually in government laboratories, universities, or other not-for-profit institutions. In recent years some of the OECD governments have expanded programs to subsidize R&D in technically progressive industries for the purpose of establishing or preserving competitive advantage. For the most part these industries overlap those supported by defense and space R&D. Outside of these industries, none of the OECD governments are a major source of funds for the development of general industrial technology.

However, government policies have a significant impact on incentives and constraints for private R&D in this broader area. In the first place, governmental demands comprise a large share of the market for goods and services in many sectors, and government demands, as private demands, tend to draw the attention of R&D entrepreneurs. Generally, privately funded R&D efforts compete with or complement publicly funded ones in arenas where the demands are public.

One of the most striking developments of the last decade has been a growing attempt to defend or enhance nonmarket values in sectors selling goods and services to the general public through various regulatory regimes. Prominent here are the environmental and safety regulations of the United States and several other OECD countries. These regulatory structures have an important effect on R&D incentives. In addition, in some fields, prominently pharmaceuticals and pesticides, R&D is now regulated directly, and an extension of the arena of "technology assessment" and direct regulation of new technologies has been proposed by some analysts. These new mechanisms for regulating technical advance, indirectly or directly, reflect a growing tension in the OECD countries regarding the relative importance of market and nonmarket values. What is at stake is the nature of future economic growth.

The effect of the new regulatory regimes on R&D and technical advance is well recognized if not well understood. What has not been as well recognized, however, is that more general government regulatory, competitive, and trade policies strongly influence the incentives for R&D. In the analysis which follows, considerable stress will be placed on the effects upon R&D and technical advance of the economic slack that governments have permitted to persist over the past five years.

The Era of Rapid Growth

This section will discuss certain aspects of the postwar era of rapid growth. First, I will consider general contributing factors and then turn to intercountry and intersectoral differences.

The Era of Rapid Growth: Contributing Factors

The period between the mid-1950s and the early 1970s was one of remarkably rapid growth. Kuznets, Maddison, Denison, and others all have shown that growth of measured GNP per worker and per capita was faster during this period, in virtually all of the OECD countries, than during any other past era of comparable duration.[3] The key question is, What lay behind this growth acceleration?

Certainly, the initial conditions set the stage for rapid growth. Many of the OECD countries had experienced devastating physical losses during World War II. Most had experienced economic stagnation during the prior depression. Thus all of the nations came out of the war with a perception of large unmet needs for private and public goods, capital shortages, and a shelf of unused technical advances which had accrued over the years of depression and war, a situation virtually guaranteeing a high rate of return on investment and rapid productivity growth as capital expanded. The economic policy problem clearly was to set institutional conditions so that capacity and productivity could expand rapidly, and preserve balance between demand growth and potential output growth.

And yet roughly the same conditions held after World War I, but growth during the 1920s was erratic, and ended abruptly in the depression of the 1930s. What was different?

Some commentators have ascribed the difference to the fact that between these two postwar periods economists had revised their thinking regarding how government fiscal and monetary policies could keep economies from sliding into depressions, and that after the Second World War governments were attuned to Keynesian advice.[4] Yet some of the most rapidly growing economies—those of Germany and Japan for example—had governments that certainly did not put forth Keynesian rhetoric, and operated under regimes of legal and institutional constraints that would have made Keynesian remedies difficult to implement had they been needed. The United States and Great Britain, the two countries most explicit in their adherence to Keynes, experienced the slowest growth rates of the major OECD countries.

One can posit that the balancing tasks of fiscal and monetary policy are eased in eras where investment is booming because of high rates of return, and productivity growing rapidly. High investment relieves government policy of the need actively to provide demand stimulus which may entail politically vulnerable deficits. Rapid productivity growth means that pressure in a high employment economy towards sharply rising wages need not result in high inflation rates. But again, the question arises as to why the post–World War I boom aborted so soon. I believe that economists and politicians did learn from the earlier bad experience and that the new, call it Keynesian, understanding did prevent governments from making the same kinds of mistakes they made in the earlier era. In any case, a characteristic of the later era is that after the initial, sometimes chaotic, adjustments that marked the immediate postwar period, almost all of the OECD countries managed to avoid both sustained unemployment and high and sustained inflation rates until the late 1960s.

During the era of rapid growth, investment rates were high and the capital stock grew rapidly. Productivity was enhanced by newer machines and more machines per worker. The capital-labor ratio rose in almost all sectors in almost all countries during this period. High investment rates also permitted relatively rapid reallocation of the capital stock. In general capital grew much more rapidly in the high-productivity sectors like manufacturers and public utilities than in the lower-productivity sectors like agriculture.[5]

This shifting of capital facilitated a parallel shifting of labor from low- to high-productivity sectors. In particular, over this period, virtually all of the OECD countries experienced a significant outflow of labor from agriculture to the other sectors. Several analysts have commented that flexibility of the work force, the ability of labor allocation to respond to changing patterns of demand, was an important ingredient of the rapid growth recipe.[6] In addition to an outflow of labor from the farms, in the United States and Canada labor force flexibility was enhanced by an indigenous labor supply growth. In several of the European countries guest workers were a significant part of labor supply. Thus, during the early part of the rapid growth era, manufacturing expanded employment without running into labor bottlenecks. Later, part of the bulk of employment increases were in the service sectors.

During this period the young people entering the labor market tended to have significantly higher levels of educational attainment than did the prior generation; thus education and training bottlenecks tended to be averted. However, as we shall see later, certain explanations for the more recent productivity growth slowdown ascribe a portion of the blame to growth in the fraction of young and inexperienced (if well-educated) workers in the work force.

While all of the OECD countries entered the postwar era with a catalogue of new technologies that had not yet been incorporated widely in practice, this source of productivity growth and high returns to capital sooner or later had to run out. But research and development spending in all of the OECD countries was strikingly large during the rapid-growth era compared with earlier periods, and the list of important inventions that occurred during the period is impressive. Many analysts have proposed that technical progress was significantly higher postwar than earlier. In view of the slowdown in recent years, several of the more contemporary commentators have referred to these years as the upswing and high point of a Kondratief cycle.[7] But one can ask if rapid technical progress during this period can be considered an independent and exogenous factor. As indicated earlier, the environment for technical progress was highly stimulating and facilitating.

Rising educational attainments, shifting of the labor force from low-productivity to higher-productivity sectors, widespread and rapid technical advance, high investment activity—all were going on together and reinforcing each other during this period. This booming economic environment may well have been facilitated by governmental commitments to keep unemployment low and demand growing. At the same time these underlying dynamic conditions undoubtedly made it easier for full employment policies to be associated with high investment rates, and for rapid growth of money wages to be largely offset by rapid productivity growth. It is this salutary package which came unravelled during the 1970s.

However, before considering the unravelling, it is important to look beneath the surface aggregates. There were significant differences among the OECD countries in their rates of growth. There were striking intersectoral and interindustry differences in rates of productivity growth.

Intercountry Variation

In the late 1950s the United States stood far above the rest of the major OECD countries in gross national product per worker, and the limited available data are consistent with the proposition that the productivity advantage of the United States extended sector by sector and industry by industry. The United Kingdom, Germany, and France tended to cluster together in their productivity levels at about half that of the United States. Japan and Italy lagged far behind.

There was a strong negative correlation between initial productivity level and productivity growth rate over the period in question. The United States and Canada experienced the slowest productivity growth rates, Japan and Italy the fastest. However there was considerable variation of productivity growth rates among countries which originally had roughly the same productivity levels. Germany and France experienced much more rapid productivity growth than did Britain. Because of the rough tendency for the countries that initially had the lowest productivity levels to experience relatively rapid productivity growth, and for the country with the highest initial productivity level to lag, there was a considerable convergence of productivity levels during the period. However, significant differences among countries remain.

Some analysts have looked to differences in R&D spending as an explanation for intercountry differences. However, the two countries which initially had the highest ratios of R&D to GNP—the United States and the United Kingdom—experienced the slowest productivity growth rates. The apparent negative correlation is to a considerable extent obviated by the fact that much of the higher R&D to GNP ratio of the United States and Britain stemmed from defense R&D spending. If that is eliminated from the R&D figures, the United States' lead in R&D spending is significantly reduced and Britain drops back into the pack. And it is significant that the major OECD countries with the most rapid productivity growth—Japan, Germany, and France—significantly increased their R&D to GNP ratio during this period, and by 1970 had nondefense R&D to GNP ratios very close to those of the United States and Britain.[8]

However, one should not really expect productivity growth rates across countries to be correlated with the ratio of their (nondefense) R&D to GNP. Particularly in the postwar era, technological knowledge flowed easily across borders. Countries that are behind the pack are able

TABLE 4.2
Productivity Growth in the OECD Countries: 1963-1974

Country	Productivity Growth Rate	Growth Rate of Capital Stock Per Employee
Belgium	4.3%	3.8%
Canada	2.2	-0.3
Denmark	2.9[a]	2.6[a]
France	4.1	5.6
Germany	4.2	4.6
Italy	5.3	5.0
Japan	11.3	10.2
Netherlands	4.1	4.5
United Kingdom	2.7	2.0
United States	1.4[b]	0.5

Source: Data taken from Table S.1 in John P. Stein and Allen Lee, Productivity Growth in Industrial Countries at the Sectoral Level, 1963-1974 (Santa Monica: The Rand Corporation for Council on International Economic Policy, R-2203-CIEP, July 1977).

[a] 1965-1974.

[b] 1963-1973.

to take or buy much of their new technology from the leaders. One would expect that the technologically leading countries like the United States would have to spend significantly more on research and development than the lagging nations in order to have comparable productivity growth rates.

Physical investment is much more country specific in its impact on productivity than is R&D. Over the era of rapid growth there was a strong positive correlation between the growth of capital per worker in a country and growth of productivity, as shown in Table 4.2, adapted from Stein and Lee. As suggested earlier, rapid capital growth carried many benefits—more tools per worker, more modern tools, and the means to shift the allocation of labor. In the most rapidly growing countries capital expansion was sufficiently rapid so that employment expanded significantly in manufacturing. This was so in Japan, Italy, Germany, and France. In contrast, by the early 1960s the two growth laggers—the United States and the United Kingdom—were experiencing a decline in manufacturing employment.[9]

In turn one can ask, What characterized the countries where this complex interactive process worked most forcefully? Mancur Olsen has put forth the proposition that the countries which experienced the most rapid productivity growth in the postwar era were those whose social and governmental structures were most shaken up by the war.[10] He suggests that in the normal run of events societies tend to ossify, economic interests tend to become vested, and changes become throttled. It is true that of the major OECD countries the two productivity growth laggers, the United States and Great Britain, probably came out of the war with significantly less social and political shaking up than the productivity growth leaders, Japan, Germany, France, and Italy. However, Sweden and the Netherlands, both of whom experienced rapid productivity growth, appear to have displayed considerable social and political continuity. But the question posed by Olsen, of the compatibility of rapid growth with institutions that protect interests, is an important one, and will be raised again later in this paper.

Intersectoral Differences

I stressed above that intersectoral and interindustry differences in productivity levels growth rates played an extremely important role in driving and patterning postwar economic growth. While the OECD countries differed significantly among themselves in terms of growth of GNP per worker as shown in Table 4.3 (taken from Stein and Lee), there were strong similarities among the nations regarding which industries experienced the most rapid and which the slowest productivity growth.

In many of the countries, agriculture, while having low initial productivity growth leaders—Japan, Germany, France, and Italy. is often overlooked on the list of technically progressive sectors, from 1963 to 1974 considerable resources were directed to R&D on agricultural processes and inputs. Rapid productivity growth in agriculture, in the face of price-inelastic demands, freed up labor which moved into manufacturing where initial productivity levels were higher.

On the average, growth of productivity in manufacturing was quite rapid over the period as it also was in public utilities and transport. In almost all countries measured, productivity growth in the service sectors and construction was slow. But within both services and manufacturing there were significant differences. For example, the electric power and airline services industries are sometimes counted as "services" because they are not engaged in manufacturing, agriculture, or mining as traditionally defined. Productivity levels and rates of productivity growth in these two sectors have been high in large part because input

TABLE 4.3
Rank Order of Labor Productivity Growth, 1963-1974[a]

Sector	Belgium	Canada	Denmark	France	Germany	Italy	Japan	Netherlands	United Kingdom	United States	Average
1. Agriculture	2.5	3	3	2	10	1	6	4	2	1	3.45
2. Mining	5	5	10	5.5	1.5	7	2	2.5	8	4	4.9
3. Manufacturing	2.5	4	2	5.5	4	3	7	2.5	4	3	3.75
4. Utilities	1	1	1	3	1.5	3	10	1	1	5	2.75
5. Construction	8	8	7	4	5.5	8	8	8	6	10	7.25
6. Trade	9	7	5	9	7	3	4.5	7	5	7	6.35
7. Transport	6	2	4	1	3	6	9	5	3	2	4.1
8. Finance	4	9	8	9	9	9.5	1	9.5	9	9	7.7
9. Services	10	10	9	9	8	9.5	4.5	9.5	10	8	8.75
All sectors	7	6	6	7	4.5	5	3	6	7	6	5.75

Source: Table taken from Stein and Lee, Productivity Growth in Industrial Countries, p. 21.

[a]Where two or more sectors had the same growth rate in a particular country, or where sectors were aggregated, the average rank for these sectors is indicated in the position of each sector. The government sector was not included in these rankings because in no country were data on labor productivity available in this sector.

suppliers have been R&D intensive. A nontrivial fraction of that part of the service sector that is growing most rapidly may have similar characteristics. Within the manufacturing sector productivity growth was unusually rapid in electronic equipment, aircraft production, pharmaceuticals, and a variety of other chemical products. It was slow in such traditional industries as leather products and furniture products.

Interindustry productivity growth patterns not only were similar across the different OECD countries, they also tended to persist over time. In contrast, the intersectoral flow of resources was showing significant differences toward the latter part of the period from the pattern during the earlier part. In particular, the flow of labor out of agriculture slowed to a trickle, largely reflecting that in most of the OECD countries only a small fraction of the work force was left in agriculture. More important, manufacturing employment stopped growing in virtually all the OECD countries, and began declining in most, with the service industries increasingly absorbing the growth of employment. But I am now getting into phenomena that may have to do with the slowdown of productivity growth over the past half decade. It is time to shift the focus to the recent economic malaise.

Stagnation

Even during the heyday of rapid growth, voices were raised saying that such growth over the long run was not sustainable, or desirable, or both. The central issues involved the values being enhanced and eroded by growth, and the human costs involved. Environmental costs of growth began to be sharply debated in a variety of arenas and, somewhat later, the issues of product and job safety became prominent in many countries. In many of the OECD countries the polity debated and divided on the extent to which individual and family real living standards ought to be insulated from the vicissitudes of labor markets. Throughout the postwar years policies and institutions were being put into place that moderated or augmented raw market incentives, and which shielded persons and groups from economic adversity. At the end of this section I will propose that these changes significantly changed the environment for productivity growth.

The late 1960s were marked by a deceleration of productivity growth rates in a number of the OECD countries. Table 4.4, taken from a recent OECD report, shows a sharp relative decline in productivity growth after 1969 in the United States, Italy, and Sweden, and some tendency for the most rapid growers in the earlier period to slow down as well. The slowdown was connected with an increase in inflationary tendencies at

TABLE 4.4
Growth of Labor Productivity

	Agriculture		Industry		Other		Total	
	1960-69	1969-73	1960-69	1969-73	1960-69	1969-73	1960-69	1969-73
Canada	4.6%	4.4%	3.7%	3.1%	1.5%	1.5%	2.5%	2.0%
United States	6.1	5.0	2.9	3.4	1.9	.3	2.6	1.6
Japan	6.3	8.2	9.1	7.5	7.2	6.6	8.9	8.1
France	5.0	7.3	5.2	5.0	3.3	2.6	4.9	4.4
Germany	5.9	8.2	5.4	4.4	3.3	2.7	4.8	4.2
Italy	9.0	5.7	5.8	3.8	4.2	2.4	6.5	4.2
United Kingdom	5.6	7.4	3.3	3.9	.9	1.7	2.3	2.7
Netherlands	6.3	7.1	6.0	8.0	2.5	2.5	3.6	4.2
Sweden (1962-69)	5.2	4.9	5.8	3.4	2.3	1.2	3.8	2.0

Source: Data from Organization for Economic Co-operation and Development, Towards Full Employment and Price Stability (Paris: June, 1977).

Note: Owing to difference of definition the figures are not strictly comparable across countries.

TABLE 4.5
Output Per Man-Hour in Manufacturing in the OECD Countries

	U.S.	Japan	Germany	France	Italy	Canada	U.K.
1970	100	100	100	100	100	100	100
1971	106	104	104	105	102	107	105
1972	110	114	111	114	111	111	112
1973	113	133	117	121	125	117	118
1974	116	136	121	125	130	119	119
1975	118	131	126	121	123	121	119
1976	124	148	135	135	134	125	123
1977	127	158	139	139	142	131	121
1976 I	122	141	135	133	135	124	121
II	124	148	136	133	133	125	124
III	126	151	136	135	136	126	123
IV	126	154	136	135	135	125	124
1977 I	126	154	138	141	147	130	123
II	126	156	138	137	136	131	120
III	128	158	138	137	146	130	121
IV	128	163	140	138	140	132	122
1978 I	127						122

Source: Organization for Economic Co-operation and Development
Note: Index numbers, 1970 = 100.

low levels of unemployment, efforts in the United States and several other countries to damp that inflation, and, partly as a result of such policies, a rise in unemployment rates. But prior to 1973 these later characteristics were much less marked in the other OECD countries than in the United States.

Nineteen seventy-three clearly marks a break in trend. The sharper inflationary forces, higher unemployment, slowdown of growth of GNP and GNP per employed worker that have occurred since then have been much discussed. This syndrome marks virtually all of the OECD countries, although in varying degrees. Tables 4.5 and 4.6, taken from a recent OECD report, display two prominent manifestations, a

TABLE 4.6
Industrial Production in the OECD Countries

		OECD Total	U.S.	Canada	Japan	Sweden	West Germany	U.K.	France	Italy	Netherlands	Belgium
1968		91	99	92	76	88	83	95	88	90	82	88
1969		98	103	98	88	94	94	100	94	94	91	97
1970		100	100	100	100	100	100	100	100	100	100	100
1971		102	102	106	103	101	102	100	104	100	106	103
1972		109	111	113	110	104	106	102	112	104	111	109
1973		119	120	124	127	111	113	111	120	115	119	116
1974		120	120	127	122	117	111	109	123	119	125	120
1975		110	109	121	110	115	105	103	114	108	119	109
1976		120	120	127	122	114	113	104	124	121	126	118
1977		124	127	132	127	111	116	106	126	121	127	117
1976	I	117	118	126	117	112	111	103	123	117	124	114
	II	119	120	128	121	114	113	104	123	121	126	119
	III	120	121	127	124	115	114	104	125	123	127	118
	IV	122	122	128	125	115	115	106	125	128	129	119
1977	I	124	124	131	127	113	117	107	129	131	127	120
	II	124	127	132	126	110	116	105	125	122	128	119
	III	124	128	132	126	111	116	106	125	121	124	114
	IV	125	129	133	128	109	117	105	124	119	127	116
1978	I	126	130	133	132	109	117	107	127	124	126	119
1978	Jan.	126	129	132	131	110	120	106	126	122	127	121
	Feb.	126	129	134	131	109	116	107	125	126	126	120
	Mar.	127	131	134	133	108	115	107	129	126	126	117
	Apr.		133	133	134	107	117	109	131	122	129	122

Source: Organization for Economic Co-operation and Development, Industrial Production, various issues.

Note: Index numbers, 1970 = 100, seasonally adjusted.

deceleration of growth of output per man-hour in manufacturing that has occurred in most countries, and an even sharper and more pervasive reduction in growth of industrial output. The overall deceleration of productivity growth reflects both a slowdown in productivity growth in the several sectors, and a particularly sharp falloff in output growth and employment in high-productivity sectors like manufacturing.

Investment as a fraction of GNP has been significantly lower since 1973 in most of the OECD countries than it was, on average, in the earlier period. At least one study attributes a nontrivial share of the slowdown of productivity growth to the falloff in growth of capital per worker.[11] Symmetrically with the period of high investment rates, the falloff of investment cuts against productivity growth in a variety of different ways. In particular, low investment is associated since 1973 with stagnation or decline of employment in industry.

R&D activity also has decelerated significantly. In the United States R&D began to decline as a fraction of GNP in the late 1960s. However, until 1973, this largely reflected a reduction in government spending on defense and space R&D and was localized in the aerospace and electronics industries. France experienced a similar cutback in government R&D activity in the late 1960s. But as shown in Table 4.7, in the other OECD countries R&D held up as a percentage of GNP through the early 1970s. And until 1973 industry-financed R&D continued to rise at a constant or increasing rate in most of the major OECD countries.

Since 1973 the rate of growth of real business-financed R&D has been significantly slower than earlier. R&D to sales ratios have held up pretty well. However, the slowdown of output growth has been associated with a parallel slowdown of R&D growth. Further, data from the United States suggest strongly that the period since 1973 has seen a significant change in the objectives to which industrial R&D has been directed. Part of that change is associated with higher energy prices, regulations relating to the environment and safety, and other changes in the incentive systems that reflect durable changes in social values and which have, appropriately, changed the allocation of R&D attention. There has been as well a shortening of R&D time horizons, and a shifting of industrial R&D out of long-range exploratory research, out of the search for new products and new markets, into projects with short-term payoffs, and efforts concentrating on the improvement of existing products.[12] These changes almost certainly reflect the generally bearish and uncertain business conditions.

It is easy enough to identify the proximate causes for these interdependent developments—slowdown of productivity growth,

TABLE 4.7
Trends in Total Expenditures on R&D As a Percentage of Gross
National Product

Country	1963/4	1967	1969	1971
Belgium	0.9 %	1.1 %	1.1 %	1.2 %
France	1.7	2.2	1.9	1.8
West Germany	1.4	1.7	1.7	2.1
Italy	0.6	0.7	0.8	0.9
Netherlands	1.9	2.1	2.0	2.0
United Kingdom	2.3	2.4	2.3	2.3
United States	2.7	3.1	2.8	2.5
Canada	1.0	1.3	1.3	1.2
Japan	1.3	1.3	1.5	1.6
Sweden	1.3	1.4	1.3	1.6

Source: Organization for Economic Co-operation and Development,
Patterns of Resources Devoted to Research and Experimental
Development in the OECD Areas, 1963-71 (Paris, 1975).

reduction in the rate of investment with a particularly heavy falloff in manufacturing investment, a decline in manufacturing employment, a slowing down and conservative redirection of research and development activity. These developments are largely the result of restrictive fiscal and monetary policies that have been pursued, with intermittent relaxation, in all of the OECD countries since 1973.

In turn these policies can be traced to governmental concerns about inflation and balance of payments deficits. As recounted above, these problems were experienced more frequently in the late 1960s and early 1970s than earlier in the rapid growth era, but they certainly were greatly exacerbated by the surge of raw materials and especially oil prices in 1973. Domestic prices and wages shot up in response as firms and individuals sought to protect their profits and real incomes. Prior to 1973, periods when governments were actively spurring demand alternated with periods when policy aimed to check demand growth. Since 1973, the dominating policy objective has been to restrain inflationary tendencies and protect the balance of payments. The result has been that virtually all the OECD economies have been on a tight leash, resulting in unemployment rates that are high compared with the 1960s and slack capacity in many industries. While governments have certainly not sought to damp incentives on investment and entrepreneurial R&D or to retard productivity growth, they have not proved clever enough to avoid these concomitants of restrictive economic policies. It should be noted that, to the extent policies to damp inflation hinder productivity growth, they partially nullify their effect on inflation.

Too few economists, and fewer laypersons, appreciate the strength of the connection between output growth and productivity growth, not only in the economy as a whole, but industry by industry. In a recent paper, Richard Ruggles presents data for the United States that show there has been no tendency since the early 1970s for productivity growth rates to decline in industries whose output growth rates have been sustained; rather the slowdown in overall productivity growth is associated with the fact that fewer industries have been expanding output rapidly, and many more are increasing output slowly or retrenching.[13] In the short run, with plant and equipment and overhead personnel relatively fixed, the feedback of decelerated output growth to deterred productivity growth is direct and obvious. Over the longer run, while short-run rigidities may dissolve, slow output growth shifts downward expectations of future market size, and deters investment in new plant and equipment and in R&D.

Most analysts, I believe, would agree with the above general diagnosis that the slowdown in productivity growth, investment, and R&D has been in good part the consequence of restrictive policies, and that the negative effects on productivity growth make the task of holding back inflation harder. Analysts tend to divide on how much of the productivity growth slowdown is attributable to restrictive policies. And analysts are not in accord about the underlying causes of inflationary pressures.

The most optimistic interpretation is that the major change during the last half decade is the oil price rise, that the OECD countries (particularly the United States) have been more sluggish than expected in adapting, but that the problem is working itself out. This may be part of the story, but most surely it is not all of it. Inflation in the OECD countries already has wiped out some of the relative increase in oil prices that occurred in 1973-74. And, while most of the OECD countries have cut down their rates of inflation from the staggering levels of 1974 through 1976, there is little sign of further deceleration, in spite of the fact that unemployment rates continue to be very high by historical standards.

Some analysts have proposed that the problems are due largely to inept and indecisive fiscal and monetary policies. In general such arguments include the observation that inflationary troubles were occurring in the United States significantly before 1973 and in several of the European countries as well, and that the oil crisis may have exacerbated the problem, but it is not the source of the problem. The source, according to this view, is government spending that has been allowed to rise, and deficits that have been financed by printing money.[14] The restrictive responses to inflation have not been deep or sustained enough to really halt monetary growth and change inflationary expectations. Skeptics respond at two levels. First, they point to the fact that unemployment has been high in virtually all of the OECD countries but that, except in a few nations like West Germany, inflation remains stubborn. Second, they suggest that it is not lack of nerve that sustains government programs, but real political demands. Of course one can ask whether growth, as we have experienced it, is possible with a significantly higher level of government spending and taxing than marked the early 1960s. But this poses the problem in terms of economic structures and policies that are or are not compatible with rapid growth, rather than in terms of the weakness of policymakers. I shall return to this issue later.

Some analysts have suggested that there are factors behind the scene, independent of the post-1973 recession, and independent of governmental spending increases, that would have led to deceleration of productivity growth. Demographic and labor force trends, changes in the nature of technological advance, and changed overall values and structures all have been mentioned.

One factor which has been noted is the rapid increase in the percentage of the work force accounted for by young, inexperienced, and female workers. The productivity of these workers, at least initially, is less than that of more experienced workers.[15] However, before assigning very heavy weight to this proposed cause, one should recall that many analysts earlier had argued that availability of a work force not committed to particular jobs and industries, and willing and able to shift into the expanding sectors, was an important factor behind the rapid growth experienced during the 1960s. Perhaps the 1970s differ from the 1950s in that the OECD countries now are much more education rich, and hence high education of a young worker does not compensate as well now for lack of experience. However, certainly the inexperienced and female worker explanation for the productivity slowdown needs more skeptical scrutiny than it generally receives.

Some analysts have proposed that technical advance was changing its character significantly prior to the 1973 slump. It is suggested that sometime in the early 1960s the number of major innovations which opened up broad new product fields tended to decline relative to minor product-improving or cost-reducing innovations. According to this view, whereas the boom of the 1960s could be attributed to the upswing of a Kondratief cycle, since the early 1970s we have been in a downswing.[16] Certainly a falloff in the rate of technical progress, and a shift from major invention to minor invention, could have an effect on productivity growth directly, and also indirectly. Indirectly the effect would work through a falloff in the rate of expansion of profitable investment opportunities, a decline in profit rates at existing investment rates, and a tendency for investment rates to fall unless offset by a comparable decline in the cost of capital. This hypothesis is consistent with much of the data.

But except for the arguable evidence for a decline in major inventing that started during the 1960s, the data also are consistent with an increase in economic slack originating from other sources (for example, restrictive government monetary and fiscal policies) feeding back to deter both investment and R&D, and to make businessmen cautious and conservative about the R&D projects they finance. Of course it is not a question of one explanation or of the other. A Kondratief cycle well could result in economic slack which in turn feeds back to deter invention.

It has been proposed that an important force behind the overall productivity growth slowdown has been a shift in the allocation of the work force away from high productivity growth sectors, particularly industries in manufacturing, to low productivity growth sectors, particularly certain service industries. One study, which examined data from the United States and attempted to distinguish between productivity growth deceleration within particular sectors and the shift in allocation of the work force among different sectors as causes of the overall productivity growth decline between 1968 and 1973, attributed almost all of the decline to the latter.[17] Since 1973, of course, sector by sector declines have become more pervasive, but the sectoral shift continues.

It is important to try to understand why allocation has shifted. A portion of the shift away from manufacturing since 1973 probably reflects depressed economic conditions which, among other things, have deterred demand for new equipment. My conjecture is that if aggregative demand were closer to potential output, manufacturing would comprise a large share of employment. However, there certainly are more durable forces at work. Manufacturing employment was declining relative to service employment long before 1973.

Part of the cause almost certainly resides in the fact that some of the slow productivity growth sectors are characterized by high income and low price elasticity of demand. Private housing and many personal services are examples. As incomes rise, a larger share of private incomes flows into these kinds of sectors *because of* their slow productivity growth. The "real political demand" view of the increases in public spending involves an argument that there is high income and low price elasticity of demands for many publicly provided services, like garbage collection, police protection, and education, which, like private services, have experienced low productivity growth. Thus while in earlier years the pattern of income and price elasticities of demand resulted in a shift of resources into sectors with high productivity and rapid productivity growth, in recent years the shift has been into sectors that, in the past at least, have not been marked by rapid productivity growth. According to this interpretation, to some extent at least the productivity growth slowdown has to do with changes in demand and supply conditions associated with the fact that incomes had risen significantly since the 1950s but that productivity growth was very uneven and that at the margin society now values highly many of the products of the industries where productivity growth has been slow.

In assessing this interpretation, it is important to recognize that output in many of the private and public service sectors is very poorly measured. In some of these, like public garbage collection and many health care services, output is measured by input. Absent growth of nonlabor input per worker, there will be no measured productivity growth in such sectors, by accounting convention. But for some of the services, for example, medical care, there clearly have been very major technological advances over the past decades, and a number of indexes of the efficiency of medical care show that the new medical technologies do save more lives, enable more people to recover, and alleviate distress. While these improvements do not show up in measured productivity growth, beliefs of both doctors and patients that medical care now can do more than it used to do is one of the reasons why more medical care services are being bought. If output measured quality of output more adequately, measured productivity growth in such a sector would be higher, the rate of growth of prices smaller, and the demand curve estimated to be more elastic.

There is some truth in both interpretations. Resources have shifted into slow productivity growth sectors where demands are inelastic. And productivity growth has been underestimated along with demand elasticity in others of the service sectors. By the latter interpretation the overall productivity growth slowdown has been overestimated, but according to either, the slowdown in measured productivity growth reflects changes in marginal private and social values.

One can interpret another important source of productivity growth slowdown—the development and enforcement of environmental and safety legislation—as reflecting not orthogonal but similar forces. It is debatable whether the policies have gone too far or not far enough, and the sense of their design is also questionable, but it is certainly true that citizens in the OECD countries became in the late 1960s and early 1970s much more concerned about environment and safety than they had been in the past. Almost certainly this is partially the result of the fact that most citizens had much more traditional consumer goods than they had before, and could afford to pay more attention and resources to problems of environmental quality and product and job safety.

A number of studies have shown that, as was intended, the new regulatory regimes certainly have shifted R&D allocation towards projects aimed to meet regulatory requirements. To the extent that the overall R&D budget is not expanded accordingly, R&D resources have shifted away from projects aimed to enhance productivity or to better meet market demands. It has been pointed out that the new regulatory regimes also have affected the nature of new physical capital put in place, with a possible result that new equipment, while permitting environmental and safety standards to be met, has less of an effect on enhancing measured productivity than would be the case absent these constraints.[18]

A shift of relative values also is reflected in policies involving increased transfer payments and public provision of certain goods and services, and other legislation that has better shielded individual and family living standards from the pull and push of market forces. But one consequence is high tax rates which may well damp incentives to work and invest. Another possible consequence is that it may now be much harder to shift labor from activities where demand is declining to activities where demand is increasing. Governments increasingly are motivated to step in with programs to offset the effects of these kinds of demand shifts. Fewer workers are threatened with unemployment, and unemployment where it occurs is much less of a private trauma than it used to be. According to this argument, it now takes much higher unemployment rates to get labor to shift to new regions and industries. More generally, it has been proposed that the new regimes have made economic slack a far less useful instrument than it used to be in restraining demands for wage increases. According to this view the new welfare states are prone to sustained coexistence of high inflation rates and high unemployment rates. Some analysts have argued that the problem is compounded by the fact that real income targets are in terms of command over private goods and services. In a situation where government programs are leaving less and less room for private consumption as a fraction of GNP, and where productivity growth is slow, the result is further to augment the pressures for inflationary wage bargains. In turn this causes government to adopt restrictive policies which further deter productivity growth.

It is time to take stock. The productivity growth slowdown clearly has multiple causes and the causes interact. Slow productivity growth since 1973 clearly is closely associated with restrictive government policies due to concerns about inflationary pressures. But there are deeper forces impinging on productivity growth and these forces may also lie behind the greater tendency towards inflation. There has been a shift in the age-sex composition of the labor force; with time, any adverse consequences of this will work themselves out. It has been argued that there has been a falloff in basic technological progressivity, but the evidence for this is not clear. It is clear, however, that economic slack is feeding back to deter technical progress. The very unevenness of the technical advance we have experienced is now working against future rapid growth as resources are shifting to industries of slow measured productivity growth. In turn this can be regarded as reflecting changes in relative priorities which have manifested themselves, as well, in the new regulatory regimes and in policies to protect individuals and families from the losses associated with the shifts in resource allocation associated with rapid economic growth. But these changes may make rapid growth more difficult to achieve in the future both directly and indirectly by making it more difficult to control inflation.

The Challenge of Returning to Rapid Productivity Growth

It probably is not feasible to attain again the pace of productivity growth achieved over the 1955-70 period. The reason resides not so much in any physical limits to growth, but rather in the social limits to growth that we have built into our laws and institutions. In a sense the OECD societies have chosen to slow the pace of economic progress traditionally defined and measured, and to redirect the pattern of economic progress to one that better respects a variety of non-market values. At the same time they have attempted to better shield individuals and families from the vicissitudes of economic change. These choices were not the result of any detailed rational calculation in which the costs and benefits were carefully weighed, nor would one find social consensus on the relevant weights of the different values that would be involved in such calculations. Many people clearly believe that the change has gone too far, many others that the change has not gone nearly far enough. In part these differences reflect differences in values, in part differences in beliefs about the long-run consequences of the new policies. Given the uncertainties and differences in values, the result is a somewhat uneasy democratic compromise. It still is not fully clear what the compromise entails.

Most certainly the changed policies have not mandated either "no growth" or "growth of an entirely different kind." Rather I suspect that most people are hoping for a change in degree rather than in kind. The rhetoric and the realization of wage bargains over the past few years seems to reflect only modest, if any, declines in expectations and aspirations for increases in private living standards conventionally defined. I think that there may be a real problem here. It well may be that the OECD societies in their moves to protect other values have hindered the ability of their economies to achieve more conventional kinds of productivity growth to a greater extent than they bargained. If so there is trouble ahead. I am not saying here that it is so—only that the possibility cannot be dismissed out of hand.

I certainly am skeptical that we can have as much of the old as we did have, and a lot more of the new as well. But I believe strongly that we can do better than we have done over the past five years. To do this poses challenges to both macroeconomic policy and microeconomic policy.

Macroeconomics

I believe that it will be very difficult for the OECD countries to pick up the long-run rate of productivity growth unless they are able to better handle the unemployment-inflation nexus of problems. It is not inevitable that high unemployment prevents rapid productivity growth; there are a number of episodes in the past where they have co-existed. But generally in the past rapid productivity growth and low unemployment have gone together. Rapid productivity growth has been associated with a rich flow of new technologies and technological improvements spurring investment to comprise a high fraction of GNP and, directly and indirectly, strong demand for labor. In turn, with labor markets strong, labor has had less cause to be frightened of the advent of new technologies. And strong demand for goods and services and flexibility on the part of the work force has fed back to make inventive activity profitable.

During the past five years all of these interactions have been operating in reverse. It is arguable whether or not a Kondratief downturn contributed in the early 1970s to the difficulties fiscal and monetary policies began to have reconciling low unemployment with low inflation rates. But there is no question that high unemployment and erratic inflation is feeding back to make research and development more conservative.

I have no intention of adding my remarks here to the torrent of words that have been directed toward prescribing for the current macro-economic malaise. I already have indicated above that I suspect the problem may be relatively deepseated, and based on aspirations for a more rapid growth of living standards than the economies are now able to yield. But I do want to suggest that if Western societies do not somehow learn to again make low unemployment rates compatible with now acceptable inflation rates, or learn to live with high inflation rates, one of the consequences is likely to be that it is impossible to significantly improve the poor productivity growth performance of the last five years.

Microeconomic Policy Issues

A solution to the aggregate demand management problem is, I propose, a necessary condition for the achievement of a more satisfactory pattern of long-run economic growth. However, it is by no means a sufficient condition, because changed priorities call for changed directions of growth, and these in turn will call for some imaginative new policies. In the remainder of this essay I will discuss two changes which seem to pose difficult policy questions regarding how to stimulate and mold technical advance—the new regulatory regimes, and the shifted sectoral allocation of resources.

The evidence is clear enough that the new regulatory regimes are having a significant influence on technical advance in the sectors most affected. Various studies have shown an increase in the fraction of industrial investment in equipment and in R&D in such sectors as chemical products and automobile production going into efforts to meet regulatory requirements, and being pulled away from efforts that lower unit production costs. But it also is apparent that there are significant problems involved in trying to redirect private R&D expenditure through the use of regulations. In the first place, uncertainty regarding what regulatory requirements will be in the future well may deter firms from trying to develop new products and processes significantly different from present ones since the regulators may respond to their advent by prohibiting them. There is some evidence that this has been happening. Second, while regulations forbidding or requiring certain product or process attributes augment the range of values and costs considered by R&D decision makers beyond that which would be made salient by a market alone, these extensions usually are quite crude, with certain dimensions of pollution or work hazard being proscribed and others not, and with particular levels of achievement being mandated and no reward established for surpassing these.

Furthermore, these regulatory standards (it would be the same thing with deterrent taxes) tend to be set with some notions regarding the costs of meeting them and the nature of the substitutions they will evoke which may not be very well justified. Sometimes the result is that the standards are met at high cost and with very little social benefit. Sometimes the result is that the standards are challenged, and the regulators forced to back down. For example, in the American case of legislating emission standards for automobile engines, the automobile companies have been able to claim that they cannot meet these standards at reasonable costs, and the regulators have been unable to make their regulations stick.

This is not an essay on regulatory reform in general. However, I believe that three of the prominently mentioned general reforms— regulation through specification of performance standards rather than specific product or process requirements, incentives or penalties keyed to degree of performance achievement rather than a step function, and better mechanisms to balance conflicting objectives in the setting of regulatory regimes—would have an important and salutory effect on the environment for technological advances. While making a better market would be a long step forward, I propose that a more active public role in R&D is called for as well.

At the least, cases like that of automobile emission control indicate that a rather strong governmentally funded R&D program is necessary simply to enable standards to be set sensibly. Governmentally undertaken or funded R&D also is necessary if government agencies are to avoid being outclassed by the firms they are regulating in discussions regarding what are the technological options, what are they likely to cost, and what are reasonable expectations regarding performance of the companies in question. I would tentatively suggest that public responsibility for the funding of R&D aimed at furthering non-market values in market sectors might go considerably beyond this minimal information-obtaining role. Regulations might well be set more sensibly if Congress and government agencies had to face some of the R&D costs of meeting them.

Another challenge for policy regarding technical advance is posed by the shift in the allocation of resources away from manufacturing industries to other, principally service industries, where in general measured productivity growth has been slower. The shifting pattern of resource allocation has involved both private consumption decisions and public political decisions regarding the level and composition of government expenditures. In recent years the latter has been especially important.[19] For example, in virtually all of the OECD countries there has been a rise in expenditure in the health and education sectors relative to GNP. The bulk of the money financing these expansions has come from government, either directly or indirectly. In some of the service sectors quality growth and technical advance clearly have been rapid. Nonetheless, in many of the service sectors productivity growth clearly has been very slow.

Slow productivity growth in the service sector now exerts a bigger drag on income growth than it used to. Continued rapid technical progress in the sectors where progress has been rapid clearly is important, but as these sectors shrink in size productivity growth there counts for less. Conversely, the social gains from significantly enhancing productivity growth in such sectors as construction, urban mass transport, health maintenance, and education is now even more important than earlier.

Simply the shift of resources into these sectors will tend to draw greater R&D attention to them. But it is highly unlikely that market forces alone will be able to effect major improvements in technological progressivity in sectors like these. And it is doubtful that governments ought to stand idly by and wait for the market for R&D to work. For one thing, the organization of many of these sectors is mixed with government playing a large role on the demand side and often on the supply side as well. Directly or indirectly governments have a good deal of leverage over R&D in such sectors as public housing, health, education, and urban mass transport. This leverage ought to be exerted self-consciously and intelligently. For another, in many of these sectors, like private housing, demand long has been high and growing and not much has happened. Governmental action has the chance of getting something to happen.

As in the case of regulation, for the sectors where the government is heavily involved as direct or indirect demander or as supplier, the public agencies involved should spend at least enough on R&D to know what the technological options are and what they are likely to cost. But, as with the regulatory cases, I would propose that here too the fruitful public role in R&D goes well beyond that minimal requirement, and involves government finance or cost sharing of a wide range of research and development activity. In fact government R&D expenditure in these fields has increased significantly in the United States over the past decade. But satisfactory arrangements have yet to be worked out.

Where governments are major demanders of the product of an industry there are several routes for active policy. Governments can stimulate private R&D by articulating product demands and acting as an informed innovative buyer. And public contracting for R&D has much greater legitimacy when the government is the purchaser of the end product than when it is not. Similar considerations obtain in the product regulation case, where in effect the government is the demander for particular product attributes.

I suspect that it is significantly harder for active government policies to spur the growth of productivity in lagging industries where the government is not a major demander or supplier than where it is. Competition among firms in an industry seriously constrains what governments can do directly to stimulate R&D. Firms in the industry rightly complain if assistance is given to one firm but not to another.

There are several cases where governments have stimulated technical change in private industry selling to a nongovernmental market through support of cooperative or university research. But the cases are rather special. One of these is, of course, agriculture, where government funds long have supported research. But agriculture is rather special in that individual farmers are not market rivals. There can, therefore, be collective support for programs that will help them all, and little fear that such programs will help one at the expense of another. Governmental support for R&D in industries where firms are small and there is no tradition of significant technological innovation probably would have to take a form similar to that taken in agriculture, involving support of extra industry R&D efforts on projects that firms in the industry regard as having the potential for helping them all. Europeans have done this more than Americans. The programs have been modest and so have the results.

The emphasis above on trying to increase productivity growth in sectors which are growing in relative size and which have been experiencing relatively slow productivity growth is not meant to denigrate the importance of policies to sustain or enhance productivity growth in industries where technical change has been rapid. And it is interesting that the major government efforts over the last decade to spur technical advance in industries selling on a commercial market largely have been aimed at technologically progressive industries. More so in Europe than in the United States, public programs have supported developments in computers, civil aircraft, and manufacturing innovation more generally. There are some success stories but by and large the record is not very good.[20] I suspect that an important reason resides in the problem I mentioned above. In competitive industries it is politically difficult for governments to help one firm but not others. And in technically progressive industries firms tend to be skittish about cooperative research for obvious reasons. The European countries have had less difficulty with this problem than the United States, in large part because in Europe there is more toleration, indeed support, of industry planning arrangements where, in effect, the firms in the domestic industry are viewed as cooperating against foreign competition. Thus government has been able often to come in as a research partner. But even under those conditions the batting average has not been particularly high.

Prospects for Future Growth

I am quite uncertain regarding the future growth prospects of the OECD countries. In particular, I am uncertain as to whether the syndrome of restrictive governmental policies, high but damped inflation, and high unemployment which has characterized the last five years will be chronic, or whether we can resolve the underlying difficulties. It seems to me that we cannot resolve them in a way that basically revokes the new protections for environmental values, job safety, and family income security that have been put in place. The Western societies are committed to an economic structure which is significantly more regulated with the scope of markets more limited than was the case during the heyday of growth.

Critics as well as admirers of market capitalism have agreed that that system was a marvelous engine of technical progress and productivity growth. The dispute was and is about, first, the nature and the importance of the costs inflicted by that system, and second, whether a gentler, more controlled, more socialized system would be capable of a roughly comparable growth performance. Marx evaded the question by positing that socialism would arrive after technical progress was more or less complete. Schumpeter, a friend of market capitalism, despaired of the long-run political viability of that system, regarded some form of socialism as inevitable, and argued that socialism would be able to sustain rapid productivity growth.[21] I maintain that for the mixed semi-market semi-socialized systems that the OECD countries have evolved since World War II, the verdict with respect to their capacity for economic growth is still forthcoming.

Notes

1. Two of the most interesting and sophisticated are Andrew Shonfield, *Modern Capitalism* (New York: Oxford University Press, 1965), and A. Maddison, *Economic Growth in the West* (New York: Twentieth Century Fund, 1964).

2. One good reference, giving data for a number of different countries is Edward F. Denison, *Why Growth Rates Differ* (Washington D.C.: Brookings Institution, 1967).

3. For an interesting discussion see John Cornwall, *Modern Capitalism: Its Growth & Transformation* (New York: St. Martin's Press, 1977), and Maddison, *Economic Growth.*

4. See prominently Shonfield, *Modern Capitalism,* and Maddison, *Economic Growth.*

5. For a good general discussion in this spirit, with quantitative backing, see Cornwall, *Modern Capitalism.*

6. Perhaps the most often cited reference is C. Kindleberger, *Europe's Postwar Growth: The Role of Labor Supply* (Cambridge: Harvard University Press, 1967).

7. For example, see G. Mensch, *Das Technologische Patt* (Frankfort: Fischer Taschenbuch Verlag, 1977).

8. For comparative data on R&D see *Patterns of Resources Devoted to Research and Experimental Development in the OECD Areas, 1963-1971* (Paris: Organization for Economic Co-operation and Development, 1975).

9. Again Cornwall, *Modern Capitalism,* is a good reference.

10. M. Olson, "The Political Economy of Comparative Growth Rates," Manuscript, University of Maryland, 6 January 1978.

11. See Laurits Christensen, Diane Cummings, and Dale G. Jorensen, "Economic Growth, 1947-1973: An International Comparison," Discussion Paper #521, University of Wisconsin, December 1976.

12. For a discussion see P. Gwynne, "The Growing R&D Gap," *Newsweek,* 3 July 1978, p. 89.

13. See Richard R. Ruggles, "Employment and Unemployment Statistics as Indexes of Economic Activity and Capacity Utilization," Draft, September 1978.

14. The so-called McCracken Report takes a subtle version of this position. Paul McCracken et al., *Towards Full Employment and Price Stability* (Paris: Organization for Economic Co-operation and Development, June 1977).

15. See, for example, George L. Perry, "Labor Structure, Potential Output, and Productivity," *Brookings Papers on Economic Activity,* no. 3 (1971): 533-65.

16. Mensch, *Das Technologische Patt.*

17. William D. Nordhaus, "The Recent Productivity Slowdown," *Brookings Papers on Economic Activity,* no. 3 (1972): 493-536.

18. Edward F. Denison, "Effects of Selected Changes in the Institutional and Human Environment Upon Output Per Unit of Input," *Survey of Current Business* (Washington, D.C.: U.S. Department of Commerce, January 1978), pp. 21-44.

19. Robert Bacon and W. Eltis, *Britain's Economic Problem: Too Few Producing* (New York: St. Martins Press, 1976).

20. For a review of policies see *The Current International Economic Climate and Policies for Technological Innovation* (Science Policy Research Unit,

University of Sussex, and Staffgroup Strategic Surveys, TNO, Netherlands, 1978).

21. Joseph A. Schumpeter, *Capitalism, Socialism and Democracy* (New York: Harper and Row, 1960).

Commentary

M. Ishaq Nadiri

In this short paper Richard Nelson has brought together important issues related to the behavior of productivity growth in industrialized countries and has suggested some provocative ideas. I do not have much disagreement with what he has said. He stresses three basic elements: that sources of productivity growth are interrelated and the familiar accounting approach could be misleading, that there are intersectoral differences in the growth of factor productivity, and finally that there are a series of items which contribute to what he calls the "environment of productivity growth." He attributes this environment to two things: (1) a series of macroeconomic demand management type policies of monetary and fiscal nature and (2) a series of institutional habits, social demands, and government regulations. These "environmental factors" have been built into Western economies and explain both the rise and the fall of the rate of growth of productivity in the OECD countries.

I would stress a few other points in reference both to points he made and to some he has not made, and present some alternatives that we should consider. One, he reaches a fairly pessimistic conclusion, that the rate of productivity growth in the OECD countries probably will not reach its 1960s level. I therefore presume that there is a systematic or secular decline in the rate of productivity growth, but I am not sure of this, and merely pose that as a question. On the other hand, if Nelson puts so much emphasis on the demand management side, then the productivity growth decline might be a consideration of a cyclical nature. All governments have to do is clean house, put the right fiscal and monetary policies in place, and productivity will take care of itself. Nelson does not really address the important question of why the rate of growth of productivity collapsed around 1973. Why was this so sudden? I have a hunch, and there is some evidence, that the growth of productivity was slowing down, in the United States at least, but the external shocks of 1973-74 caused productivity growth to plummet. The continued slowdown of productivity is partly attributable to the supply shocks which may not have worked their way through the structure of the economy. The supply side and the supply shocks are not given as prominent a treatment in Nelson's paper as I would have liked. From this perspective, his emphasis on demand considerations as primary causes of the productivity slowdown is incomplete.

The other point which I find very disturbing is the U.S. experience, especially during this latest slowdown. It is one thing to look at the U.S. experience and consider it as a part of a general slowdown of the rate of productivity growth in all OECD countries, and another to see the magnitude of the U.S. decline. Between 1960 and 1966, and 1966 and 1976, the rate of productivity growth declined by 45 percent. That is a very large change. Given that the United States is still considered to be the technological leader among OECD countries, the sheer size and importance of the country suggests that a closer look at the U.S. experience is needed. Also it would be useful to note how the U.S. experience affects growth of productivity in other OECD countries, or vice versa.

Finally, I want to bring another issue to our attention. The structure of the world economy is changing, especially due to changes and development of third-world economies. It is well known that many of these countries are bent on building certain types of industries and exporting their products. As these countries develop and insist on larger markets for their exports in OECD economies a certain amount of adjustment in OECD industries is necessary. How this adjustment is made, at what cost, and at what trade-off will also change the whole picture of whether Western economies become more service oriented, concentrate on high technology industries, and get out of certain types of manufacturing. Growth in the developing countries will have to be monitored and integrated in any discussion concerning secular phenomena influencing rates of productivity growth in the OECD countries.

Commentary

J. Fred Weston

Professor Nelson's paper is divided into four parts:

1. Sources of productivity growth
2. The rapid growth period of the 1950s and 1960s
3. The slowdown of the 1970s
4. How to move in the direction of a higher rate of productivity growth

The general framework which Professor Nelson outlines has an overall logical development. His treatment is comprehensive and he provides a useful reference work on the subject. His analysis encompasses major factors influencing R&D growth and provides a basis for diagnosis of the periods of rapid growth and slow growth. Within his general framework some particular points invite brief comment.

He states that where price elasticities of demand have been high in rapid productivity growth sectors, resources have moved to these sectors and out of low productivity growth sectors. He further argues that where price elasticities of demand for products of industries with rapid productivity growth have been low, resources have moved out of those sectors. He does not provide data to support the generalizations here. His later discussion includes a consideration of income elasticity as well as price elasticity. An analysis of both is required to make predictions. It would be of interest to have some tests with empirical data.

He observes that in all of the OECD countries basic research is largely financed by government. He states that in recent years in some of the OECD countries there has been a rise of governmental programs to subsidize industrial R&D and technically progressive industries for the purpose of helping the competitive position of those industries. These trends pose issues for what represents fair trade practices among the industries and governments involved.

Professor Nelson observes that the rapid growth of Germany and Japan in the immediate post–World War II period did not reflect the application of Keynesian economic policy. This, of course, depends on the definition of Keynesian policy as well as a careful characterization of the economic policies followed by Germany and Japan. If Keynesian policy is defined by close government business cooperation, it could be argued that these countries represented an application of the Keynesian philosophy carried through very fully.

One of the points emphasized by Professor Nelson is that the restrictive fiscal and monetary policies, pursued with intermittent relaxation in all of the OECD countries since 1973, have been responsible for the slowing down of productivity growth rates. He expresses skepticism toward the view that the problems are due more to inadequate fiscal and monetary policies. This is an issue of broad significance and probably could not be treated fully within the scope of a paper on productivity. However, the leanings indicated by Professor Nelson were not fully supported by any systematic evidence.

One issue is whether the share of government in GNP has increased and whether this increased share has any important bearing on the performance of the economies involved. Professor Nelson himself mentions that high tax rates may have had an influence on incentives to work and invest. Professor Malkiel argues that it was not restrictive monetary and fiscal policies as such, but rather government policies which produced a general environment of increased uncertainty which caused the capitalization rates applied to new investments (including those in R&D) to be shifted unfavorably.[1]

Professor Nelson suggests that where the government has been a direct or indirect demander or supplier "government finance or cost sharing of a wide rate of research and development activity" may be called for. In other industries he observes that the government can provide financing and other subsidies of R&D activity to industry groups as is done in European countries. There the view is held that some cooperative industry activities in planning, and in areas such as sharing the costs of relatively basic R&D, do not necessarily reduce competition between firms. In addition, foreign competition is recognized as the major threat and any cooperative activity to make firms and industries more competitive in the international market is the overriding consideration. This, of course, raises issues from an international trade standpoint as to the extent to which such government help constitutes a subsidy.

I would like to underscore and emphasize one insight that Professor Nelson advances. He observes that productivity growth is maintained in industries in which high rates of growth of output are sustained. One of the reasons he suggests is that by adding equipment to provide capacity for expanding volume, increased learning and technical advance will take place in the manufacture of the new equipment. Thus growth in capacity reflects the latest technology and sustains the momentum of an ongoing learning process. This is well exemplified by the management of export growth rates by Japan in its steel and automobile industries as a method of achieving a high rate of growth in those industries and thus benefiting from the favorable relationship among growth, technological change, and capital stock increases; the net result is favorable progress in productivity improvement. This illustrates that government policies outside of R&D which help an industry to achieve a high rate of growth, either from internal domestic sales or from exports, will itself assure a high rate of productivity improvement and enhance the international competitive strength of that industry.

Professor Nelson concludes that the problem of dealing with the simultaneous challenges of inflation and high unemployment, along with government regulations for the environment, job safety, and income security, will inevitably result in "an economic structure which is significantly more regulated and the scope of markets more limited than was the case during the heyday of growth." A basic question is, How much more limited? Others hold that the basic inflation-unemployment problem is fundamentally a government macroeconomic problem and that precisely if policies in this area are improved, the general role of government can be decreased not increased. These conflicting positions reflect an issue that remains open.

Note

1. Burton Malkiel, "The Capital Formation Problem in the United States," Financial Research Center, Department of Economics, Princeton University, Research Memo No. 25, August 1978.

5

Population, Productivity, and Economic Growth in the Western World

*Julian L. Simon
and Larry D. Neal*

Introduction

This conference is about the OECD countries, but the most important of the forces that we shall be talking about—productivity increase—operates internationally throughout the developed world. Hence we shall address ourselves to the Western world as a whole.[1]

The policy questions before us are: (1) what are the effects of a higher versus a lower birth rate? (2) what are the effects of more versus less immigration into a given country? (3) what are the effects of an increase of female labor-force participation?

Except for immigration, these policy variables are not quick acting like, say, tax changes, currency revaluations, or changes in government ownership of industries. Hence our horizon is what economists consider the long run and the intermediate run, rather than the short run of the next 1-7 years or so. In fact, one of our most important tasks in this paper is to raise our eyes to the longer horizon, so that we take into account the effects of current demographic changes 20, 40, 80, even 160 years from now, because many of the demographic effects are quite different—and much more important—in the long run than in the short run.

Here we must distinguish between immigration and more children being born: additional children have at least *some* negative short-run effects upon the rest of the community, primarily the use of schools. And additional children also have the *apparent* negative effect of lowering per capita income for the community, because they are additional consumers rather than producers, and hence they reduce the ratio of output to consumers by simply increasing the denominator. Of course most of the total negative effect of the additional children is illusory; the children's families bear the brunt of the reduction in income per person, whereas other families are unaffected except by such externalities as the cost of education. And the children's families usually make the choice of the additional child willingly, and feel the better off for doing so. Hence an additional birth is hardly a social loss just because computed per capita income goes down.[2]

Beyond any shadow of a doubt, an additional person has some negative economic effect upon people other than his parents—and perhaps even upon them—for the first fifteen or twenty-five years of his life. Brothers and sisters have less of everything except companionship. Taxpayers cough up additional funds for schooling and other public services. Neighborhoods have more noise. Taken as a whole, the baby produces nothing during these early years, and the income of the economy is spread around·more thinly than if the baby were not born. And when the baby grows up and first goes to work, jobs are squeezed a bit, and the output and pay per working person go down. All this is a clear negative economic effect for other people.

Almost equally beyond the shadow of a doubt, there is also a population "boon": the taxes the child or immigrant will pay later on; the contribution of energy and resources to family and community problems; the goods and services that the grown-up child or immigrant produces for the consumption of others; what the person does to beautify and purify the environment; and, perhaps most significant of all in more developed countries the improvement that the average person makes to the efficiency of production through new ideas and contributions to knowledge.

An additional child is, from the economic point of view, like a laying chicken, a cocoa tree, a new factory, or a new house. It is a durable good in which one must invest heavily long before it begins to provide returns on the investment. The economic problem is the matter of timing. Just as "fly now, pay later" is inherently attractive because the pleasure is immediate and the piper will wait, "pay now, benefit from the child later" is inherently problematic because one must sacrifice now in order to benefit later from the child.

The real population problem, then, is *not* that there are too many people, or that too many babies are being born. The real population problem is that additional people must be supported by others *before* these additional people produce.

Which is more weighty, the "problem" or the "boon"? That depends on economic conditions, about which we shall speak at some length. But to a startling degree the calculation about whether the overall effect of a child or immigrant is positive or negative also depends on the personal values of whoever is making the judgment—values about the worth of a dollar outlay now compared to a dollar-plus-something coming back in twenty or thirty years, values about the intrinsic worth of whether more or fewer wild game are alive and more or fewer human beings are alive, and so on. Population growth is a problem but not just a problem, it is a boon but not just a boon. One's values are all important in judging the effect on balance of population growth, and whether there is "overpopulation" or "underpopulation."

Immigrants differ from additional children in that they do not impose major negative externalities on the rest of the community before becoming producers; rather, they bring costly education with them. And they do not even have the illusory but unpleasant negative effect on per capita income that children do (though immigrants have lower incomes than preexisting citizens and may thereby lower average income—or they may not, as we shall see later). Depending on the circumstances of their migration, they may have the same effect as any new entrant to the labor force—temporarily exerting downward pressure on labor productivity. But the economic costs of immigrants to the receiving country are almost entirely indirect and derive entirely from the noneconomic cost of adjustment to the trappings of an alien culture which the immigrants bring with them—foreign speech, clothing, living standards, work habits, and family patterns. Further, the social tensions created by assimilation of aliens are not usually offset by social ties with natives akin to those between parents and newborn children.

Let us talk first and mostly about additional people, because they are the harder case (though not the more complex case), and then distinguish the effects which differ depending whether the additional people are immigrants or children.

The Effects of More or Fewer People

The overwhelming general presumption is that additional people—children or immigrants—have a negative effect on the incomes of the rest of the people in industrialized countries such as the OECD as well as in subsistence-agriculture countries. The usual reason given is diminishing returns to fixed stocks of agricultural, industrial, and social capital. The dependency burden of additional children, the consequent need for additional "demographic investment," and the effects on welfare services of children (and immigrants) are usually mentioned. Because these theoretically based presumptions are so firmly held in people's minds, let us first confront the conventional theory with the data, which flatly contradict the conventional theory.

Evidence

The data suggest that in more developed countries (MDCs) population growth does not hinder economic growth. One piece of historical evidence is the concurrent explosion in Europe of *both*

TABLE 5.1
Population Growth and Output Growth Over a Century in Contemporary
More-Developed Countries

		Population Growth Rate Per Decade	Output Per Capita Growth Rate Per Decade
France	1861-70 to 1963-66	3.0%	17.0%
Sweden	1861-69 to 1963-67	6.6	28.9
Great Britain	1855-64 to 1963-67	8.2	13.4
Norway	1865-69 to 1963-67	8.3	21.3
Denmark	1865-69 to 1963-67	10.2	20.2
Germany	1850-59 to 1963-67	10.8	18.3
Japan	1874-79 to 1963-67	12.1	32.3
Netherlands	1860-70 to 1963-67	13.4	12.6
U.S.	1859 to 1963-67	18.7	17.3
Canada	1870-74 to 1963-67	19.0	18.7
Australia	1861-69 to 1963-67	23.7	10.2

Source: Simon Kuznets, Economic Growth of Nations (Cambridge: Harvard University Press, 1971), p. 11-14. Reprinted by permission.

population and economic development from 1650 onward. The failure of France to excel economically despite its low birth rate in the past 100 years is an important vignette in this history. A fuller picture is given in Tables 5.1 and 5.2, showing rates of growth per decade of population and output per capita for those contemporary MDCs for which long run data are available. No strong relationship appears, as seen in Figures 5.1 and 5.2. If one takes the worldwide perspective, however, and aggregates the data along the lines of industrializing areas rather than national boundaries, a strong and *positive* relationship does appear between rates of growth of population and output. It may disappear at the national level due to some countries imitating industrialization in neighbor countries without imitating population increase (e.g., France and Canada) and to other countries imitating the population increase but not the industrialization of their neighbors (e.g., Norway and Italy). The first group tend to be countries receiving immigrants while the second group become sending countries.

Contemporary comparisons among various countries of current rates of population growth and economic growth are another source of evidence. Many such studies have been done by now. All except one (and that one has a fairly obvious flaw in its method) conclude that

TABLE 5.2
Population Growth and Output Growth Over Half a Century in
Contemporary More-Developed Countries

			Population Growth Rate Per Decade	Output Per Capita Growth Rate Per Decade
France	1896	to 1963-66	3.5%	18.6%
U.K.	1920-24	to 1963-67	4.8	16.9
Belgium	1900-04	to 1963-67	5.3	14.3
Italy	1890-99	to 1963-67	6.9	22.9
Switzerland	1910	to 1963-67	8.8	16.1
Germany	1910-13	to 1963-67	10.4	20.5
Netherlands	1900-09	to 1963-67	14.2	15.1
U.S.	1910-14	to 1963-67	14.2	18.4
Australia	1900-04	to 1963-67	18.8	13.1
Canada	1920-24	to 1963-67	19.4	20.9

Source: Same as Table 5.1. Reprinted by permission.

population growth does not have a negative effect upon economic growth. Among these are studies by the best respected economic-demographic statisticians of recent decades; for example, Kuznets' results are shown in Table 5.3. You may verify for yourself that neither a positive nor a negative relationship is shown by the data.

These overlapping empirical studies do not show that fast population growth in any given MDC increases per capita income. But they certainly imply that one should not confidently assert that population growth decreases economic growth.

A recent piece of evidence is crude but perhaps most telling of all: contrary to common impression, the per capita income in LDCs has been growing *faster* than in MDCs, according to the World Bank.[3] And population growth in LDCs is faster that in MDCs! There is no evidence here of a negative connection between population growth and economic growth.

The foregoing studies focus on the process of population growth. If we look at the attained level of population, we see much the same effect. Evidence on MDCs is lacking. But in LDCs, Hagen and Kindleberger both show visually, and Simon and Gobin show in multivariate regressions, that higher population density is associated with higher rates of economic growth; this effect may be strongest at low densities, but there is no evidence that the effect reverses at high densities.[4] Stryker

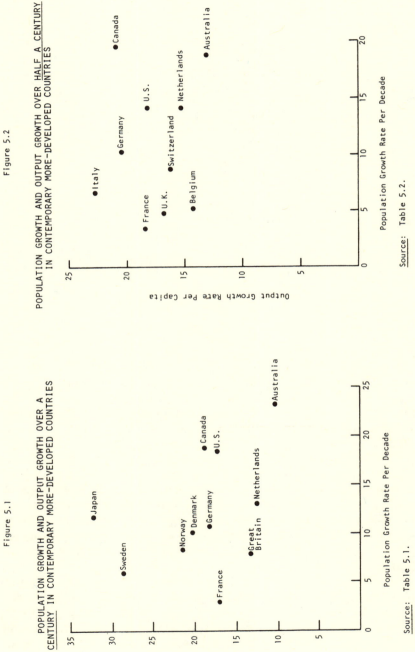

Figure 5.1

POPULATION GROWTH AND OUTPUT GROWTH OVER A CENTURY IN CONTEMPORARY MORE-DEVELOPED COUNTRIES

Population Growth Rate Per Decade

Output Growth Rate Per Capita

Source: Table 5.1.

Figure 5.2

POPULATION GROWTH AND OUTPUT GROWTH OVER HALF A CENTURY IN CONTEMPORARY MORE-DEVELOPED COUNTRIES

Population Growth Rate Per Decade

Output Growth Rate Per Capita

Source: Table 5.2.

TABLE 5.3
Annual Rates of Growth of Population and Total and Per Capita Product, Non-Communist Developed Countries (Including Japan), Post-World War II Period (Mostly From the Early 1950s to 1964)

Average rates for groups of countries arrayed in increasing order of rates of growth of population (%)

Groups	Population (1)	Per Capita Product (2)	Total Product (3)
1. 1-4	0.29%	3.66%	3.96%
2. 5-8	0.65	3.60	4.28
3. 9-13	0.94	5.07	6.05
4. 14-17	1.46	3.49	5.00
5. 18-21	2.19	2.02	4.25
Average, 21 Countries	1.10%	3.64%	4.77%

Source: Simon Kuznets, "Population and Economic Growth," in Proceedings of the American Philosophical Society 3 (1967):191.

shows the same effect for agricultural productivity.[5] Supporting evidence is provided in Figure 5.3.

Explanations

The total contradiction between observed facts and received theory has naturally provoked explanations, among which are the advantages of youthfulness in the labor force, the increased opportunities and consequent flexibility in a growing economy, and the greater mobility of the labor force in a growing economy. These speculations have not yet been pinned down empirically, so we can do little more than mention them and pass on.

Another set of factors that could explain why population growth shows unexpectedly good economic results should appeal to traditional economists: economies of scale in production. A bigger market is likely to bring bigger manufacturing plants that may be more efficient than smaller ones, as well as longer production runs and hence lower set-up costs per unit of output. A larger market also makes possible greater division of labor and hence an increase in the skill with which goods and

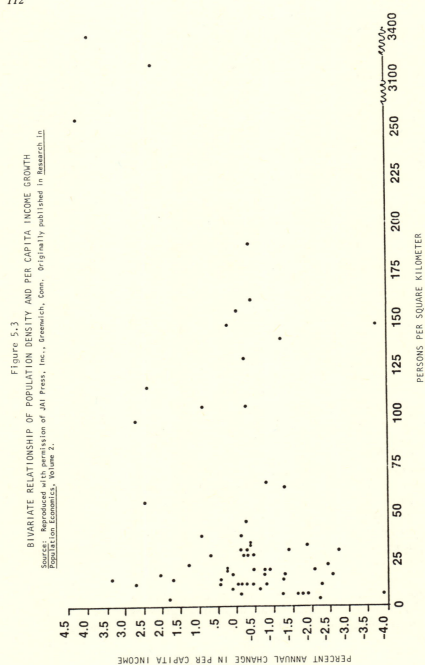

Figure 5.3

BIVARIATE RELATIONSHIP OF POPULATION DENSITY AND PER CAPITA INCOME GROWTH

Source: Reproduced with permission of JAI Press, Inc., Greenwich, Conn. Originally published in Research in Population Economics, Volume 2.

services are made. Specialization can also occur with respect to machinery. If the market for its goods is small, a firm will buy a machine that can be used in the production of several kinds of products. If the market is larger, the firm can afford to buy a separate, more specialized machine for each operation. Such economies of size seem to be exhausted at relatively modest plant sizes, however.[6] Larger markets also support a wider variety of services. If population is too small, there may be too few people to constitute a profitable market for a given product or service. In such a case there will be no seller, and people who do want the product or service will not be able to obtain it.

In more recent years, economists have also noted the influence of the size of the market—the total output and income in a market—on the decision to invest. As Nurkse put it in a famous article, "The inducement to invest is limited by the size of the market. . . . The level of productivity depends—not entirely by any means, but largely—on the use of capital in production. But the use of capital is inhibited, to start with, by the small size of the market."[7]

In addition to the usual sort of evidence on costs falling with city size in such industries as utilities and newspapers, we now have evidence that retail goods, and even most services, are distributed more cheaply in larger communities, once we allow for the wage effect.[8] And in a general study of the costs of manufacturing production, Sveikauskas[9] found an economically important advantage in efficiency in larger cities. There is also evidence, summarized by Alonso,[10] that less capital is needed to produce a given amount of output in larger cities. And the cost of capital is lower as measured by bank rates in larger communities.

Another important element is the greater density of communications and transportation networks that accompany denser population. This may be seen casually in the larger number of radio and television stations in larger cities; and in LDCs, Glover and Simon have shown in a cross-country study how denser road networks are found where population is denser, a vital factor for agricultural development.[11] Of course denser population may also imply greater congestion in transportation, and I know of no evidence on the net cost of transportation in relation to population density.

Still another possibly important element is the greater propensity to produce new ideas that accompanies living in larger cities,[12] and the greater tendency for new ideas and trends to diffuse and be adopted in larger cities.[13] Just why people are more likely to create and pick up new ideas where population is denser is still the subject of sociological speculation, but the evidence for the phenomenon is rather solid.

It may be that increased population size decreases the costs of making investments necessary to create cities, transportation networks, irrigation works, and other kinds of "infrastructure." Easterlin notes the correspondence between increases in labor force and major upswings in investment which occurred in the United States as a whole and within separate regions of the United States.[14] More recently, studies of interrelated factor demand in U.S. manufacturing in the 1950s and 1960s show that investment demand is positively correlated with demand for labor.[15] To the extent that an increased demand for labor is met by an increased supply of labor rather than a rise in wage rates, a larger population decreases the cost of investment in the manufacturing sector. It is possible theoretically that these effects could be offset by larger populations having a lower savings rate, perhaps due to higher dependency ratios. In practice, however, the downward pressure on savings rates, if it exists at all, is offset by increased income generated by harder work. The response of the immediate family of the baby is to work harder—the father takes on overtime work or a second job, the mother returns to work more quickly, the brothers and sisters enter the labor force earlier. Simon summarizes some of the evidence on this point for the United States in the 1960s.[16] Cramer finds stronger effects in a more recent study.[17] Lindert guesses that "the presence of one or more children in the home raised the father's paid work time by 50 hours a year as a rough postwar average."[18] In sum, higher birth rates, within the limits actually observed, appear to generate increases in investment (and employment) rather than decreases.

Important as the foregoing factors may be, however, the most plausible explanation of the observed lack of negative influence of population growth almost surely is the positive effect of additional people on productivity by creating additional productive knowledge. This factor also implies a positive long-run effect of additional people on the economic well-being in the OECD countries.

People and Knowledge

We are saying that, in the long run, the most important economic impact of population size and growth is the effect of additional people upon the stock of useful knowledge employed in the production of goods and services. And this positive effect is large enough (in the long run) to dominate all the negative effects of population growth. This is a strong statement, but the evidence for it seems strong. We shall now support this assertion.[19]

Let us begin with a question: Why is the standard of living so much higher in the United States or Sweden than in India or Mali, and why is the standard of living so much higher in the United States or Sweden now than it was 200 years ago? The proximate cause is that the average worker in the United States or Sweden now produces *x* times as much goods and services per day as does the average worker in India or Mali, or as did the average worker in the United States or Sweden 200 years ago, where *x* is the ratio of the standard of living now in the United States or Sweden to that in India or Mali now or the United States or Sweden then.

Though the first answer is almost definitional it points us to the important next question: Just *why* does the average worker in Sweden now produce so much more per day than does the average worker in Mali, or than did the average worker in Sweden 200 years ago? Part of the answer is that the average worker in Sweden today has available a much larger supply of capital equipment to work with—more buildings, tools, and transportation equipment. But that is only a minor factor. Striking proof of this assertion is afforded by the experience of West Germany after World War II. It is estimated that West Germany had ten million refugees to resettle from the end of the war until 1950 and gained another net three million in refugees from East Germany during the 1950s. This massive relocation of the German population into a much smaller territory actually enabled West Germany to achieve by the early 1960s the levels of output that would have been attained by the entire German economy had the prewar trends continued without the interruption of World War II. In other words, the ability of these additional people to build and produce more than offset the loss of territory, natural resources, and capital stock caused by the partition of Germany.

The all-important difference between the United States or Sweden now and those countries 200 years ago or India now is that there is a much greater stock of technological know-how available now, and people are educated to learn and use that knowledge. The knowledge and the schooling are intertwined; in India now, unlike the United States 200 years ago, the knowledge is available in books in the library— but without the schooling the knowledge cannot be adapted to local needs and then put to work. The stock of industrial capital is also intertwined with the stock of knowledge and with education; the value of much of our stock of capital such as computers and jet airplanes consists largely of the new knowledge that is built into them. And without educated workers, these chunks of capital cannot be operated and hence would be worthless.

The importace of the technological knowledge factor has clearly emerged in two famous studies, one by Solow and the other by Denison.[20] Using different methods, they calculated the extent to which the growth of physical capital and the labor force could account for economic growth in the United States and Europe. Both found that even after capital and labor are allowed for, much of the economic growth cannot reasonably be explained by any factor other than an improvement in the level of technological practice (including improved organization methods). Economies of scale due to larger factory size do not appear to be very important in this context, though in larger and faster growing industries the level of technology improves more rapidly than in smaller and slower growing industries. This improvement in productivity with technological practice did not come free, of course; much of it was "bought" with investments in research and development. But that does not alter the importance to us of the gains in technological knowledge.

How do population size and growth come into the picture? The source of improvements in productivity is the human mind, and the human mind is seldom found apart from the human body. And because improvements—their invention and their adoption—come from people, it seems reasonable to assume that the amount of improvement depends upon the number of people available to use their minds.

This is an old idea, going back at least as far as William Petty in 1682.[21] More recently, this effect of population size has been urged upon us by Kuznets.[22]

It cannot be emphasized too strongly that "technological advance" does not mean "science," and scientific geniuses are just one part of the knowledge process. Much of technological advance comes from people who are neither well educated nor well paid—the dispatcher who develops a slightly better way of deploying taxis in his ten-taxi fleet, the shipper who discovers that garbage cans make excellent cheap containers for many items, the supermarket manager who finds a way to display more merchandise in a given space, the supermarket clerk who finds a quicker way to stamp the prices on cans, the market researcher in the supermarket chain who experiments and finds more efficient and cheaper means of advertising the store's prices and sale items, and so on.

The need for additional producers of knowledge, and their potential contribution to resources and the economy, is manifest. Nobel Laureate Hans Bethe tells us that the future cost and availability of nuclear power—and hence the cost or availability of energy generally—would be a rosier prospect if the population of scientific workers were larger. Talking specifically about nuclear fusion and a device called Tokamak by the Russians, he states:

> Work on machines of the Tokamak type is also going forward in many other laboratories in the U.S., in the U.S.S.R. and in several countries of western Europe. If the problem can be solved, it probably will be. Money is not the limiting factor: the annual support in the U.S. is well over $100 million, and it is increasing steadily. Progress is limited rather by the

availability of highly trained workers, by the time required to build large machines and then by the time required to do significant experiments.[23]

For the United States in the twentieth century there is some statistical evidence. For the period 1950-62 for the United States, Denison estimated yearly growth in output of 0.76 percent due to "advances in knowledge" (which excludes the effect of education on the labor force), and 0.30 percent due to "economies of scale," for a total just over 1 percent. For Northwest Europe he estimated 0.76 percent due to "advances in knowledge," 0.56 percent due to "changes in the lag in application of knowledge, general efficiency, and errors and omissions," and 0.41 percent due to "economies of scale," for a total of something over 1.5 percent per year.[24] Solow's estimate of the increase in output in the United States due to increases in technical knowledge for the forty years from 1909 to 1949 is about 1.5 percent per year.[25]

If a larger labor force causes a faster rate of productivity change, one would expect to see this reflected in observed changes in the rate of productivity advance over time in the United States as population has grown. And indeed, Solow concludes that the yearly rate of change of productivity went from 1 percent to 2 percent between the 1909-29 and 1929-49 periods;[26] Fellner found these rates of productivity increase: 1900-29, 1.8 percent; 1929-48, 2.3 percent; and 1948-66, 2.8 percent.[27] These results are consistent with the assumption that the rate of increase of productivity is indeed higher when population is larger.

Put differently, would you bet on Sweden or Holland, against Great Britain and the USSR, to produce such great discoveries as those that will make nuclear fusion practical?

Though a bigger population produces more scientific knowledge, this does not yet show that more people mean faster technological advance, because science is not the same as applied knowledge put into operation. The fact that Sweden imports much more technology from the United States than the United States imports from Sweden is very suggestive. But one would like to have still more evidence.

A larger population implies a bigger market, all else equal. And larger markets induce faster gains in productivity, due to some combination of learning and competition. An example of the competitive effect is the January White Sale, a costless commercial innovation, which was adopted decades earlier in big cities than in small cities, on the average; the obvious explanation is the pressure of competition. As to learning, the more television sets or bridges or airplanes that a group of people produces, the more chance they have to improve their skills with "learning by doing," a very important factor in increasing productivity.

The increased efficiency of production within firms and industries as experience accumulates has been well documented in many industries starting with the air-frame industry in the 1930s. The bigger the population, the more of everything that is produced, which promotes learning by doing.

The most relevant evidence on market size and economies of scale comes from studies of industries as wholes. As mentioned above, it is an important and well-established phenomenon that industries which grow faster increase their efficiency faster, even compared with the same industries in other countries. The most recent and complete analysis, that of Clark, is shown in Figure 5.4. There we see comparisons of the productivity of U.S. industries in 1950 and 1963, and of U.K. industries in 1963, against U.K. industries in 1950. The larger the industry relative to the 1950 U.K. base, the greater is the productivity difference. This effect is very large. It is also consistent with "Verdoorn's Law," which is that productivity goes up with the square root of the change in output.[28] A subsequent analysis found similar results, as shown in Figure 5.5.

Babies do not create knowledge and improve productivity while still in their cradles, of course. And though the family bears most of the cost, society must also expend to bring the baby to productive adulthood. This means that if you do not look as far as the next twenty-five years, the knowledge benefits of someone else's baby born today do not interest you, and that baby is therefore a poor social investment for your taxes. But if you feel some interest and obligation to the longer run future, perhaps based on the fact that you yourself are today enjoying the fruits of the expenses that someone paid for 25 or 50 or 100 years ago, then the knowledge produced by today's children will be seen to be of great positive benefit.

Let us talk about transfer payments. On the one hand, a lower rate of population growth in any period implies fewer children to be educated, and fewer medical and other child-oriented services. On the other hand, a lower rate of population growth implies that later on there will be fewer working adults to support retired persons. It is this latter effect which has lately become a major concern in Europe and the United States, because it is clear that the old age social security payments are taking up an increasing proportion of the earnings of workers. This in turn creates worry that the level of support for retired persons will suffer.

The facts are, indeed, rather worrisome. Between 1950 and 2000 the ratio of retired to working persons is projected in a recent study to go up by somewhere between 40 percent and 100 percent in various European countries.[29] As the drop in the numbers of children is not relatively great, there is little positive counterbalance in transfers. Furthermore, an

Figure 5.4

THE EFFECT OF SCALE UPON PRODUCTIVITY

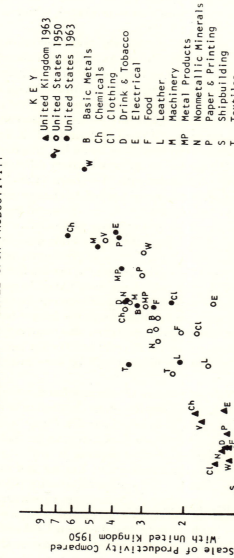

Scale of Production Compared
With United Kingdom 1950

Scale of Productivity Compared
With United Kingdom 1950

K E Y

▲ United Kingdom 1963
○ United States 1950
● United States 1963

B   Basic Metals
Ch Chemicals
Cl Clothing
D   Drink & Tobacco
E   Electrical
F   Food
L   Leather
M   Machinery
MP Metal Products
N   Nonmetallic Minerals
P   Paper & Printing
S   Shipbuilding
T   Textiles
V   Vehicles
W   Work

Source: Colin Clark, Population Growth and Land Use (New York: St. Martin's
Press, 1967), p. 265. Reprinted by permission of St. Martin's Press
and Macmillan, London and Basingstoke.

Figure 5.5

TOTAL PRODUCTION AND PRODUCTIVITY PER MAN
IN VARIOUS INDUSTRIES
U.K. 1950 = 1

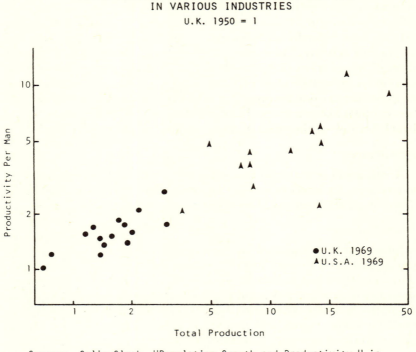

Source: Colin Clark, "Population Growth and Productivity," in
         Julian L. Simon, ed., Research in Population Economics, Vol. 1
         (Greenwich, Conn.: JAI Press, 1978). Reprinted by permission
         of the publisher.

added retired dependent makes a much larger demand upon public funds than one child fewer saves.[30] So the reduction in population growth in recent time indeed has troublesome implications from the standpoint of transfer payments.

In the long run, the way out of this dilemma is to have a higher birth rate. In the short and intermediate run the only selection is immigration, to which we now turn.

Immigrants

So far we have talked about additional people without distinguishing between those born into OECD countries and the rest of the industrialized world, or those who immigrate into it. But immigrants differ from native-borns in some important ways: (1) they generally immigrate after their education is complete, (2) they differ in skills and education from native-borns, (3) they send remittances back to their countries of origin, (4) many of them return home after some time, and (5) they have different needs for welfare services and different claims on the welfare systems. These characteristics may affect such factors as: (1) unemployment rates of native-borns, (2) the balance of payments, and (3) outlays for welfare services including education. Let us take up some of these matters one by one. Our comments should be understood as being drawn from analyses of Great Britain, United States, Canada, and Israel, because of the good studies available for those countries.

Remittances

Remittances sent abroad by immigrants or guest workers are similar to payments for imports, except that labor instead of goods is imported. There is no difference in their effect on the balance of payments.

Unemployment

Immigration is opposed by various occupational groups because immigrants tend to work at price-cutting rates and hence lower wages throw natives out of work in some occupations. Certainly there must be *some* negative impact of immigrants on *some* workers, and to say that the native workers can eventually find work in other occupations does not salve their wounds very much. Yet to our knowledge no study has shown massive or even important effects on any occupation. In the United States, for example, interesting evidence comes from two experimental programs designed to fill with citizens or legal aliens those jobs formerly held by illegal aliens. We have not been able to obtain the original description by Villalpando, and therefore we quote from Cornelius:

> The Los Angeles program consisted of an attempt by the State Human Resources Development Agency to fill some 2,154 jobs vacated by the apprehension of illegal aliens. The Agency's efforts to recruit citizen residents of the Los Angeles area to fill these jobs reportedly failed because (1) most of the employers paid less than the minimum wage rate; (2) the low-status job categories did not appeal to local residents; and (3) applicants were discouraged by the difficulty of some jobs and the long hours demanded by the employers. The "Employer Cooperation Program" conducted by the I.N.S. in San Diego from November, 1975, to April, 1976, had a similar outcome. As described by Villalpando, the purpose of this program was to "assist employers to identify illegal aliens

on the job, remove them from the payroll, and fill the job slots with local unemployed residents." A total of 340 illegal aliens were identified and removed from their jobs during the six-month program, most of whom had been working in hotel maintenance, food handling and processing, and laundry services, earning wages ranging from $1.75 to $7.05 per hour. The 340 jobs were eventually filled, but not by unemployed citizens of San Diego. Instead, 90 percent of the positions were occupied by [legally entering] "commuter workers" from Baja California, Mexico.[31]

Immigrants also have the positive (for native-borns) employment effect of buffering economic fluctuations. Immigrants are usually the first to be fired and the last to be hired.[32] And they tend to go home when employment ends, especially guest workers and most especially the illegals, whose return to Mexico is well documented.

As to welfare services, the data for Britain and Canada suggest that immigrants use a below-average quantity of services, largely because of the "favorable" age and sex composition of the immigrant groups. For the illegals in the United States, the evidence is clear and strong: illegal aliens do not use welfare services, both because they are young, mature, and strong, and also because they cannot use such services without fear of the law. For example, in the North and Houston survey, the data are as follows:

Used hospitals or clinics	27.4%
Collected one or more weeks of unemployment insurance	3.9%
Have children in U.S. schools	3.7%
Participated in U.S.-funded job training programs	1.4%
Secured food stamps	1.3%
Secured welfare payments	0.5%

And of the 27.4 percent who used hospitals, only 17 percent of the visits were not paid for by the alien or his insurance payments, i.e., less than 5 percent received public hospital services.[33]

Taxes

Immigrants tend to pay quantities of taxes that exceed the costs of the public services they use. In the United States, despite the fact that the illegal Mexican immigrants use almost no public services (except the time and energy of the Border Patrol), they do pay taxes. In the North and Houston survey, 73.2 percent of the aliens had federal income taxes withheld and 77.3 percent had social security insurance withheld (which the immigrants can never collect).[34] The Villalpando study of San Diego County estimated that illegal aliens paid $48.8 million in taxes per year, to be compared with approximately $2 million in social services used by them—a ratio of twenty-four to one.[35]

Other Factors: Immigrants and the Cost of Children

The main contrast between immigrants and children as the source of new population is that immigrants are "instant labor" while children must be reared and educated. The delay for the population boon from today's children is absent in the case of immigrants. If one assumes that immigrants today simply replace babies that would have been born otherwise so that the total population remains the same, an estimate can be made of the actual size of the resource pool which immigrants make available to the receiving country. The assumption that population size is determined independently of the origin of the population may or may not be realistic in the case of a particular economy (see discussion in Shergold for nineteenth-century United States);[36] it is adopted here only to determine the effects on an economy of immigration compared to native natality independently of the effects of greater or lesser population size.

The size of the resource pool released for other uses in the receiving economy is given by the following equation, where C is the total costs of producing an immigrant replacement, S the subsistence costs, E the educational costs to the society, n the interest rate, t the year of immigration, i the age of the immigrant at the time of immigration, and j the number of years of equivalent schooling of the immigrant in the host country.

$$C = \sum_{t-1}^{t} S_m (1 + n)^i + \sum_{t-1}^{t} E_k (1 + n)^j$$

Once the size of this resource pool has been calculated, another assumption must be made about the disposition of these extra resources in the receiving country. The two limiting assumptions are that the resources are either entirely consumed or entirely saved. The first assumption may make sense from the viewpoint of a household deciding what to do with its income that was committed to child raising and then is freed from that commitment, say, by death of the infant at birth. It does not make sense from the viewpoint of the economy as a whole within which these expenditures are made. The second assumption may also seem responsible from a household's viewpoint and is consistent with

Friedman's permanent income hypothesis; it quickly leads to absurd results for specific economies.[37]

The two empirical studies which have been made of immigration on the basis of this model both assumed that the resource pool was allocated between consumption and saving precisely in the same proportions as observed for total income. In the case of the United States in the period from 1790 to 1912, Neal and Uselding concluded that as of 1912 between 13 and 42 percent of the capital stock of the American economy could be attributed to the savings provided by taking immigrants as a major source of labor supply rather than natives.[38] In the very short period of 1957 to 1973, Blitz calculated for Western Germany that over 1 percent of the German national wealth in 1973 could be attributed to this source of savings.[39]

Whatever the precise proportions, the fact remains that this phenomenon explains an interesting feature about most economies which receive major parts of their labor force from immigration. This is the high capital-labor ratio which characterizes them by comparison with other countries at similar levels of per capita income but without major inflows of immigrants. A high capital-labor ratio is not necessarily associated with higher rates of economic growth, but it is associated with higher levels of labor productivity and hence of real wages.

Return to Capital

We should also note that immigrants represent a benefit to the owners of capital. Immigrants are paid only their own incremental output, while at the same time there is also an incremental return to the capital. This increases the income of the capital owners.

Female Labor-Force Participation

Nothing has been said about female labor-force participation, for a variety of reasons. First, this is a complex topic, intertwined with effects through changes in the birth rate. Second, the trend toward more female participation is very slow-acting with little fluctuation. Third, there is little opportunity for social manipulation. The effects on per capita income in the short and long run are almost completely positive, because, as with immigrants, expenditures on women's education are largely independent of their labor force participation. And women in the labor force tend to buffer unemployment. Of course, there is a social loss in leisure when women go to work, and perhaps in the quality of child raising. But these matters are beyond our scope here.

It is interesting to note, however, that there may well exist a behavioral interaction between immigration and births which, if it operates, works through the effects of immigration upon female participation in the labor force. The effect may be positive or negative, depending on the composition of the immigrant stream. In the last thirty years, major changes in the fertility patterns of women have occurred in all Western societies. The most striking and most nearly universal empirical association with these dramatic changes in fertility behavior has been the rising participation rates of women in the labor force. This association has been clearly illustrated in a large number of studies.[40]

Some demographers have argued that the striking inverse correlation between fertility and labor force activity of women is solely the result of less fertile women being released from the time-consuming tasks of child rearing for participation in the labor force activities outside the home.[41] Some economists, on the other hand, have argued that the availability of women's jobs and the wage rate paid them determines female activity in the labor force, and, therefore, their rate of fertility.[42] Most should agree, however, with Willis that both effects operate, one through the tastes of women for labor force participation and the other by determining the set of opportunities available for them in the labor market.[43] And one economist argues quite convincingly that female participation in the labor force and fertility are correlated only because they are both responses to a third phenomenon—changes in the age-composition of the labor force.[44] The presence of alien immigrants may operate on both preferences and opportunities of native women for joining the labor force.

Preferences

Women's preferences for work in the marketplace appear to be affected by the availability of domestic help. Bowen and Finegan, for example, found that it was the presence of children under six years of age that most strongly deterred women from the labor market.[45] This effect, however, was greatly weakened when a teenage child was present in the home. Ben-Porath, in a study of Israeli fertility, found that the increase in fertility of highly educated women was greater for nonworking wives, but whether working or not, they had a sharp increase in expenditures on domestic help.[46] The importance of domestic help may explain why the fertility rates of the European-American group of immigrants in Israel rose most noticeably when there was an upsurge of immigration from Asia and Africa.[47] This line of argument suggests that native natality of highly qualified women may be positively influenced if there are immigrants suitable for domestic help—females coming from lower income countries and classes. On the other hand, for less highly qualified native women the increased availability of domestic help may encourage quicker reentry into the labor force after a first child is born and thereby delay the birth of second and later children. In the first case, the effect on native natality is positive; in the second case it is negative.

Opportunities

Opportunities for employment of native women in satisfactory jobs may also be affected by the presence or absence of foreign immigrants. If the immigrants are highly concentrated in occupations which are complementary to women's employment, immigration should encourage labor force participation by native women, and therefore decrease their fertility. On the other hand, if the immigrant workers are lower priced substitutes for native women in their occupations, immigration will discourage labor force participation and encourage fertility by native women. Determination of complementarity and substitutability requires knowledge of the relative importance of the various occupation categories for native women as well as for the immigrant workers. Low income, female immigrants best qualified for domestic help are clearly complementary to native women's employment. A high concentration of immigrant women in Paris, for example, helps explain the extraordinarily high participation rate of women in that region.[48] Both native women and foreign women have their participation rates increased in this situation and both, as a consequence, have unusually low fertility rates.

A Stripped Long-Run Model[49]

Now let us return to additional people generally, and take a view that includes only the most important factors for the long run. If the economist is to be worth his keep, he must take account of the size and importance of the various effects, and calculate the net effect. One can only obtain a satisfactory overall assessment by constructing an integrated model of the economy, and then comparing the incomes produced by the economy under various conditions of population growth.

If one adds to the simple, neoclassical model another fundamental fact of the economic growth of nations—the increase in productivity due to additional people's inventive and adaptive capacities—one arrives at a very different result from the standard Malthusian model. The analysis is outlined in Figure 5.6, where the elements of the usual economic demographic model for MDCs are shown in solid lines, and where the

Figure 5.6

SCHEMATIC OF MDC MODELS WITHOUT EDUCATION

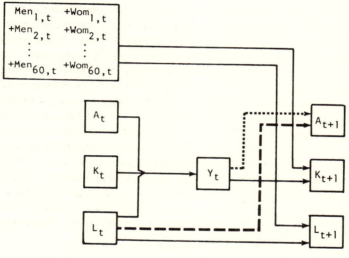

Where

A_t = Level of Technology in Year t

K_t = Capital

L_t = Labor

Y_t = National Income

Source: From Julian L. Simon, <u>The Economics of Population Growth</u>, copyright © 1977 by Princeton University Press, Fig. 6-1, p. 109. Reprinted by permission of Princeton University Press.

Note: The line with long dashes from L_t to A_{t+1} represents the feedback effect in the Residual model, whereas the line with the short dashes from Y_t to A_{t+1} represents the feedback effect in the Verdoorn model.

knowledge-feedback elements are shown in dotted lines. That is, this model embodies not only the standard classical and neoclassical capital effects, but also the effects of knowledge advance, economies of scale, and natural resource use. These latter elements have been omitted from population models in the past, but they are crucial to a balanced understanding of the problem. The analysis is conducted with two separate ways of introducing the effect of population size upon the production of productive knowledge, the residual model and the Verdoorn model.

The residual model derives an estimate from the "residual" found in studies that attempt to explain U.S. economic growth. The residual is the unexplained portion of economic growth left after inputs of capital and labor have been accounted for, and is commonly associated with technological advance. The residual model assumes that the size of the residual is a function of the size of the labor force considering the industrialized world as a whole, so that the question of a small country riding the coattails of other countries does not arise. In this formulation the residual is positively influenced by population growth.

A variant of Verdoorn's law provides a second approach to our subject. The Verdoorn model embodies the effect of the size of an economy—as measured by changes in its labor force—upon the rate of increase in productivity. Additional workers certainly are not the only cause of increased outputs. But over any period longer than the business cycle, the size of the labor force is a major influence upon total output. And if one holds constant the capital endowment and the original level of technological practice in the analysis, then population size is the *only* influence upon total output. Therefore, it is reasonable to think of Verdoorn's law as a proxy for the labor force-productivity change relationship; that is, output itself does not change productivity, but rather the people engaged in producing that output change productivity (and in fact, Verdoorn explains his law as caused by learning). One may, of course, also think of Verdoorn's law simply as an empirical estimate of economies of scale without specifying a behavioral mechanism. Either interpretation is quite consistent with the work described here.

Results: High Population Growth
Implies Faster Economic Growth

Five different rates of population growth were investigated in the simulation: ZPG has zero population growth; BASE has 1 percent population growth per year; PLUS-HALF has a 50 percent jump in the birth rate above BASE in year zero and subsequent years; TWO has 2 percent population growth per year; TEMP has a one-year temporary increase in the birth rate. The results for the five demographic structures with the residual model are shown in Figure 5.7; corresponding results for the Verdoorn model are not shown but are similar.[50] The most important outcome is that under every set of conditions, demographic structures PLUS-HALF and TWO with the more rapid population growth come to have higher per-worker income than structure BASE in less than eighty years, even with a base rate-of-change technology as low as one percent. And in every run, structure TWO, which reaches a labor force (in thousands, say) of 23,769 in year $t = 160$ from the starting point of 1,000 in year $t = 0$, has a higher per-worker income structure than structure PLUS-HALF, which reaches a labor force of 7,346 in $t = 160$. (For comparison, the labor force for structure BASE in year 160 is 4,913.) And population-growth structure ZPG holds its advantage over the BASE structure only about as long as BASE holds its advantage over faster population growth; thereafter, it does much worse.

In many runs the higher fertility structures overtake the BASE structure's per-worker output after only thirty years—that is, only about ten years after the entrance of the first additional children into the labor force. It is true that the long run—thirty to eighty years—is a long way off from now, and therefore is of less importance to us than is the short run. But we should remember that our long run will be someone else's short run, just as our short run was someone else's long run. Some measure of unselfishness should impel us to keep this in mind as we make our decisions about population policy. Furthermore, the short-run economic differences between the various demographic structures are small by any absolute measure, though the long-run differences are large.

The time horizon is sufficiently short so that any possible major changes in the natural resources situation may be disregarded. But it is sufficiently long so that the delayed effects of knowledge increase can come to play their role. It is appropriate to think of this analysis as applying to the developed world as a whole, because of the scientific and technological interdependence among the MDCs.

Summary and Conclusions

The short-run effect of a higher birth rate in OECD countries is an increase in social costs. But these costs are small relative to any standard, and can have positive stimulating effects on business activity.

When additional persons—natives or immigrants—enter the labor force there is some dilution of capital with a consequent reduction in wages paid to labor (though not necessarily in per capita income across

Figure 5.7

OUTPUT PER WORKER WITH VARIOUS RATES OF
POPULATION GROWTH

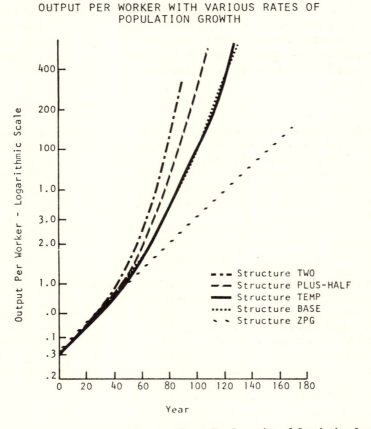

Source: From Julian L. Simon, <u>The Economics of Population Growth</u>,
copyright © 1977 by Princeton University Press, Fig. 6-4,
p. 132. Reprinted by permission of Princeton University
Press.

the economy). But this capital-dilution effect is outbalanced by the positive effect of additional persons and additional total output upon productivity and hence upon output and income per worker. That is, additional persons in the labor force lead to faster technical progress through formal knowledge creation, learning by doing, faster diffusion of ideas, and related mechanisms. There are also positive effects on investment and on economies of scale.

Immigrants to OECD countries have the additional advantage that the flow of them is responsive to immediate cyclical demands. They tend to pay more taxes than the cost of the social services they consume. And their benefits are immediate, in contrast to additional children for whom there is a social cost years before the social benefit occurs.

Notes

1. This paper draws upon: Julian Simon, *The Economics of Population Growth* (Princeton: Princeton University Press, 1977); Julian L. Simon, "Additional People Improve the Standard of Living Through Knowledge Creation, and Productivity Increases," Testimony given to Select Committee on Population of the U.S. House of Representatives, June 2, 1978; Julian L. Simon, "Immigrants Don't Cost, They Pay," Paper delivered to Population Association of America, April 1978.

2. In this connection there is illumination in Wilfred Beckerman's remark, "The instant a calf is born, per capita income rises, but the instant a baby is born, per capita income falls." Wilfred Beckerman, *In Defense of Economic Growth* (London: Jonathan Cape, 1974).

3. David Morawetz, "Twenty-Five Years of Economic Development," *Finance and Development* 14 (September 1977), p. 10.

4. Everett E. Hagen, *The Economics of Development* (Homewood: Irwin, 1975); Charles P. Kindleberger, *Economic Development*, 2nd ed. (New York: McGraw-Hill, 1965); Julian L. Simon and Roy Gobin, "The Relationship Between Population and Economic Growth in LDC's," in Julian L. Simon and Julie Da Vanzo, *Research in Population Economics*, vol. 2 (Greenwich: JAI Press, 1979).

5. J. Dirck Stryker, "Optimum Population in Rural Areas: Empirical Evidence from the Franc Zone," *The Quarterly Journal of Economics* 41 (May 1977):177-93.

6. See F. M. Scherer, *Industrial Market Structure & Economic Performance* (Santa Monica: Rand Corporation, 1978).

7. Ragnar Nurkse, "Growth in Underdeveloped Countries," in A. N. Agarwala and S. P. Singh, *The Economics of Underdevelopment* (New York: Oxford, 1963), p. 20.

8. Douglas Love, "City Sizes and Prices" (Ph.D. dissertation, University of Illinois, 1978).

9. Leo Sveikauskas, "The Productivity of Cities," *Quarterly Journal of*

Economics 89 (1975):343-413.

10. William Alonso, "The Economics of Urban Size," in *Regional Policy Readings in Theory and Applications*, eds. John Freidmann and William Alonso (Cambridge: The M.I.T. Press, 1975).

11. Donald R. Glover and Julian L. Simon, "The Effect of Population Density Upon Infrastructure: The Case of Roadbuilding," *Economic Development and Cultural Change* 23 (April 1975).

12. Robert Higgs, "American Inventiveness, 1890-1920," *Journal of Political Economy* 79 (1971):661-67; and Allen Kelley, "Scale Economies, Inventive Activity, and the Economics of American Population Growth," *Explorations in Economic History* 10 (1972):35-52.

13. Claude S. Fischer, "Urban-to-rural Diffusion of Opinions in Contemporary America," *American Journal of Sociology* 84 (July 1978):151-59; and Julian L. Simon and Leslie Golembo, "The Spread of a Cost-Free Business Innovation: The Case of the January White Sale," *Journal of Business* 40 (October 1967):385-88.

14. Richard A. Easterlin, *Population, Labor Force, and Long Swings in Economic Growth* (New York: National Bureau of Economic Research, 1968).

15. M. I. Nadiri and Sherwin Rosen, *A Disequilibrium Model of Demand for Factors of Production* (New York: National Bureau of Economic Research, 1974).

16. Simon, *Economics of Population Growth*, pp. 55-62.

17. James C. Cramer, "The Effects of Fertility on Husband's Economic Activity: Evidence from Static, Dynamic, and Non-Recursive Models," in *Research in Population Economics* 3, eds. Julian L. Simon and Julie Da Vanzo (Greenwich: JAI Press, 1979).

18. Peter Lindert, *Fertility and Scarcity in America* (Princeton: Princeton University Press, 1978), p. 274.

19. For a more detailed presentation of the evidence see Simon, *Economics of Population Growth*, chapters 4 and 6.

20. Robert Solow, "Technical Change and the Aggregate Production Function," *The Review of Economics and Statistics* 39 (1957):312-20; and Edward F. Denison, *Why Growth Rates Differ* (Washington: The Brookings Institution, 1967).

21. William Petty, *Another Essay in Political Arithmetic* (1682), in *The Economic Writings of Sir William Petty*, ed. Charles H. Hull (Cambridge: At the University Press, 1899), p. 474.

22. Simon Kuznets, "Population Change and Aggregate Output," in Universities National Bureau of Economic Research, *Demographic and Economic Change in Developed Countries* (Princeton: Princeton University Press, 1960).

23. Hans Albrecht Bethe, "The Necessity of Fission Power," *Scientific American* 234 (January 1976):16.

24. Denison, *Growth Rates*.

25. Solow, *Technical Change*.

26. Ibid.

27. William Fellner, "Specific Interpretations of Learning by Doing,"

Journal of Economic Theory 1 (1969):119-40.

28. P. J. Verdoorn, "Factors that Determine the Growth of Labor Productivity," trans. G. Thirlwall and A. P. Thirlwall in Julian Simon and Julie Da Vanzo, *Population Economics;* originally in *L'Industria,* no. 1, 1949, pp. 45-46.

29. Pierre Guilmot, "The Demographic Background," in Lounat of Europe, *Population Decline in Europe* (New York: St. Martin's Press, 1978).

30. Robert L. Clark and Joseph J. Spengler, "Dependency Ratios: Their Use in Economic Analysis" in Simon and Da Vanzo, *Population Economics.*

31. Wayne A. Cornelius, "Illegal Migration to the United States: Recent Research Findings, Policy Implications, and Research Priorities," Mimeographed (Cambridge: Center for International Studies, M.I.T., May 1977), p. 10; his quotes are from M. Vic Villalpondo et al., *A Study of the Socio-Economic Impact of Illegal Aliens, County of San Diego* (San Diego: Human Resources Agency, County of San Diego, January 1977).

32. K. Jones and A. D. Smith, *The Economic Impact of Commonwealth Immigration* (Cambridge: At the University Press, 1970).

33. David S. North and Marian F. Houston, *The Characteristics and Role of Illegal Aliens in the U.S. Labor Market: An Exploratory Study* (Washington: Linton and Company, March 1976), p. 142.

34. North and Houston, *Characteristics and Role.*

35. Cornelius, *Illegal Migration,* p. 12.

36. Peter Shergold, "The Walker Thesis Revisited: Immigration and White American Fertility, 1800-1860," *Australian Economic History Review* 14, no. 2 (September 1974):168-89.

37. Milton Friedman, *A Theory of the Consumption Function* (Princeton: National Bureau of Economic Research, 1975); see also Corrado Gini, "Europe und Amerika: Zei Welten," *Weltwirtschaftliches Archiv* 52 (1940):1-30.

38. Larry Neal and Paul Uselding, "Immigration: A Neglected Source of American Economic Growth, 1790-1917," *Oxford Economic Papers* 24 (1972):66-88.

39. Rudolf Blitz, "A Benefit-Cost Analysis of Foreign Workers in West Germany," *Kyklos* 30, no. 3 (Fall 1977):479-502.

40. See, for example, William G. Bowen and T. Aldrich Finegan, *The Economics of Labor Force Participation* (Princeton: Princeton University Press, 1969); Glen G. Cain, *Married Women in the Labor Force: An Economic Analysis* (Chicago: University of Chicago Press, 1960); William B. Clifford and Patricia L. Tobin, "Labor Force Participation of Working Mothers and Family Formation: Some Further Evidence," *Demography* 13 (February 1976):115; L. Tabah, "Rapport sur les relations entre la fécondité et la condition sociale de la famille en Europe," Council of Europe, 2nd Population Conference (Strasbourg, 1971); Yves Tugault, *Fécondité et Urbanisation,* Cahier no. 74 (Paris: INED, 1975); R. H. Weller, "Employment of Wives, Role Incompatibility and Fertility," *Millbank Memorial Fund Quarterly* 46:507-526; Pascal Whelpton, A. A. Campbell, and J. E. Patterson, *Fertility and Family Planning in the United States* (Princeton: Princeton University Press, 1966).

41. See, in particular, Weller, "Employment of Wives."

42. Bowen and Finegan, *Labor Force Participation*, may perhaps be read this way.

43. Whelpton et al., *Fertility and Family Planning*.

44. Richard Easterlin, "What Will 1984 Be Like? Socioeconomic Implications of Recent Twists in Age Structure," *Demography* 15 (November 1978):397-432.

45. Bowen and Finegan, *Labor Force Participation*.

46. Yoram Ben-Porath, "Fertility in Israel," in T. W. Schultz, ed., *Economics of the Family: Marriage, Children, and Human Capital* (Chicago: University of Chicago Press, 1974), pp. 209-210.

47. Ben-Porath, "Fertility in Israel," p. 293, Table 1.

48. Tugault, *Fécondité*, p. 133.

49. This model, and the empirical support for it, are described in Simon, *Economics of Population Growth*, chapters 4 and 6.

50. The results shown in Simon, *Economics of Population Growth*, chapter 6; the Verdoorn model uses a function based on the *absolute size* of the labor force rather than the *rate of change* of the labor force, as Verdoorn has it. This became clear to me only with Thurlwall's recent translation of Verdoorn's original paper from the Italian (forthcoming). It seems more reasonable that productivity change is a function of the size of the labor force rather than its rate of change; the latter implies zero productivity growth if there is zero growth in the labor force, which does not accord with reality. But most of the available parametric estimates relate the rate of change of the labor force in the spirit of Verdoorn's formulation. The intercountry comparison—the sort of data presented over Clark's name earlier—is ambiguous in this connection.

Commentary

Selma Mushkin

A useful theory of human behavior, be it positive or normative in content and purpose, must assume some rationality. Choices of individuals and government policy officials must be directed to achieve some objective or goal that is rationally within grasp. This paper poses three questions: What are the effects of higher versus lower birth rates? What are the effects of more versus less immigration? And what are the effects of an increase in female labor force participation? Except for the last question, which is considered in terms of net effect on population growth, the other two questions are answered in terms of the economic benefit that flows from more people, and particularly "the improvement that the average person makes to the efficiency of production through new ideas and contributions to knowledge." I would contend that any gain assumed does not happen automatically, because incentives are all wrong. It is irrational to assume that additional production will be achieved through new ideas and advances in knowledge, just because there are more people.

I agree entirely with the view of the authors that an additional child is a durable good, in which one must invest heavily. The critical investment question to which I take exception is, What is the size of the investment return on that durable good? Will the investment return reflect the add-on of new knowledge and advances in productivity, or would it be a constant unchanged return per labor member because the added child, now adult, works with existing knowledge and technology and does not necessarily contribute to it?

Expansion in technology and advances in the scientific base that can contribute to such technological change are of great importance to this nation and to many countries of the OECD. I therefore think we have to take any discussion of it most seriously. The rate of return on investment in babies, or in any other investment, requires newly designed organizational structures that can encourage and support new scientific achievement and assure implementation of new advances in technology. Again, nothing happens automatically. Research and development needs to be financed on a more generous basis. Today R&D growth from year to year is about equal to the price change, so that added resources are not going into technological advance. Further, a longer run perspective is needed on R&D. At high interest rates, myopia has set in concerning returns to R&D, which I think affects not only private industries but also government.

At one point the authors note, "Improvement in productivity with technological practices does not come free. Much of it is bought with investments in R&D." They also contend, however, that technological advance can come from persons who are neither well educated nor well paid. I need to know why these people would bother with a change. There has to be something in it for them, and that means the incentive of higher pay or of greater profits. Unless there is a structure in an organization for change, and rewards for change, it seems to me irrational for someone to choose to make a change. Innovators are not popular people; they always subject themselves to firing rather than reward. If the intent is to reward technology and innovation, the system has to be structured to do just that. Western nations have come to emphasize the limits of scientific growth at the very time that those nations need to learn how to foster acceleration of scientific advance, gain implementation of new technologies, and achieve the advantage that would permit them to run harder and more successfully in the international trade race.

It is the automaticity of the concept of growth, tied to long-run population movements, to which I take strong exception. Furthermore, it seems to me that the paper assumes that population growth is spread uniformly over age groups. In fact, population developments have been characterized by great unevenness in growth rates. The size of the different age cohorts cannot but have differential impacts on the economy. At present our own wartime babies have contributed to high youth unemployment and the high cost in alienation that such high unemployment rates produce. Europe has a somewhat similar experience that has in some places disrupted traditional apprenticeships and added to the problem of education being out of step with industrial needs. As the wartime babies pass through the decades, we are going to have another type of crisis—the crisis of social security benefit financing and provision of medical services for the aged. The long run perspective on population developments requires counterpart analysis of the evenness or unevenness of the spread in population itself, and most of the analysis presented completely neglects this problem.

Let me make an additional observation. In this case it is not a quarrel with what was said, but rather what was not said. Throughout the discussion of factors that contribute to economic growth, long-term population increases, and so on, there is no mention of sickness or health in the population—the impact of reduced deaths and reduced disabilities on productivity and economic growth. The omission of health considerations stands out, particularly in the discussion concerning important differences between the United States and Sweden now and 200 years ago. I agree that there is a greater stock of technological knowledge now available, and that people have learned to use this knowledge, but there is also no smallpox, plague, or pellagra, there is a little bit of dysentery, and tuberculosis is not so prevalent. I would contend that the vitality of the population, the extent to which sickness requires loss of time from work or loss of energy while at work had something to do with economic growth.

Commentary

Angus Maddison

This paper is very ambitious in scope. It goes into the sort of topics dealt with in Professor Nelson's paper as well as with the problem of population. Even if it were restricted only to population, the treatment strikes me as too simplistic. You cannot make judgments about the impact of population on growth or welfare simply by juxtaposing densities or growth rates with corresponding levels of real income. I also find it a little odd that the paper refers to "received theory" on population, because I thought that since Mrs. Boserup wrote her book in 1965 there had been a high degree of agnosticism about what optimal population policy or theory would be.[1] A recent article by Goran Ohlin for the International Economic Association reviews the state of population theory, and this confirms my feeling that demographers are somewhat agnostic.[2] In any case my first point is that the underlying theory should be clearly stated at the beginning.

The second point is that our focus is on OECD countries, in the period since the war. The paper includes developing countries whose population problems are really rather different. To my mind, the rate of population growth in OECD countries is not now high enough to have much effect one way or the other on growth of per capita product. Further I do not really think it a legitimate field for public policy in these countries. The government does not need to have a view as to what optimum population growth should be. It is a matter of personal choice whether you have children or not. The main scope for public policy is to provide facilities for birth control and abortion for those who want it or need it.

In a recent OECD study on demographic trends and their social and economic implications,[3] the most striking conclusion was the drop in the birth rate which occurred in all countries (except Ireland) around the beginning of the sixties. And it was quite a big drop—some countries now have negative population growth. That is true of Germany where it is expected that population will decline by several million over the next fifteen years. In Great Britain, there has also been a slight decline in the past year or two. The growth of the working-age population has not decelerated as much as total population. Therefore, the likelihood is that the ratio of the population which is in the labor force will increase. In normal circumstances this would be good for welfare because it would reduce transfer costs. However, if you have a problem of unemployment, and lower population growth, it makes welfare problems worse. Transfer payments will go to the unemployed as well as to the aged and children. This view of the outlook is a little different from that of Simon and Neal.

On immigrants and children, I also disagree with Simon and Neal. It seems to me that immigrants do bring considerable benefits in some cases, but I think costs are understated. It seems clear that, at least in Western European countries, immigrants do change the wage structure. All of the dustmen in Paris are immigrants, and the wages of dustmen in Paris relative to the average wage are quite different from what they are in Oslo. There are huge slum areas around Paris which cause great social problems; European countries are acquiring some of the social tensions which the United States has experienced. Some of these social costs are not treated seriously in the paper.

As far as children are concerned, it is not clear exactly what is meant. But I do not think children can be regarded only as investments. They are a consumer good too, and any lifetime view of the population problem would produce a totally different answer. You may need somebody else's children to honor your pension.

Notes

1. E. Boserup, *The Condition of Agricultural Growth*, (London: Allen and Unwin, 1965).

2. G. Ohlin, "Economic Theory Confronts Population Growth," in A. J. Coale, *Economic Factors in Population Growth* (London: Macmillan, 1976).

3. Organization for Economic Co-operation and Development, *Demographic Trends: Their Economic and Social Implications* (Paris: Organization for Economic Co-operation and Development, 1979).

6

Development of the Service Sector in OECD Countries: Economic Implications

Maurice Lengellé

Since the breakdown of the Bretton Woods Agreement, Western economies have been hit in different ways: inflation, market instability, slower economic growth, increased unemployment, etc. It is interesting to analyze the behavior of the service sector during this period of unrest, in comparison with agriculture and manufacturing.

Recent Employment Trends

The rate of growth of employment began to decline in the OECD countries in 1973: from 1973 to 1977, *the civilian labor force*[1] increased by 17.0 million, i.e., an average annual rate of 1.34 percent compared with 1.36 percent between 1969 and 1973. But *civilian employment*[2] rose by only 8.4 million from 1973 to 1977, i.e., an average annual rate of 0.68 percent compared with 1.09 percent per annum during the four preceding years.

The gap between the trends in the civilian labor force and civilian employment obviously explains the rise in unemployment: 8.6 million between 1973 and 1977.[3] From 6.7 million unemployed in OECD countries in 1969, this figure rose to 9.6 million in 1973 and 18.2 million in 1977.

Without doubt, the most interesting feature concerns the development of employment in the service sector:[4] during 1973-77, it increased by 15.6 million, i.e., an average growth rate of 2.48 percent per annum compared with 2.78 percent during the four preceding years. Different

Mr. Lengellé is principal administrator in the Organization for Economic Co-operation and Development. The views expressed in this article are those of the author, and not necessarily those of the OECD.

from the two other sectors, the service sector has been almost unaffected by the economic slump.[5]

A comparison among the various regions within the OECD area shows that the fall in employment was particularly noticeable in the EEC (a decline of 335,000 in civilian employment), although service employment developed more rapidly than the civilian labor force. In fact, it is the only OECD region where the service sector has increased in proportionate terms so sharply during the period under review (Table 6.1).

Employment in Service Sector

Over ten years ago, for a special OECD study on the service sector,[6] a comprehensive questionnaire was circulated to member countries and specific data were collected on trends in employment in a dozen major groups of activities.[7]

Unfortunately, the statistics currently available are far less comprehensive, since the series stops at the year 1976 and covers only four main activities.[8] In addition, a number of countries have not replied to the annual questionnaire circulated by the OECD on the labor force; the two most important are the United States and Canada.

From 1973 to 1976, the number of people employed in activities of the service sector in fifteen countries rose by 4.4 million. Once again it is in the EEC that the increase in the number of people employed is proportionately the lowest. As regards employment in restaurants and hotels taken as a whole, the numbers actually declined in the EEC (by 258,000). A more detailed analysis shows that employment declined most in the United Kingdom (by 16,000) and Germany (by 285,000). The number of people employed in transport and communications in the EEC also fell (by 25,000); in the United Kingdon the decline was 33,000 and in Germany 53,000. There were increases in all the other countries. As regards the activities relating to finance and services to firms, all countries covered by the survey report substantial increases, the highest being in the social, community, and personal services (Table 6.2).

Trend in Employment by Sex

Data on employment by sex in the various economic activities are even less comprehensive, since only a dozen countries were in a position to supply the necessary information. In addition to the United States and Canada, no reply was received in particular from France, New Zealand, and Spain.

In all the countries for which data are available, the number of people employed between 1973 and 1976 has declined in agriculture and

TABLE 6.1
OECD Employment (Increase from 1973 to 1977 in thousands)

	Civilian Labor Force (1)	Civilian Employment (2)	Difference (1) - (2) (3)	Civilian Employment in Activities other than Agriculture and Industry (4)	(4) as % of (2)
North America	+9,982	+7,089	+2,893	+7,581	106.9%
Japan	+1,260	+830	+430	+2,200	267.5
Australia	+635	+385	+250	+427	110.9
New Zealand	+79	+78	+1	+49	62.8
OECD Europe	+5,039	+40	+4,999	+5,294	13,235.0
of which:					
- EEC	(+3,153)	(-335)	(+3,488)	(+3,832)	(---) (a)
Europe excl. EEC	(+1,886)	(+375)	(+1,511)	(+1,462)	(390)
OECD Total	+16,995	+8,422	+8,573	+15,551	184.9%

Source: Organization for Economic Co-operation and Development, Labour Force Statistics, 1965-1976 (Paris: 1978).

(a) During this period, employment in activities other than agriculture and industry increased as total civilian employment decreased.

TABLE 6.2
Employment in Activities other than Agriculture and Industry (change from 1973 to 1976 in thousands)

Activities	OECD Europe (12 Countries)	Of which EEC (7 Countries)	European Countries other than EEC (5 Countries)	Italy Apart	Japan	Australia	New Zealand
6 (Trade)	-116	-258	+142	+61	+660	+173	+3
7 (Transport)	-9	-25	+16	+78	+40	+18	+7
8 (Financing)	+452	+291	+161		+160	+54	+7
9 (Community, Social and Personal Services)	+1,606	+1,226	+380	+569	+600	+37	+31
	+1,933	+1,234	+699	+708	+1,460	+382	+48

Source: Same as Table 6.1.

industry taken together: the decline affected both men and women. But employment increased in the service sector for both sexes. No doubt the most interesting observation is that in all countries except Japan more new jobs were offered to women than to men (Table 6.3). Although the figures available are incomplete, it may be observed that these results partly confirm the OECD study of 1966. As in 1966, a relatively close link may be established between the feminization of the service sector and the gradual importance taken by the activites of this sector in which women are more and more numerous: education, health, social services, child care, etc.

Development of Employment and Production in the Three Economic Sectors

Civilian employment and contribution to the gross domestic product[9] in the six groups of OECD member countries were classified into three broad sectors:

- agriculture (including forestry, hunting and fishing)
- industry (mining and quarrying; manufacturing; construction; transportation; electricity, gas, water, and sanitary services)
- commerce and services

For each group of countries employments and production in each of these sectors were calculated as a percentage of total civilian employment and gross domestic product. Three figures were thus obtained and are reported in Tables 6.4 and 6.5:

A = Percentage in agriculture, forestry, hunting, and fishing
I = Percentage in industry and transport
S = Percentage in commerce and services
A + I + S = 100.

To determine any relationship which may exist between A, I, and S, triangular graphs were used on the following principle: An equilateral triangle ABC, with point M inside and with lines Ma, Mb, and Mc drawn parallel to AB, BC, and CA, respectively, has the following properties: the lines form three angles of 120°, and the sum of the lengths of Ac, Ba and Cb is constant. Any three values whose sum is constant can thus be represented by varying the position of point M. Thus, lines drawn parallel to the guidelines meet the axes at points which sum to 100 percent.

In Figures 6.1 and 6.2, the A, I, and S values for each group of countries

TABLE 6.3
Civilian Employment by Sex and Industry (Change from 1973 to 1976 in thousands)

Countries	Females		Males	
	Agriculture and Industry	Other Activities	Agriculture and Industry	Other Activities
Japan	-890	+420	-450	+1,040
Australia	-8	+147	-82	+135
Belgium, Germany, Italy and United Kingdom	-786	+992	-1,851	+360
Finland, Norway, Spain and Sweden	-98	+429	-483	+111
Total 10 Countries	-1,782	+1,988	-2,866	+1,646

Source: Same as Table 6.1.

TABLE 6.4
Civilian Employment by Sector (percent of total: I = Agriculture, II - Industry, III - Other Activities)

Years	Southern European Countries			North Western European Countries			EEC			Japan			Australia and New Zealand			USA and Canada		
	I	II	III	I	II	III	I	II	III	I	II	III	I	II	III	I	II	III
1969	39.3%	31.7%	29.0%	9.6%	42.9%	47.5%	11.2%	43.8%	45.0%	18.8%	35.1%	46.2%	9.0%	36.9%	54.1%	5.0%	33.4%	61.7%
1973	35.0	32.1	32.9	7.5	42.3	50.2	9.2	42.8	48.0	13.4	37.2	49.4	8.0	34.9	57.1	4.3	31.4	64.3
1974	33.8	32.8	33.4	7.6	41.8	50.6	8.9	42.6	48.5	12.7	37.0	50.1	7.7	35.1	57.2	4.3	30.9	64.8
1975	33.0	33.0	34.0	7.2	40.7	52.1	8.4	41.8	50.0	12.7	35.9	51.5	7.4	32.9	59.7	4.2	29.0	66.8
1976	32.3	32.7	35.0	7.0	40.0	53.0	8.2	41.0	50.8	12.2	35.8	52.0	7.4	33.3	59.3	4.0	29.0	67.0
1977	31.1	31.8	37.1	6.8	39.6	53.6	8.2	39.8	51.9	11.9	35.4	52.8	7.5	32.8	59.7	3.8	28.9	67.3

Source: Same as Table 6.1.

TABLE 6.5
Contribution to the Gross Domestic Product (percent of GDP
at current prices: I = Agriculture, II = Industry,
III = Other Activities)

	1970			1973			1976 [a]		
	I	II	III	I	II	III	I	II	III
Canada	4.3%	36.6%	59.1%	5.2%	37.0%	57.8%	4.2%	35.6%	60.2%
USA	2.8	34.7	62.5	4.0	34.0	62.0	2.9	33.4	63.7
Denmark	8.0	40.8	51.2	8.3	39.6	52.1	7.2	37.7	55.1
Finland	13.9	43.2	42.9	12.0	44.4	43.6	11.5	42.5	46.0
Germany	3.5	54.0	42.5	3.2	51.6	45.2	2.9	52.0	45.1
Greece	18.2	31.4	50.4	20.4	33.2	46.4	18.8	30.2	51.0
Italy	9.0	43.1	47.9	8.7	42.8	48.5	8.2	44.6	47.2
Norway	6.8	35.7	57.5	6.0	34.2	59.8	6.5	38.1	55.4
Portugal	18.0	41.6	40.4	16.1	43.8	40.1	15.8	42.7	41.5
Spain	11.8	39.4	48.8	11.1	39.8	49.1	9.7	40.0	50.3
Sweden	4.5	42.7	52.8	4.3	41.8	53.9	5.0	39.9	55.1
Turkey	28.1	29.4	42.5	26.4	28.2	45.4	28.5	27.1	44.4

Source: Organization for Economic Co-operation and Development,
National Accounts (Paris: 1978).
[a] The figures for Portugal and Spain are from 1975.

are represented on such a diagram for three different years.[10]

Examination of Figure 6.1 shows that during the first eight years of the 1970s the proportion employed in agriculture declined in all OECD countries. After 1973 in particular, industrial employment fell except in the countries of southern Europe. Expansion in the service sector continued regularly over that period.

Figure 6.2, which is in the same form as Figure 6.1 but deals with the contribution of each of the three sectors to the GDP of a number of countries, shows movements that are far less regular and of a lesser amplitude. From 1973 onwards, different movements appeared in the breakdown of the GDP. Obviously the new economic conditions then prevailing partly explain these irregular movements. From 1970 to 1973, for example, the policy of high agricultural prices and the sharp rise in raw material prices on the world market (cereals and oilseeds, in particular) account for the fact that the share of agriculture in the GDP did not decline. After 1973, market instability and further losses (livestock producers in particular) partly account for the decline in the

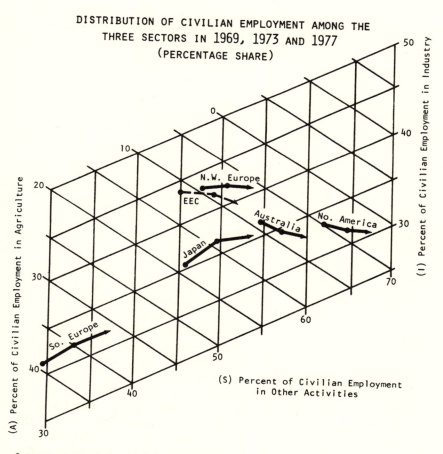

Figure 6.1

DISTRIBUTION OF CIVILIAN EMPLOYMENT AMONG THE
THREE SECTORS IN 1969, 1973 AND 1977
(PERCENTAGE SHARE)

Source: Table 6.4.

Figure 6.2

CONTRIBUTION OF THE THREE SECTORS TO GROSS DOMESTIC
PRODUCT AT CURRENT PRICES IN 1970, 1973 AND 1976
(PERCENTAGE SHARE)

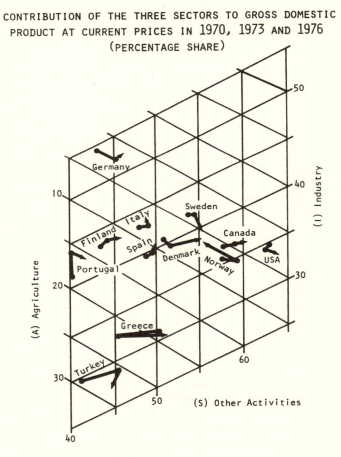

Source: Table 6.5.

share of agriculture in the GDP.[11] The share of the service sector rose sharply in most OECD countries after 1973 (except in Norway, Italy, Germany, and Turkey), partly as a result of difficulties encountered in the two other sectors.

Analysis of Figure 6.2 shows the influence of short-term economic factors on the breakdown of the GDP among the three sectors. A comparison between this figure and the previous one also indicates that as far as employment is concerned, structural changes appear to be partly independent of current economic conditions.

Recent Trends in Prices and Labor Productivity

Statistics currently available enable annual growth rates to be calculated, though only for a dozen countries, for the years 1970-73 and 1973-76 for the following items:

1. production—defined as the contribution, at constant prices, of the three sectors to the GDP;
2. implicit prices—obtained by dividing the contribution of each of the three sectors calculated at current prices by this same contribution calculated at constant prices;
3. productivity of labor—obtained by dividing the values of production by the numbers employed in each of the three sectors.

The annual rates thus calculated are set out in Table 6.6.

After 1973, a decline in production growth rates is observed in all countries, with only a few exceptions; this decline is particularly marked in the industrial sector. Similarly, the rate of price increase accelerated, thus illustrating the stagflation common to most OECD countries after 1973.

As regards rates of labor productivity growth, the decline observed is striking. In four countries (Canada, Greece, Portugal, and Sweden) there was a decline in the manufacturing industry, and in three other countries (United States, Italy, and Spain) growth was negligible.

A comparison between the rates of increase in labor productivity in the industry and service sectors shows divergent trends. This is not a new feature but merely a confirmation of results obtained every time research workers have endeavored to compare the trends in production (based on national accounts) with those in employment (based on population statistics).[12] In Canada, Greece, Portugal, Spain, and Sweden, rates of increase in productivity currently appear to be much sharper in the service sector than in the manufacturing industry. A reverse situation is observed in the United States, Denmark, Finland, Germany, Italy, Norway, and Turkey.

TABLE 6.6
Production, Prices and Labor Productivity (Average Annual Rates of Change:
I = Agriculture, II = Industry, III = Other Activities)

		Gross Domestic Product at Constant Prices			Implicit Prices (a)			Productivity of Labor (b)		
		I	II	III	I	II	III	I	II	III
Canada	1970–1973	+1.2%	+10.6%	+6.0%	+19.9%	+6.4%	+6.1%	+3.0%	+3.5%	+1.6%
	1973–1976	+2.0	+1.4	+4.4	+5.6	+12.9	+12.5	+2.6	-1.6	+1.3
USA	1970–1973	+2.2	+5.2	+4.2	+24.1	+8.9	+9.5	+2.3	+3.5	+1.2
	1973–1976	-0.1	-0.9	+2.4	-1.8	+8.7	+10.3	+1.4	+0.8	-0.4
Denmark	1970–1973	+1.2	+3.6	+3.2	+13.4	+10.8	+12.7	+6.6	+6.5	-1.6
	1973–1976	+0.7	+0.4	+3.0	+7.7	+11.4	+15.2	-0.2	+2.7	+1.4
Finland	1970–1973	-3.4	+6.2	+6.4	+13.4	+9.2	+8.7	+5.7	+4.5	+2.5
	1973–1976	+0.2	+0.6	+3.5	+16.6	+16.1	+16.6	+7.0	+1.5	+0.6
Germany	1970–1973	+3.8	+3.8	+3.8	+4.1	+5.0	+8.9	+9.0	+4.4	+2.2
	1973–1976	-1.9	+1.9	+0.1	+5.2	+5.1	+6.3	+2.0	+5.6	+0.6
Greece	1970–1973	+2.9	+12.2	+8.0	+19.5	+7.5	+6.7	+8.1	+7.9	+5.1
	1973–1976	+2.8	+0.7	+4.4	+12.5	+14.3	+17.3	+8.2	-1.0	+1.3

Italy	1970–1973	−0.2	+6.1	+4.3	+11.0	+7.7	+8.2	+4.1	+4.3	+2.9
	1973–1976	+0.9	+1.5	+2.6	+16.9	+19.6	+15.4	+3.6	+0.7	−0.4
Norway	1970–1973	+1.7	+4.9	+4.8	+5.4	+5.1	+8.5	+5.0	+4.8	−2.5
	1973–1976	+7.1	+5.6	+3.8	+9.9	+12.8	+7.9	+11.4	+3.6	−0.6
Portugal	1970–1973	−0.4	+10.9	+10.7	+12.7	+7.0	+5.3	+3.7	+18.7	+11.6
	1973–1976	−2.0	−2.5	+0.7	+17.5	+17.5	+17.1	−15.0	−7.8	+3.7
Spain	1970–1973	+3.8	+9.5	+6.8	+10.9	+7.3	+9.9	+6.4	+7.0	+4.1
	1973–1976	+1.6	+2.3	+4.0	+10.4	+18.6	+17.3	+7.4	+0.7	+3.8
Sweden	1970–1973	+1.4	+2.7	+2.3	+5.0	+4.9	+6.8	+5.6	+3.9	+0.5
	1973–1976	−0.5	+0.2	+3.2	+21.0	+12.1	+8.7	+2.8	−0.3	+0.2
Turkey	1970–1973	+0.8	+8.8	+9.1	+23.0	+14.6	+18.6	+1.2	+4.2	+0.8
	1973–1976	+9.6	+8.5	+8.3	+22.1	+18.9	+19.7	+10.7	+5.5	+4.5

Source: Organization for Economic Co-operation and Development, Labour Force Statistics, and National Accounts (Paris: 1978).

(a) GDP at current prices divided by GDP at constant prices.

(b) GDP at constant prices divided by civilian employment.

In regard to prices, it seems that they increased at a faster rate between 1973 and 1976 in the service sector than in manufacturing in the United States, Denmark, Germany, and Greece. On the other hand, they rose at a lower rate in services than in manufacturing in Italy, Norway, Spain, and Sweden. Agricultural prices were more inflationary than those of the service sector, either because of agricultural policies or world price increases prior to 1973. However, the reader should refrain from drawing too many conclusions from Table 6.6.

Prospects for the Service Sector

Analysis of the statistical data currently available supports the idea that development of the service sector, sometimes called the "Révolution Tertiaire," has not been affected by the world crisis.

The role played by the service sector as a partial check to unemployment and its social and political importance (albeit unintentional) in the Western countries has been recently underlined in two studies, one by the European Commission and the other by the French Economic and Social Council.[13]

The question of whether a more general and sufficiently deep economic slump might affect the service sector has been asked in Europe. However, it would be necessary to have much more information on the sensitivity of the service sector to the business cycle to be in a position to give a serious reply. Data drawn from statistics published by the OECD (Table 6.7) suggest that the service sector (calculated by the contribution of the activities listed under 6-0 of NISIC to the GDP) is quite sensitive. It should be noted in particular that this contribution has declined since 1974 in the United States, Japan, Greece, and the United Kingdom and in eight European countries in the single year 1975. This observation is consistent with the time schedule of the world economic crisis and with what is known of the time lag between its occurrence in the non-European and the European OECD countries.

However, employment in the service sector appears to have been little affected by the world crisis. It will be observed that employment declined in only a very limited number of countries and (except in Germany) for a very short period. The apparent lack of sensitivity of employment in the service sector has always been observed and is an enigma.[14] It is undeniable that certain methods of assessment lead to a purely artificial smoothing of trends (Greece, France, and the Netherlands). On the other hand, it is obvious that certain categories of personnel in the service sector (largely family labor and employees paid on a monthly basis) are less exposed to unemployment than personnel of the manufacturing

TABLE 6.7

Annual Indices of Growth of GDP at Constant Prices and of Employment in Activities other than Agriculture and Industry (previous year = 100)

Country	Gross Domestic Product in Purchase Value at Constant Prices				Civilian Employment in Activities other than Agriculture and Industry			
	1973	1974	1975	1976	1973	1974	1975	1976
Canada	107.5	103.6	100.9	105.2	105.4	104.7	102.6	101.9
United States	105.4	98.7	99.0	105.8	102.9	102.7	101.9	103.6
Japan	109.8	99.0	102.4	106.0	103.4	101.0	102.5	101.9
Australia	105.5	101.4	102.7	103.9	104.2	103.3	102.4	105.3
Austria	105.8	104.1	98.0	105.2	101.5	106.5	99.1	102.2
Belgium	106.6	104.8	104.5	105.3	102.7	102.3	101.0	101.1
Denmark	102.8	100.2	97.4	105.3	102.6	101.1	100.3	103.5
Finland	106.5	104.3	100.9	100.3	106.1	103.9	102.5	102.1
France	105.4	102.6	99.9	105.6	102.8	102.3	102.2	102.2
Germany	104.9	100.5	97.4	105.6	99.5	98.8	99.3	100.5
Greece	107.3	96.4	106.1	105.9	99.5	103.0	103.0	103.0
Italy	106.9	103.9	96.5	105.6	103.0	103.0	102.7	102.9
Netherlands	105.9	104.2	98.8	104.6	103.8	104.0	102.7	101.4
Norway	104.1	105.3	103.5	106.0	101.3	101.4	101.3	101.4
Portugal	110.9	100.7	96.3	106.2	102.4	101.3	104.9	106.9
Spain	108.4	105.3	100.7	102.1	100.6	90.7	104.0	104.4
Sweden	103.5	104.0	100.9	101.5	105.0	102.5	98.1	103.0
Switzerland	103.0	101.5	92.6	97.9	101.0	102.6	103.9	102.8
Turkey	104.4	108.5	108.8	108.5	101.7	100.9	98.7	97.6
United Kingdom	106.6	99.4	98.4	102.6	110.4	102.3	104.1	104.4
					103.2	101.2	102.5	100.6

Source: Same as Table 6.6.

industry. However, this is only an assumption and it should be recognized that only a relatively detailed study would confirm the lack of sensitivity of employment to the cycle and, if so, for what reasons.

Although some people recognize the social and political importance of the developments just described, it is surprising that very few conclusions have been drawn by member countries, and hardly any reaction has been observed in response to the world raw materials crisis by accelerating the setting up of a services economy on a model similar to what has been called the "Swedish model."[15]

One of the reasons for this situation lies in the absence of sufficiently broad studies on all problems raised by changes in the service sector as a whole. Various reliable studies have been carried out on a number of activities of the service sector: for example, health, teaching, transport, telecommunications, and leisure. However, it is undeniable that the economic and political world does not possess an overall view of the specific problems common to all these activities, raised by the supply of "nongoods." In our previous studies, we have endeavored to show that the real problems facing economic agents in this sector and their methods of work throw light on each other.

The scarcity of regular global studies on trends in the structure of the service sector, particularly on capital needs following increasing mechanization, is remarkable.[16] The increasingly complex interactions between the service sector and the other two sectors are hardly known.[17] It seems that modernization of the service sector and its ramifications for the economy in general remain little known.

Prices and productivity are the two main problems which, obviously, have still to be solved. It was mentioned above that the data available so far do not provide any explanation. It came as a great surprise to many participants in the symposium on services in Puerto Rico to hear various speakers describe important productivity gains obtained in various activities of the service sector, thanks to constantly improving management and increasing mechanization.[18] The problems raised by the socio-professional origin of the workers in the service sector and the conditions in which they are trained, in particular, are equally almost unknown.

Finally, the extremely rapid development of the service sector in developing countries in recent years was also a surprise for the participants of the Puerto Rico symposium. An earlier observation made by the OECD Development Center was thus confirmed.[19] The most interesting factor is, no doubt, the large transfer of technology from OECD countries to the developing countries for the supply of facilities for tourism, the mechanization of management services, the planning of large scale public facilities, etc. China has just adopted a similar strategy in a rather spectacular manner.

It is hoped that the developments and problems mentioned in this modest contribution will lead governments and research workers to pay more attention to the service sector's effects on the world economy.

Conclusions

The discussion on development prospects in the service sector gives rise to many conclusions. If employment in the service sector of the OECD countries had not continued to rise after 1973, there would be 33.7 million unemployed today instead of 18.2 million. A standstill in growth of the service sector would have aggravated the current economic crisis and provoked an economic slump probably of the same magnitude as that of the early 1930s.[20] The service sector in the Western economies has played the role of a protective net; a role which Allan Fisher had forecast it would play in 1935.[21]

It is obvious that many observers have been surprised by the events which have taken place since the end of 1973. Various interpretations and forecasts based on sound and famous theories have been upset. After this new type of crisis, many will have to scrap some of their ideas. New theories will have to be constructed, and it is obvious that the service sector will have to be introduced therein as an important factor; in addition, many of these new theories will no doubt break away from the previous ones. In this connection, I have in mind the theory put forward by Phillips in 1958:[22] to what extent has a strong demand for services and a large supply of labor in this sector contributed to upset the expected effects of unemployment on prices and income? In addition, if, as observed by Professor Maddison and myself, the large gaps among income and productivity levels in the three sectors are being reduced, it is no longer compulsory to retain the idea that the rise in demand for services (inflationary by nature) distorts the sharing of fruits of productivity between workers and consumers.

I believe that by focusing on these problems, we can stimulate studies of a sector which has become the foremost employer in Western economies.

Notes

1. The civilian labor force is comprised of all civilians who fulfill the requirements for inclusion among the employed or the unemployed with the exceptions of persons intending to establish businesses on their own accounts

and unpaid family workers who had ceased working and were not seeking work for pay or profit.

2. Civilian employment includes all persons above a specified age with the exception of workers laid off without pay and persons without jobs who had arranged to start a new job at a date subsequent to the period of reference.

3. This is the difference between the civilian labor force and civilian employment.

4. Services are defined as in the New International Standard Industrial Classification—activities 6 to 0. The armed forces are not included in services (code no. 9).

5. From 1973 to 1977, the overall loss of employment in the agricultural sector of the Organization for Economic Co-operation and Development countries reached 3,237,000 compared with 3,813,000 in the manufacturing industry. In the four preceding years, numbers employed in industry had increased by 3,337,000.

6. Maurice Lengellé, *The Growing Importance of the Service Sector in Member Countries* (Organization for Economic Co-operation and Development, Paris: 1966).

7. Business Services (NISIC Major Group 83), education (Group 822), medical and other health (Group 822), banks, insurance and real estate (M.G. 62, 63, and 64), wholesale trade (Group 611), where employment appeared to be expanding most rapidly.

Retail trade (Group 6123), restaurants, cafes, and hotels (Group 852 and 953), recreation (M.G. 84), miscellaneous personal services (Group 854 to 859), where employment was increasing slowly.

Domestic service (Group 851), where employment was on the decline.

8. NISIC code no. 6 (wholesale and retail trade and restaurants and hotels), no. 7 (transport, storage and business services), no. 9 (community, social and personal services) and no. 0 (activities not adequately defined).

9. *Sources*: Organization for Economic Co-operation and Development, *Labor Force Statistics, 1965-1976*, (Paris: 1978), and idem., *National Accounts of OECD Countries* (Paris: 1978).

10. For more detailed information on this type of graph, see Maurice Lengellé, *Growing Importance of the Service Sector*, and idem., "The Role of the Service Sector in the World Economic Slump and its Possibilities of Recovery" (Paper delivered at the International Symposium on the Service Sector of the Economy, University of Puerto Rico, San Juan, June 25–July 1, 1978).

11. It is interesting to note that in Sweden, where the government accepted a relaxation of price controls with effects from 1973, farmers were in a position to maintain their overall income.

12. Cf. Mr. Lengellé: *La Révolution Tertiaire* (Paris: Editions M. Th. Genin, 1966).

13. Cf. "Minutes of the Proceedings of the Meeting of the French Economic and Social Council," Paris, France, March 14, 1978, and *Direction Générale de l'Emploi et des Affaires Sociales—Chiffres significatifs de l'évolution sociale*

dans la Communaute Européenne depuis 1960 (Bruxelles: CCE, Octobre 1978).

14. Similar patterns of black market labor developed in the service sector. See Louis Ferman and Louise Berndt, *Irregular Economy* (Ann Arbor: The University of Michigan Press, 1978). This "black market labor" has been described in a similar way in France by Bernard Cazes and Alain Cotta in two recent articles in *Le Figaro*, January 13-14, 1979.

15. Lengellé, *Révolution Tertiaire*.

16. Mechanization includes use of computers, modifications to buildings, increased number of selling points, washing equipment, communication satellites, etc.

17. Service to firms, services included in foods (convenience foods), after sales service, etc. It may be recalled that already in 1959, Charles L. Schultze described the development of nonproductive employment in the industrial sector in "Employment Growth and Price Levels" (Washington D.C.: Joint Economic Committee, U.S. Congress, 1960).

18. Lengellé, "Service Sector in World Slump."

19. Derek W. Blades, Dereck D. Johnston, and W. Marczewski, *Service Activities in Developing Countries* (Paris: Organization for Economic Co-operation and Development, 1974).

20. On the differences between the two world crises, see Bertrand de Jouvenal, *Les Deux Crises, Bulletin SEDEIS* (Paris: Etudes et Documentation Economiques, Industrielles et Sociales, 1978).

21. Allen G. B. Fisher, *The Clash of Progress and Society* (London: 1935).

22. A. W. Phillips, "The Relation Between Unemployment and the Rate of Change of Money Wage Rates in the United Kingdom, 1861-1957," *Economica* 25 (November 1958):285.

Commentary

Irving Leveson

Maurice Lengellé indicates many reasons for the great intensification of interest in the service sector which burst forth in 1978. These include:

1. traditional concern with the effects of a large and/or rapidly growing service sector on the rate of growth of prices, output, and productivity in the economy as a whole
2. implications for stability of employment

3. its value in absorbing supplies of labor (not only of women but also youth and the disadvantaged)
4. basic questions about the nature of society and work
5. measurement of economic performance
6. problems with helping professions
7. planning public facilities (and expenditures and services)
8. implications for the Phillips curve (and control of the money supply, which, given all the changes that have taken place in banking, could involve some serious problems)

I would like to focus on the question of stability of employment, which receives considerable attention in the paper as a result of the rocky road that many of the OECD countries have traveled in the last few years. Mr. Lengellé suggests that the stability of employment remains an enigma. I would agree it is, to the extent that we do not have specific quantification of which of the many possible reasons for more stable employment in the service sector are actually making the difference. But there has been some thinking around for a long time which implies that employment in the service sector should be more cyclically stable than employment in industry, and there are some additional reasons for greater stability related to recent growth trends.

The most widely discussed reason for greater employment stability is the greater flexibility of compensation systems in service industries, because of commission payments in many sales activities, tips for waiters and waitresses, incomes of the self-employed, and the more limited presence and influence of unions. Furthermore, lower capital intensity means less of a tendency toward overexpansion of capital with subsequent adjustments which affect employment.

Also, in a number of service industries there is a large element of firm-specific training. Firm-specific training induces firms to retain more employees when demand falls, so that it will not be necessary to incur costs to develop that knowledge when conditions improve. The government and nonprofit sectors are relatively insensitive to changing market conditions, and this includes the health sector for which insurance premiums act like a broad base tax. Furthermore, there is greater disguised unemployment in service industries, especially among the self-employed.

As a result of these conditions, even though output is less cyclical in service industries as a whole than goods, employment tends to fluctuate less, to an even greater extent. Hence, service industries tend to have greater cyclical variation in productivity.

In the present economic climate, rapid growth of service employment has been affected by a number of other developments, including the increase in female labor in many countries and the increase in the number of youth in countries which had baby booms after World War II, particularly the United States, Canada, and Japan. This conclusion can only be inferred from observations on such developments as the growth of the fast food industry and the huge increase in self-employment among women in the United States between 1975 and 1978.

Service industries are on average less affected by the cost of energy because they are less capital intensive, although availability is clearly a problem for travel and tourism. Also, services tend to be less influenced by environmental regulation, and also by problems of financing and taxation in an inflationary environment. Lower capitalization requirements are an advantage in an era in which extra risks make long-term capital projects less attractive. Thus it is not surprising that U.S. data show a genuine acceleration in the rate of growth of service employment relative to goods employment in the last few years, even after allowing for differences in cyclical sensitivity.

I should like to concentrate the rest of my remarks on the question of the relative productivity changes in goods-producing versus service-producing industries. In June 1978 I testified before the Joint Economic Committee of Congress that the service industries are entering a new era, an era in which they are moving from being a lagging sector to an advanced one. In this new era, nongovernment services may do as well in productivity growth as goods-producing industries, or may even surpass them.[1] With the heightened interest in improving government efficiency, there may be some carryover effects of a similar nature in government as well. Examples such as fast goods, electronic funds transfer, and medical diagnostics are the beginning of a major shift toward a progressive service sector.

Unfortunately, measurement problems make it impossible to find these kinds of results in the data. In fact, the latest attempt at quantification has argued exactly the reverse. At the service sector symposium in Puerto Rico in June 1978, Colin Clark suggested that relative productivity change in services was slowing down with economic growth. The developing countries were doing much better than had been believed, but in stages of development in which per capita GDP was about a thousand U.S. dollars or more, there suddenly was a rapid acceleration of prices of services relative to goods. If we plot the ratio of a price index of services to a price index of goods on the vertical axis, versus GDP per capita on the horizontal axis, the price ratio is roughly constant (a horizontal line) up to about a thousand dollars. Then there is a very rapid rise in the price of services relative to goods.[2]

There is a potentially serious bias in the method of analysis which may account for the result. Clark uses the method proposed by Denison and others, of measuring output per unit of total factor input by relative prices. This concept of productivity allows for changes in capital per worker, labor quality, and inputs. However, the method of comparing prices depends on the assumption that a composite index of the prices of factors of production changes at the same rate in goods-producing industries as in service-producing industries.

Clark's results could have been obtained if the costs of labor tended to rise less rapidly to the service sector than to the goods-producing sector during early stages of economic development. That situation may well arise as a result of the demographic transition, with rapid population growth and large movements of labor off the farms, when a limited number of workers are able to benefit from opportunities in highly automated factories, and others concentrate on the fringes of industrial areas.

Changes in output per man, unlike relative prices which may have this bias, yield exactly the opposite conclusion. Angus Maddison's data from 1870 to 1950 show that the average rate of change of output per man in service industries in industrial countries was one-third the rate of growth in goods-producing industries. From 1950 to 1976, the rate of change in output per man was one-half for the same group of countries. Subperiod comparisons with Fuchs's data for the United States also tend to show an acceleration.[3] The measurement problems are so great the data cannot be used as evidence of an acceleration, but neither is it possible to conclude that the reverse is true.

An acceleration of productivity growth in services relative to goods has a number of critical implications.

1. More and more of the rapid growth of employment in services occurs because prices have become relatively lower and more output is sold rather than because productivity is not rising and the services are demanded anyway.

2. The rate of growth of productivity, both in the service sector and in the national economy, can be significantly understated and the rate of rise of prices can be significantly overstated.

3. In Richard Nelson's paper, the statement is made that slow productivity growth now exerts a bigger drag on income growth than it used to. Income data can be used as a test of what happened to productivity when output data are misleading. Interindustry differences in productivity growth tend to be associated with

interindustry differences in wage changes at the major industry level,[4] and in the short run, differences tend to be especially great. If there are real improvements in productivity growth in services relative to goods, relative incomes in services should be higher than predicted from past relationships between income and measured relative productivity growth.

4. Nelson suggests that there are less price elastic demands in leading sectors today than in the past. Yet, measurement biases cause the growth of output to be understated and the growth of price to be overstated. It looks as if the service sector is not responding as much to price changes, when in fact it may be doing exactly what we expect a leading sector to do.

5. When we start talking, as both Professors Lengellé and Nelson did, about the possibility of inducing a shift in R&D spending, I would caution very strongly against an increase in government intervention. It seems to me that R&D has already shifted. Economists have gone too far in taking an industry approach to measuring productivity change. The people in the computer industry know that they are developing products for an economy-wide market. Nobody had to tell them, as the induced innovation incentive effects were playing themselves out, that they had to think about banking and hospitals as potential areas of application. I think the real question is one of keeping government out of something that is doing very nicely, and seeing that some of the long-standing regulations which protect markets, such as in financial areas, do not get in the way of rapidly changing technology. It would be wise to deregulate, as in the airlines, much more extensively.

Finally, for the purposes of this conference it is essential to recognize the implications of rapid service sector employment growth for economy-wide adjustment. If employment growth slows down in both goods-producing and service-producing industries, the adjustment problems are a good deal more manageable than if there are absolute employment declines in industry and rapid increases in services. The shift in employment that takes place because of differences in demand and productivity alters the size and severity of the adjustment problem.

Notes

1. Irving Leveson, "The Service Economy: Entering a New Era," *Special Study on Economic Change, Part 3*, Joint Economic Committee, U.S. Congress

(Washington, D.C.: U.S. Government Printing Office, 1978), pp. 767-70.

2. Colin C. Clark, "Productivity in the Service Industries," paper presented at the International Symposium on the Service Sector of the Economy, University of Puerto Rico, June 25–July 1, 1978.

3. Victor R. Fuchs, *The Service Economy* (New York: National Bureau of Economic Research, 1968), Chapter 3, and idem, "The Service Industries, and U.S. Economic Growth Size, World War II," Working Paper #211 (Stanford, Ca.: National Bureau of Economic Research, November 1977).

4. Fuchs, *The Service Economy*, Chapter 3.

7

Structural Problems and Economic Policy: The U.S. Experience

Edward M. Bernstein

Summary and Conclusions

In the past ten years, the United States has had a slowing of the growth of output, an accelerated inflation of prices, an intractable deficit on current account, and a considerable depreciation of the dollar. The persistence and the severity of the problems indicate that they are to a considerable extent due to structural changes in the U.S. economy and the world economy. From 1967 to 1977, the growth of U.S. output averaged 2.8 percent a year compared with 3.9 percent in the preceding twenty years. That is because productivity increased much less than in the past. From 1967 to 1977, productivity in the nonfarm business sector increased at an average annual rate of 1.5 percent compared with 2.6 percent in 1957-67. Similar changes in the growth of output and the increase of productivity have occurred in other large industrial countries. While the increase of productivity may not return to previous rates, it may be greater than it has been recently. Some of the factors that slowed the increase in productivity will be less important in the next few years. The government can facilitate a return to a higher rate of increase of productivity by encouraging investment.

The U.S. payments position has deteriorated sharply in the past three years as shown by the trade deficit of over $34 billion in 1978. While this may be partly due to differences in cyclical developments in the United States and other industrial countries, the main reason is probably the structural changes that have occurred in the world economy. Some other countries have tried to meet the increased cost of imported oil by increasing their trade balance with the United States. The slower growth of domestic demand in other industrial countries has induced some of them to maintain employment by exporting more of their output to the United States. Because of the weaker payments position, it has not been possible to attract a net inflow of capital sufficient to finance the U.S. current account deficit and the dollar has depreciated considerably.

Nevertheless, the payments position has not improved as yet. If the trade deficit is not reduced substantially it may be necessary to limit imports from the large surplus countries to avoid a further depreciation of the dollar.

The present inflation originated in the excessive demand caused by the Vietnam war and it could have been prevented by firmer fiscal and monetary policies. In 1966 the demand inflation became a cost inflation. The difficulty in halting the cost inflation was aggravated by the failure of real spendable earnings to increase at the expected rate because of adverse structural changes—the smaller increase of productivity, higher prices of food and energy, and the depreciation of the dollar. The emphasis on high levels of output and employment inhibited the authorities from taking more positive measures to slow inflation. The administration has adopted a new antiinflation program that relies on standards for limiting wage and price increases. To induce labor to cooperate in the new program, the administration proposes to compensate wage earners that abide by these standards if the rise of consumer prices exceeds 7 percent over the next year. This is a risk it is necessary to accept, but it requires the administration to follow cautious fiscal, monetary, and exchange rate policies.

Structural Change

The structure of a dynamic economy is constantly changing. That is inevitable, as it is inconceivable that every sector of the economy could or should grow at the same rate. If structural changes take place gradually and in a pattern to which the economy is prepared to move, there need be no difficulty in adjusting to them. In fact, the structural changes may have a stimulating effect, increasing the growth of output and employment, and raising productivity and real income. Thus, one aspect of technical progress is the change in the industrial structure of the economy and the occupational distribution of the labor force.

There are structural changes, however, to which the economy is unable to adjust, or can adjust only with difficulty and after considerable delay, and these become structural problems. For example, the unemployment rate for young people of both sexes is about four times as great as for adult men, and more than twice as great for young black workers as for young white workers. Measures to expand aggregate demand do increase the employment of young workers, but even in boom times their unemployment rate remains exceptionally high. In his inaugural lecture, Professor J. R. Hicks, the Nobel laureate, said of such problems that "if the difficulty which we find is purely monetary, it ought to be possible to find a means of doing something about it; but if the monetary problem hides a real problem, no monetary wizardry can conjure it away."[1] This is a convenient test of structural problems— those that cannot be solved satisfactorily exclusively by monetary or fiscal policy.

In the past ten years, the United States has been confronted with the most serious economic problems it has had since the Great Depression. The growth of output and the increase of productivity have slowed; and inflation of prices and costs has accelerated. The international payments position has deteriorated and the dollar has depreciated relative to the currencies of the other large industrial countries. These problems are probably interrelated in part and that has aggravated their severity. They are not ordinary cyclical problems that could be expected to correct themselves in the next phase of the business cycle. Their persistence and their severity indicate that they are to a considerable extent caused by changes in the structure of the U.S. economy and the world economy. For this reason, they are not as responsive to monetary and fiscal policies as would be expected. That does not mean, however, that the problems cannot be solved or their adverse effects alleviated. Nor does it imply that there is no positive role for monetary and fiscal policies in dealing with these structural economic problems.

Output and Productivity

In the United States, as in other large industrial countries and in many developing countries, the postwar period was one of exceptionally rapid growth. In recent years, however, the growth of output in the large industrial countries has slowed to a marked extent. In the ten years from 1947 to 1957, the gross national product of the United States in constant (1972) dollars increased at an average annual rate of 3.8 percent. In the following ten years to 1967, however, the growth of output slowed to an average rate of 2.8 percent, with the growth somewhat slower in the second half than in the first half of this decade. The recent slowing of the growth of output is not limited to the United States. A similar change has occurred in all of the large industrial countries, in some of which the growth of output has been even slower than in the United States since 1975 (see Figure 7.1).

The slower growth of output is not due to a smaller increase in the labor force. On the contrary, private nonfarm payroll employment increased more in 1967-77 (23.4 percent) than in 1957-67 (20.3 percent) and 1947-57 (17.9 percent). Even allowing for the shorter workweek, aggregate hours worked by all persons in the nonfarm business sector

Figure 7.1

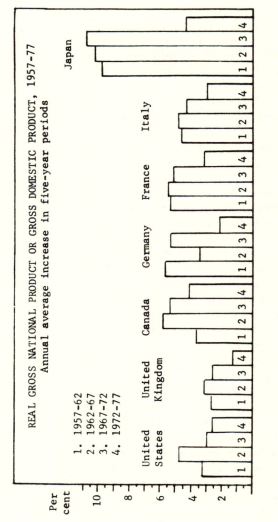

REAL GROSS NATIONAL PRODUCT OR GROSS DOMESTIC PRODUCT, 1957-77
Annual average increase in five-year periods

1. 1957-62
2. 1962-67
3. 1967-72
4. 1972-77

Source: International Monetary Fund, <u>International Financial Statistics.</u>

increased considerably more in 1967-77 than in the preceding decades. As this shows, the slower growth of output was due to the much smaller increase in productivity. Between 1947 and 1957, output per hour of all persons in the nonfarm business sector increased at an average annual rate of 2.4 percent (see Table 7.1). In 1957-67, this productivity increased at an average rate of 2.8 percent. In the following ten years to 1977, however, productivity increased at an average rate of only 1.5 percent. The smaller increase of productivity was particularly marked in the five years from 1972 to 1977 when it increased at an average annual rate of only 1.0 percent. The rate of increase declined in all major nonfarm industries, although more in nonmanufacturing than in manufacturing, and within manufacturing more in the durable than in the nondurable goods industries.

There have been such vast changes in the U.S. economy in the past ten years, particularly since 1973, that it is difficult to determine precisely the causes of the smaller increase of productivity, although some of them are apparent. The greater proportion of women and young people in the labor force held down the increase of productivity. This is also evident in the change in the industrial distribution of the labor force. Between 1967 and 1977, the increase in private nonfarm payroll employment was somewhat greater in the low-wage (low-productivity) industries than in the high-wage (high-productivity) industries. If the growth of productivity had been precisely the same in each major industrial group, the shift in the proportion of workers in the high-wage and low-wage industries, weighted by average hourly earnings in 1967, would have held down the growth of output by 1.8 percent over the ten years to 1977. Such changes in the occupational distribution of the labor force, as in the industrial pattern of output, have been going on throughout the postwar period.

Another reason for the smaller increase in productivity appears to be the employment of more productive resources to provide safer working conditions and a healthier environment. The costs incurred for these purposes contribute to the social product, to use a welfare-economics term, but not to the private business product as measured by output. The effect of such costs on productivity is difficult to measure, although their importance is indicated by the large amount of investment in new plants and equipment for pollution abatement. In the six years from 1973 to 1978, such investment amounted to a cumulative total of $38.3 billion and constituted 5.2 percent of total fixed business investment. The ratio was higher in manufacturing (7.7 percent) and much higher in electric utilities (9.9 percent). This is not a measure of the operating costs involved in pollution abatement which must have necessitated the use of

TABLE 7.1
Output and Productivity, 1947, 1957, 1967 and 1977

| | 1967 = 100 | | | | | | Percent Change Per Annum, Ten Years To | | | | | |
| | Output | | | Productivity[a] | | | Output | | | Productivity[a] | | |
	1947	1957	1977	1947	1957	1977	1957	1967	1977	1957	1967	1977
Nonfarm business sector	47.5	67.5	133.6	60.0	76.1	115.8	3.6%	4.0%	2.9%	2.4%	2.8%	1.5%
Durable manufacturing	43.5	65.5	121.4	59.1	76.6	120.8	4.2	4.3	2.0	2.6	2.7	1.9
Nondurable manufacturing	47.9	67.0	135.7	51.8	73.1	135.3	3.4	4.1	3.1	3.5	3.2	3.1
Iron mining, crude ore	64.4	88.5	86.5	43.2	53.3	104.6	3.2	1.3	-1.4	2.1	6.5	0.5
Copper mining, crude ore	66.1	99.2	198.8	53.1	67.8	128.7	4.2	0.8	7.1	2.5	4.0	2.6
Coal mining	131.8	97.1	116.0	35.1	50.8	70.6	-3.0	0.3	1.5	3.9	7.0	-3.4
Other nonmetallic minerals	--	72.1	117.0	--	72.2	116.7	--	4.9	1.6	--	3.3	1.6
Steel	70.8	93.4	102.1	70.3	84.3	118.2	2.8	0.7	0.2	1.8	1.7	1.7
Primary copper, lead, and zinc	107.4	130.4	129.4	71.0	96.0	144.9	2.0	-2.7	-0.4	3.1	0.4	3.8
Primary aluminum	17.7	52.0	131.2	43.6	59.2	112.5	11.4	6.8	2.8	3.1	5.4	1.2
Canning and preserving	47.3	66.8	128.0[b]	54.8	74.9	132.4[b]	3.5	4.1	2.8[b]	3.2	2.9	3.2[b]
Bakery products	75.5	87.0	106.0	66.3	74.7	115.9	1.4	1.4	0.6	1.2	3.0	1.5
Sugar	60.1	67.5	113.9	42.9	62.7	129.7	1.2	4.0	1.3	3.9	4.8	2.6
Candy and confectionary	64.2	70.7	93.5	54.6	70.0	112.2	1.0	3.5	-0.7	2.5	3.6	1.2
Malt beverages	66.2	71.8	150.8	42.0	54.1	188.5	0.8	3.4	4.2	2.6	6.3	6.5
Soft drinks	--	68.3	162.3	--	86.3	147.4	--	3.9	5.0	--	1.5	4.0
Tobacco products	74.2	83.5	99.2	50.3	69.4	118.9	1.2	1.8	0.1	3.3	3.7	1.7
Synthetic fibers	--	49.7	205.0	--	68.6	226.3	--	7.2	7.4	--	3.8	8.5
Hosiery	52.6	57.7	124.3	36.9	49.2	211.4	0.9	5.7	2.2	2.9	7.4	7.8
Footwear	82.5	99.5	67.5	70.6	91.5	102.4	1.9	0.0	-3.8	2.6	0.9	0.2
Petroleum refining	44.8	73.2	133.6	31.4	51.0	132.7	5.0	3.2	2.9	5.0	7.0	2.9
Paper and products	41.8	63.1	127.4	47.9	66.6	138.6	4.2	4.7	2.5	3.3	4.1	3.3
Tires and tubes	60.1	66.6	167.1	45.3	61.0	128.6	1.0	4.1	5.3	3.0	5.1	2.5

TABLE 7.1 cont'd
Output and Productivity, 1947, 1957, 1967 and 1977

| | 1967 = 100 | | | | | | Percent Change Per Annum, Ten Years To | | | | | |
| | Output | | | Productivity[a] | | | Output | | | Productivity[a] | | |
	1947	1957	1977	1947	1957	1977	1957	1967	1977	1957	1967	1977
Motor vehicles and equipment	--	65.0	176.0	--	68.9	150.4	--	4.4	5.8	--	3.8	4.2
Major household appliances	--	53.9c	132.7	--	58.3c	155.9	--	7.1c	2.9	--	6.2c	4.5
Household furniture	--	69.6c	127.0	--	83.5c	123.8	--	4.1c	2.4	--	2.0c	2.2
Sawmill products	--	96.5	115.2	--	73.1c	116.6	--	0.4c	1.4	--	3.5c	1.5
Metal cans	45.1	68.9	126.5	59.8	79.5	131.6	4.3	3.8	2.4	3.3	2.3	2.8
Glass containers	56.7	66.4	126.3	77.4	81.5	118.6	1.6	4.2	1.7	3.0	2.1	1.7
Railroad freight transportation	112.1	88.4	105.0	41.5	53.0	130.8	-2.3	1.2	0.5	2.5	6.6	2.7
Intercity trucking	--	56.6	164.0	--	78.2	142.6	--	5.9	3.6	--	2.5	3.6
Air transportation	6.5	27.1	181.1	18.4	47.0	153.6	15.3	14.0	6.1	9.8	7.8	4.4
Petroleum pipelines	25.2d	55.3	149.2	16.5d	39.0	165.6	8.2d	6.1	4.1	9.0	9.0	5.2
Telephone communications	29.2	46.7	211.7	37.0d	49.4	175.5	8.2d	7.9	7.8	4.9d	7.3	5.8
Gas and electric utilities	20.8	51.8	154.9	26.2	53.7	137.9	9.6	6.8	6.5	7.4	6.4	3.3
Gasoline service stations	--	71.3c	132.6	--	77.5c	160.7	--	3.8c	2.9	--	2.9c	4.9
Eating and drinking places	--	78.8c	138.9	--	91.3c	105.2	--	2.7c	3.3	--	1.0c	0.5
Hotels, motels, etc.	--	68.8c	127.9	--	76.8c	106.5	--	4.2c	2.5	--	2.9c	0.6
Laundry and cleaning services	--	86.1c	63.9	--	83.9c	110.4	--	1.7c	-4.4	--	2.0c	1.0

[a]Output per hour of all employees, except intercity trucking and air transportation which is output per employee, and gasoline service stations, eating and drinking places, hotels, and motor courts, and laundry and cleaning services which are output per hour of all persons. The productivity data for the nonfarm business sector and for durable and nondurable manufacturing are output per hour of all persons.

[b]Index is for 1976 and increase per annum in output and productivity is from 1967 to 1976.

[c]Index is for 1958 and increase per annum in output and productivity is from 1958 to 1967.

[d]Index is for 1951 and increase per annum in output and productivity is from 1951 to 1957.

Source: U.S. Department of Labor, Bureau of Labor Statistics, Productivity Indexes for Selected Industries, 1978 Edition, Bulletin 2002 (Washington, D.C.: 1979).

additional labor and a consequent reduction in productivity from what it would otherwise have been.

The rise in energy prices may have been a factor holding down the increase of productivity. In the gas and electric utilities, for example, output per employee hour, which had increased at an average annual rate of 5.2 percent from 1967 to 1972, increased at a rate of only 1.4 percent between 1972 and 1977 as the high cost of energy reduced the growth of such output from an average annual rate of 7.1 percent (1967-72) to 1.9 percent (1972-77). Measures to economize in the consumption of oil and energy may have added to other costs and reduced the increase in productivity. The trade deficit, to which oil imports were a major contributor, held down the growth of goods output in this country relative to the growth of domestic demand, and thus had an adverse effect on the increase of productivity, particularly in recent years. Between 1975 and 1977, the absorption of domestic goods (goods output minus exports) increased by $132.9 billion (22.9 percent) in current dollars while the absorption of import goods increased by $53.6 billion (54.7 percent). The adverse effect on total output was largely offset by a more expansionary budget, but the goods component of output, with higher than average productivity, was less than it would otherwise have been.

There is a great deal of apprehension that the smaller increase in productivity may be the result of a lag in technical innovation. As this involves new products or new methods of production, the changing importance of innovation should be reflected in part in the ratio of investment in new plants and equipment to output (see Table 7.2). In the ten years to 1957, fixed investment averaged 9.4 percent of the nonfarm business product. The ratio declined to 8.9 percent in the ten years to 1967, but rose again to 9.4 percent in the following period to 1977. In manufacturing the ratio of fixed investment to output was much higher in 1967-77 (12.5 percent) than in the preceding twenty years (10.8 percent). Surprisingly, the investment ratio in manufacturing averaged 13.1 percent in 1973-77 when the growth of output slowed. Investment by gas and electric utilities is very large relative to output. It also averaged more in 1966-77 (56.9 percent) than in the preceding twenty years (45.4 percent). The investment ratios in manufacturing and utilities are exaggerated by the requirements for pollution abatement, but even allowing for this, the investment ratios in these two sectors have been high in recent years. In other nonfarm industries, however, the ratio of investment to output in recent years was by far the lowest of the postwar period (see Figure 7.2).

Because the growth of output and the increase of productivity have slowed in all of the large industrial countries, it has been suggested that

TABLE 7.2
Nonfarm Product and Fixed Business Investment, 1947-77

	Billion Dollars								Fixed Business Invest. as Percent of Product			
	Nonfarm Business Product[a]				Fixed Business Investment[b]							
	Total	Mf'g	Util.	Other	Total	Mf'g	Util.	Other	Total	Mf'g	Util.	Other
1947	188.0	66.2	3.8	118.0	19.33	8.44	1.54	9.35	10.28%	12.75%	40.53%	7.92%
1948	212.7	74.8	4.3	133.6	21.30	9.01	2.54	9.75	10.01	12.05	59.07	7.30
1949	211.7	72.1	4.8	134.8	18.98	7.12	3.10	8.76	8.97	9.88	64.58	6.50
1950	235.5	83.8	5.2	146.5	20.21	7.39	3.24	9.58	8.58	8.82	62.31	6.54
1951	267.4	98.7	6.0	162.7	25.48	10.71	3.56	11.21	9.53	10.85	59.33	6.89
1952	282.5	103.0	6.6	172.9	26.43	11.45	3.74	11.24	9.36	11.12	56.67	6.50
1953	301.2	112.2	7.2	181.8	28.20	11.86	4.34	12.00	9.36	10.59	60.28	6.60
1954	301.3	106.4	8.0	186.9	27.19	11.24	3.99	11.96	9.02	10.56	49.88	6.40
1955	332.8	121.0	8.7	203.1	29.53	11.89	4.03	13.61	8.87	9.83	36.32	6.70
1956	354.3	126.9	9.4	218.0	35.73	15.40	4.52	15.81	10.08	12.14	48.09	7.25
1957	372.3	131.5	10.0	230.8	37.54	16.51	5.67	15.36	10.19	12.56	56.70	6.66
1958	370.7	123.8	10.7	236.2	31.89	12.38	5.52	13.99	8.60	10.00	51.59	5.92
1959	408.9	140.8	11.8	256.3	33.55	12.77	5.14	15.64	8.70	9.07	43.56	6.10
1960	423.0	143.9	12.8	266.3	36.75	15.09	5.24	16.42	8.69	10.49	40.94	6.17
1961	433.4	143.8	13.5	276.1	35.91	14.33	5.00	16.58	8.29	9.97	37.04	6.01
1962	465.9	157.5	14.2	294.2	38.39	15.08	4.90	18.41	8.24	9.56	34.51	6.26
1963	492.2	166.3	14.9	311.0	40.77	16.22	4.98	19.57	8.28	9.75	33.42	6.29
1964	529.2	178.6	15.8	334.8	46.92	19.34	5.49	22.09	8.88	10.83	34.75	6.60
1965	573.8	196.3	16.6	360.9	54.42	23.44	6.13	24.85	9.48	11.94	36.93	6.89

TABLE 7.2 cont'd

1966	625.0	215.9	17.6	391.5	63.51	28.20	7.43	27.88	10.16	13.06	42.22	7.11
1967	658.8	241.3	18.5	419.0	65.47	28.51	8.74	28.22	9.94	12.88	47.24	6.74
1968	720.2	241.8	20.0	458.4	67.76	28.37	10.20	29.19	9.41	11.73	51.00	6.37
1969	776.2	254.6	21.5	500.1	75.56	31.68	11.61	32.27	9.73	12.44	54.00	6.45
1970	808.6	250.3	22.7	534.6	79.71	31.95	13.14	34.62	9.87	12.76	57.89	6.48
1971	867.9	261.5	25.3	581.1	81.21	29.99	15.30	35.92	9.36	11.47	60.47	6.18
1972	955.8	288.8	28.0	639.0	88.44	31.35	17.00	40.09	9.25	10.86	60.71	6.27
1973	1055.2	321.8	30.5	702.9	99.74	38.01	18.71	43.02	9.45	11.81	61.34	6.12
1974	1139.9	334.6	31.3	776.0	112.40	46.01	20.55	45.84	9.86	13.75	65.65	5.92
1975	1232.6	350.1	38.8	843.7	112.78	47.95	20.14	44.69	9.15	13.70	51.91	5.30
1976	1385.6	402.8	43.3	939.5	120.49	52.48	22.28	45.73	8.70	13.03	51.45	4.87
1977	1544.0	451.6	46.9	1045.5	135.80	60.16	25.80	49.84	8.80	13.32	55.01	4.77
1978c	1700.8				150.05	65.81	28.55	55.69	8.82			

Source: For nonfarm business product and components, U.S. Department of Commerce, The National Income and Product Accounts of the United States, 1929-74, pp. 178-83; idem, Survey of Current Business (July 1978), pp. 51-52. For expenditures on new plant and equipment, idem, Business Statistics (1977), pp. 12-13; idem, Survey of Current Business (December 1977)), p. S-2.

aGross domestic product.

bExpenditures on new plant and equipment.

cAnnual rate, first three quarters of 1978.

Figure 7.2

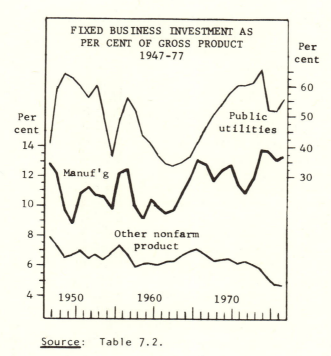

FIXED BUSINESS INVESTMENT AS
PER CENT OF GROSS PRODUCT
1947-77

Source: Table 7.2.

the world economy may have entered the protracted low phase of the long waves described by Kondratief. It is doubtful whether the forces that generated the long waves in the past have been operating on the world economy since the Great Depression. The conjuncture of forces that slowed the growth of the U.S. economy will not continue indefinitely. Some of the structural changes, as in the age-sex composition of the labor force, are nearing an end. Much of the adjustment to higher standards of safety and pollution abatement has been made and requirements for further change may be moderated. The U.S. balance of payments is not likely to get worse and it could get much better. The growth of output and the increase of productivity may not return to the high rates of the earlier postwar period, but they can be higher than they have been in recent years. It would help to achieve this if the government encouraged and facilitated a higher level of investment. It would also help if the rate of inflation could be brought down. That would restore the customary rewards for efficiency and penalties for inefficiency.

Balance of Payments and Exchange Rates

The deterioration in the U.S. balance of payments and the depreciation in the foreign exchange value of the dollar must in large part be due to structural changes in the world economy. Since April 1971, the foreign exchange value of the dollar has fallen by over 60 percent relative to the Swiss franc, by 50 percent relative to the Deutschemark, and by 45 percent relative to the yen. The dollar has fallen nearly as much relative to the guilder and the Belgian franc and somewhat less relative to the French franc and the Swedish krona. It has risen relative to sterling, the Canadian dollar, and the lira. Most of the fall of the dollar in terms of the strongest currencies has occurred since the adoption of floating exchange rates in March 1973.

One reason for the depreciation of the dollar relative to the strongest currencies is that prices and costs rose more in the United States than in the other countries. As the depreciation of the dollar was in excess of the difference in the rate of inflation, the rest must have been due to the deterioration in the U.S. payments position. One aspect of this was the emergence of a very large deficit on current account, entirely due to the enormous trade deficit. The other aspect was the change in the preference for holding assets denominated in dollars relative to assets denominated in the strong currencies. Because of this, the net inflow of capital has not been adequate in recent years to match the deficit on current account. As a consequence, the balancing of U.S. payments in the past few years has depended on the exceptionally large accumulation of dollar assets by foreign monetary authorities which they undertook to avoid an even larger depreciation of the dollar than actually occurred.

The U.S. balance of payments has been very volatile in the past ten years. The emergence of a deficit on current account from the second quarter of 1971 to the first quarter of 1973 necessitated the two devaluations of the dollar, and when they did not succeed in restoring the payments position the exchange rate for the dollar was allowed to float. The balance on current account shifted to a surplus in the second quarter of 1973 and remained in surplus until the fourth quarter of 1976, in spite of the increase in the cost of imported oil. Since then, the balance on current account has been in deficit—$15.3 billion in 1977 and probably more than $16.5 billion in 1978. The trade deficit, which was $31.1 billion in 1977, was probably over $34.0 billion in 1978 (see Table 7.3). The weakness in the current account, particularly the trade deficit, is the main reason for lack of confidence in the dollar.

It is difficult to explain the persistence of the huge trade deficit. In part it is the result of the large increase of imports of petroleum and products.

TABLE 7.3
Exports, Imports, and Trade Balance, Large Industrial Countries, 1967-78

					Million Dollars				
	1967	1971	1972	1973	1974	1975	1976	1977	1978
Exports, fob									
United States	30,666	43,319	49,381	71,410	98,306	107,099	114,694	120,576	101,843[a]
Canada	10,902	18,419	21,093	26,363	34,335	33,910	39,979	43,267	23,530[b]
Japan	10,231	23,567	28,032	36,262	54,488	54,734	66,028	79,333	69,570[a]
Belgium	5,970	10,493	12,710	18,340	24,592	24,726	26,635	30,211	17,625[b]
France	11,260	20,677	26,149	35,883	45,828	50,943	54,551	62,086	37,084[b]
Germany	21,741	37,419	40,813	65,006	87,509	88,616	99,452	113,935	65,403[b]
Italy	8,601	14,888	18,496	22,064	30,107	34,508	36,839	44,534	
Netherlands	6,843	12,470	15,479	21,840	30,255	32,216	36,791	39,808	22,187[b]
Sweden	4,485	7,421	8,699	12,108	15,796	17,259	18,286	18,911	
Switzerland	3,688	5,909	7,096	9,722	12,154	13,223	15,036	17,839	
United Kingdom	14,109	22,311	23,916	30,080	39,227	43,745	46,231	56,593	33,302[b]
Imports, fob									
United States	26,806	45,579	55,797	70,499	103,649	98,041	124,047	151,706	129,884[a]
Canada	10,361	15,360	19,011	23,371	32,396	34,288	38,318	40,227	21,934[b]
Japan	9,071	15,779	19,061	32,576	53,050	49,704	56,138	62,021	49,975[a]
Belgium	5,848	9,662	11,695	17,116	23,713	24,178	27,508	31,343	18,462[b]
France	10,957	19,568	24,850	35,107	49,690	49,433	59,236	64,819	36,416
Germany	16,578	30,642	36,453	49,539	65,336	70,939	82,763	94,535	54,190
Italy	8,468	14,308	17,656	25,746	38,528	35,657	41,081	44,392	

TABLE 7.3 cont'd

Netherlands	7,415	13,090	15,044	20,840	29,690	30,901	35,016	40,029	22,683[b]
Sweden	4,339	6,528	7,488	9,835	15,189	16,504	17,845	18,652	
Switzerland	4,038	7,095	8,365	11,407	14,263	13,125	14,597	17,691	
United Kingdom	15,616	21,424	25,397	35,485	50,954	50,327	52,051	59,125	34,223[b]
Trade Balance, fob									
United States	3,800	-2,260	-6,416	911	-5,343	9,047	-9,353	-31,130	-28,041[a]
Canada	541	3,059	2,082	2,992	1,939	-378	1,661	3,040	1,596[b]
Japan	1,160	7,788	8,971	3,686	1,438	5,030	9,890	17,312	19,595[a]
Belgium	122	831	1,015	1,224	879	543	-873	-1,132	-837[b]
France	303	1,109	1,299	776	-3,862	1,510	-4,685	-2,733	669[b]
Germany	5,163	6,777	8,360	15,467	22,173	17,677	16,689	18,551	9,213
Italy	133	580	840	-3,682	-8,511	-1,149	-4,242	142	
Netherlands	-572	-620	435	1,000	565	1,315	1,775	221	
Sweden	146	893	1,211	2,273	607	695	441	259	-496[b]
Switzerland	-350	-1,186	-1,269	-1,685	-2,109	98	429	148	
United Kingdom	-1,507	887	-1,481	-5,405	-11,727	-6,582	-5,820	-2,532	-921[b]

Source: For 1967, country pages of International Monetary Fund, International Financial Statistics, May 1978; for 1971–78, country pages of International Financial Statistics, January 1979.

a
Three quarters of 1978.

b
Two quarters of 1978.

In part it reflects differences in cyclical developments in the United States and other large industrial countries during the past three years. Much of it may be due to structural changes in the world economy that have had a greater adverse effect on the United States than on other countries. In fact, structural changes in the U.S. payments position have been going on for twenty years or more and they have been the main reason for the recurrent payments difficulties of the United States. In many ways, 1957 is a convenient point for marking the structural change in the U.S. payments position. The trade surplus in that year ($6.3 billion) was the largest since 1947 and since then has been exceeded only twice (1964 and 1975). The gold reserves of the United States at the end of 1957 ($22.8 billion) were larger than they had been at any time since mid-1950. That meant that the growth of monetary reserves of all other countries in 1950-57 was met out of newly-mined gold not absorbed in industrial uses and private hoards and by the accumulation of modest amounts of dollars.

The change in the U.S. payments position after 1957 was the result of the remarkable economic recovery in Europe and Japan. Ordinarily, the growth of output and income in other countries is helpful to the U.S. balance of payments, provided their domestic consumption and investment increase proportionately. The recovery in Europe and Japan did not follow this pattern. Their savings in the first half of the 1950s were not adequate for their domestic investment plus the moderate accumulation of monetary reserves because their output was relative to their unusually large reconstruction needs. The rapid increase in output thereafter enabled the European countries as a group to meet all of their domestic investment needs, to accumulate very large monetary reserves, and to resume their traditional role as a capital-exporting region. Economic developments in Japan followed a similar pattern, even more dramatic although somewhat later.

The remarkable growth of output and the great increase of productivity in Europe and Japan seem to have created a conflict between their balance of payments objectives and that of the United States. The U.S. economy had developed in a direction that required a large current account surplus to absorb part of the output of its export industries and to finance the foreign loans and investments to which its financial institutions and business firms had adapted their operations. Rapid growth in Europe and Japan resulted in a change in the structure of their economies to resemble that of the United States, with the same major industries using much the same methods of production. In the automobile industry, for example, first Europe and then Japan became the largest exporters, with the United States their principal export market. In theory, the adverse impact of the heightened competition with Europe and Japan could be met by an adjustment of exchange rates and that was the reason for the two devaluations of the dollar and its further depreciation under the regime of floating exchange rates.

The conflict between the balance of payments objectives of the United States and some other industrial countries was exacerbated in the past few years by two new developments. The first was the increase in the price of imported oil which placed great pressure on the payments position of oil-importing countries. Any one country could offset or moderate the adverse effect this had on its balance of payments by an increase in exports to or decrease in imports from oil-exporting countries or by an increase in exports to or decrease in imports from other oil-importing countries. To the extent that the increase in exports was to or the decrease in imports was from other oil-importing countries, it merely shifted to them more of the aggregate current account deficit with the oil-exporting countries. Because of U.S. passivity on the balance of payments, much of the aggregate current account deficit with the oil-exporting countries was ultimately shifted to the United States.

The other development that intensified the conflict in balance of payments objectives was the recent slowing of the growth of output in Europe and Japan. In the past three years, producers in these countries found that the growth of their capacity far outstripped the growth of home demand, and in order to maintain output and employment they increased their exports. As the United States is a very large market for all types of manufactured goods, a deficiency in home demand could be offset by capturing a moderately larger share of the U.S. market. One reason for the deterioration of about $43 billion in the U.S. trade balance between 1975 and 1978 was the larger increase of imports from members of OPEC than of exports to them, although that accounted for only one-fourth of the change in the trade balance over these three years. Another reason was the larger increase of imports of basic commodities, other than petroleum and products, than of exports of such commodities. Most of the deterioration in the trade balance, however, was due to the much larger increase of imports of finished manufactured goods (about 100 percent) than of exports of such goods (about 32 percent) between 1975 and 1978. Not all of this, however, was in trade with the large industrial countries.

It has been argued that the trade deficit of the United States and the surplus of some industrial countries are a result of the difference in cyclical developments since 1975. To some extent this must be so, although the deterioration in the U.S. trade balance is much too large to be solely a cyclical phenomenon. The depreciation of the dollar relative to the currencies of the surplus countries has had no effect on the trade deficit so far. Perhaps it takes even longer for trade to respond to changes in exchange rates than has been assumed. The measures taken by the Treasury and the Federal Reserve to strengthen and support the dollar have brought a modest recovery in its foreign exchange value. If the dollar is to become strong, however, there will have to be a substantial reduction in the trade deficit. Perhaps that will happen as a result of the previous depreciation of the dollar and the slackening of economic activity this year.

The dollar will be subject to recurring pressure until the exchange market is convinced that the United States has restored an acceptable balance of payments. Official intervention can sustain the foreign exchange value of the dollar for a time, as it has in recent months. From November 1978, when the new measures were taken, to January 10, 1979, the marketable U.S. government securities held in custody by the Federal Reserve Banks for foreign official and international accounts increased by $13.2 billion. That is an indication of the magnitude of official intervention, probably mainly by foreign monetary authorities for their own account. Such large-scale support for the dollar is helpful, but only as an intermediate stage while the payments position is restored. That requires a substantial reduction in the trade deficit in the next few months. If that does not occur, it may become necessary to limit imports from the large surplus countries. Otherwise, the dollar may depreciate further and make it much more difficult to achieve the administration's goal of slowing the inflation of prices and costs.

Structural Aspects of Inflation

Traditionally, inflation has been regarded as a monetary phenomenon in the sense that it was caused by monetary expansion and could be terminated by monetary restriction. That is certainly true of a demand inflation. The present protracted inflation originated in the excessive demand that accompanied the Vietnam war. The effect of the increased government expenditure could have been largely offset by an increase in taxes and its stimulus to investment could have been minimized by a tighter monetary policy. Nevertheless, the price inflation was very modest until 1966 and there was no cost inflation until that year. It is worth noting that unit labor costs in manufacturing—the best test of monetary stability under a system of fixed parities—were precisely the same in 1966 as they had been in 1958. The rise of the consumer price index at an annual rate of 3.8 percent in the first quarter of 1966, however, inevitably led to demands for larger wage increases to offset the higher prices. This initiated the cost inflation in which a larger increase of wages than the increase in productivity was said to be justified by the prior increase of prices, and a further increase of prices was said to be necessitated by the prior increase of labor costs.

Once the cost inflation acquired this self-perpetuating rhythm it would have required much more restrictive monetary and fiscal policies to halt the rise in prices and costs than the monetary authorities could or would take. The difficulty in halting the cost inflation was aggravated by the failure of real spendable earnings to increase at the expected rate because of adverse structural changes, some of which have been noted. First, the increase of productivity, which is the source of the increase in real wages, slowed materially after 1967. Second, prices of farm products rose much more than prices of other goods and services, in part because of supply conditions abroad. Third, prices of import goods rose more than prices of domestic goods because of the depreciation of the dollar. Furthermore, stricter regulations of occupational safety and environmental conditions added somewhat to the increase of costs in the past ten years.

Other structural changes held the increase of real spendable earnings to less than the increase in productivity. Although labor's share of the nonfarm business product increased from 58.6 percent in 1967 to 61.2 percent in 1977, the ratio of nonwage labor compensation to wage and salary payments increased from 5.1 percent to 9.2 percent. The ratio of personal social insurance contributions to wage and salary payments increased from 4.8 percent to 6.2 percent and employer contributions increased correspondingly. In addition, personal tax and nontax payments increased from 13.1 percent in 1967 to 14.8 percent in 1977. As a consequence, the spendable real weekly earnings of a married worker with three dependents who earns the average wage is only slightly higher now than it was in 1967. Income is being shifted from the active to the nonactive sector of the population through transfer payments. The ratio of transfer payments in personal income rose from 12.3 percent of wage and salary payments in 1967 to 21.2 percent in 1977. Labor took no account of these structural changes in its expectations on real wages. Instead, the attitude has been that if expectations on real wages could not be met by a 5 percent increase in wages, then it was necessary to have a 10 percent increase in wages.

The inability of the monetary authorities to deal satisfactorily with the cost inflation is in large part due to the change in the objectives of monetary policy. Until the Great Depression, the primary objective of monetary policy in the United States and in all other large industrial countries was to maintain the immutable gold value of the currency. This was achieved through limiting the money supply on the basis of the gold reserves and providing for the convertibility of money into gold. This approach to monetary policy was radically changed in the 1930s although it was not fully recognized at the time. The Gold Reserve Act of February 1934 raised the dollar price of gold. The convertibility of the dollar into gold was terminated for private holders of dollars, but not for foreign monetary authorities. The gold reserve requirements on the money supply were retained, but in fact the gold reserve was never thereafter a limitation on the expansion of the money supply. In June 1945, when the wartime expansion of the money supply brought the reserve ratio close to the legal minimum, the reserve requirements were reduced. They were reduced again later when the outflow of gold and the expansion of the money supply brought the reserve ratio close to the new limit, until the reserve requirements were abandoned entirely in March 1968.

The attitude of the U.S. monetary authorities toward the foreign exchange value of the dollar also changed radically. Because of its persistent payments difficulties, the United States abandoned the initial par value of the dollar and its gold convertibility in 1971. In subsequent negotiations, the United States undertook to establish a new par value but not to restore the convertibility of the dollar. Instead other members of the Group of Ten and Switzerland agreed to support the dollar. As the first devaluation did not succeed in adjusting the U.S. payments position, the dollar was devalued again in February 1973. And when this did not halt a flight from the dollar, the United States gave up the maintenance of a par value and allowed the dollar to float. Until recently, the U.S. attitude was that it was not concerned with fluctuations in the foreign exchange rates for the dollar except to avoid disorderly market conditions. The exchange market regarded this as an indication that the maintenance of an acceptable exchange rate was not an objective of U.S. monetary policy. That was probably a contributing factor in the large depreciation of the dollar in 1977-78 until the announcement on November 1, 1978, of the measure being taken to support and strengthen the dollar by the Treasury and the Federal Reserve.

The change in the traditional role of fiscal policy also occurred in the Great Depression. The Roosevelt administration accepted the view that the budget should be used to stimulate recovery, although the deficits on the present consolidated basis were small because of the surplus in the social security funds. The Employment Act of 1946 gave statutory authority for the use of economic policy to maintain high levels of output and employment. Actually, there was little active use of the budget for this purpose until the 1960s. Since fiscal 1961, there has been only one year in which the budget was not in deficit and recently in large deficit. Whatever the cause of a decline in output, the accepted remedy was an expansionary budget. The 1978 *Economic Report of the President* took the view that the deterioration in the trade balance by $18 billion in 1976 and by $22 billion in 1977 necessitated reduction in taxes to offset their effect on output and employment. The administration has since adopted a policy of reducing the budget deficit substantially in order to slow the inflation.

If it is not a contradiction in terms, these changes in the objectives of fiscal and monetary policies could be said to be of a structural character. Without saying that the old objectives were superior (and they were not), it is reasonable to suggest that the new objectives have made it much more difficult to deal with inflation problems. The fact is that the monetary authorities have been reluctant to use very restrictive policies to slow the inflation. No doubt that is because they believe that a recession would have little effect in moderating wage increases, particularly those in major collective bargaining agreements. Moreover, although the public regards inflation as the most urgent economic problem, it is uncertain whether the American people would accept a protracted recession in order to slow the inflation. That is why the administration has felt that it must rely on standards for limiting wage and price increases in order to slow the inflation.

To induce labor to accept the limit of an average increase of 7 percent in wages, the administration is proposing to make compensating payments to wage earners who accept this limitation if the rise in the consumer price index exceeds 7 percent over the next year. This is a remarkable innovation that is not without economic risk. Prices could rise more than the standard if productivity does not increase as much as expected, if farm supplies are less than expected, or if the dollar depreciates further. The justification for accepting the risk is that it is essential to have labor cooperation in the new program. For its part, the administration must avoid policies that could contribute to a larger rise of prices. That is why the budget deficit will have to be brought down, monetary policy will have to remain restrictive, and a further depreciation of the dollar will have to be avoided.

Note

1. J. R. Hicks, "An Inaugural Lecture," in *Oxford Economic Papers* 5 (June 1953):117-35.

Part 3
Adjustment Pressures
and Policies

8

Capital Formation and Investment Policy

Victoria Curzon Price

It is frequently argued that capital formation in OECD countries is at present inadequate to maintain full employment and initiate structural change. This paper will be divided into three sections. The first section will review recent trends in aggregate investment behavior in developed countries in order to determine whether the recent drop in investment levels is largely cyclical or secular in nature. The second section will discuss some of the macroeconomic policies and structural factors currently in force that promote or discourage private productive investment. The last section will draw some conclusions with respect to the medium-term prospects for the relative competitive positions of certain OECD countries and the declining rate of profit.

Investment Decline: Secular or Cyclical?

Everybody knows that investment has been remarkably sluggish during the last five years. So depressed has it been that theories about long-term "Kondratief" cycles have been taken off the shelf, dusted, and put back into circulation once again, much to the surprise of those who thought that modern economics had relegated them for good to the status of antique curiosities.

At first glance, however, the figures do not support the thesis of abnormally low levels of investment, considering the fact that most governments have been trying to reduce the rate of inflation—some gradually, others brutally—for the past two to five years.

We know that if residential construction is not a particularly volatile component of domestic demand, private investment in productive resources is. If demand is growing, this component of total investment is likely to grow much faster, because machines and plants are expected to have a useful economic life extending over several years.[1] On the other hand, if demand merely stops growing quite so fast, let alone if it stagnates or actually falls, investment in productive resources will dwindle rapidly to zero, since installed capacity will be quite enough to cope with demand. If there is anything in this well-worn theory of the investment accelerator, or in newer theories, such as the flexible accelerator (which relates a firm's investment behavior to the gap between the existing and desired capital stock), then one would expect investment to have mirrored the rather disappointing economic performance of most OECD countries in the 1974-77 period.

If one examines real gross fixed capital formation from 1973 to 1977-78, taking 1973 to be the last year before the oil crisis and attempts to return to a minimum of price stability and 1977-78 to be the last years for which figures are available, one is struck by the fact that investment in the principal developed market economies experienced three bad years (1974, 1975, 1976) but, with the exception of the United Kingdom and Italy, began to revive in 1977 and continued to do so during the first half of 1978 (see Table 8.1). Moreover, even during the bad years, investment

TABLE 8.1
Real Gross Fixed Capital Formation
(Billions of U.S. dollars, 1970 prices and exchange rates)

	1970	1973	1974	1975	1976	1977	1978[a]
France	33.11	40.60	41.15	39.75	41.74	43.03	43.9
Germany	47.63	52.56	47.34	45.35	47.64	50.00	53.4
Italy	19.67	20.72	21.45	18.66	19.08	19.38	18.80
Japan	69.16	94.51	84.91	82.61	85.61	90.75	101.77
Switzerland	5.79	6.87	6.58	5.68	5.07	5.61	-5.72
UK	22.68	24.69	24.64	24.04	23.28	20.18	20.1
USA[b]	170.21	205.73	192.52	188.61	178.23	204.63	225.38

Source: Organization for Economic Co-operation and Development, National Income Accounts, 1976; International Monetary Fund, International Financial Statistics, for 1977 and 1978 reducing the nominal rate of growth by the investment goods price index (where available) or the industrial goods price index (if necessary), or the wholesale price index (as a last resort).

[a]Seasonally adjusted annual rate.

[b]Private investment only.

did not fall below its 1970 level except in Germany and Switzerland.

The picture is therefore one of a *prolonged* recession, but not of a particularly *deep* one. Of course, in terms of the twenty-five years that preceded it, it was the longest and the deepest we have experienced, but a generation is not a long time even in terms of most people's life spans, and compared with other "Great Depressions," the 1974-77 experience does not merit this appellation.

An alternative measure (the proportion of gross fixed capital formation as a percentage of GDP, both at current prices and without attempting to reduce everything to a common currency) tells much the same story, but with some differences (see Table 8.2). Gross fixed capital formation, both public and private, averaged 19.2 percent from 1968 to 1972 in the United States. It dipped to 17.9 percent in 1973, rose to 20.8 percent in 1974, and vacillated between these two extremes thereafter. The difference between the high and the low—1.3 percentage points—does not strike me as particulary startling. The same could be said of the United Kingdom, Italy, and half a dozen other countries listed in Table 8.2. Some countries even raised the share of investment in GNP (Finland, Norway, Iceland, Ireland, Canada). However, Japan, Germany, and Switzerland stand out from all the others as having sustained a substantial drop in the ratio of investment in GDP: from an average of 38.7 percent for 1968-72 to 30.8 percent in 1975 for Japan; from 25.9 percent to 21.1 percent for Germany; and from 27.8 percent to 20.7 percent (1976) for Switzerland. In absolute dollar terms (Table 8.1) this experience shows up as a considerable real drop in absolute investment levels of 10 percent for Germany and Japan from 1973 to 1974, a further drop in 1975 and a gradual revival thereafter. According to this rough measure, Germany, Japan, and Switzerland are in trouble and the rest are not doing too badly. But this measure has its limitations, especially the fact that the rate of inflation for capital goods is probably much lower than the consumer price index, so it may be safer to return to a "real" deflated measure of investment.

It is of interest for the purpose of intercountry comparison, to look at real absolute levels of investment in dollar terms on a per capita basis (see Table 8.3). The spread between the highest and lowest levels of per capita investment has widened considerably and the ranking of various countries has changed. Italy, which invested $366 per capita in 1970, was managing only $332 in real terms by 1978. (It is one of the few European countries with an expanding population.) The United Kingdom which invested $408 per capita in 1970, was down to $360 in real terms by 1978 (with a stationary population). These two countries clearly have an "investment problem" to which we return in the next section.

TABLE 8.2
Public and Private Gross Fixed Capital Formation as Percentage
of GDP (Current Prices)

	1968/72 (average)	1973	1974	1975	1976	1977	1978
Australia	25.8%	23.1%	24.0%	23.8%	23.7%	25.1%	28.5%
Austria	29.0	28.1	28.0	26.7	26.0	30.3	
Belgium	20.8	21.0	22.3	22.0	20.0	22.0	
Canada	21.4	22.2	23.2	24.2	23.1	26.0	26.0
Denmark	23.6	23.0	21.9	19.9	21.5	n.a.	
Finland	24.1	27.7	29.0	30.2	27.0	29.1	
France	26.3	23.8	25.1	23.4	23.1	22.5	
Germany	25.9	24.5	22.5	21.1	20.7	20.8	21.4
Greece	25.7	28.0	21.7	20.2	21.5	24.5	
Iceland	28.7	30.0	32.5	33.2	29.5	28.3	
Ireland	24.2	24.0	24.9	23.8	24.5	25.3	
Italy	19.8	20.8	23.4	20.8	20.3	19.8	
Japan	38.7	36.6	34.3	30.8	29.6	30.0	
Netherlands	25.3	23.0	22.2	21.3	19.7	21.1	
Norway		29.7	32.1	35.4	36.3	35.8	
Portugal	19.0	20.4	19.3	19.6	23.9	19.2	
Spain	24.2	23.6	25.0	24.1	22.9	22.6	
Sweden	23.1	21.6	22.0	20.7	20.6	20.2	
Switzerland	27.8	29.3	26.1	24.0	20.7	21.1	
UK	19.6	19.5	20.1	20.0	19.2	18.0[a]	18.2[a]
USA	19.2	17.9	20.8	19.4	18.8	17.9[a]	18.5[a]

Source: Organization for Economic Co-operation and Development,
National Accounts, 1976; and International Monetary Fund,
International Financial Statistics, various issues.

[a]Public investment estimated at 2.82 of GDP (average of last
four years).

TABLE 8.3
Real Fixed Capital Formation Per Capita
(U.S. Dollars, 1970 prices and exchange rates).

	1970	1973	1974	1975	1976	1977	1978
France	652	778	784	753	788	810	826
Germany	785	848	763	733	774	814	870
Italy	366	377	387	334	339	343	332
Japan	669	869	770	740	759	797	894
Switzerland	924	1068	1021	887	799	886	905
UK	408	441	439	429	416	361	360
USA[a]	830	978	908	883	828	944	1038

Source: Same as Table 8.1.

[a]Private investment only.

Japan and France have been running neck to neck with per capita real investments of $669 and $652, respectively, in 1970, and $894 and $826 in 1978. Since both countries have also experienced fairly satisfactory growth rates even during the worst of the recession (down to a catastrophic 3.5 percent real growth of GDP for Japan and an equally unheard-of 2.9 percent real growth for France in 1975), we must spare our sympathy for others. But for whom? For struggling Switzerland, whose per capita real level of investment fell from $924 in 1970 to $905 in 1978? For embattled Germany, for whom this measure stood at $785 in 1970 and $870 in 1978? Or for the poor United States, who saw real per capita investment rise from $830 in 1970 to $1,038 in 1978?

The rich and successful, however, do have their problems. Though they cannot really worry very much about the level of investment (but they do), then can (and do) worry about its marginal productivity. Are we investing more and more and reaping less and less per dollar spent? Is the free enterprise system entering its final phase, predicted with gloomy certitude by Ricardo and with elation by Marx, characterized by the declining marginal rate of profit? We shall return to this fascinating question in the last section. In the meantime, there are more figures to wade through. Table 8.4 splits gross capital formation (the basis for Tables 8.1, 8.2, and 8.3) into residential construction on the

TABLE 8.4
Gross Fixed Capital Formation as Percentage of GDP:
Residential Construction and Productive Investment-
Selected Countries

		1968/72 Average	1974	1975	1976
France	resid.	6.5%	7.3%	7.3%	5.8%
	prod.	19.8	17.8	16.1	14.9
Germany	resid.	5.2	5.3	4.5	5.8
	prod.	20.7	16.2	16.6	15.7
Italy	resid.	5.9	7.1	6.1	5.8
	prod.	13.9	16.3	14.7	14.5
Japan	resid.	6.6	8.0	7.8	7.9
	prod.	32.1	26.3	23.0	21.7
Switzerland	resid.	7.1	(5.5)	(5.5)	(5.5)
	prod.	19.7.	(20.6)	(18.5)	(15.2)
UK	resid.	3.5	3.9	4.0	3.8
	prod.	16.1	16.2	16.0	15.4
USA[a]	resid.	3.5	3.9	3.3	3.9
	prod.	13.5	13.6	13.0	12.3

Source: Organization for Economic Co-operation and Development, annual country studies.

[a]Private investment only.

one hand and productive investment on the other. Since residential investment is a fairly constant proportion of national income, this split highlights variations in productive capital formation. Unfortunately, the OECD is late with its 1977 national accounts, the United Nations is even later, and the International Monetary Fund (IMF) does not descend to such detail, so Table 8.4 takes us only to the end of 1976. However, in all fairness, one must admit that productive investment as a percentage of GDP has taken a nose dive from 1968-72 to 1976 in all large OECD countries except the United States, the United Kingdom, and Italy.

One can worry about the level of productive investment, or about its marginal product, but one cannot worry about both at once since they are inversely related to one another. In Germany, Japan, Switzerland,

and France the level of productive investment has fallen, so one must not be too surprised to find that the growth in the national product had been lower than in the recent past, and one need not seek the cause in a mysterious secular pendulum. In the United States, the level of productive investment as a percentage of GDP has not fallen, and it has experienced rather satisfactory historical rates of growth (4.7 and 5.7 percent in 1976 and 1977, compared wih the long-term 1960-74 trend rate of 3.6 percent). Output per unit of labor has risen less rapidly than in the past, a phenomenon which the OECD, for one, attributes half to cyclical and half to "structural" factors.[2] However, with the micro-processor revolution about to hit our mechanical-based economies, one cannot take the productivity Cassandras too seriously—at least in the United States.

Only Italy and the United Kingdom present the paradoxical picture of having succeeded in maintaining the level of productive investment as a proportion of GDP over the past ten years, but having enjoyed little or no growth from it since 1974. In these two countries the marginal product of capital really does seem to have fallen off most alarmingly. Why?

The reasons are obviously complex, but can probably be summarized under the heading "excess of ill-advised government intervention." If one looks at the share of public investment in total fixed capital formation (see Table 8.5) one can distinguish between those countries where it is relatively low (United States, Germany, Canada) at between 14 and 16 percent and those where it is much higher (24 percent and up). In this latter group, the United Kingdom outpaces its companions by a substantial amount (its current share is down from 52 percent in 1975 to 37 percent in 1977). One of the reasons for this appears to be the dearth of private residential investment, which is probably due to a combination of longstanding local government spending on housing and newer and growing disincentives to owners of rented accommodation, and which may also help to explain the decline in absolute levels of investment mentioned earlier. But other countries also have high rates of public investment—France and Japan for example—which suggests that it is not only the quantity but also the quality of public investment which one must try to account for.

Turning now to current trends and future prospects, Table 8.6 sets forth the change in the components of fixed investment over the previous year. It shows in a general way—allowing for the fact that investment also changes over time—that if public investment grows, private investment, whether residential or productive, grows less rapidly or falls. This process shows up clearly, for example, in the case of the

TABLE 8.5
Breakdown of total fixed investment by sector, 1977 (Percentage)

	Total	Public	Private resi- dential	Private manu- facturing	Ratio publ/priv manu- facturing
USA	100%	13.7%	28.1%	58.2%	.235
Japan	100	30.4	23.4	46.2	.658
Germany	100	16.1	28.3	55.6	.29
France	100	24.0	33.1	42.8	.56
UK	100	37.3	9.0	53.7	.69
Canada	100	14.5	26.2	59.3	.24
Italy	100	27.8	25.1	47.1	.59

Source: Organization for Economic Co-operation and Development, Economic Outlook (Paris: December, 1978).

United Kingdom, where for two years (1976-77 and 1977-78) public investment fell by 13.9 percent and 8.76 percent, respectively, while private manufacturing investment grew by 7.5 percent and 10 percent. In 1978-79, however, public investment grew by 4 percent, while private manufacturing investment failed to grow. If this were the result of planned counter-cyclical investment policies, one could only applaud. However, it is equally possible that the reverse is true, namely, that public investment in nationalized industries and bankrupt companies is "crowding out" private investment in viable concerns and is thus accentuating rather than diminishing the oscillations of the normal business cycle.

It is, incidentally, worthy of note that in a general sense we seem to be returning to the normal pattern of unsynchronized investment cycles, after an exceptional period of uniform recession after the oil price shock. Thus, while private manufacturing investment growth has tapered off in the United States, it has grown in Canada, Europe, and Japan. This will greatly help the process of balance of payment adjustment and is a

TABLE 8.6
Change in total fixed investment by sector (percent change
from previous year)

	1977 (%)	1978 (%)	1979 (%)
U.S. Total	n.a.	n.a.	n.a.
Public	n.a.	n.a.	n.a.
Private resid.	20.5	3.25	-9
Private manuf.	9.1	7.25	2.75
Japan Total	3.7	11	11.5
Public	10.4	20.5	23.25
Private resid.	1.3	12	6.75
Private manuf.	1.2	5	5.75
Germany Total	4.1	4.5	5.5
Public	-3.8	6.75	2
Private resid.	3.5	3.75	5
Private manuf.	6.9	4.5	6.75
France Total	-0.6	0.5	2.5
Public	2.5	5	5

TABLE 8.6 cont'd

Private resid.	-2.0	-2.75	-2
Private manuf.	-1.1	0.75	4
UK Total	-3.7	2	1
Public	-13.9	-8.75	4
Private resid.	-13.2	-1.25	-4.75
Private manuf.	7.5	10	0.25
Canada Total	0.3	0.5	2.75
Public	2.6	1	1
Private resid.	-4.6	-4	2.25
Private manuf.	1.7	1.75	3.5
Italy Total	0.1	-2	3.25
Public	-7.2	-5	2.25
Private resid.	-2.1	-2	1
Private manuf.	6.2	-0.25	5

Source: Organization for Economic Co-operation and Development, Economic Outlook, December 1978.

TABLE 8.7
Net Public Sector Borrowing, as Percentage of
Gross Domestic Product

	1973	1974	1975	1976	1977
	(%)	(%)	(%)	(%)	(%)
France	negl.	-1.1	-2.5	-0.5	-0.8
Germany	0.6	1.1	3.5	1.8	1.8
Italy	9.5	8.8	14.3	10.2	13.0
Japan	1.4	1.5	2.8	1.9	6.2
Switzerland	0.06	1.0	1.3	3.3	0.6
UK	3.9	2.4	7.6	4.5	7.7
USA	0.6	0.8	5.6	4.1	3.0

Source: International Monetary Fund, International Financial Statistics, October 1978.

welcome sign that the world economy is returning to normal.

Turning now to the share of net public sector borrowing as a percentage of GDP (Table 8.7) we see that this measure of the excess of public expenditure over receipts has climbed steadily from 9.5 percent in 1973 to 13.0 percent in 1977 in Italy; and from 3.9 percent to 7.7 percent in the United Kingdom during the same period. Other countries have maintained a much better balance in their public accounts, although Japan adopted expansionary policies in 1977, largely at the request of the United States. Again, if it were true that public expenditure merely substituted for private expenditure which was not forthcoming, then one could view Italian and British public sector deficits as the correct counter-cyclical policy to adopt. It is difficult to believe this, however, since unemployment has grown most rapidly in precisely these two countries. Quite the contrary, one is forced to concede, at least in part, the validity of the "crowding out" hypothesis, namely, that the growth in public expenditure takes place at the expense of, and not in addition to, private expenditure in consumption and especially in investment.

An excess of public expenditure over receipts has an immediate impact on private investment because of government borrowing which, if it is at all substantial, raises interest rates above what they would have been in its absence. The size of the government as a borrower in the market can be seen from Table 8.8. It fluctuates considerably from one year to the next, but it is everywhere substantial, especially in recent

TABLE 8.8
Public sector borrowing as a percentage of total credit
raised by end-users

	1973	1974	1975	1976	1977	1978
USA	10.5%	14.5%	47.4%	32.4%	24.3%	21.3%
Japan	18.6	24.8	36.9	40.4	47.3	71.8
Germany	16.1	21.9	42.8	30.6	26.5	31.8
UK	17.8	40.5	61.1	32.2	49.6	

Source: Organization of Economic Co-operation and Development,
Economic Outlook 24 (Paris: December, 1978), p. 29.

years. If the government absorbs over 40 percent of new credit raised in the economy, as has been the case in the United Kingdom, Italy, and Japan, it is difficult to argue that this has had no effect on interest rates or people's marginal propensity to save and consume.

Policy and Structural Factors Influencing Private Investment

Cyclical Factors

The patterns of investment described in the previous section can partly be explained by the counter-cyclical measures taken by governments in the wake of the 1973 oil price rise. Each government reacted differently. Germany, for instance, adopted a mixture of expansionary fiscal policies and restrictive monetary policies. Its budget moved from comfortable surplus in 1973 to an unheard-of deficit in the succeeding years, while the rate of increase in the money supply dropped from 10 to 8 percent. In 1977-78 the mixture was reversed and fiscal policy became more restrictive while the money supply rose, mainly as a result of the appreciation of the DM. Japan seems to have adopted much the same mixture of restrictive and expansionary policies. France, on the other hand, pursued the opposite strategy. Its budgetary policy remained extremely conservative with a very small deficit developing in

1975 which was reduced again in 1976 to negligible proportions, while monetary expansion, vacillating between 14 and 17 percent, was generous.

The result was a gratifying drop in inflation from 5.9 percent in 1974 to 3 percent in 1978 in Germany, and a rather less successful drop from 15.2 percent to 9 percent in France, accompanied by a substantial increase in unemployment from a long-term average of 1.4 percent to 4.4 percent for Germany[3] and from 1.6 percent to 4.9 percent for France.

The United States was the only OECD country which can be said to have experienced a "normal" recession-recovery cycle, perhaps because a presidential election occurred in 1976 and the incumbent administration pumped up the economy in anticipation thereof. In any event, the result was enviably successful in terms of real GNP growth and increase in employment; the only drawback being rising inflation, a depreciating exchange rate, and a disturbing reduction in the rate of productivity growth. Restrictive policies were reluctantly introduced in October 1978 to cope with the first two problems but, since 1979 is once again a pre-electoral year, one awaits the next moves with skeptical interest.

Switzerland pursued restrictive monetary *and* fiscal policies and as a result brought the rate of inflation down from a raging 10 percent in 1974 to a modest 1.4 percent in 1976—but at a considerable cost in terms of real lost production (-7.4 percent in 1975, -2.1 percent in 1976), expelled foreign workers (amounting to 10 percent of the working population), and a rapidly appreciating exchange rate. In mid-1978 the government altered its policy by holding down the Swiss franc and allowing the money supply to expand (at an annual rate of 12 percent compared with only 2 to 4 percent in 1977). The change in government policy is too recent to show up in any national aggregates as yet.

In the United Kingdom, the government adopted fairly restrictive policies to cope with inflation, which was generated during a period of disastrous laxity in 1973.[4] The extent of the turnaround was impressive (the rate of monetary expansion fell from a peak of 29 percent at one point in 1973 to 13 percent in 1977) but partial and short-lived. In 1978 the money supply rose by over 20 percent. Moreover, the government did not have the courage to carry its restrictive policies through in budgetary terms and, as mentioned above, the government's net borrowing as a percentage of GDP rose from 2.4 percent in 1974 to 7.6 percent in 1975, 4.5 percent in 1976, and 7.7 percent in 1977, despite growing revenues due to oil. Inflation, which had dropped from a peak of 25 percent per annum in 1975 to 8 percent in 1978, has started to rise again, while unemployment has continued to increase.

The case of Italy is even clearer. The rate of money supply growth stood at a substantial 20 percent in 1973. It rose to 24 percent in 1975-76, and has dropped back to 20 percent since then. Fiscal policy has been no more conservative, as mentioned above. As a result, the rate of inflation has remained high, falling from 25.3 percent in 1974 to 21.8 percent in 1976 and 20 percent in 1977. Since then, stabilization policies introduced at the insistence of the IMF and EEC have brought the rate of inflation down to a more reasonable rate of 12 percent, mainly by restrictive monetary policies, while government spending continues unabated. Unemployment has risen from 4 to 7 percent.

Insofar as it is possible to generalize at all, one can discern two broad categories of governmental behavior: the strict stabilizing countries on the one hand (Switzerland, Japan, and Germany) and the accommodating countries on the other (Italy, United Kingdom, and the United States), with France somewhere between the two extremes.

And what about the collective behavior of individuals in different countries? While government behavior may sometimes be difficult to understand, it is not usually difficult to see in which way it is going. Collective consumer and business behavior is much harder to penetrate. However, at the risk of offending the purists, one could suggest that government policies on the whole reflected consumer behavior in each country. In Germany, Japan, and Switzerland, the population, faced with economic uncertainty, tightened its belt and saved for the rainy day that was there anyway, thus helping to generate those extraordinary trade surpluses and exchange rate appreciations, and thwarting various half-hearted attempts by the authorities to raise aggregate demand by normal Keynesian methods. In Britian and Italy on the other hand, the population, faced with economic uncertainty, decided to spend its way out of its troubles—especially on Japanese and German goods. The net result was that in neither the stabilizing nor in the accommodating countries (with the exception of the United States) was there any net increase in aggregate demand, and therefore, any reason to invest.

Structural Factors Affecting Investment

Although cyclical factors can explain part of the differences in investment patterns, they are clearly not enough. However, identifying significant structural differences between countries requires detailed knowledge of their economies. For this reason, I shall leave the United States to those more familiar with it and shall concentrate on the contrast in Europe between two generous accommodators (the United Kingdom and Italy), a stern stabilizer (Germany), and a mild stabilizer (France).

These four countries present interesting institutional nuances which help to account for differences in their capacity to adjust and, therefore, differences in their attractiveness for private investment.

Banking Systems

One of the most important differences among these four countries seems to lie in their respective banking systems. The German banking system is unique in that it is a source of both short- and long-term finance, since banks may become shareholders in public corporations. The banks play an active role in the restructuring of German industry by being in a position not only to spot firms in difficulties at an early stage, but also to suggest a solution and impose it, if necessary, on an unwilling management by virtue of their capacity as interested shareholders. German banks also have a reputation for being willing to lend money on the strength of a good idea and little else—a throwback to early postwar years when German entrepreneurs had nothing else to offer in the way of security.

In France, all large banks are nationalized. They are the principal instrument through which the government's industrial policies are implemented, feeding or starving firms or industries of credit according to the overall government strategy. Nevertheless, the French banking sector has been severely criticized of late (by the government, of all things) for having, in the recent past, lent too much money too freely to too many firms with too many commercial prospects. In a word, the banks are being blamed for the fact that many firms are now bankrupt and that unemployment is rising. They are, indeed, a convenient scapegoat, but the government can hardly disclaim all responsibility. The French banks could not have lent money they did not have. If a decade of easy money policies might very well account for many of today's structural problems in France, the responsibility must lie first and foremost with the government itself. As for the alleged lack of discernment in their lending policies, this may have been due (a) to excess liquidity and (b) to their status as nationalized bodies, supposed to act in the public interest and not from crude profit motives. The problems raised by the efficiency of the French state banks as allocators of the nation's savings, however, are suggestive.

In Italy banks are also nationalized and play an active part in rescue operations on behalf of the state. For instance, when the privately owned Sidonia group (building contractors) went bankrupt in 1978 (total assets amounted to $200 million, total debts to $580 million) even the Instituto per la Riconstruzione Industriale (IRI, the principal state holding company) refused to take it over. A "private" solution was proposed, which involved foreign capital and in which IRI was even prepared to sell its own building firm (one of its few profitable subsidiaries) to secure agreement. In any event, the scheme fell through, and instead a bank consortium was formed to reschedule these debts and improve the balance sheet prior to absorption by IRI. In 1978 a bill was passed to define this process in law. Firms which are overburdened by debt but basically profitable may reschedule their short-term debt into long-term debt at lower interest rates or into bank equity. When a banking system has responsibilities of this type and magnitude, one cannot expect many resources, in real terms, to be available for profitable ventures.

In Britain, banks are privately owned but while they are first rate in organizing finance for tungsten mines in Timbuctoo, they are reputedly cautious and difficult when it comes to domestic borrowers. It is reported that this is due to the serious banking crisis of 1974-75, when some important banks collapsed as a result of unwise or unlucky credit policies and were rescued collectively and absorbed by the major British banks.[5] Since then, they have been extremely cautious lenders. It is symptomatic that many of the small firm success stories reported on regularly in the *Financial Times* are based on financial support from outside the classical banking system, in particular multinational fairy godmothers or the state-sponsored National Enterprise Board (NEB) described below.

Clearly there is a happy medium to be discovered between excessive profligacy (as in France or Italy) and excessive caution (as in Britain)—a middle way which perhaps the German banking system has found.

Government Ownership of Industry

Governments in Europe are entrepreneurs. They produce many goods and services of a non-public-goods nature, such as steel, ships, automobiles, aircraft, jet engines, petroleum products, chemicals, fibers, and so forth. Interesting enough, the relative size of the public industrial sector does not differ widely from one country to another, at least as far as the four "big" European states are concerned. Public enterprises employ 8.1 percent of the labor force in Britain, 6.6 percent in Italy, 7.3 percent in France, and 7.2 percent in Germany.[6]

The size of the public sector in Germany is accounted for by the fact that many basic industries were nationalized during the Nazi era. To this day, the German government has a substantial stake in industry, either as a major shareholder (as in Volkswagen) or outright owner (as in IVG, Salzgitter, VIAG, or VEBA).

France has extensive state involvement in such sectors as banking, insurance, telecommunications, electricity, gas, coal, oil transport, steel, chemicals, and automobiles. Lately, the state sector has been acting as an "investment motor." With probably scant exaggeration, *The Economist* claims that "without the nationalized sector, investment in French industry would be at a standstill."[7]

In France and Germany the origins of state entrepreneurial involvement are to be found in the historical past or, more recently (in France), in the reluctant acquisition by the state of a large ailing industry—steel. In Britain, on the other hand, state entrepreneurship has been politically motivated, since the nationalization of the means of production is laid down in the statutes of the British Labour Party as one of its basic political objectives. However, it was, paradoxically, a Conservative government which saved Rolls Royce from bankruptcy in 1971 and blazed the trail for the Labour government's nationalization of British Leyland after 1974. This was a straightforward rescue operation, and not "planned" like the nationalization of the British Steel Corporation and various shipyards.

In 1975 the Labour government established the National Enterprise Board, a state investment company to support the more dynamic sectors of industry. Given the unpropitious economic climate, however, the NEB ended up spending most of its money on distinctly unprofitable ventures, such as, inter alia, British Leyland. This has clearly limited the funds at its disposal for investment in dynamic "new" sectors, but in 1978 the NEB announced that it was to establish a 100 percent government-owned micro-processor firm, with an initial capital of 50 million.[8] Well-established firms in the industry have greeted this move with some skepticism ("It's like if you jump off a building fifty stories high and say: 'I must learn to fly.'"—Mr. Bob Heikes, Vice-President of Motorola). But Inmos (as it is named) may have galvanized domestic British firms into action, for English General Electric subsequently announced a joint venture with Fairchild in the same line of business. However, if this had been intended by the NEB, the mere threat to enter the field might have been sufficient. One awaits the outcome of this incursion of the state into a highly competitive, rapidly changing market with interest—and some concern.

In Italy, state capitalism is credited with having propelled the country out of its secular agrarianism and into the modern industrial era. The IRI was founded by Mussolini in the 1930s to rescue the country's banking system from collapse. In postwar years, IRI expanded into industry and services: steel, shipbuilding, broadcasting, telecommunications, motor cars (Alfa Romeo), engineering, public works—the list is endless. Another state company, Ente Nazionale Idrocarbure (ENI) controls energy, chemicals, and textiles; while Ente Partecipazioni e

Finanziamento Industria Manifatturiera (EFIM) is involved in the railways and rolling stock production, hotels, tobacco, food, and motorcycles. Is there anything left for private enterprise? The answer is yes, but not much. The state holding companies reportedly account for 50 percent of all fixed investment, and employ 25 percent of the industrial labor force.[9]

Although the state sectors do not differ in terms of relative size from one country to the next, it is clear that they are run with different objectives in mind. In Germany the enterprises in which the government has a majority shareholding usually compete alongside privately owned firms, even in the troubled coal and steel sectors. There is no question of running them as public utilities. (When Volkswagen was faced with bankruptcy in 1975 and turned to the government, its principal shareholder, for help, Hans Apel, then minister for industry, is said to have remarked, "One common agricultural policy and one federal railway system is quite enough for me.")[10] Similarly in France, state-owned companies are managed on sound business principles. Even when they have to "carry the flag" (as Air France does when it flies the Concorde) or are not permitted to rationalize productions (as when Charbonnages de France keeps noneconomic mines open for social reasons) a careful line is drawn between their commercial and political responsibilities. The latter are costed and the state provides the appropriate amount in the form of a grant, after which the enterprise is expected to turn in a normal commercial return on investment.

In addition, French state-owned enterprises do not usually have a monopoly outside the field of utilities, such as electricity. They share the market with privately owned firms and are expected to compete with them. "In contrast to their counterparts in the U.K., Sweden, and Italy, they are rarely accused of gross inefficiency or of maintaining employment at the expense of profits."[11]

In Britain, on the other hand, "social and political considerations exert heavy pressure."[12] Nationalized industries, such as steel, shipyards, and British Leyland, are not expected to yield a market rate of return on capital invested. A 1978 white paper stated that government enterprises should achieve a "required rate of return" of 5 percent on all new investments. Although this is nowhere near the true opportunity cost of capital in the United Kingdom, such a target rate of return represents a welcome departure from the "nudge and fudge methods of the past,"[13] and some recognition on the part of the government that even politically motivated investments must pass a minimum test of viability in economic terms.

In Italy even this minimum test is absent. Here state enterprises are subject to even greater social and political pressures and are only expected to attempt to limit their losses, not turn in a profit. Since the recession, it is virtually unquestioned that the state enterprises should pick up any sizeable firm which is in danger of collapse. Partly as a result of this, and partly because they were already unprofitable, the state enterprises have been losing a lot of money: IRI alone lost $900 million on its manufacturing activities in 1977, and $500 million in 1976.

Besides having to undertake noneconomic investments in the depressed South, it is out of the question for IRI to adapt existing industrial plants to newer, labor-saving methods of production. The trade unions simply will not agree to it. At the end of the 1960s, Italy's trade unions and students became very militant, as they did all over Europe; however, in Italy they seem to have remained so, perhaps because IRI, ENI, EFIM, and company were such large sitting ducks for attack. Militant worker groups could get directly through to the government, via its own enterprises, thus short-circuiting the malfunctioning parliamentary procedures; and the government was never strong enough to resist their political pressure.

Germany, France, Britain, and Italy thus each have their own way of running their fairly extensive state enterprises, ranging from Germany, where the government accepts the market as an allocator of state-owned resources, all the way to Italy, where public funds are allocated according to militant social and political forces, with France and Britain somewhere in between.

Industrial Policies

Besides being active entrepreneurs in their own right, all four countries under discussion have extensive and highly individualistic industrial policies directed at the private sector. Again, they range from discreet "nudging" of investment towards certain geographic areas, to straightforward subsidization of particular industries, active involvement in "restructuring," and, increasingly, temporary stop-gap relief to prevent large-scale redundancies, not to mention state-supported export credit and insurance schemes. The proliferation of such measures in Europe is partly due to the fact that if one country starts, others feel obliged to follow. The EEC, for its part, has attempted to prevent sterile competitive subsidization of industry by its member states, by setting ceilings and campaigning for "transparency" (in which it has not been entirely successful). As a result, EEC member states all subsidize up to the permitted levels, and then discover various nontransparent ways of stealing a march on their neighbors. Even if the EEC Commission catches up with them in the end, as for instance happened with the

British "Temporary" Employment Subsidy, they have gained time and can find alternatives.

Despite the basic similarity of industrial policies all over Europe, some interesting differences emerge when one looks at the attitude of government to the problem of structural change. Of all the countries under discussion here, Germany accepts the need for structural change most readily. There is a certain amount of "investment steering" (in the words of the Federal Finance Minister, Mr. Matthofer), that is, selective state encouragement of *desirable* investments in high-technology infant industries, but there is little active resistance to market forces (except in coal and shipbuilding) in low-technology geriatric sectors. Firms in difficulty are left to the tender mercies of the banking system and have, on the whole, not fared too badly: AEG-Telefunken and Volkswagen, for example, were pulled back from the brink of disaster in 1975 and are now flourishing.

Despite an impressive number of bankruptcies, Germany is the only major European country with less than one million unemployed, which suggests that this positive attitude toward restructuring by the market creates more jobs in the long run than ad hoc emergency attempts to preserve jobs in the short run. Nevertheless, strikes in the engineering, printing, and steel industries in 1978-79 suggest that hitherto unheard-of social resistance to structural change is beginning to develop in Germany. Luckily, the government is in a position to be able to stimulate the economy without running the risk of inflation, and may be able to defuse the issue.

In France a special government body, the Comité Interministériel pour l'Aménagement des Structures Industrielles (CIASI), was set up in 1974 precisely to promote structural change and help firms to adjust. The CIASI does not have funds of its own, but since it is composed of the president, the prime minister, and the principal regional, economic, and industrial ministries, it can call on the Fonds de Développement Economique et Social (FDES) or the Institut pour le Développement Industriel (IDI), the former for short-term loans or interest subsidies, and the latter for longer term finance on a loan or equity basis. (Unlike Britain's NEB, however, France's IDI may only acquire shares in a private company on a temporary basis, and must try to return them to private hands as soon as possible.)

Whenever it can, the CIASI will attempt to find a solution which does not involve the use of public funds: it will appoint an administrator to draw up a rationalization plan, lean on the state-owned banks to provide credit, and look for a viable firm in the same sector to take over the company in distress. For instance, when the large Boussac textile group was finally declared bankrupt in the summer of 1978, the CIASI selected the Willot brothers to take over the Boussac assets, despite the fact that their terms included the loss of 700 jobs because they did not ask for a government subsidy. The rival offer had included fewer redundancies, but a request for government funds.

When a "rationalization" plan involves a significant loss of jobs in an area of above-average unemployment, the French government will frequently decide to step up public works in order to ease the process of structural change. For instance, simultaneously with the sale of the Boussac assets to Agache Willot, the government announced an expansion of the road-building program in the Vosges region to the tune of Fr 500 million (U.S. $100 million).

Earlier in the year, the French government had made clear (through no less a person than the prime minister himself) that it would not subsidize inefficient sectors: "We must not hesitate to cut out the dead wood, that is, the sectors where we cannot compete. The future of France does not depend on the number of ships which we build at a loss, nor on the production of steel which we cannot sell. . . . The role of the state is to say to the 'patrons': so you want to do such and such? We'll help you. But if in five years you have not succeeded, we'll drop you. There must be a (market) sanction."[14]

Unfortunately, within the next three months the situation in the steel sector became so critical, France's eight steel companies had clocked up a total outstanding debt of Fr 40 billion (about U.S. $8 billion), that the government got cold feet and stepped in to save it. The plan was that outstanding loans to the government would be converted to equity, new government finance amounting to Fr 12 billion would be provided for "rationalization," and the work force would be reduced by 16,000. This plan has been greeted with scorn by Mr. Attali, the economic advisor to the head of the Socialist party, who pointed out in a recent article[15] that the work force in the French steel industry would have to drop from its present level of 154,000 to 38,000 before it could hope to compete with Japan or the Philippines. Ironically, it is the socialist opposition which is warning the government that the French steel industry will soon be a museum piece.

The dilemma of the French government in confronting the problem of structural change in the steel industry is repeated in many other European countries. Despite basic acceptance of the need to adapt existing industrial structures, some sectors are so large, face such enormous changes, and are so geographically concentrated, that it is not worth people's political skins to allow the changes to move forward at anything but a snail's pace. The prospect of losing 16,000 jobs in the steel industry in the coming year has caused serious rioting and deep discontent in the affected areas—and it would take eight years of similar redundancies to bring productivity up to international levels. One is obliged to conclude that the pace of restructuring will, in fact, be much slower and that Europe's steel industry will need protection at least until the end of the century, if not beyond.[16]

In Britain, the government is naturally in favor of restructuring industry, and has even devised an "industrial strategy" to bring it about. This is drawn up by the National Economic Development Board (affectionately known as Neddy) which is composed of representatives from both sides of industry, as well as government officials. Neddy has given birth to some four dozen "mini-Neddies," or sector-working parties, concerned with devising industrial strategies for as many "key sectors" of British industry. It is too early yet to judge whether this detailed sectoral approach will work. Each sector identifies its market, the extent of import penetration, the size of export markets, and future prospects for improving competitiveness. One objective is to identify potential bottlenecks in key industrial inputs before they actually occur. Another is to encourage firms to "buy British" whenever terms are competitive. Another is to identify sectors "in difficulty" and to devise restructuring plans.

Perhaps the most significant innovation in Britain's industrial policy is its attempt to involve both business and labor in the debate. If it succeeds in convincing Britain's labor unions of the need to accept change the process will have been extremely valuable. But one must also ask whether this could not have been achieved more simply by improving communications between labor and management.

Even if Neddy succeeds in improving productivity and competitiveness in its forty "key sectors," one must ask why firms did not adopt such improvements spontaneously; either the improvements are economically justified, in which case firms were asleep and do not deserve help, or the improvements are technically feasible but not economically useful, in which case it is a mistake for the government to force them on firms.

In Italy there is a series of stop-gap emergency measures which do not add up to an industrial policy—rather the reverse, in fact. The social and political situation is so tense and unstable that no government dares to grasp the nettle of structural change. For instance, it is virtually impossible for firms in Italy, whether in private hands or state owned, to dismiss workers (as described in the next section); it is also virtually impossible for a large firm to go bankrupt. Thus Italy has almost no flexibility left in its industrial structures, at least as far as large firms are concerned (the family concern, which manages to escape various social overhead costs, as well as most taxation, continues to thrive and helps to explain the "Italian paradox"). The arsenal of measures to prevent a large firm from declaring itself bankrupt was augmented in the summer of 1978, when the government, faced with the threat of the imminent collapse of two chemical companies—Liquigas and Societa Italiana Resine—rushed through a bill to stave off bankruptcies. It applies to companies with accumulated debts of over 50 billion lira (U.S. $45 million) and unable to meet current commitments. In the first instance, a consortium of creditors is to be formed to take over and produce a plan for restructuring. If the creditors are unwilling to undertake this thankless task, then the government will appoint a commissioner for it. Only if the latter can produce no viable program will the company be wound up. This statute only ratifies the existing situation, namely, the virtual impossibility, in practice, to shut down an operation in Italy. Is it reasonable to expect a publicly appointed commissioner (or anybody for that matter) to close down a firm, knowing that the Red Brigades would be waiting for him the next morning?

Countries clearly have different capacities for structural change, depending not only on the flexibility of the work force, and the availability of other jobs, but also on the flexibility of management and its ability to seek out more promising alternative occupations for its productive resources. Since the cost of avoiding structural change is high and grows with time, the aim of government structural policy should be to improve the flexibility of both sides of industry, in order to increase the system's capacity to adapt. The danger, however, is that the brunt of the state's efforts will be directed towards slowing down the pace of change to the system's existing capacity for adaptation, with very little effort devoted to improving it. There is also a danger that because the need for the state to ease the process of adjustment when confronted with really huge structural problems is virtually unquestioned in Western Europe (except perhaps in Switzerland and Germany), the state will be asked for help to solve more manageable structural problems as well. Western Europe is in the process of experiencing this escalation of government policies for structural adaptation which, other things remaining equal, can only blunt the edge of the market's inherent ability to adapt to all but the most catastrophic economic discontinuities. This follows not from any prejudiced view concerning the efficiency of government per se, but from our natural human response to certain stimuli: if the state is there to help us cope with all market fluctuations, why should we exercise great ingenuity and effort in coping with them ourselves? The consequences in terms of productivity and growth are only too predictable.

Dismissal Provisions

Employment protection legislation made great strides in continental Western Europe in the 1970s, as workers began to negotiate for various nonmonetary benefits rather than simple improvements in wages and working conditions. Such legislation has serious implications for structural change, because it reduces labor mobility from declining to expanding sectors: the former find it difficult to dismiss workers and the latter are reluctant to engage them. A vicious circle is then created, for as new job openings become scarcer, people hang onto their existing occupations with increasing tenacity.

All countries in Western Europe, including the four under discussion here, have precise laws regulating dismissals. All require that the public authorities be notified well in advance (ranging from one to several months' notice) so that a maximum can be done for their redeployment. Furthermore severance pay makes it extremely unattractive, in some cases, to dismiss workers and raises the cost of restructuring accordingly.

Dismissal provisions are comparatively lenient in Germany and the United Kingdom, become stricter in France (where prior permission must be obtained from the government for mass layoffs), and reach a paroxysm of worker protection standards in Italy. According to the 1970 Statute of Workers Rights in Italy, severance pay (at the modest rate of 3 weeks' pay for each year of service) must be paid even if the employee resigns voluntarily. The sting, however, lies elsewhere in the statute: workers cannot be dismissed for absenteeism, or unproductiveness, and firms may not check up on a worker who is absent or on sick leave. If a worker can prove that he or she was unjustly dismissed (which is easy) the employer must either rehire him/her or pay 5-12 months' salary over and above regular severance pay.

How Europe is to face the major structural changes ahead, carrying such a heavy handicap, is by no means quite clear.

Conclusions and Medium Term Prospects

The Fall in Investment: Cyclical or Structural?

There can be no clear-cut answer to this question. However, the purpose of the preceding section was to build up a picture of business conditions in four European countries (admittedly in caricature, highlighting the most prominent features) so as to be able to support the following tentative generalization: though no country is free of structural rigidities, some are freer than others. In these, the fall in investment, while severe, has been largely cyclical, and because they accept and encourage structural change, they will in due course pick up and start growing again. It is inconceivable, with the developing countries taking the most laborious tasks off our backs on the one hand, and micro-processors taking the load of repetitive and boring work from our shoulders on the other, that productivity and real income should fail to grow—for those who accept the need to adapt to changing circumstances.

However, there are other countries with very severe structural rigidities, which find it virtually impossible to cope with change. In recent years they have had to cope with recession, a change in the price of energy relative to other inputs, and a rapid rise in the price of labor; they are now confronted with competition from developing countries and a major technological revolution. These countries will become increasingly unattractive to private investment because, by resisting change, they will have high cost structures relative to those which do accept change. These countries will suffer a structural decline in investment, and will gradually move from a private enterprise to a public enterprise economic system.

Declining Rate of Profit?

Several studies have shown that industrial earnings in relation to capital, or in relation to turnover, or as a proportion of GNP, have been declining for some time, at least since the early 1960s, well before the current recession. Inversely, the return to labor, in terms of the share of earned income in GNP, has risen slowly but surely, after having been one of the most amazing economic constants of all.

This gradual shift in the relative price of labor and capital can be partly attributed to a change in underlying factor supply conditions which are part of the natural process of growth—an increasing abundance of capital relative to labor, or a movement along the marginal-product-of-capital (MPK) curve. However, part of the relative price change can also be attributed to growing market rigidities, antipollution legislation, and social protection laws, which have the effect of shifting the MPK curve backwards towards the origin, or reducing marginal output per unit of input.

In the past, technological advance, which reduced the demand for labor per unit of output, was a sufficient counterforce to the gradual change in underlying factor supply conditions to prevent the return to capital from falling relative to that of labor. In graphical terms, technological change shifted the MPK curve outwards from the origin.

The question today is whether the technological advance will be sufficient to offset both the effect of a growing abundance of capital and the effect of political and social policies, both of which work towards reducing the return to capital, and, by implication, real economic growth. Who knows? When one hears that Fiat's robot assembly process "Robogate" reduces the work force on a typical motor car assembly line from 128 to 28, or that an industrial sewing machine marketed by Singer can be programmmed to undertake 50 separate steps automatically, or that there are some 25,000 applications for micro-processors which have been patented, one cannot take too pessimistic a view.

Quantity vs. Quality of Investment

Capital *formation* is not a problem in an advanced industrial state. If private investors, for either cyclical or structural reasons, do not invest enough, the government has no difficulty in stepping in. The marginal propensity to save is surprisingly constant, and if private entrepreneurs refuse to borrow, the government certainly can and has an endless list of worthy public projects on which the money could be spent. The problem lies in the *allocation* of these (scarce) resources, so that their return reflects their full opportunity cost. Where the government takes a large share of national savings as in Italy and the United Kingdom, the marginal rate of return on investment in terms of productivity growth is close to zero. Both countries are saving some 20 percent of GNP just to stay in the same place, whereas in Germany a 20.8 percent rate of investment yielded a 2.9 percent rate of growth, in France, 22.5 percent yielded 3 percent growth, and in the United States, 18 percent yielded 1.3 percent in real productivity growth in 1977.[17]

Since the overall rate of investment as a proportion of GNP does not vary much from one developed country to another (with the exception of Japan), while the marginal rate of return clearly does, one is forced to conclude that some countries allocate their investment resources better than others. The United States does so better than France or Germany, and the latter do so better than the United Kingdom or Italy. The quality of investment is far more important than its quantity; therefore, what policies could be adopted to improve its allocation?

In the United Kingdom, an attempt is being made to oblige public sector enterprises to achieve a "required rate of return" as mentioned above, but as long as the government remains their owner, they are easy targets for trade union action and it is difficult to see the government taking any drastic steps if a public enterprise fails to meet the "required rate of return." The only long-term answer, for Britain and Italy, is for the state to withdraw, at least in part, from the industrial sector, and allow private enterprise to compete with the government, so as to set a standard by which to measure its performance. As far as public investment proper—i.e., infrastructure—is concerned, the cherished belief that any investment, or more than that, any public expenditure, is good enough to trigger off the multiplier process and raise national income, needs to be abandoned. It leads to nightmarish combinations of Keynes and Kafka which are both wasteful and absurd.

In countries where the quality of investment is clearly higher, as in France and Germany, what steps could be taken to improve its allocation? There are two large grey areas of misallocation where much could be done to improve matters, namely, agriculture and textiles.

People in France and Germany spend, on average, 20 percent of GNP on food and 5 percent on clothing. Food prices are much higher in Europe than elsewhere, as any world traveller can testify, because a long tradition of protection has created strong vested interests in farming. Even if prices are only 50 percent higher than they would otherwise be without the EEC's Common Agricultural Policy (and this, in my view, is a conservative estimate) the Common Market as a whole and France and Germany in particular, are spending between 6 and 7 percent of GNP—which could be spent on "other things"—on food.

Investment in industries or services producing "other things" would yield a far greater return than investment in agriculture, which produces, at the margin, surpluses which have to be burned, given away as food aid, or "sold" to the USSR at 10 percent of their cost. Much the same could be said for textiles and clothing, where recent moves to stabilize the growth of LDC exports to the Common Market will undoubtedly raise the price of clothing to European consumers well above world market levels.

Protection of food and clothing alone (not to speak of steel, machinery, household appliances, and a host of other products) probably costs Western Europe at the very least something on the order of 10 percent of GNP per annum. Therefore, any shift of investment away from these sectors and into "other things" would immediately improve its overall quality. Such a shift may in fact be a prerequisite if Europe is to be able to afford its generous social protection legislation and meet its own environmental standards.

Notes

1. Most tax authorities, when they are not using artificial rates of depreciation for reasons of policy, allow depreciation on machinery at a rate of 10 percent per annum on a straight line basis, and even less for buildings.

2. *Economic Outlook* (Paris: Organization for Economic Co-operation and Development, December 1978), p. 15.

3. The figure for Germany is distorted downwards by net emigration of foreign workers whose work permits were not renewed when they lost their jobs.

4. One can only liken this conduct to that of a prisoner released after fifty years of bondage to fixed exchange rates. After having gone on a monumental bender, the subject came to its senses, but still has a frightful hangover and may have permanently damaged its insides.

5. *Investment, Licensing, and Trading Conditions Abroad, Britain* (Geneva: Business International, July 1977), p. 4.

6. "Public Sector Enterprise," *The Economist*, 30 December 1978, p. 40.

7. "Public Sector Enterprise," *The Economist*, p. 53.

8. *Financial Times*, 19 September 1978, p. 31.

9. "Public Sector Enterprise," *The Economist*, p. 49.

10. *Quarterly Economic Review, Federal Republic of Germany*, no. 2 (London: The Economist Intelligence Unit, 1975), p. 11.

11. *Investment, Licensing and Trading Conditions Abroad, France* (Geneva: Business International, June 1978), p. 5.

12. *Investment, Licensing, Britain*, p. 5.

13. "Public Sector Enterprise," *The Economist*, p. 41.

14. *L'Expansion*, no. 117, April 1978, p. 20 (author's translation).

15. Jacques Attali, "L'Année de l'autruche," *Le Monde*, 27 December 1978.

16. The long and short term costs of this policy are detailed in a forthcoming publication, Victoria Curzon Price, *Industrial Policy in Western Europe* (London: Macmillan, for the Trade Policy Research Centre, 1979-80).

17. *Economic Outlook*, p. 15.

Commentary

Thomas A. Pugel

The paper "Capital Formation and Investment Policy" by Dr. Victoria Curzon Price presents a survey of recent investment conditions and behavior in a number of OECD countries. This paper represents an attempt to combine analyses of recent, short-run investment behavior with a discussion of the long-run conditions affecting investment and real economic growth. The paper first discusses macroeconomic investment behavior in a number of OECD countries over the most recent business cycle, 1973 to the present. It then presents a survey of conditions affecting investment decisions in each of four countries— Germany, France, Britain, and Italy. The concluding section then attempts to combine the analyses of conditions and short run trends into an outlook for investment and real economic growth in these four countries.

My discussion focuses, as does the paper, on Germany, France, Britain, and Italy. Dr. Curzon Price proceeds to analyze the underlying conditions affecting investment in each of these countries, in order to examine whether the recent rather poor investment behavior in each of these countries is cyclical or reflective of longer run forces. In doing so, she highlights three conditions which may explain recent investment behavior and which have important long-run implications. These conditions are (1) government attitudes toward the operation of governmentally owned enterprises, (2) government attitudes toward the restructuring of industry, and (3) the behavior of labor unions.

In all four countries government ownership of enterprise is extensive. In Germany and in France, the enterprises are run in a relatively commercial manner, but in Britain and Italy the enterprises are run substantially to satisfy political imperatives.

Government attitudes toward restructuring of industry also vary among these countries. In Germany, the government allows market forces to operate much more than in the other three countries. In France, government "steering" of new investment encourages restructuring. Nonetheless, substantial government subsidy efforts sometimes block restructuring, although the government prefers private rescue of failing firms. In Britain and Italy, government rescue of failing firms has become standard practice.

Third, the industrial and political power of trade unions is stronger in Britain and Italy. Trade unions are strong enough to inhibit restructuring in both Britain and Italy by extracting large side payments to permit mass layoffs of their members.

Dr. Curzon Price encounters difficulties in attempting to relate recent investment behavior to the underlying investment conditions. Basically, she fails to draw a sufficient distinction between short-run macro-economic events and long-run economic growth conditions. Thus, she argues that because productivity has not grown in Britain and Italy during the last few years, their investment must be of low "quality," while because productivity has grown more rapidly in the United States, its investment must be of a higher "quality." Since the return to current investment is spread over many years and many other influences affect current, short-run growth rates, such conclusions have little meaning.

Rather, long-term economic growth depends, other things equal, on the aggregate quantity of real investment and its average quality, which may be summarized as the social marginal product of capital (SMPK). Along these dimensions Dr. Curzon Price presents too little analysis. She does argue that, in resisting structural change, government policies are inducing new investment in relatively low SMPK uses, to the detriment of long-run growth. Although this argument is most appropriate to Britain and Italy, protection of the agricultural and textile sectors in France and Germany is also evidence of resistance to restructuring. She notes that the operation of government enterprises for political ends also likely leads to new investment in low SMPK uses, thus reducing real economic growth.

Dr. Curzon Price's analysis of the unattractiveness of Britain and Italy as locations for private investment may require modification. Although she argues that the unattractiveness is due to resistance to structural change, her analysis more clearly leads to the conclusion that the unattractiveness is due to trade union power in these countries. In fact, given trade union power in these countries, public investment may be the only way in which any significant quantity of investment can be achieved. Thus long-term growth prospects in Britain and Italy may depend crucially on the ability of the government to invest in relatively high SMPK uses.

Three other areas of great importance to the rates of real investment and long-term economic growth are treated only peripherally in the paper. First, the increase in the relative price of energy may inhibit capital formation to the extent that energy is a complement to capital in the production process.[1]

Second, corporate taxation policies may inhibit capital formation during periods of inflation.[2] Of special importance are rules requiring depreciation on the historic cost of capital equipment rather than replacement cost. Use of historic cost depreciation results in depreciation reserves which are insufficient to purchase replacement machinery and in corporate taxation of "phantom" profits. The ability to deduct the full nominal cost, rather than just the real cost, of debt borrowing offsets this bias to some extent. Nonetheless, efficiency in corporate decision making requires an indexed/replacement cost corporate tax system.

Third, the effects of environmental laws on the cost of new capital equipment, the delay of new investment projects, and the allocation of new investment to environmental protection rather than productive uses are not discussed by Dr. Curzon Price. A Chase Econometrics study concludes that alternative private investments in the United States are reduced by forty percent of the cost of pollution abatement investment.[3] Of course, a full analysis of the social worth of environmental protection requires a net measure of the benefits from pollution reduction relative to its economic costs, including the likely reduction in long-run GNP growth.

Notes

1. See, for example, E. A. Hudson and D. W. Jorgenson, "Energy Policy and U.S. Economic Growth," *American Economic Review* 68 (May 1978), pp. 118-123.

2. See, for example, M. Feldstein and L. Summers, "Inflation, Tax Rules, and the Long Term Interest Rate," *Brookings Papers on Economic Activity*, no. 1 (1978), pp. 61-99.

3. As discussed in the survey article by R. H. Haveman and V. K. Smith, "Investment, Inflation, Unemployment, and the Environment," ed. P. R. Portney, *Current Issues in U.S. Environmental Policy* (Baltimore: Johns Hopkins University Press, 1978).

Commentary

Paul Wachtel

Perhaps a more appropriate title for this paper would be: "Are the 1970s Different?" It is an important question for policymakers concerned with formulating policy responses to current problems that will be appropriate for the succeeding decade or two. However, it is also a question whose answer is not yet apparent. In this paper we do find some provocative suggestions which merit closer examination. I will comment briefly on Dr. Curzon Price's position and try to show why the question posed is such a difficult one to answer.

The decade of the 1970s can be viewed either as a period of severe random shocks to world economies or as a period of major structural changes for the worse. If the first view is correct, we should be able to show that world economies will be returning to "normal" and if the second is correct, we should be able to explain why they occurred. These tasks might be impossible because, as Professor Nelson noted earlier, structural change and cyclical buffeting may well be inseparable phenomena. Nevertheless, it is worth looking at the data.

For the United States, at least, the 1970s may be viewed as a cyclical episode. By 1978, investment levels in the United States were as high as they would have been if investment grew at a steady 4 percent per year since the prerecession year of 1973. However, the cumulative loss from five years below trend, the amount of capital not created is about equal to one year's investment output. Thus, although the cycle may be finished, its legacy is large enough to affect the trend. For the European economies, the recovery of investment to its growth trend has not yet taken place.

Before we conclude that there has been a structural decline in levels of capital formation, we should note that for most countries the proportion of output devoted to capital formation did not decline in the mid-1970s.[1] In these cases, low levels of investment can be attributed to low levels of demand; a simple response to the business cycle and the existence of excess capacity.

Dr. Curzon Price prefers to attribute low growth to capital formation problems rather than aggregate demand problems. Clearly, there are elements of both—the oil price increases induced structural changes in the midst of the business cycle. Dr. Curzon Price's view is interesting and I could be convinced by some evidence which demonstrates that the capital formation problem is due to structural changes which make investment unattractive.

The evidence presented is in the form of catastrophe scenarios for four European countries. To an American, her descriptions of restrictive manpower policies and costly subsidies to nationalized industries are a source of relief. One can relax with the knowledge that things are much worse elsewhere. But my crucial concern is that her travelogue of economic inefficiencies does not quite prove the point. These catastrophes have long been with us—even the United States has its share of allocative inefficiencies.

In order to attribute the decline in growth rates and levels of capital formation in the 1970s to allocative inefficiencies, it is necessary to show that the extent of these inefficiencies has increased. Surely the British unions have been intransigent since the fifteenth century. What new structural rigidities were introduced in the 1970s to transform Italy from a high growth to a no growth economy? I suspect that Dr. Curzon Price is correct, there have been increases in structural inefficiencies, but we need some hard evidence of *change* in the structure. In some way one needs to quantify characteristics of the economy which indicate that there has been an erosion of the social contract, or an increase in allocative inefficiencies or uneconomic subsidies.

The answers provided by Dr. Curzon Price are primarily descriptive and require more investigation. In particular, her concern with the "crowding out" of private investment by public investment is of great interest. The cross-country comparisons need to be bolstered by time series analyses extending back to the 1960s. Her description of industrial, manpower, and nationalized industry policies in recent years provides a strong argument that recent policy moves have created growth deterrents. On the other hand, structural differences in the banking industry, although important, do not seem to me to be responsible for changes in growth trends. The need for a formal quantitative analysis of these various factors is clear.

It is surprising that there is so little growth accounting research that could help us attribute recent low growth rates to various sources. Even for the United States, there is little current work of this kind. This is probably due to the difficulties in allocating growth to sources other than directly measured inputs (capital and labor) and to the underlying interrelationships among the various factors. However, some progress can be made and John Kendrick has recently released some interesting estimates.[2] Although very little is said about methodology, the results are worth repeating. The average annual rate of growth in U.S. real gross domestic business product declined from 3.5 percent in 1966-73 to 2.0 percent in 1973-77. This change in the growth rate of 1.5 percentage points is allocated in the following way:

Total factor input	-.6%
Total factor productivity	-.9%
Advances in knowledge	-.2%
Changes in labor quality	+.3%
Age/sex composition	+.3%
Education, training, and health	0.0%
Resource reallocations	-.4%
Intensity of demand	-.4%
Impact of government regulation	-.2%
Other	0.0%

Kendrick allocates almost half the decline in the rate of growth of total factor productivity to the recession. Major structural factors are the increased impact of regulation and the reduced contribution of resource reallocations towards more productive sectors. These structural impacts can be viewed as favorable developments or evidence of crises. Government regulation that produces social goods unmeasured in aggregate product (e.g., clean air) need not be criticized. Similarly, if resource reallocations provide a smaller growth contribution because there are few resources remaining in inefficient sectors, one can hardly blame the nation's investment policy for failing to produce high growth rates.

The complex issues raised in Dr. Curzon Price's paper require considerable research on growth accounting for the European economies. Perhaps inefficiencies arising from government policies towards the nationalized industries and labor redundancies are the major culprits, but the economics profession must go a long way towards demonstrating this.

An alternative approach suggested by Dr. Curzon Price is to examine rates of return to private capital formation. For the United States, there has been considerable controversy about whether the rate of return has been declining. Inflation creates severe measurement problems that make the profit share of national income an inadequate answer to this question. Thus, another research issue that needs to be pursued is whether the marginal return to investment in the private sector in Britain and Italy is really zero as Dr. Curzon Price suggests. Once again, I suspect she is correct, but need to be convinced.

In conclusion, Dr. Curzon Price's paper should be viewed as catalytic. By jumping to conclusions, she should provoke a great deal of further research. That work is clearly overdue and may very well demonstrate the perceptiveness of her intuition. For that reason alone the paper is valuable. The work that follows will provide an important and necessary basis for formulating and evaluating investment policies.

Notes

1. Using the data in Dr. Curzon Price's Table 8.2, we see that Germany and Japan are notable exceptions:

	U.S.	U.K.	Japan	Germany
1968-1972	19.2%	19.6%	38.7%	25.9%
1973-77	18.9%	19.1%	32.3%	21.8%

2. See John W. Kendrick, "Sources of Productivity Growth and of the Recent Slow-down," for the study by the New York Stock Exchange, *Reaching a Higher Standard of Living,* mimeographed, 1979.

9

LDC Manufacturing Production and Implications for OECD Comparative Advantage

Anne O. Krueger

Among the most prominent of the consistent themes of the period since World War II has been the urgency of the need to raise living standards in developing countries. Prior to the war, there had been little experience with conscious policies designed to affect living standards and rates of growth of real income. Also, knowledge about techniques and measures that would accelerate growth rates was extremely limited. As experience accumulated, thinking and opinion about the development process and its interrelationship with the world economy has undergone pronounced twists and turns.

In the early years, attention tended to focus upon the remarkable similarities among poor countries. A conspicuous regularity among the features was the degree to which exports of developing countries were dominated by primary commodities. This empirical regularity gave rise to a number of theories and policy prescriptions, most of which were based explicitly or implicitly upon some sort of "export pessimism"— the notion that developed countries had an overwhelming and unchallengeable superiority in manufacturing production and that, if there was to be industrialization in the developing countries, it must come about through some sort of import substitution mechanism. This view essentially rejected reliance upon the international marketplace as a major stimulus to the development effort. Indeed, most early growth models of the world economy assumed that developed countries exported manufactures to the developing countries in exchange for raw materials, both agricultural and mineral.

Export pessimism was almost universal in the 1950s, but by the 1970s it virtually met its demise. A number of factors has contributed to the rejection of this viewpoint, including the failure of import substitution strategies to generate sustained growth rates that were regarded as

Parts of this chapter are based on a paper given at the September 1978 meeting of the International Economics Study Group in Sussex. I am indebted to the participants in that group, to Professors James M. Henderson and Richard Snape, and to James Mulligan for helpful comments and suggestions.

satisfactory by policymakers. A key factor, however, was the reversal of the import substitution strategy by a number of developing countries, and the spectacular success those countries achieved both in attaining rapid rates of growth of exports, especially industrial exports, and in raising their real income growth far in excess of that which most observers had earlier believed to be the maximum attainable.

Those countries, most notably Brazil, South Korea, and Taiwan, have based their growth strategy on export promotion. Although there can be arguments as to the exact nature of the mechanism through which export growth is linked to the overall growth rate, there can be little doubt that the successful export performance achieved by those countries was a major factor contributing to spectacular growth performance.

The success of the "super exporters" has raised a number of issues. On one hand, there are those in the OECD countries who are concerned with the impact of the rapid growth of manufactured exports from LDCs on the domestic economies of their countries. On the other hand, the very success of the super exporters has been observed carefully by policymakers in other developing countries, and there is every prospect that they will attempt to emulate the Brazilian-Korean-Taiwanese export-oriented growth strategy in the future. This, in turn, raises a variety of questions as to the probable impact of rapidly rising LDC-manufactured exports on OECD countries.

It is the purpose of this paper to review the issues involved, and to assess the extent to which past and prospective future developments in LDC manufacturing production have affected and will affect the comparative advantage of the OECD countries. In the first section, there is a brief discussion of the process of economic growth, and how comparative advantage changes as it proceeds. This, in turn, highlights the importance, for both developed and developing countries, of maintaining a liberal international economy. The second section then examines the evidence with regard to the impact of LDC manufactured exports on structural change in the developed countries in the 1970s. A third section then is devoted to consideration of the ways in which future impacts of LDC manufacturing on the OECD countries might differ, either qualitatively or quantitatively, from past experience. A concluding section then summarizes the main issues and evaluates policy alternatives.

Growth and Industrial Structure

Although our understanding of the growth process is far from complete, there is universal recognition that economic growth, by its very nature, entails significant changes in economic structure. On the one hand, these changes are a necessary part of the growth process and, on the other hand, they impose costs on some members of society.

At a descriptive level, economic growth is accompanied by a shift in the composition of economic activity, first from agriculture to industry, and then from industry to services. Invariably, economic growth has been accompanied by rising agricultural productivity both per man and per unit of land. Productivity growth, in turn, has exceeded the growth of demand for agricultural output, and thus there has been a reduction in employment in agriculture as a concomitant of economic growth. The share of agriculture in income and output has invariably declined. In the early stages of economic growth, to be sure, population growth may be so rapid that the rural population actually increases. But in any sustained process of raising per capita incomes and living standards, the rate of growth of nonagricultural output and employment has exceeded that of agriculture. At a later stage in the growth process, productivity increases in industry are more rapid than those in services, and there is thus a tendency for a shift in employment and the share of output from industry toward the service sectors. In addition to this broad structural shift, there are other changes which equally entail both economic growth and costs for components of society.

Without spelling them out in detail, these shifts encompass a variety of phenomena which dislocate individuals and regions: there is generally a shift away from small-scale, final consumer goods manufacturing production toward greater emphasis on large-scale consumer durables and other manufacturing processes. Some activities, such as cottage industries, diminish while others increase rapidly. These shifts entail both regional and occupational changes. In the United States, for example, the early-settled region of New England has long been an area of displacement and factory closings as both the industry mix and the shifting nature of demand impacted upon the region. At a national level, some occupations such as horseshoers and railroad engineers declined in importance as automobiles and trucks replaced earlier modes of transportation.

Some of the causes of these shifts during the course of economic growth are obvious: as real incomes rise, individuals are enabled to spend larger fractions of their income on goods other than basic food, clothing, and shelter. As their expenditure patterns shift, so must the composition of industry and output. Obviously, too, innovations such as the telephone and electricity can outmode entire occupations and activities, such as the pony express and whaling.

But there are some more fundamental processes at work in the course of economic growth. In particular, the process of increasing output per man (which is, by definition, increasing per capita income) is accomplished by providing more resources for individuals to work with and enabling them to make better use of those resources. These processes generally entail increasing investments in man, in machines, and in other instruments of production. The skill level of the labor force systematically increases with economic growth, as does the amount of capital stock available for the individual worker to enhance his productivity. Much of the labor force is eventually shifted away from manual labor, where machines can replace men to a large degree, into skilled and organizational jobs. Thus, economic growth of the OECD countries has been accompanied by (as well as caused by, at least in a simplistic sense) a drastic shift in the educational and occupational composition of the labor force: unskilled, illiterate workers are really a thing of the past. As the labor force's training and skills become more productive, the real wage increases, since men are becoming scarcer relative to machines and to other resources.

All of these phenomena are part of the growth process which has enabled most of the population of the OECD countries to achieve standards of living, life expectancies, and health standards never previously realized in human history.

The other side of that coin has been that industries and sectors relying heavily upon manual labor and unskilled workers have been disadvantaged during the process of economic growth. In particular, as real wages rise, those who are "left behind" want increases in their standards of living as well. Those increases, in turn, put pressures on industries which use unskilled labor to modernize. Moreover, costs rise rapidly as the labor-intensive industries are confronted with higher wages. When, as has happened in many instances, the industries using unskilled labor are also those producing commodities for which demand does not increase rapidly with income, the consequence has been falling income and employment in firms and towns where production is concentrated on those activities.

This phenomenon is well illustrated with historical data from the United States. Table 9.1 gives data on the composition of consumption expenditures and employment for 1929, 1940, and selected postwar years. As can be seen, the proportion of consumption expenditures devoted to nondurable items has been falling since 1940, while the share of consumption expenditures devoted to services has been rising since 1950. The rate of growth employment in any given industry depends on the rate of growth of demand (itself a function of real incomes and of changing relative prices) and the rate of growth of labor productivity (which influences the rate of change in relative prices). As can be seen,

TABLE 9.1
Changing Composition of Output and Employment in the U.S. (Percentages)

	1929	1940	1950	1960	1970	1977
Expenditure Composition						
Durable Goods	11.9%	10.9%	16.0%	13.3%	13.7%	14.8%
Nondurables	48.8	52.1	51.1	46.5	42.7	39.7
(Food)	(25.2)	(28.4)	(28.1)	(24.9)	(22.0)	(20.4)
(Clothing and Footwear)	(12.2)	(10.6)	(10.2)	(8.2)	(7.5)	(6.8)
Services	39.2	36.9	32.8	40.2	43.5	45.5
(Housing)	(15.1)	(13.7)	(11.3)	(14.8)	(15.2)	(15.2)
(Transportation)	(3.4)	(2.9)	(3.2)	(3.2)	(3.4)	(3.4)
Employment Composition						
Agricultural	21.9	20.1	12.2	8.3	4.4	3.6
Nonagricultural	78.1	79.9	87.8	91.7	95.6	96.4
Wage and Salary Workers						
Manufacturing	34.1	33.9	33.7	31.0	27.3	23.8
(Durable goods)	n.a.	(16.6)	(17.9)	(17.4)	(15.8)	(13.9)
(Nondurable goods)	n.a.	(17.4)	(15.8)	(13.5)	(11.5)	(9.8)
Mining	3.4	2.9	2.0	1.3	.9	1.0
Construction	4.8	4.0	5.2	5.3	5.0	4.7
Transportation and utilities	12.5	9.4	8.9	7.4	6.4	5.6
Wholesale and retail trade	19.5	20.8	20.7	21.0	21.2	22.2
Finance, insurance and real estate	4.8	4.6	4.2	4.9	5.2	5.5
Services	11.0	11.4	11.9	13.7	16.4	18.7
Government	9.8	13.0	13.3	15.4	17.7	18.4

Source: 1978 Economic Report of the President (Washington, D.C.: Council of Economic Advisors, 1978), pp. 272, 288 and 296.

agricultural employment has fallen sharply, from over one-fifth of employment in 1929 to less than one twenty-fifth in 1977. This decline was so sharp that it was reflected in a decline in the absolute number of persons engaged in agricultural employment—it fell from 10.4 million in 1929 to 3.2 million in 1970. The fact that the share of consumption expenditures on food fell less drastically than agricultural employment reflects several growth-related phenomena: agricultural productivity grew very rapidly, and at higher levels of per capita income, individuals purchased more highly processed food, both in the form of packaged and ready-made items and in the form of restaurant and fast-food prepared meals.

While the declining numbers and share in agriculture probably reflect the sharpest decline in any sector, other sectors have also been adversely affected. The number of employees in mining has fallen (from 1.1 million in 1929 to 0.6 million in 1970, rising somewhat during the 1970s), while employment in transportation and utilities has remained approximately constant, reflecting in part offsetting trends in the bus-railroad and airline-truck segments of the transportation industry.

To be sure, these declines were necessary to enable the huge expansion that took place in the service sectors of the economy. Without those declines, the expansions in output and employment in the latter sectors would have been less rapid, with an attendant reduction in the rate of economic growth. For present purposes, however, the main points of the discussion are three: (1) economic growth has necessarily entailed structural shifts, especially away from labor-intensive, unskilled-labor-using industries, toward human-capital-intensive and service-oriented activities, as productivity growth and the substitution of machines for men have replaced manual labor; (2) the main causes of structural change have been, and will continue to be, internal to the growth process itself; and (3) there are inevitably gains and losses in the growth process. In terms of social costs, it is usually the loss of employment opportunities in declining sectors which are thought to impose the greatest hardship.

Thus, it is necessary to consider the ways in which opportunities for international trade affect growth and structural change. Here, consideration must be given to two separate but related issues: the effect of trade on the developed countries and the impact of the international economy on the developing countries.

Turning to the developed countries first, the main benefits of trade are generally fairly independent of the issues discussed above. Trade enables countries to obtain goods more cheaply than they can produce them themselves; it provides increased competition for domestic industries and it permits division of labor and specialization along the lines of

individual countries' comparative advantage. Most trade in manufactures is among countries with similar levels of per capita income:
two-thirds of all U.S. exports go to other developed countries
and more than one-half of all imports originate from other developed
countries. When raw materials are excluded from the figures, the
dominance of developed countries in the trade pattern of the United
States is even more pronounced. A similar picture holds for Western
Europe and other developed regions. Until very recently, therefore,
evaluation of future growth prospects for developed countries was
undertaken almost independently of considerations pertaining to
international trade. Even when trade prospects were considered, it was
generally in the context of the likely availability of raw materials and
other needed inputs, and without regard to the impact of trade on the
domestic structure of production.

The growth of manufactured exports from LDCs has, however,
changed the nature of the discussion somewhat. The success the super-
exporters have met in selling their exported manufactured goods to the
developed countries has raised questions as to the impact those
countries' exports have on the structure of industry within the developed
countries.

Generally speaking, the LDCs have been successful in exporting a
range of products, finished and partially processed, which use relatively
more unskilled labor and fewer design and engineering skills than do
the products they import. Because they have lower per capita incomes (a
result in part of the less skilled labor force and smaller available capital
stock per worker), it naturally follows that their best export prospects are
to be found, by and large, in those industries and activities which
employ unskilled labor in abundance and are not heavy capital users.
Those are precisely the same industries which in the developed countries
are most likely to be adversely affected by the domestic growth process.

The fact that it is the same general run of industries and lines of
employment which are likely to be adversely affected by economic
growth as by import competition from LDCs makes it extremely
difficult to assess the role of LDC manufactured imports in structural
change. On a priori grounds, one would expect that LDC competition
would intensify difficulties that the affected industries would in any
event encounter. However, to the extent that LDC competition may keep
the prices of labor-intensive commodities lower than they would otherwise be, consumption in developed countries will be greater than would
be possible in the absence of imports. Moreover, because structural
adjustment in the developed countries is in any event necessary for
economic growth, it can be cogently argued that competition from LDC
imports will in fact speed up the growth process.

All of these considerations imply that there is no simple, straight-forward way of estimating the impact of LDC imports in the past, much less assessing their precise future contribution to structural change in developed countries. Although the available data are examined in the next section, with a view to providing an idea of the order of magnitude of LDC import competition in manufactured goods, it should be borne in mind that the presence of LDC imports does not imply that domestic consumption and prices (not to mention real income) would have been the same in the absence of those imports.

From the viewpoint of the LDCs, one of the motives prompting the change to an export-oriented strategy on the part of the successful exporters was the failure of the import substitution strategy to generate a satisfactory or sustainable rate of economic growth. While it is beyond the scope of this paper to delve in detail into the reasons why LDC growth prospects are so integrally connected to prospects for access to the developed country markets,[1] there is overwhelming evidence that for countries beyond the very early stages of development further progress is exceptionally difficult through an inner-oriented growth strategy. This is because an inner-oriented strategy entails development of multiple production lines for small-scale, economically inefficient sizes of production runs; involves development of capital-intensive and skill-using industries at an early stage of development when the resources for those activities are simply not available in sufficient supply domestically; and results in an absence of competition and thus inhibits productivity growth.

Indeed, there is beginning to be considerable evidence that an efficient growth pattern entails the gradual evolution of industrial specialization, starting with unskilled labor-intensive, low-skill, low-technology industries, and progressing over time toward the more capital-intensive, and finally more skill-intensive activities (in the sense of requiring engineering design, and innovative abilities). For later consideration, this notion of progression through stages of comparative advantage is of some importance. For, if countries such as first Japan and now Korea, Taiwan, and Singapore gradually lose their comparative advantage in labor-intensive industries, other developing countries can start producing those products. Much of the international market for those countries can result not through displacement of developed countries' industry or through further structural adjustments, but rather through structural adjustments in the developing countries as they progress from reliance upon their abundance of unskilled labor to the development of industries with a higher value-added component.

We are thus left, on a priori grounds, with the conclusion that successful development of manufactured exports from LDCs may intensify the difficulties that the labor-intensive industries in developed countries will encounter, but will not cause them, and may accelerate the growth rates of the developed countries. It also follows that those industries would, in any event, be facing problems of structural adjustment. A major question, therefore, is the relative importance of the domestic adjustments confronting the labor-intensive industries contrasted with the pressures put upon them by imports. That question cannot be answered by theory alone, but requires examination of the empirical evidence, a topic to which we now turn.

Growth of LDC Manufactured Exports

Aggregate Manufacturing

It was already mentioned that the bulk of world trade is between industrialized countries. This can be clearly seen in Table 9.2, which gives data on developing countries, and total exports for selected years between 1955 and 1977. The share of non-oil-exporting developing countries in world trade was just over 20 percent in 1955, and fell sharply until the late 1960s. Thereafter, exports from non-oil-exporting LDCs have grown somewhat more rapidly than exports of developed countries, although the increased share of the oil exporters in world exports resulted in a significant diminution in the share of both in 1974. During the years 1974-78, LDCs increased their share of world exports relative both to developed countries and to oil-exporting developing countries.

The picture with respect to manufactures is similar. LDC exports of manufactures grew more slowly than world exports of manufactures until the late 1960s. Since that time, LDCs have increased their share continuously, with manufactured exports rising from $6 billion in 1967 to $32 billion in 1974 and $56 billion in 1977.[2]

Thus for the period 1960-75 as a whole, world exports of manufactures at constant prices are estimated to have grown at an average annual rate of 8.9 percent.[3] For industrialized countries, the corresponding rate was 8.8 percent while, for LDCs, it was 12.3 percent. In terms of growth rates, therefore, the LDCs fared very well. However, because that growth was from a small base, the share of LDCs in world exports was still only 7 percent in 1974, compared to about 4 percent in the mid-1960s. This same phenomenon can be seen even more clearly when another statistic is examined: of the total increase in manufactured imports by

TABLE 9.2
World Exports, 1955 to 1977

	1955	1960	1967	1974	1977
Billions of dollars					
Industrial countries	61.6	88.1	153.7	556.1	743.5
Oil exporting countries	5.9	7.3	12.1	117.8	145.6
Other developing countries	17.2	19.2	26.8	98.1	134.6
Total	84.8	114.6	192.7	772.0	1023.7
Percent					
Industrial countries	72.6%	76.9%	79.7%	72.0%	72.6%
Oil exporting countries	6.9	6.4	6.3	15.3	14.2
Other developing countries	20.3	16.8	13.9	12.7	13.1

Source: International Monetary Fund, International Financial Statistics, May 1978.

Note: "Industrial countries" includes the IMF category of that name plus "Other Europe" and Australia, New Zealand and South Africa.
Columns may not sum to totals due to rounding errors.

industrialized countries, only 9 percent originated in LDCs. Interestingly enough, of the increase in industrialized countries' manufactured exports, 29 percent went to the developing countries.

At an aggregate level of total manufactured exports, therefore, the LDCs have not as yet reached a sufficient size to have a quantitatively significant impact upon the manufacturing sector of industrialized countries. Even if the manufactured exports of LDCs should continue to grow at the rapid 12.3 percent rate of the 1960-75 period while those of the industrialized countries were to continue to expand at 8.8 percent, the LDC share in world exports of manufactures would be only 9 percent in 1975 and would reach only 20 percent in 2013.[4]

Before turning to the composition of manufactured exports, one other aggregate phenomenon should be noted. Not only are the industrialized countries still dominant in manufactured exports, but the growth in the share of the LDCs has resulted predominantly from the export-promotion countries—a small subset of all developing countries. Thus,

OECD countries accounted for 80.5 percent of world exports of manufactures in 1963, 82.3 percent in 1973, and 82.8 percent in 1976. Seven developing countries—Brazil, Korea, Mexico, Singapore, Taiwan, Yugoslavia, and the Crown Colony of Hong Kong—accounted for 2.5 percent of world exports of manufactures in 1963, 6.4 percent in 1973, and 7.2 percent in 1976.[5] The same general pattern holds if one examines the share of different countries and regions in manufacturing production: the same countries increased their share of manufacturing production from 4.1 percent in 1963 to 6.8 percent by 1976.[6]

Exports by Individual Sectors

It seems clear, simply because of the small share, that LDC manufactured exports have not yet become sufficiently large in the aggregate to affect the size of the manufacturing sector as a whole in industrialized countries. Indeed, exports of manufactures from developed to developing countries far exceed those from developing to developed countries. Without North-South trade, the aggregate size of the manufacturing sector in OECD countries would certainly be smaller than it in fact is. Indeed, as will be discussed in the next section, a major source of stimulus to the further growth of manufacturing industry in the OECD countries will originate in the demand generated by the LDCs if their growth is sustained.

Insofar as there is any issue of structural adjustment resulting from manufactured exports from LDCs, it arises in individual industries within manufacturing, and not in the overall volume of LDC exports, at least for the foreseeable future. Table 9.3 provides some data on the composition of manufactured exports, and the LDC share in specific sectors. The commodity groups listed are those for which the LDC share was largest in 1977. As can be seen, only in three groupings—leather, footwear, and travel goods; wood and cork manufactures; and clothing—did the LDC share of imports to OECD countries exceed 25 percent. Those three commodity groups accounted for about 8.5 percent of OECD imports of manufactured goods in 1977. Of course, the LDC share of manufactured exports to the OECD rose in each commodity grouping, as is to be expected on a small base with rapid growth. Nonetheless, the LDC share of OECD markets was less than 10 percent for chemicals, paper, metal manufactures, rubber products, nonelectrical machinery, and transport equipment. Of the "sophisticated" manufacturing industries, only for electrical machinery was the LDC share of OECD markets in excess of 10 percent.

It thus seems clear that the effects of rapid growth of LDC exports on OECD countries must have been felt, to the extent they were, in the

TABLE 9.3
OECD Imports, by Commodity Groups and Origin, 1963 and 1977 (Percentages)

Commodity Group and SITC Number	Seven Exporting LDCs	Other non-OECD LDCs	Industrial OECD Countries	Total OECD	Share of OECD Imports
Chemicals (5)					
1963	1.2 %	3.5 %	90.8 %	91.7 %	12.1 %
1977	1.4	4.1	91.2	92.3	12.9
Leather, Footwear and Travel Goods (61, 83 and 85)					
1963	4.9	7.6	81.4	83.7	2.2
1977	23.4	7.8	56.6	64.5	2.4
Rubber Manufactures (62)					
1963	.3	.7	97.6	97.8	1.1
1977	3.4	.7	90.0	94.2	1.3
Wood and Cork Manufactures (63)					
1963	6.1	8.7	74.0	80.2	1.4
1977	19.1	7.4	65.1	69.8	1.2
Paper (64)					
1963	.2	.3	98.4	98.5	4.5
1977	1.2	.1	96.5	97.5	2.9
Textiles (65)					
1963	3.3	11.4	80.5	82.9	8.9
1977	7.9	8.6	74.8	79.0	5.3
Nonmetallic Mineral Manufactures (66)					
1963	1.9	3.3	84.0	84.8	3.9
1977	3.4	7.0	73.4	74.9	3.3

TABLE 9.3 cont'd.
OECD Imports, by Commodity Groups and Origin, 1963 and 1977 (Percentages)

Commodity Group and SITC Number	Seven Exporting LDCs	Other non-OECD LDCs	Industrial OECD Countries	Total OECD	Share of OECD Imports
Iron and Steel (67)					
1963	.8%	.8%	91.7%	92.2%	9.3%
1977	2.4	1.7	87.9	90.3	6.4
Metal Manufactures (69)					
1963	1.0	.4	97.3	97.8	3.7
1977	5.4	.9	89.9	91.9	3.4
Nonelectrical Machinery (71)					
1963	.1	.3	98.5	98.7	20.1
1977	1.8	.4	95.3	96.3	16.6
Electrical Machinery (72)					
1963	.6	.5	98.0	98.2	8.3
1977	11.0	2.0	84.8	85.8	10.3
Transport Equipment (73)					
1963	.5	.8	97.5	98.0	12.2
1977	1.1	.4	95.8	97.5	18.2
Miscellaneous Finished Manufactures (81, 82, 86, 89)					
1963	3.5	.8	92.8	93.5	9.0
1977	9.9	1.4	84.3	85.6	10.2
Clothing (84)					
1963	16.1	3.0	77.3	78.5	3.3
1977	34.0	8.2	46.8	51.9	4.9

Source: Organization for Economic Co-operation and Development.

industries where the share of imports from LDCs was large enough to affect the overall size of the market. Since, within each category there are some noncompeting items and some degree of nonsubstitutability for some subcategories of those groups, a 10 percent level of imports is probably the lowest at which structural changes can conceivably have been effected. By that criterion, leather and footwear, wood and cork manufactures, electrical machinery, and clothing are the sectors in which there could have been significant effects from LDC imports. Those sectors are, by and large, usually labor-intensive, and so the question arises as to the degree to which it was the process of domestic economic growth which led to structural difficulties, and the extent to which imports affected output and employment for the OECD countries.

To examine that question, it is necessary to analyze the data for individual countries, and to reconcile domestic production statistics with available trade data. That is a time-consuming and laborious process, as production and employment statistics by industrial sector must be reconciled with trade data on a commodity basis. Although efforts to examine the question have been made for a number of OECD countries and sectors,[7] it will suffice for present purposes to examine the data for the United States.

Effect of LDC Manufactured Exports on U.S. Output and Employment[8]

As already indicated, primary concern with structural changes arises from the belief that workers may be displaced and unemployed as a consequence. For that reason, focus is usually upon employment changes and their origins. As mentioned before, the rate of growth of output is a function of the rate of growth of domestic demand and the rate of price change within individual industries. Although much discussion has centered upon imports from LDCs, their importance remains sufficiently small to make it difficult to provide any quantitative estimates of their impact. For that reason, it seems to make sense instead to focus here upon the orders of magnitude of the total effects of all imports and all merchandise trade for the United States.

To estimate demand and cost equations for individual industries is extremely difficult and time-consuming, although such an undertaking would be required if one were to attempt to estimate the extent to which output and employment were casually affected by the foreign trade sector.[9] A simpler procedure provides an estimate of the orders of magnitude involved. One can decompose the observed increase in domestic consumption into the component satisfied by domestic output increases, and that met by imports. The growth of output is then a function of those two variables plus the growth of exports. The rate of growth of employment is then equal to the rate of growth of output less the rate of growth of labor productivity, and one can partition, in a definitional accounting sense, changes in employment in particular industries into components—exports, imports, domestic demand, and labor productivity. These estimates of the "contribution" of each component are not estimates of causality—more rapid growth of labor productivity may be associated with more or less import competition, and more rapid growth of domestic consumption will generally occur when prices are declining, as may be the case in industries where imports are increasing rapidly. Nonetheless, the exercise is a useful first step in providing an indication of the orders of magnitude of the effect of imports on output and employment. Appendix A provides a derivation of these relationships.

Table 9.4 provides data on U.S. output, employment, exports, and imports for two-digit SIC manufacturing industries in 1970 and 1976.[10] Appendix B gives details of the sources of these data. Choice of 1970 as an initial year was dictated by several factors. First, most observers have claimed that the effect of imports has been felt in recent years, and use of an earlier starting year would have resulted in smaller estimates of the effect of imports (since the estimated growth rate of imports would be lower over a longer period). Use of the year 1970 as an initial year thus provides a virtual upper-bound estimate of the effects of imports. Secondly, the 1970 data are free of the difficulties that surround 1971 estimates, where dollar devaluation in midyear affects the price series being used. Third, there is a fairly comparable set of estimates for the period from 1963 to 1971 provided by Charles Frank.[11] Using 1976 as a terminal year was necessary because 1977 data were not available at the time the empirical work was undertaken (summer 1978).

As can be seen from the data in Table 9.4, there were only five two-digit industries for which imports exceeded 10 percent of domestic output in 1976. They were leather products (24.2 percent), apparel (11.4 percent), transportation equipment (11.3 percent), miscellaneous manufacturing (15.8 percent), and electrical and electronic equipment (11.4 percent). Even in those sectors, exports were often a significant offset to imports: exports almost equalled imports in electrical and electronic equipment and exceeded imports in transportation equipment.

Table 9.5 provides the decomposition of employment changes into its various components. As can be seen, the magnitude of imports, even in this extreme form where exports are not taken into account, was

TABLE 9.4
Production, Trade, and Employment, U.S. SIC 2-Digit Industries 1970 and 1976

SIC CODE	Industry Name	1970				1976			
		Output (millions of 1970 dollars)	Exports	Imports	Employment (thousands)	Output (millions of 1970 dollars)	Exports	Imports	Employment (thousands)
20	Food Products	103,631	2,520	3,562	1,574	111,892	3,826	4,019	1,536
21	Tobacco Products	5,528	191	17	67	5,965	364	36	65
22	Textile Mill Products	24,030	461	1,059	907	23,869	954	924	876
23	Apparel	25,025	251	1,287	1,319	28,328	642	3,228	1,271
24	Lumber Products	14,931	687	989	530	13,774	953	1,076	629
25	Furniture and Fixtures	9,754	48	217	436	10,465	152	388	426
26	Paper and Paper Products	25,458	1,106	1,548	632	28,753	1,508	1,985	615
28	Chemicals	51,873	3,997	1,256	849	57,094	5,389	2,075	851
29	Petroleum and Coal Products	26,935	575	1,560	141	30,830	478	2,639	145
30	Rubber and Plastic Products	17,044	341	661	544	21,106	901	1,222	627
31	Leather Products	5,218	64	702	274	4,597	145	1,114	247
32	Stone, Clay and Glass Products	18,535	445	542	583	18,612	638	673	599
33	Primary Metals	53,067	2,323	3,915	1,169	52,633	1,748	4,683	1,106

TABLE 9.4 cont'd.
Production, Trade, and Employment, U.S. SIC 2-Digit Industries 1970 and 1976

SIC CODE	Industry Name	1970				1976			
		Output (millions of 1970 dollars)	Exports	Imports	Employment (thousands)	Output (millions of 1970 dollars)	Exports	Imports	Employment (thousands)
34	Fabricated Metal Products	42,026	1,361	799	1,279	47,844	2,522	1,364	1,471
35	Nonelectrical Machinery	55,560	7,880	1,999	1,744	64,502	12,855	3,620	1,960
36	Electrical and Electronic Equipment	49,168	2,971	2,716	1,659	53,142	5,876	6,056	1,579
37	Transportation Equipment	89,920	6,486	6,362	1,621	97,799	12,497	11,027	1,668
38	Instruments	12,276	1,294	659	382	18,905	3,008	1,692	518
39	Miscellaneous Manufacturing	10,122	485	1,196	411	11,469	993	1,810	410
	TOTAL MANUFACTURING	644,083	33,486	31,046	16,119	681,083	55,927	50,098	16,599

Source: Department of Commerce Bureau of the U.S. Census, U.S. Commodity Exports and Imports as Related to Output 1970 and 1969 and 1975.
Annual Survey of Manufacturers, 1970 and 1976.
Output and trade data for 1976 were deflated by the Department of Commerce 2-digit SIC deflators contained in Wholesale Prices and Price Indices Data for January 1977. Data for January 1971, and December 1976 figures were used.

TABLE 9.5
Contribution of Demand, Imports, and Labor Productivity to Rate of
Employment Change 1970 to 1976 (continuous percentage rates)

SIC CODE	Industry Name	Demand Growth	Labor Productivity	Imports	Employment
20	Food Products	1.30%	-1.68%	- .02%	- .41%
21	Tobacco Products	1.32	-1.78	- .05	- .51
22	Textile Mill Products	-0.20	-0.47	.09	- .58
23	Apparel	3.03	-2.68	- .96	- .62
24	Lumber Products	-1.16	4.20	- .18	2.85
25	Furniture & Fixtures	1.41	-1.56	- .24	- .39
26	Paper & Paper Products	2.16	-2.48	- .13	- .45
28	Chemicals	1.80	-1.56	- .20	.04
29	Petroleum & Coal Products	2.68	-1.78	- .43	.47
30	Rubber & Plastic Products	3.87	-1.20	- .30	2.37
31	Leather Products	- .60	.38	-1.51	-1.73
32	Stone, Clay & Glass Products	.18	.38	- .11	.45
33	Primary Metals	.01	- .79	- .23	- .92
34	Fabricated Metal Products	2.32	.17	- .16	2.33
35	Nonelectric Machinery	2.81	- .54	- .32	1.95
36	Electrical & Electronic Equipment	2.20	-2.12	- .90	- .82
37	Transportation Equipment	2.04	- .92	- .64	.48
38	Instruments	7.75	-2.12	- .56	5.08
39	Miscellaneous Manufacturing	2.66	-2.12	- .58	- .04

Source: Same as Table 4.

generally fairly small relative to either labor productivity growth or domestic demand growth. Only in leather products was import growth quantitatively greater than labor productivity growth. As analysis of the growth process suggests, variations in rates of demand growth and labor productivity growth exceeded import growth rates in accounting for rates of growth of output and employment.[12] When the same calculations are repeated, using the net trade balance rather than simply imports to estimate the effect on sectoral employment, the size of the trade variable appears even smaller.

The conclusion can be illustrated by calculating the rate of growth of employment that would have occurred had demand and labor productivity both increased as they in fact did, while import growth or the behavior of the net trade balance was such that the domestic share of output was the same in 1976 as it was in 1970. The results of these calculations are reported in Table 9.6. The effect of holding the import, or net trade balance, share constant is reported in columns (2) and (3) of the table. As can be seen, apparel, electrical and electronic equipment,

TABLE 9.6
Hypothetical Changes in Employment if Import or Trade Balance Share
had Remained Constant

SIC CODE	Industry Name	Actual Rate of Employment Change (1)	Rate if Import Share Constant (2)	Rate if Trade Balance Share Constant (3)	Number of Jobs Implied by: (2) (4)	(3) (5)
		(continuous percentage rates)			(thousands)	
20	Food Products	-.41%	-.39%	-.28%	.3	2.0
21	Tobacco Products	-.51	-.46	-.13	.2	1.5
22	Textile Mill Products	-.58	-.67	-.97	-.1	-.7
23	Apparel	-.62	.34	.15	78.2	62.4
24	Lumber Products	2.85	3.03	3.04	5.8	6.1
25	Furniture & Fixtures	-.39	-.15	-.48	6.3	-2.4
26	Paper & Paper Products	-.45	-.32	-.44	4.9	.4
28	Chemicals	.04	.24	.12	10.2	4.1
29	Petroleum & Coal Products	.47	.90	-.08	3.7	-4.7
30	Rubber & Plastic Products	2.37	2.67	2.43	9.9	1.9
31	Leather Products	-1.73	-.22	-.46	26.0	21.7
32	Stone, Clay & Glass Products	.45	.56	.50	3.8	1.7
33	Primary Metals	-.92	-.69	-.50	16.2	29.8
34	Fabricated Metal Products	2.33	2.49	2.51	12.4	13.9
35	Nonelectric Machinery	1.95	2.27	2.50	33.8	58.5
36	Electrical & Electronic Equipment	-.82	.08	-.68	92.0	14.0
37	Transportation Equipment	.48	1.12	.71	63.4	22.5
38	Instruments	5.08	5.64	5.36	13.0	6.5
39	Miscellaneous Manufacturing	-.04	.54	-.05	14.5	- .2

Source: Calculated as described in the text.

and miscellaneous manufacturing are the only sectors which would hypothetically have reversed declining employment had the import share of output not risen. In addition, the rate of decline of leather products employment would be—in the same hypothetical sense—substantially diminished.

When attention turns to translating these hypothetical alterations in growth rates to an absolute number of jobs, the numbers are once again relatively small. Only in apparel (6.1 percent), leather (10.5 percent), and electrical and electronic equipment (5.8 percent) is the number greater than 5 percent of 1976 employment, and in most other sectors the percentage implied is less than 1 percent. Even in those three sectors, exports were sufficient to offset part of the impact of an increased import share. When it is recalled that some of the domestic consumption increase would not have occurred had prices been higher, the conclusion once again is reinforced: import competition may have intensified adjustment difficulties and the pace of structural change, but those difficulties would have been present even in the absence of that competition. Of course, this conclusion would be even further strengthened if the calculations were performed separately for imports from LDCs.

It can be argued that these results are a function of the fact that even two-digit disaggregation may fail to reveal the impact of imports on particular specialized industries. In textiles, for example, the net effect of imports appears to have been positive over the 1970-76 period as the synthetics' share of consumption (in which American firms appear to be more competitive and for which exports are significant) more than offset the increased imports of natural fibers.

An offsetting factor, of course, is that the greater the degree of disaggregation, the higher are the substitution elasticities in consumption between commodities likely to be, and the more consumption patterns would probably have shifted in the absence of increased imports. Nonetheless, it appears worthwhile to use the same procedures for subsectors of the two-digit industries which most observers believe to have been adversely affected by import competition. The results are presented in Table 9.7. There, for textiles, apparel, leather products, and electrical and electronic equipment, data are given for all subsectors at a four-digit level for which comparable estimates of output, employment, imports, and prices could be obtained. As is to be expected, there are considerably wider swings in all variables because of the finer level of disaggregation. Nonetheless, the pattern that emerges is not significantly different from that found at the two-digit level: generally speaking, the industries which suffered the most rapid changes in employment were those where demand growth, labor productivity, and the trade sector all combined to work in the same direction. The most rapid rate of decline of any subsector was electronic receiving tubes: there, demand growth (minus 12 percent), labor productivity growth (minus 7 percent), and import growth (minus 1.3 percent) all combined to result in a continuous rate of decline in employment of more than 20 percent.

It is also noteworthy that employment and output trends varied significantly within individual two-digit industries, as well as between them. This accords once again with the general expectations set out at the beginning: that in the process of economic growth there will be individuals adversely affected, both because of changes in demand, technology, capital, and real wages, and because of regional differences

TABLE 9.7
Four-Digit Industry Results (continuous percentage rates)

SIC CODE	Industry Name	Demand Growth	Labor Productivity	Imports	Employment
2211	Cotton Weaving Mills	6.48%	-10.18%	- .56%	- 4.26%
2221	Synthetic Weaving Mills	1.90	- .25	.10	1.74
2231	Wool Weaving Mills	-10.18	- 2.10	.22	-12.07
2252	Hosiery Mills, n.e.c.	2.74	- 5.87	.57	- 2.57
2272	Tufted Carpets & Rugs	6.29	- 5.90	.02	.40
2281	Yarn Mills	3.86	- 1.74	.03	2.15
2283	Wool Mills	-16.73	1.32	- .51	-15.93
2297	Combing Plants	21.54	-12.28	7.59	16.86
2298	Cordage & Twine	5.35	.06	-1.20	4.19
2311	Mens' & Boys' Suits & Coats	-.85	- 1.73	-1.21	- 3.79
2321	Mens' & Boys' Shirts	5.06	- 2.55	-2.38	.15
2327	Mens' & Boys' Pants	.35	- 2.76	.65	- 1.76
2328	Mens' & Boys' Work Clothing	6.32	- 1.47	-1.45	3.41
2341	Womens' & Childrens Underwear	.23	- 3.05	- .03	- 2.84
2342	Corsets & Allied Garments	-.30	- 7.20	-1.33	- 8.84
2369	Childrens' Outerwear	8.30	- 5.08	-4.37	- 1.15
2386	Leather & Sheepskin Clothing	9.03	1.49	-6.81	3.72
2392	House Furnishings	.69	- 2.01	- .12	- 1.45
3131	Footwear Cut Stock	-10.28	2.99	- .81	- 8.09
3161	Luggage	7.94	- 5.32	-1.65	.95
3171	Womens' Handbags	7.76	- 4.39	-1.89	1.52
3172	Personal Leather Goods n.e.c.	2.26	- 4.95	-1.03	- 3.72
3612	Transformers	-1.38	- 2.24	- .19	- 3.80
3621	Motors & Generators	-1.01	- .34	- .86	- 2.23
3623	Welding Apparatus	2.65	- .23	- .19	2.23
3624	Carbon Products	-1.08	.73	.35	.00
3632	Household Refrigerators	-2.80	- 3.03	- .26	- 6.09
3633	Household Laundry Equipment	.80	- 4.13	- .02	- 3.34
3634	Housewares & Fans	5.82	- 5.83	.02	.01
3635	Vacuum Cleaners	6.82	- 5.26	.07	1.59
3636	Sewing Machines	1.51	1.98	1.31	4.79
3639	Household Appliances n.e.c.	7.51	- 5.72	-2.86	- 1.07
3641	Lamps	.20	- 2.32	- .21	- 2.73
3643	Current Carrying Wiring Devices	1.51	- .30	-1.22	.00
3644	Non-current Carrying Wiring Devices	-2.11	.15	.02	- 1.96
3651	Radio & TV Sets	9.18	- 9.70	-3.20	- 3.72
3652	Phonographs	10.51	-11.21	- .19	- .90
3671	Electronic Receiving Tubes	-12.12	- 7.45	-1.32	-20.88
3684	Semi-conductors	19.85	-15.60	-1.82	2.43
3691	Storage Batteries	5.83	- 4.29	- .02	1.51
3692	Primary Batteries	4.29	- 2.26	- .28	1.76
3693	X-ray Apparatus	15.26	- 1.10	- .66	13.52

Source: Calculated as described in the text.

in the impact of growth and change. While imports may intensify (or offset) these dislocations for some parties, it is extremely difficult to pinpoint any sector or subsector as being one where imports have caused major structural changes which otherwise would have been entirely avoided. To date, in any event, the dislocations generated by imports into the United States do not appear to have been an identifiably major source of structural change. When focus is upon LDC exports alone, there can be little question that the effects must have been confined to relatively small subsectors, with the possible exceptions of the apparel and footwear industries. Even there, imports from other industrialized countries and domestic demand conditions were probably more important in bringing about the adjustment difficulties that have occurred.[13] The question, of course, remains as to whether that will continue to be the case in the future.

Potential LDC Exports

Attempting to forecast the likely course of future LDC exports is exceptionally hazardous, and cannot be undertaken at all without considering and forecasting other economic events, including the rate of growth of OECD countries and the extent to which the new protectionism affects both developed country demands and policies within LDCs.

The analysis and data presented above all suggest that, to date, exports of manufactures from LDCs cannot have had as pronounced an effect on the structure of production and employment in OECD countries as protectionist advocates would have us believe. The question remains, however, as to whether that will continue to be the case in the future, especially as countries attempt to emulate the success stories of Japan, Korea, Taiwan, Brazil, and the other early exporters.

Despite the difficulties inherent in forecasting, there are some broad considerations that serve to indicate the probable range of manufactured export expansion from the LDCs, abstracting of course from the restrictionist policies undertaken by developed countries, and also their likely impact on OECD countries' comparative advantage. First, and perhaps the consideration about which most can be said, is the set of issues pertaining to the future export levels of the countries which have already established themselves as exporters. The second consideration is the probable future rate of growth of the OECD countries. Finally, there is the question as to the likelihood of emergence of other exporting developing countries, and their effects on the structure of world trade and comparative advantage.

Shifting Comparative Advantage within the Exporting LDCs

Although Japan is by now a developed country, it is often forgotten that her per capita income was extremely low after World War II, and that the early period of Japanese export expansion was one during which Japanese comparative advantage lay in the production of textiles, apparel, and other labor-intensive commodities. Indeed, early protectionist cries were focussed upon Japanese exports, as the rapid growth of the Japanese economy accelerated and exports increased rapidly. As Japanese per capita income and wages rose, Japan's comparative advantage began shifting away from the labor-intensive goods toward commodities, such as steel and metal products, which utilized considerably more capital per man than did the early exports. Still later, the Japanese have moved into still more human-capital-using industries, and are facing many of the same structural adjustments as are other OECD countries.

During this process, the Japanese have naturally (and necessarily for the continuation of their rapid growth) lost much of their comparative advantage in such low value-adding lines as textiles, apparel, footwear, and steel. Indeed, a sizeable proportion of the expansion of textile exports from LDCs was offset by reduced exports from Japan. It is often alleged that the reason quotas on textiles were "effective" is that the Japanese significantly (and with anticipation, if not deliberately) underfilled their quotas, permitting countries such as Korea and Taiwan and the Crown Colony of Hong Kong to overfill their quotas. Japan is now facing the same difficulties in other unskilled-labor and capital-using industries such as shipbuilding and steel and many of those pressures would be present even without competition from the developing countries.

This same sort of internal adjustment is beginning to take place in Korea, Taiwan, and other successful exporting countries, and will inevitably be repeated whenever an exporter is successful: the mark of success is a rising real wage, capital accumulation, the development of a more highly skilled labor force, and thus a shift in comparative advantage away from the industries in which exports are initially most profitable.

As Japan's comparative advantage continues to shift,[14] she will undoubtedly become a market for the exports of the new exporting countries. And, at a later date, Korea, Brazil, and the other countries whose skill levels and capital per worker have risen will also find their domestic industries less and less economic, thereby providing still further markets.

Thus, to the extent that Japan, Korea, Brazil, Taiwan, and other countries shift their comparative advantage, they are increasing the size of the market for any new exporters of those commodities both by adding their own demand and by reducing their exports.[15] From the perspective of the United States, manufactured imports in the 1950s and early 1960s were originating both from Europe and Japan and the export-promotion LDCs. By the 1970s, Europe and Japan had themselves become markets which could absorb some of the manufactures of other countries that attempt export-promotion strategies. Simultaneously the world market need not expand as fast as it did historically to provide for the same rate of growth of exports for newly-exporting low-wage LDCs simply because part of their exports can replace the exports of the countries whose comparative advantage has shifted away from the labor-intensive industries.[16]

It seems evident, therefore, that the adjustments in the economies of the already successful exporters will enable a more rapid rate of growth of exports of labor-intensive commodities in the future with no more impetus to structural change in the OECD countries than there has been in the past. How much more rapid growth can be will depend, of course, on the extent to which OECD markets remain open to imports and the degree to which the successful exporters are willing to open up their internal markets, although if they only reduce their level of exports the effect will be there. There is already evidence that Korea is planning to shift her resources more and more away from the extremely labor-intensive industries and into such areas as shipbuilding, automobiles, metal products, and chemicals. Taiwan has already shifted to a considerable degree, and there is every reason to believe that successful growth and rapidly rising real wages will force continuing adjustments.

The second factor is the rate of growth of the OECD countries. To the extent that growth rates for those countries remain similar to their levels of the past decade and a half, there is little basis for believing that the pressures of structural adjustment will be any more severe than they have been in the past. As already mentioned, sustained economic growth will require shifting resources in exactly the same direction as do imports of unskilled-labor-intensive commodities. The problem would be more severe, however, if the growth rate of OECD countries slowed significantly. For, when growth slows down, any shifts in the labor force and in the composition of output are effected with increased difficulty, as profitable alternatives to existing activities become harder to find.

Finally, there is the question of the probable orders of magnitude involved in the emergence of other export-promotion strategies in the still poor countries. Here, a distinction must be made between relatively slow-growth countries whose living standards and wage levels are already in the medium income range—such as the oil-exporting countries of the Middle East, Venezuela, and Argentina—and the low-wage countries such as India and Indonesia. While the former group may well adopt policies which induce rapid growth of manufactured exports, their wage levels will preclude them from specializing in the very labor-intensive commodities where adjustment problems are most severe. Indeed, if the oil-exporting countries and other resource-rich regions with high wage levels move toward export promotion policies, their skill levels combined with their ability to acquire a fair amount of capital equipment per worker will probably imply that they are competing with the middle-income countries, producing the same sorts of labor- and capital-using goods as the Japanese did in the late 1960s and the Koreans are producing currently.

While this development could intensify the adjustment difficulties of such industries as shipbuilding and steel, it is more likely that the comparative advantage of those countries would lie in industries using their abundant raw materials—as petrochemicals in the case of Middle East countries and products produced with animal materials, for example, in Argentina and Uruguay. A still further consideration along this line is that the resource-rich developing countries are by and large not heavily populated, and, relative to the size of the international market, it is unlikely that their exports would either be sufficiently alike or large enough in volume to result in observable dislocations in the OECD countries.

Any potential for increased pressures on the OECD countries would therefore originate, if at all, in the low-wage, heavily populous countries, primarily China and South and Southeast Asia. That Southeast Asia will embark upon the export-promotion strategy seems fairly clear, although it is likely to be less intensive than the Far Eastern pattern due in part to the much better endowment of Southeast Asian countries with natural resources than the Far Eastern countries. Moreover, the Southeast Asian countries, even including Indonesia, probably could not together generate an efficient growth of exports of labor-intensive commodities equal to the rate realized in the 1960s for any period of time; except for Indonesia, it would not be long before rising real wages began choking off comparative advantage. Indonesia's low base and the large size of her internal market both suggest that it would be difficult to achieve even the rate of growth Korea did, much less that of the Far Eastern exporters combined. Many of the same considerations apply to China and India: their large sizes are somewhat misleading in terms of export potential, both because transport distances to external markets are so great and because the large size of the country indicates that an efficient pattern of trade would never absorb as large a fraction of GNP as it does in Japan and Korea (whose natural resources are far inferior).

However, even if all of those countries did embark upon export-promotion strategies simultaneously, it should be observed that they would surely increase their imports at least as rapidly as their exports. Whereas Japan's increased imports were both manufactured goods and raw materials, it seems evident that China and South and Southeast Asia would import manufactured goods almost exclusively. The rate of shift in the composition of OECD countries' industries would undoubtedly be faster with such a pattern than without it. However, to the extent that the markets of the new exporters provided a stimulus to growth in the OECD countries, their own rates of growth of manufacturing output could increase, thereby easing the adjustment process relative to what it was in the case where growth originated almost entirely from the internal market and was slow overall.

Conclusions and Policy Issues

Structural change is an inevitable and necessary part of the process of economic growth. Despite widespread beliefs that imports are in large measure responsible for the difficulties encountered in some sectors and regions, the evidence suggests that the role of imports is, at most, to accelerate the process of structural change which will occur in any event.

The emergence of the rapid-growth LDCs relying upon exports has led to a new set of concerns about the effect of imports on the industrial structure of developed countries. In fact, there are sound reasons for believing that imports from the labor-abundant, low-wage LDCs would consist of commodities similar to those produced by industries most prone to losing their shares of output and employment independently of the international market. To the extent that imports from LDCs enable more rapid growth of demand for the expanding industries, they provide a benefit to consumers by enabling them to maintain higher consumption levels of labor-intensive commodities, and simultaneously provide a market for the commodities toward which the OECD countries' comparative advantage is shifting.

Despite the widespread belief that much structural change has been generated in the OECD countries by imports from the LDC export promotion countries, examination of the data does not confirm this. Indeed, there is every reason to believe that the general pattern of change in the composition of output and employment would have been much the same in the absence of the rapid growth of imports. At most they have intensified the difficulties encountered by the industries disadvantaged in the process of economic growth.

Consideration of future prospects suggests that the impact of exports from LDCs probably will not be significantly greater than it has been in the past unless OECD growth rates decline. Assuming continued growth in those countries (which could itself be augmented by the spur of increased demand for imports from the successfully exporting LDCs), the fact that the previous exporters are partially shifting out of labor-intensive industries as their comparative advantage shifts provides a buffer for exports from other labor-abundant countries that shift toward an export promotion policy.

These conclusions enable evaluation and assessment of the major policy concerns arising from the increased manufactured imports from LDCs. First and foremost, the pressure for increased protection from LDC imports is greatly overstated, simply because many of the pressures result from internal, rather than external, causes. To the extent that there are individuals and groups disadvantaged by the process of growth and structural change, there is an excellent case for policy measures to ease the adjustment process. But it is not obvious that the policies for smoothing adjustment should be different for industries where the primary sources are internal than for those where imports appear to have penetrated the market to a greater extent. In this regard, it should be noted that, for the manufacturing sector as a whole, it is likely that increased trade with LDCs will take place primarily in manufactures. For this reason, any policies which serve to reduce trade between developed and developing countries will most likely result in a smaller overall size of the manufacturing sector than would be realized without protectionist measures.

A second conclusion is equally obvious, although, like the first, it is not confined to imports. That is the fact that the process of structural change (and adapting to increased import demands) will be considerably easier against the background of a higher growth rate of real output within the OECD countries. Relocating displaced workers is a vastly simpler task in the context of growing employment and output than it is in the context of stagnation. Ironically, it may well prove that trade with the developing countries, and expansion of capital goods exports to them, could provide one of the main stimuli to that growth. If protectionist measures resulted in lower growth rates for the developing countries and forced them to rely upon their internal productive facilities for capital goods and other manufactures, the net result could well be increased difficulty in adjustment.

Finally, questions are often raised as to the extent to which intra-LDC trade can take pressures off the structural adjustment process in the developed countries. For reasons outlined in the first section of this paper, such an alternative does not promise great hope. To be sure, there are regional opportunities for trade between LDCs, just as there are many opportunities for interregional trade among European countries. But the chief opportunities for export in the international division of labor necessarily lie in trade between developed and developing countries, simply because differences in comparative advantage are greater.

APPENDIX A:
Employment-Output-Import Relationships

One can write the identity

$$C_{it} \equiv Q_{it} - X_{it} + M_{it}$$

where C_{it} is domestic consumption of the *ith* good in period t, Q is domestic output, X is exports, and M is imports. Consumption refers to all uses of a particular commodity, whether for final utilization, for investment, or for inventory accumulation. All variables are in physical terms, or, equivalently, in constant prices. At any time t, labor has an average productivity a_{it}, which is defined as

$$a_{it} \equiv Q_{it}/L_{it}$$

where L_{it} is employment in the *i*th industry or sector at time t.

We now wish to decompose the growth of employment into its component parts. To do so, define s_t as the ratio of output to domestic consumption ($s_t \equiv Q_t/C_t$), and assume that the domestic share of domestic consumption, s, labor productivity, a, and consumption, C, all grow at constant continuous rates:

$$s_t = s_o e^{\alpha t}$$

$$a_t = a_o e^{\rho t}$$

$$C_t = C_o e^{\beta t}$$

Combining relations, employment L_t can be expressed as

$$L_t = a_t^{-1} s_t C_t = a_o^{-1} e^{-\rho t} s_o e^{\alpha t} C_o e^{\beta t}$$

$$= E_o \, e^{(\alpha + \beta - \rho) t}$$

The rate of growth of employment is thus, definitionally, the sum of three components, the rate of growth of domestic consumption, the rate of growth of the domestic share of output in consumption, and the rate of growth of labor productivity. Any of these three components can be positive or negative. The larger is ρ, the lower will be the rate of growth of employment for any given rate of growth of demand and imports. The smaller are α and β, the lower will be the rate of growth of output and employment. A negative sign for α indicates that the fraction of domestic consumption satisfied by domestic production declined, and α can be interpreted, definitionally, as the additional (continuous positive or negative) growth rate of employment that would have been experienced had the share of domestic output in domestic consumption remained constant, i.e., had imports risen only at the rate of growth of domestic consumption.[17]

It should be noted that the continuous formulation is necessary in order to yield these identities: if annual rates of growth are employed, there are sizeable interaction terms among the variables and the sum of growth rates no longer is identically equal to the rate of growth of employment.

Because continuous rates need to be employed, there are several possible interpretations of the s variable. On one hand, if one wishes to examine the impact of imports on employment, domestic consumption is defined as domestic production plus imports. If it is recognized that export demand is related to import demand, the appropriate procedure is to compute domestic consumption as domestic production plus imports less exports. Neither of these procedures imputes causality, both because employment is a function of real wages and because one would have to specify the underlying model of industry demand and output in order to make those interpretations.

In the text, continuous growth rates are taken to be the rates defined by using 1970 as the initial year and 1976 as the terminal year. An alternative procedure would have been to gather yearly data on the variables and to compute a regression estimate of the time trend of the variables. The empirical difficulties of reconciling the trade data with production and employment data precluded the use of the latter procedure. For some purposes, the regression estimate might be considerably superior, as for example, when there were large year-to-year fluctuations in the variables. For purposes of this paper, however, it is not believed that use of the alternative procedure would have altered the results significantly.

APPENDIX B:
Sources of Data

The major difficulties encountered in linking production, employment, and trade data result from the fact that domestic output is reported in terms of the Standard Industrial Classification (on a sectoral basis) while trade data are reported on a commodity basis. Neither of these sets of data conform to the same classification system as most price indices, and yet a set of price deflators must be used if estimates of labor productivity are to be meaningfully made.

Fortunately, the Department of Commerce has in recent years provided some estimates of trade data and industrial output on a common basis, and their data were used for trade and output estimates, from *U.S. Commodity Exports and Imports as Related to Output, 1970-1969* and *1976-1975*. These data are on the same basis as the *Annual Survey of Manufactures,* from which employment data were taken. For two-digit industries, Department of Commerce estimates of price deflators were used. The significant difficulty arose when it was attempted to obtain price deflators to disaggregate to a four-digit basis. For a few subsectors, Department of Commerce estimates of price deflators were available. For others, a pairing was made with a component of the wholesale price index, and the exact matching is available upon request. For some industries, however, it was deemed impossible to obtain a reliable price deflator. When results are reported for four-digit SIC industries in the text, those results cover all four-digit subsectors of the pertinent two-digit industries for which trade data and price deflators were available.

Notes

1. See Anne Krueger, *Foreign Trade Regimes and Economic Develop-*

ment: Liberalization Attempts and Consequences (Cambridge: Ballinger Press for the National Bureau of Economic Research, 1978), chaps. 11 and 12, for a discussion of these issues.

2. Data are from *Prospects for Developing Countries 1978-85* (Washington, D.C.: World Bank, November 1977). Estimates for 1977 are provisional. Classification as to what is manufactured varies from one source to another, and there does not appear to be any universally agreed upon set of numbers. For a different set of estimates, see United Nations Conference on Trade and Development, *Handbook of Trade and Development Statistics 1977*, Supplement (New York: United Nations, 1977).

3. This estimate, and the data used in this paragraph, are taken from *World Development Report 1978* (Washington, D.C.: World Bank, August 1978), p. 9.

4. If these growth rates were sustained for that period of time, it would imply an increase in the rate of growth of world trade (as the more rapidly growing sector was increasing its share) in manufactures; it would also imply that the LDC imports of manufactures from developed countries were growing very rapidly.

5. Eastern bloc trade has also declined—from 13.4 percent in 1963 to 9.7 percent in 1976, as reported by the General Agreement on Tariffs and Trade.

6. The shift in the Japanese–U.S. shares was quantitatively greater than the combined shift from the seven developing countries. The Japanese share of world manufacturing production rose from 5.5 percent in 1963 to 9.1 percent in 1977, while the U.S. share fell from 40.2 percnt in 1963 to 36.9 percent in 1977.

7. See, among others, V. Cable, "British Protectionism and LDC Imports," *Overseas Development Institute Review*, no. 2 (1977).

8. This section draws upon Anne O. Krueger, "Impact of LDC Exports on Employment in American Industry," the International Economics Study Group Conference (Sussex, September 1978).

9. Even that approach would not be entirely satisfactory, for at least two reasons: (1) demand is a function of real income, which is affected by trade flows and other variables; and (2) if imports were altered, exports would be also, and that too would affect employment and output.

10. Printing and publishing (SIC 27) is omitted throughout because of the absence of an appropriate price deflator.

11. Charles R. Frank, Jr., *Foreign Trade and Domestic Aid* (Washington, D.C.: Brookings Institution, 1977), chap. 3. Frank took 207 five-digit SIC industries for which imports exceeded 3 percent of domestic output or $10 million for any year between 1963 and 1969. He used annual, and not continuous, growth rates, estimating labor productivity as a residual. Although his estimates are therefore not comparable in several regards, his conclusions as to the relative importance of imports contrasted with productivity growth are similar to those suggested by the data presented here.

12. In a simple regression of the rate of growth of employment on the sum of domestic variables, the coefficient was 0.88 and the R^2 in excess of 0.9.

13. It is an interesting question, but one well beyond the scope of this paper, whether the import competition in the apparel industry was not greater because of attempts to contain textile imports: to the extent that textile prices became

higher to American producers because of protectionist measures, American apparel producers were undoubtedly at a comparative disadvantage relative to foreign producers with access to cheaper inputs.

14. The extreme rapidity of Japanese development has meant that machinery and equipment have been relatively new even in the labor-intensive industries. It is probable that the rate of decline of those industries will increase sharply as machinery replacement is uneconomic.

15. For an elaboration of the "stages" of comparative advantage, see Bela Balassa, "A Stages Approach to Comparative Advantages," mimeo, 1977. See also Anne O. Krueger, "Growth Distortions and Trade" (Princeton: International Finance Section, Princeton University Press, 1977).

16. This set of very important considerations points up the urgency of maintaining access to markets in all industrialized countries. If some adopt strong protectionist measures, the pressure for those measures will be greater in others.

17. This does not imply that slower growth would have resulted in offsetting faster domestic output growth; domestic consumption would also have changed.

Commentary

Emilio Pagoulatos

Professor Anne O. Krueger has provided us with an excellent paper on manufacturing production in the LDCs and its effect on the comparative advantage of OECD countries. In my view, the major strength of this paper is that it introduces a much needed element of moderation in the debate on the role of import competition in bringing about the structural transformation of domestic industry, and on the relative importance of the "new" successful LDC exporters as a source of import supply into OECD countries. I am hard pressed to find points of disagreement, although there is always room for different interpretations of economic forces and events. I will, therefore, attempt to extend the analysis of a couple of points and in the process indicate some of the complexities of assessing the impact of foreign competition on domestic industry that may not have been fully reflected in the paper.

The paper begins with a very useful survey of the nature of structural transformation that accompanies the process of economic growth and the role of international trade on growth and structural change. Next, Professor Krueger presents a summary of available evidence on the impressive growth of manufactured goods exports by a small number of LDC countries in recent years. The data clearly show that there has been a very marked expansion in the value of manufactured exports from the LDCs over the last fifteen years. These exports are especially concentrated in a handful of countries (South Korea, Taiwan, Mexico, India, Brazil, Singapore, and the Crown Colony of Hong Kong) that have been following export oriented rather than import substituting policies. Despite this impressive growth of exports, imports of manufactured products from LDCs into OECD countries amounted to only 9 percent of imports from all sources in 1976.

Only a small number of industries (wood and leather products, textiles, footwear, and travel goods) are now under competitive pressure as a result of increased imports from LDCs. These products, as Professor Krueger points out, are the traditional labor-intensive LDC export goods. If present trends were to continue over the next decade, certain other industries are likely to come under increasing pressure from LDC exports that are not as easily characterized as labor-intensive. The likely candidates are such sectors as plastic materials, rubber manufactures, nonelectrical machinery, metal manufactures, scientific instruments, and photographic equipment. It is in these sectors that OECD imports from LDCs have been growing significantly faster than imports from industrialized countries.

Finally, Professor Krueger presents some estimates of the effects of total imports on U.S. manufacturing output and employment. I would have preferred an econometric model approach in order to isolate the role of domestic demand, labor productivity, and imports in affecting employment. Nonetheless, Professor Krueger's results do serve as a useful first approximation of the magnitude of these effects on employment and output. This evidence leads to the conclusion that domestic forces are significantly more important than import competition in influencing changes in output and employment in U.S. manufacturing industries.

I agree with Professor Krueger that increased trade does not appear to have had major adverse effects on the structure of OECD manufacturing industry with the exception of specific firms or industries (such as textiles). It is also clear that structural change and other difficulties faced by some firms, sectors, or regions are less the result of changes in trade patterns than such domestic factors as demand and technology changes. Indeed, evidence on the effects of trade liberalization on OECD industry suggests that trade has expanded according to intraindustry or two-way trade specialization. This type of specialization reflects the importance of product differentiation and scale economies as major factors influencing changes of trade patterns following tariff reductions. As a result, firms or sectors have faced fewer hardships and adjustment problems than might have been anticipated, since factors of production have been able to move to different products within the same industry rather than to an entirely different industry.

Commentary

Robert E. Baldwin

It is a pleasure to comment on Professor Krueger's paper. She starts out by presenting a superbly lucid account of the structural changes that accompany economic growth in industrial economies, and shows how the growth of manufacturing exports from developing countries fits into this broader picture of total growth. In particular, she emphasizes that manufacturing exports from these countries are likely to be concentrated in the very industries subject to considerable adjustment pressure by domestic growth in the developed countries. She then traces the phenomenal success of the developing countries in exporting manufactures and indicates how this has basically changed the views of economists toward the growth process and patterns of trade over time. The more rapid growth in exports of manufactures from the LDCs than DCs in recent years is particularly noteworthy and encouraging from a viewpoint of obtaining a more equitable distribution of world income, since for years the opposite has been true. Although the most important quantity gains in LDC exports have been in such labor-intensive sectors as footwear and clothing, as Table 9.3 shows there have also been very important percentage gains in such higher technology areas as machinery and transport equipment.

In order to put the employment effects of the increased imports of manufactures in the context of the entire development process, she divides observed changes in employment in particular U.S. industries into statistical components contributed by the change in output (which in turn can be divided into the change in consumption, minus the change in imports, plus a change in exports) and by the change in labor productivity. For a two-digit analysis of these components, imports are the most important factor only for leather products. In a four-digit breakdown, imports are not the most important factor in any sector. Labor productivity and demand growth are generally more significant. This is the main point of her analysis. She emphasizes that this analysis does not imply causal relationships. More rapid labor productivity growth may be associated with more or less import competition. In other words, one can think in terms of two-way causality between all of these variables.

Although this is a statistical exercise, it is difficult not to draw some kind of causal conclusions. For example, after making her statement about noncausality, she nonetheless says that such exercises are a useful first step in providing an indication of the order of magnitude of the effect of imports on output and employment. That is not quite inferring causality, but it comes close.

When it is pointed out to businessmen that in such analyses labor productivity changes usually dominate employment changes related to imports, they sometimes respond by claiming that increased imports have forced them to introduce more modern equipment to increase productivity. Thus, they argue, part of the employment effect from productivity changes should be attributable to import changes. The problem with this argument is that they must admit the existence of some monopolistic elements in the industry prior to the import increase, or else they would have introduced the new equipment anyway.

It would be interesting to know if there is actually any relationship between changes in imports and changes in productivity. One might find that in industries where imports rise most rapidly, productivity actually declines since innovative talent leaves and capitalists begin to shift their funds to other fields. When one looks at the analysis in this way, one is almost tempted to conclude that low productivity growth is good because it does not displace labor. In other words, the crude mercantilistic Keynesian bias of this approach becomes evident. There is no need to pay any attention to macro or micro adjustment mechanisms, even though we are discussing a fairly long period, since it is simply an accounting breakdown of the components of employment changes. If we really leave out all theory, perhaps we should not even hint at a conclusion about the effect of imports on employment. However, if we do wish to move towards some conclusions, should we not make the theory explicit and begin to test it in the complex way that is required? Why not set up an explicit model and try to make some statements about causality among the variables? Make a few of them autonomous, but then build some theory about the effects of imports on productivity or consumption. We could then make an interdependent model and start testing it econometrically. Of course Professor Krueger recognizes this, and although her approach is very worthwhile, I would hope that her very interesting results encourage her to carry on to more complicated, interdependent analysis at which she is an expert.

Finally, let me comment on her point concerning the future prospects for adjustment pressures stemming from LDCs. She points out very properly that, as the more developed countries like Japan and Korea shift out of labor-intensive products, this will produce more LDC exports, but not necessarily greater imports into countries like the United States since part of them will be going to places like Japan and Korea. Thus, perhaps some of the older industrial countries will not have more adjustment pressure in these labor-intensive products. However, some of the LDCs are planning to move into many more high technology items; Japan has already done so. Thus, we may have more adjustment problems, perhaps not in labor-intensive commodities but in some of the high technology products.

The future that I see is one in which world trade in industrial products consists largely of complex intraindustry trade. But it is going to take a long time to reach this point. In the process there is going to be more and more pressure on some of our high technology industries. Unfortunately from a political point of view, as these industries, which are now somewhat supportive of exports and more liberal trade policies, come under competitive pressure, they will line up with traditionally protectionist industries who have long been under pressure.

10
International Competition, Industrial Structure, and Economic Policy

J. Fred Weston

Alternative approaches may be taken to analyze international competition. The most general is an explanation of the determinants of the commodity structure of trade.[1] Traditional Heckscher-Ohlin theory holds that exports from a country will employ relatively more intensively the country's relatively abundant factors of production. In 1953 Leontief presented evidence that a lower capital-labor ratio was found in U.S. exports as compared with import-competing goods despite the presumed relative abundance of capital goods. A number of explanations have been offered for the apparent paradox, but subsequent research has been consistent with the relatively lower capital-labor ratio in U.S. export goods. This literature is valuable and represents a line of inquiry that provides valuable inputs for a study of industrial structure change.

Another approach is an analysis of international trade performance related to a number of explanatory variables. The general procedure is to calculate a measure of international trade balances by industry, then seek to explain differential performance of individual industries by variables such as cost trends, price trends, productivity change, growth rates in domestic and foreign markets, technological change, and relative factor intensities. Such studies also provide useful inputs.

In the present paper, the interaction of international competition and domestic industry structures is assessed. First, the rationale for the topics treated will be given. Second, some estimates of the impact of international dimensions of markets on measures of U.S. industry structure will be made. Third, case studies of individual industries will be presented as pilot studies of factors to be considered in assessing the dimensions of international competition.

The Dominant Structure-Performance-Conduct Paradigm[2]

The structural theory of industrial organization holds that when a

255

small number of firms account for most of an industry's sales they will recognize their interdependence resulting in collusion on price and output decisions. Because of the dominance of structural theory in both academic literature and U.S. public policy it is important to consider measures of industry structure that recognize the international scope of markets.

The structural approach emerged as a result of the failure of more analytically sound methodologies to yield generalizable results about industry competitiveness. The structural approach has focused on four main hypothesized relationships:

1. Concentration and profits should be positively related.
2. Advertising to achieve product differentiation and make entry difficult should be positively related to concentration.
3. Concentrated industries should be a source of inflation.
4. Concentration and innovation should be negatively related.

Concentration-Profit Studies

The structural theory holds that high concentration facilitates collusion which in turn results in higher profits for the industry. Hence a positive association between concentration and profits could be argued to be evidence consistent with the theory that concentration leads to some form of shared monopoly. The basic reference study was published by Professor J. S. Bain in 1951 utilizing data for the period 1926-40.[3]

Subsequent studies are divided into those that investigate the simple relationship between concentration and profits and others which study the influence on profits of a number of variables in addition to concentration. Most of the studies of the simple relationship show a positive correlation which is only marginally significant from a statistical standpoint.[4] Furthermore, concentration seldom explains more than 10 percent of the variation of profitability across industries.

Generally, the relationship between concentration and profits is to be even weaker in the second group of studies. For example, Comanor and Wilson found that the influence of concentration on industry profitability was smaller than the influence of four other variables: growth of demand, capital requirements, economies of scale, and advertising per firm.[5] When Comanor and Wilson combined these variables in a multiple regression equation seeking to explain variations in profit rates across industries, the influence of concentration was no longer statistically significant. When a number of factors were taken into consideration, Ornstein found that profit rates were statistically related to economies of scale in production and to the growth rates of both the industries and firms.[6] However, the net relation between concentration and profit was not significant. He concluded that there is no support in theory or fact for the positive concentration-profit nexus upon which the structural theory is based.

Collusion or shared monopoly in concentrated industries, if it exists, should produce high profit rates for the smaller firms which are not parties to the cartel, and can thrive under the umbrella provided by the large firms. The facts, however, are the reverse of the shared monopoly theory.

Professor Demsetz finds that the largest firms have higher profit rates than the smaller firms in both unconcentrated and concentrated industries.[7] Since the large and small firms charge the same prices, the higher profits of the larger firms must result from their lower costs, possibly due to economies of scale, greater efficiency, fortuitous circumstances, or the cumulative effects of a capable management organization developed over a period of years.

The many studies using the price-cost margin data provided by the Bureau of the Census do show a positive relationship between concentration and profits. However, this measure suffers from serious defects since no account is taken of advertising, R&D, capital costs, central office and administrative expenses, and other fixed costs. Thus industries with high advertising or R&D or those which are highly capital intensive would have margins biased upward. Strong evidence of the biases in the use of the price-cost margin is provided in a study by Professor Ornstein.[8] The price-cost margin without corrections should not be employed by serious students of industrial organization. To the extent that the structural theory rests upon the concentration-profit connection, it remains far from established by systematic economic evidence.

Product Differentiation and Advertising as Barriers to Entry

High profits in an industry would stimulate entry which would erode profit differentials. Hence the structural theory needs barriers to entry to explain the persistence of high profits wherever they may be found. The greatest emphasis has been placed on product differentiation and advertising as barriers to entry. Other barriers to entry that have been identified include capital barriers, scale economies, absolute cost advantages, and legal barriers. It is argued that product differentiation enables firms to lower short-run demand elasticity for their individual products, thus increasing monopoly power.

Empirical studies of the influence of product differentiation from advertising have centered on the relationship between advertising and concentration, and advertising and profitability.[9] There appears to be a positive relationship between advertising and profitability that does not disappear when other variables are introduced into a multiple regression analysis. However, the question of causality remains. Empirically, the influence of profitability on advertising is greater than the influence of advertising on profitability. Some studies suggest that product superiority fosters increased advertising as a method of profit maximization.

Concentration and Innovation[10]

Two sharply divergent views are found on the relation between concentration and innovation. One view holds that whenever a significant innovation is traced back to its ultimate beginning the originator is found to be one or two individuals or a small firm. It is further argued that a monopolist does not have the economic pressure to innovate because he is content to exploit the existing markets already under control.

An alternative view is that large size and concentration are necessary prerequisites for conducting successful innovation because research and development activity requires that huge outlays must be placed at substantial risk. Since research and development outlays are uncertain, a large number of projects are necessary to have enough successes to make the activity financially possible and justifiable. Further, modern research requires large fixed expenditures. Economies of scale are so substantial that only large firms can finance the substantial fixed outlays required to initiate research and development activity. Also, the uncertainty of R&D efforts requires that the firm have a large number of product areas to which a broad underlying technological base is related. The wider the range of products the firm possesses the more likely it is to develop new products that will fit into its production or marketing activities.

An overview of the data indicates that most R&D outlays take place in the largest firms and in the most concentrated industries. National Science Foundation surveys consistently show that the 400 to 500 largest companies having 5,000 or more employees account for nearly 90 percent of private R&D expenditures. This sample of companies accounts for only 25 to 30 percent of total employment or total sales.

Five industry groups alone have consistently accounted for nearly three-fourths of all privately financed R&D. These are chemical and allied products, electrical equipment and communication, motor vehicles and transportation equipment, machinery, and aircraft and missiles. These data suggest that the bulk of R&D expenditures do in fact take place in large firms in concentrated industries.

Regression studies of R&D expenditures in relation to the level of industry concentration have yielded mixed results.[11] Generally, a positive association between R&D intensity and industrial concentration exists, but it is weak. Some have argued that when the four-firm concentration ratio exceeds some threshold level such as 50 percent or 55 percent, the ratio of R&D effort to sales may level off or even decline. Regressions of R&D expenditures to company size yield a similar result. The ratio increases up to a critical level of firm size, varying with the industry. Beyond that point the ratio of R&D expenditures to sales by firm may actually decline.

Empirical studies of innovation and concentration do not permit a conclusion that strongly supports either of the two alternative hypotheses stated at the start of the discussion.

Concentration and Inflation

The persistence of worldwide inflation since 1966 has made inflation a major antitrust issue in the United States. Legislative proposals in the antitrust area have included reference to the need to restructure industries to succeed in the fight against inflation.

But at the theoretical level there is no valid basis for a relationship between concentration and inflation. The most general position of economists on the relation between concentration and inflation has been set forth clearly by George Stigler. He stated, "The traditional economic theory argues that oligopoly and monopoly prices have no special relevance to inflation."[12] The general price level is determined by the interaction of aggregate demand and aggregate supply, modified by pervasive influences such as the grain sales and oil embargo. While there is disagreement on the relative importance of monetary policy versus fiscal policy, there is less disagreement with the proposition that the two together have the major responsibility for movements in general price levels.

For a test of the proposition that inflation problems cannot be solved until the structure of the economy is changed, consider the period 1959-65 in contrast to the period 1965-76. During the period 1959-65 the wholesale price index increased by less than 0.5 percent per annum. In the ensuing period it increased at a rate of over 8 percent per annum. Industrial concentration and unionism showed no significant change between the two periods. Therefore, industrial structure is not likely to be the explanation for rising inflation.

A number of studies have been made on the relation between industrial concentration and price change. They show that the degree of price change is lower the higher the degree of concentration. The superior price performance of concentrated industries results from the underlying technological and economic factors that produce concentration.[13] Concentrated industries have substantially higher capital intensity ratios than unconcentrated industries. Higher capital intensity of the concentrated industries is associated with a higher rate of labor productivity increase. The superior performance of concentrated industries in price changes is not unique to the United States. Similar studies of concentration and price change for Western European countries have obtained similar results.[14]

To summarize to this point, none of the four major hypotheses of the structuralist theory receive strong support in the empirical literature. Inefficiencies and abuses due to monopolistic powers may exist, but there is no simple relationship based on structure (concentration). Indeed if concentration results from a number of elements of efficient production (capital intensity, economies of scale, etc.), then the preconceptions of the structuralist theory can lead to a dismemberment of just those firms that represent the leading edge of economic growth. A closer look at certain overlooked characteristics of concentration in specific markets will clarify this argument.

Concentration in Individual Markets

Concentration in individual industries is generally measured by the share of production of some specified number of firms in relation to a measure of overall activity in individual industries. The most frequently used measure is the market share of the largest four firms. The assumption here is that if four firms account for a high percentage of the industry's activity, they will have considerable influence and market power over all of the other firms in the industry no matter how many there may be. Over a long period of years since the end of World War II, the average level of four-firm concentration for all manufacturing industries in the United States fluctuated within a narrow range at somewhat under 40 percent.

Industrial concentration is not a phenomenon unique to the United States but characteristic of all developed nations of the world. Indeed, studies of international comparisons of concentration have established that concentration is high in the same industries in all of the developed countries.[15] Table 10.1 presents data for concentration ratios in the United States compared with four other industrialized nations. The industries listed are major industries in terms of their economic importance due either to the total volume of investment or employment

TABLE 10.1
Concentration in Five Industrial Nations

	United States	West Germany	Japan	United Kingdom	France
Agricultural Equipment	38%	91%	-	. 40%	-
Aircraft	47	-	-	47	62%
Aluminum	100	71	100%	43	100
Electrical Products	57	65	-	-	-
Flat Glass	90	55	100	51	-
Motor Vehicles	99	92	76	98	79
Paper & Paper Goods	19	-	30	-	14
Petroleum Refining	32	75	41	93	72
Pharmaceutical Products	-	-	55	24	-
Soap	-	47	32	-	-
Steel Ingots	64	83	52	32	40
Tractors	73	94	-	-	76

Sources: West Germany, Economic Concentration, Concentration Outside the United States, Hearings before the Subcommittee on Antitrust and Monopoly, Ninetieth Congress, Second Session, Part 7A, Annex to Statement of M. Jacques Houssiaux, pp. 3971-3977.

Others from J. S. Bain, International Differences in Industrial Structure (New Haven: Yale University Press, 1966).

The data are generally for the mid-1950s or early 1960s.

The concentration ratios are for four firms for the U.S. and West Germany, but for the top three firms for the other countries.

that takes place in those industries.

While the pattern of this small sample of industries is illustrative in establishing relatively high concentration ratios for most countries, more comprehensive statistical analysis has been performed. The study by F. L. Pryor concludes as follows:

The data show that the average four-firm, four-digit concentration ratios among large industrial nations are roughly the same; and also that concentration in these nations is less than among smaller nations.

Underlying the results is a previously determined empirical relationship showing that average enterprise size (both for manufacturing as a
whole and for individual industries) and total market size appear to be
highly correlated. And this correlation appears to be the result of the fact
that establishment size and the degree to which industries are characterized
by multi-establishment enterprises are correlated with GNP.[16]

We have observed that capital intensity is greater for concentrated
than for less concentrated industries in all of the industrialized nations
of the world. This is a universal phenomenon, not one peculiar to the
U.S. economy. Other pieces of evidence corroborate the proposition that
concentration is the result of underlying economic and technological
factors rather than managerial motives.

International Competition

The previous sections have set forth the structural theory of industrial
organization and some empirical tests of its predictions. The evidence at
a minimum raises serious doubts that the structural theory provides a
sound basis for a public policy that seeks to restructure concentrated
industries. Indeed one can argue that concentration is consistent with
competitive behavior and performance.[17] Now the implications of
international competition for public policy toward domestic industry
structures will be considered. First, the impact of international markets
on concentration measures will be considered. Second, the nature of
international competition in some major industries will be analyzed in a
series of case studies.

Impact of International Competition
on Concentration Measures

Measures of concentration in domestic markets must be adjusted
when international competition is taken into account. Accordingly,
estimates of the influence of international competition on U.S. four-
firm concentration ratios were made.[18] To apply an initial screening
rule, we calculated the sum of the import and export shares in an
industry's domestic production plus imports. For those industries
whose imports plus export shares in new supply was 4 percent or more
we sought to determine the size of the world market.[19] In order to match
international and U.S. industry classifications as closely as possible,
sometimes it was necessary to combine two or three international
industries or two or three domestic industries to obtain one matching
U.S.–international industry. For a final sample of seventy-five matching
industries, we were then able to develop the data in Table 10.2.

TABLE 10.2
U.S. Four-Digit Concentration Ratios Adjusted for International Markets, 1963

Standard Industrial Classification (SIC)	Industry Name	Percent Imports and Exports Combined	Percent U.S. to Total Production	U.S. CR4[a]	Adjusted CR4
2011	Meat packing plants	6%	19.7%	31%	6%
2022	Cheese, natural and processed	3	19.6	44	9
2031	Canned and cured seafoods	23	10.3	38	4
2041	Flour	9	11.4	41	5
2045	"				
2061	Sugar	23	8.4	61	5
2062	"				
2063	"				
2111	Cigarettes	4	25.6	80	20
2283	Wool yarn mills	5	13.2	26	3
2611	Pulp mills	57	39.1	48	19
2815	Cyclic intermediates and crudes	14	29.3	53	16
2821	Plastics materials and resins	10	38.5	35	13
2822	Synthetic rubber	19	62.3	57	36
2871	Fertilizers	7	40.0	34	14
2911	Petroleum refining	8	39.6	34	13
3011	Tires and inner tubes	5	49.0	70	34
3031	Reclaimed rubber	5	74.4	93	69
3141	Shoes, except rubber	3	47.5	25	12
3312	Blast furnaces and steel mills	7	37.4	48	18
3313	Electrometalurgical products	7	30.5	79	24
3316	Cold finishing of steel shapes	7	44.8	36	16

TABLE 10.2 cont'd

Standard Industrial Classification (SIC)	Industry Name	Percent Imports and Exports Combined	Percent U.S. to Total Production	U.S. CR4	Adjusted CR4
3331	Primary copper	28	27.8	78	22
3332	Primary lead	14	15.1	95	14
3333	Primary zinc	12	26.5	57	15
3334	Primary aluminum	15	49.5	95	47
3421	Cutlery	9	44.0	66	29
{3443 3511	Steam engines and turbines, and boiler shops	12	35.9	44	16
3481	Miscellaneous fabricated wire products	4	69.2	13	9
3519	Internal combustion engines, not elsewhere classified	16	50.9	49	25
3522	Farm machinery	19	48.6	43	21
3531	Construction machinery	33	62.8	42	26
{3532 3533	Mining and oil field machinery "	27	57.7	29	17
3534	Elevators and moving stairways	2	44.6	62	28
3535	Conveyors and conveying equipment	10	54.9	28	15
3536	Hoists, cranes, and monorails	8	17.7	35	6
3537	Industrial trucks and tractors	10	64.2	54	35
3541	Machine tools: metal cutting	20	36.9	20	7
3542	Machine tools: metal forming	23	48.4	22	11
3551	Food products machinery	22	46.0	22	10
3552	Textile machinery	29	31.8	35	11
3553	Woodworking machinery	15	32.7	35	11

Code	Industry				
3554	Paper industries machinery	25	41.4	41	17
3555	Printing trades machinery	23	51.3	44	23
3561	Pumps and compressors	14	57.4	26	15
3562	Ball and roller bearings	9	51.8	57	30
3567	Industrial furnaces and ovens	10	41.7	28	12
3572	Typewriters	20	69.3	76	53
3573	Electronic computing equipment	18 %	88.5 %	n.a.	--
3574	Calculating and accounting machines	18	56.4	n.a.	--
3581	Automatic merchandising machines	6	84.0	55 %	46 %
3582	Commercial laundry equipment	20	62.0	47	29
3585	Refrigeration machinery	9	64.4	25	16
{3611, 3622	Electrical measuring instruments and industrial controls	10	51.5	44	23
3613	Switchgear and switchboard apparatus	6	54.7	51	28
3623	Welding apparatus	12	78.7	41	32
3632	Household refrigerators and freezers	5	46.2	74	34
3635	Household vacuum cleaners	4	53.2	81	43
3636	Sewing machines	63	19.1	81	15
{3641, 3642	Electric lamps and lighting fixtures	5	59.6	42	25
3651	Radio and TV receiving sets	11	41.7	41	17
3652	Phonograph records	7	41.9	69	29
{3671, 3672, 3673	Electron tubes and valves	8	63.0	76	48
3674	Semiconductors	12	78.3	46	36
3679	Electronic components, not elsewhere classified	7	74.0	13	10
3692	Primary batteries, dry and wet	7	54.2	89	48
3693	X-ray apparatus and tubes	29	41.5	67	28
3694	Engine electric equipment	9	57.7	69	40
{3711, 3714	Motor vehicles, parts and accessories	9	45.6	77	35

TABLE 10.2 cont'd

Standard Industrial Classification (SIC)	Industry Name	Percent Imports and Exports Combined	Percent U.S. to Total Production	U.S. CR4	Adjusted CR4
3721	Aircraft	14	85.5	59	50
3722	Aircraft engines and engine parts	11	74.7	57	43
3729	Aircraft propellers, parts, and equipment, not elsewhere classified	15	93.4	38	35
3731	Ship, boat building, and				
3732	repairing	3	37.1	43	16
3741	Locomotives and parts	11	64.6	97	63
3742	Railroad and street cars	11	67.5	53	36
3751	Motorcycles, bicycles, and parts	34	29.3	56	16
3831	Optical instruments and lenses	18	58.2	41	24
3841 3842 3843	Medical instruments and supplies " "	11	83.3	47	39
3861	Photographic equipment and supplies	13	52.4	63	33
3871	Watches, watchcases, and				
3872	clocks	16	16.6	47	8

Source: J.F. Weston, "Do Multinational Corporations Have Market Power to Overprice?," in The Case for the Multinational Corporation: Six Scholarly Views, ed. by Carl Madden. (New York: Praeger Publishers, 1977), pp. 24-26. Copyright © 1977 by the National Chamber Foundation. Reprinted by permission of Praeger Publishers, a sub-division of Holt, Rinehart and Winston.

a Four Firm Concentration Ratio.

Table 10.2 lists the seventy-five four-digit industries (approximately) from the U.S. Standard Industrial Classification (SIC). For each industry, column 1 presents the SIC number; column 2 presents the industry name; column 3 presents the percent imports and exports to an industry's new supply; column 4 shows the percent U.S. to total world production, which we calculated; and column 5 sets forth the U.S. four-firm concentration ratio. Column 4 is then multiplied by column 5 to obtain the U.S. four-firm concentration ratio adjusted for international markets, shown in column 6.

The impact of the adjustments in Table 10.2 are summarized in Table 10.3. The average concentration ratio for the seventy-five industries on an unadjusted basis is approximately 51 percent. When adjustments are made for international markets, the adjusted four-firm concentration ratios become 24 percent, representing a decline of over 50 percent.

We also analyzed the distribution of the seventy-five industries by concentration quartile on both the unadjusted and adjusted basis. On an unadjusted basis 40 percent of the industries had four-firm concentration ratios of over 50 percent. On an adjusted basis only 4 percent of the

TABLE 10.3
Effect of International Markets on U.S. Four-Firm Concentration Ratios

Concentration Ratio	Unadjusted		Adjusted	
Average Concentration Ratio for 75 Industries	50.9%		24.1%	
Distribution by Concentration Quartile	Number	Percent	Number	Percent
Over 75 percent	13	17.3%	0	.0%
51-75	20	26.7	3	4.0
26-50	35	46.7	27	36.0
Less than 26	7	9.3	45	60.0
Total	75	100.0%	75	100.0%

Source: Table 10.2

industries exhibited concentration ratios exceeding 50 percent. The remaining 96 percent of the industries had concentration ratios of less than 50 percent, with 60 percent having adjusted concentration ratios of 25 percent or lower.

These adjustments, however, are subject to an overstatement. Some production outside the United States is, of course, carried on by U.S. firms. Hence, the four firms in the U.S. four-firm concentration ratio would also account for a portion of production outside the United States.

A rough estimate of the upward adjustment in the adjusted four-firm concentration ratios may be made with the help of the *Fortune* directory of the 300 largest corporations outside the United States. In 1974, for the first time, *Fortune* listed separately the foreign subsidiaries of U.S. companies. The ratio of sales of the foreign subsidiaries of U.S. companies to the total sales of the largest 300 foreign firms was 7 percent. I have moved this percentage up to 10 percent as a generous estimate of the average proportion of foreign production accounted for by foreign subsidiaries of U.S. corporations. When this is done, the effects on the adjusted concentration ratios are shown in Table 10.4.

There is now one industry in the over 75 percent concentration ratio. There are six with a concentration ratio from 51-75 percent for a total of seven with concentration ratios over 50 percent. This would represent less than 10 percent of the seventy-five industries. More careful refinements will be made in the individual industry concentration ratios

TABLE 10.4
Frequency Distribution of 75 Industries after Adjustments for World Markets and Adjustments for U.S. foreign Subsidiaries

Concentration Ratio	Number	Percent
Over 75 percent	1	1.3%
51-75	6	8.0
26-50	29	38.7
Less than 26	39	52.0
Total	75	100.0%

Source: Table 10.2, adjusted as described in the text.

in the future. However, the evidence presented indicates that the U.S. four-firm concentration ratios greatly overstate the actual concentration ratios that take international markets into account. Thus, even if one takes a structural approach to an analysis of markets, the major industries have much lower concentration ratios than those generally attributed to them. Industries characterized by international competition have an average (unadjusted) U.S. four-firm concentration ratio of 50 percent, which is 25 percent higher than the average for all four-digit manufacturing industries. Thus the most concentrated industries are subject to international competition. If the theory that structure determines conduct and performance were valid, it would predict competitive behavior when international markets are taken into consideration. However, these broad statistical measures may miss dynamic economic processes taking place in individual industries. Therefore, some individual case studies will next be analyzed.

The Petroleum Industry

No discussion of international competition can ignore the role of oil in the current economic environment. U.S. oil imports continue to run over $40 billion per year. The issues are complex, with a long history of interaction between economic and military-diplomatic considerations. In the 1920s U.S. tax policies encouraged domestic production and the State Department stimulated and facilitated the participation of major U.S. oil companies in operations in the Middle East, a strategic area in which balance of power struggles between major powers have been taking place for centuries.

A major characteristic of the American petroleum industry is the pervasive participation of federal and state agencies in every phase of the business. Some generalizations can be developed from the proliferation of government intervention. In earlier years, the industry was aided by special tax provisions such as percentage depletion and write-offs of intangible drilling expenses. Major oil companies were aided in penetrating the dominant control of Middle East oil activities of the British and French after World War I. After World War II, U.S. government policy responded to the pressures of independent oil producers and refiners to maintain their market positions versus the major oil companies. This resulted in a long history of encouraging refining operations of less than efficient size. The oil import quotas between 1959 and 1973 protected domestic production, but were disadvantageous to the major oil firms with substantial foreign crude oil production.

Coming to the more recent period of the emergence of the energy shortage in the early 1970s, a substantial portion of responsibility is attributable to government price controls on natural gas and complex government regulations that developed imbalances in supply by individual oil product categories and by geographic areas in the United States. The "energy shortage" that emerged in the early 1970s helped make OPEC effective and led to the quadrupling of the price of oil.

The U.S. response has been a substantial substitution of administrative regulations and controls for the price system to allocate and distribute scarce and expensive resources. Policies to date have used prices to modify demand and some taxes to encourage conservation. The requirements for complying with complex laws, regulations, and rules, and a vast bureaucracy involves costs, both direct and indirect, of very substantial magnitudes. While any assessment is subject to some differences in judgment, the persistent weakness of the U.S. dollar in foreign exchange markets results at least in substantial degree from the widely recognized inadequacies of the U.S. response to the increased costs of energy. In addition, unsound policies in the energy field may produce unnecessarily rigid requirements in other industries, notably the automobile industry considered next.

The Automobile Industry

In 1977 imports of motor vehicles and parts totaled $18.8 billion, exports were $13.0 billion, yielding a deficit of $5.8 billion. An outstanding characteristic of the automobile industry is its global dimensions. This recognition was summarized effectively as follows: "A new internationalism is sweeping through the world's automobile industries. National differences in auto design and styling are being narrowed, fostering cross-border supply of components and a marked trend toward so-called 'world cars'—standardized autos designed to be built and sold in any major market with few changes."[20]

Although characterized by product differentiation, the world automobile industry is developing models to be sold in all markets of the world. At the same time parts and components will be sourced on a worldwide basis to achieve standardization and economies of scale. An important stimulus for the global strategy adopted by major automotive companies throughout the world is the trend in world automobile markets. The North American market including Canada and Mexico represented 43 percent of the $26.5 billion car sales in 1976. It is projected to decline to a little more than a third of the world market by 1990. While the growth in automobile sales in Europe is projected to be greater in absolute terms than in North America the share of Europe in the world market is also expected to decline somewhat. The combined share of

North America and Europe, which was over 77 percent of the world market in 1976, is projected to decline to 66.6 percent of the world market by 1990. Thus the more vigorous growth in the world automobile market will take place outside traditional markets, primarily in developing countries. The major automobile companies are developing strategies and plans for penetration of third world markets. Their success in these objectives will also influence their ability to compete in their own domestic markets against foreign competitors.

The strong implication of the foregoing is that a preoccupation with market shares of U.S. firms in the domestic market is not meaningful. Whatever concentration ratios are calculated will have to be divided by a factor of at least three in view of developing trends in the world automobile market. Even when production abroad by U.S. firms is taken into account, concentration ratios in the world automobile market demonstrate the artificiality and unreality of the structural approach to industrial organization. The relevant issues are the much more fundamental strategic developments that have been taking place.

Of great significance has been the sharp increase in the cost of fuel. This influence alone would have shifted more of the market in the United States toward smaller cars. However, fuel economy standards set by the federal government make a substantial volume of production and sale of small cars by U.S. firms mandatory. This is consistent with efforts toward the development of a global car. But one can argue that perhaps this would have occurred at a different and more competitively efficient pace if the market system had been used to a greater extent for oil and oil products. It has been estimated that expenditures by the American automobile industry to meet government standards by 1985 will be $80 billion. The outlays required are estimated to add costs of at least $1,000 per car on the average.[21]

Even without government-imposed standards, the development of global cars to compete in the world automobile market requires substantial capital outlays by automobile companies throughout the world. The nature of the response in other countries will differ somewhat from that in the United States because of the different structure of ownership and interaction in foreign countries. First, a substantial portion of the motor vehicles industry is owned by the government in other countries such as Britain, France, West Germany, Holland, Italy, and Mexico. Among the Western European governments which are either owners or substantial shareholders in major automobile companies are France in Renault, the United Kingdom in British Leyland, West Germany in Volkswagen, Italy in Alfa Romeo, and Spain in SEAT. Direct ownership is one form of government participation, financing below the market is another. Sometimes government financing is indirect and takes place through a complex set of relationships between the central bank and financial groups as in Japan. For example, in Japan in 1956 a major piece of legislation, the "extraordinary measures law for the rehabilitation of the machinery industry" enabled MITI to channel government funds to particular industries. With respect to automobile parts manufacturing, for example, a substantial program of borrowing took place between 1956 and 1966. Under the MITI-established criteria large firms were favored over small, specialized over diversified, with the aim of developing large specialized firms within a system of vertical affiliation with motor vehicle producers.

Another fundamental approach to increasing structural efficiency in foreign countries has been efforts at "rationalization." This rationalization includes mergers, elimination of duplication and product offerings, standardization of automobile parts and components, and coordinated marketing and distribution procedures. There are numerous instances of the merger aspect of rationalization. These include the union of British Motors and Leyland, Volkswagen's acquisition of Auto Union and NSU, and Fiat's acquisition of Autobianchi, Lancia, and Ferrari. A recent merger took place between Peugeot and Citröen. At the same time Citröen's truck division was sold to the French government-owned Renault. In the mid-60s in Japan, Nissan and Pryce merged. At the same time Toyota, Diahatsu, and Hino engaged in bilateral arrangements exchanging minority shares and eliminating overlapping production.

A substantial amount of coordination also takes place among foreign firms. Peugeot, Renault, and Volvo have collaborated in the development and production of a common V-6 engine. In 1975 Fiat joined Renault's truck subsidiary, Saviem, and Alfa Romeo in building a $250 million diesel engine plant in Foggia, Italy. A Dutch-based holding company, the Industrial Vehicles Corporation (IVECO), was created to coordinate the planning and operations of Fiat, OM, Lancia, UNIC, and Magirus-Deutz in the production of trucks. In contrast, in the United States in October 1969 a judgment was entered by the courts against General Motors, Ford, Chrysler, American Motors, and the Automobile Manufacturer's Association enjoining them from pooling technical information relating to emission control devices. The separate and duplicate efforts to deal with emission controls in the United States resulted in increased costs. This decreases the competitiveness of U.S. manufacturers in comparison with foreign manufacturers which have been encouraged by their governments to organize joint ventures for various purposes.

During the next five years in the world automotive market, financial factors are likely to be of significant influence on the relative competitiveness of manufacturers in the different countries. The requirements to achieve the federal government's fuel economy standards by 1985 require capital outlays of some $80 billion for American manufacturers. At the same time there are needs and opportunities for capital outlays in foreign locations if an effective strategy for penetrating the growing third-world automotive markets is to be implemented effectively. The domestic retooling required threatens the financial viability of both Chrysler and AMC. Chrysler has sold off its European production operations in the effort to help finance its development of a small car line in its U.S. operations. AMC has entered marketing and manufacturing agreements with Peugeot. The required foreign investments in addition to the costs of the substantial domestic retooling efforts pose substantial financial risks for both General Motors and Ford. It appears that General Motors will take these risks in foreign investments. However Ford, which was an early leader in standardizing and coordinating foreign automotive operations, has indicated that overhauling their car designs at home to meet fuel economy standards must have a priority call on its corporate resources.[22]

In contrast to the wide range of government encouragement and sponsorship found in foreign countries, the largest American automobile companies must allocate resources to defend themselves from a doctrinaire position that a high share of the U.S. automotive market raises an implication of anticompetitive behavior and shared monopoly. The assistant attorney general in charge of antitrust, Mr. Shenefield, has stated a number of times during 1977 and 1978 that greater efficiency may enable a company to be "entrenched" against loss of its market position to other firms, establishing a basis for antitrust action by the government. It has also been proposed that counteractions be taken against domestic firms which successfully penetrate foreign markets. "The primary connection between multinationalization and monopolization is simple: the technological and marketing advantages which allow a few firms to dominate the market also serve as a springboard for entering foreign markets."[23] On the basis of higher profitability of multinational groups as compared with domestic groups of industries the question is raised whether "foreign investment significantly increases the domestic monopoly power of multinational firms."[24] The comment is then made that American antitrust policy is deficient in that "its greatest failures have come in attacking market power inherent in economies of scale, technological know-how, and other basic elements of industry structure."[25]

A public policy remedy is proposed in the following terms:

> Every cloud has its silver lining, and this one is no exception. In trying to find an effective remedy for this type of monopoly power, antitrust authorities often look for natural ways to split dominant firms into self-sufficient entities, just as a jeweler looks for a natural way to split a diamond. In this search we would hope that antitrust authorities would not overlook the obvious opportunities to split the large and more sufficient foreign subsidiaries from their American parents. Although these subsidiaries are not current participants in U.S. product markets, they are often credible entrants. Is IBM Europe not a credible contender in the U.S. computer industry? Is General Motors, Canada not a potential entrant in the United States auto industry? In fairness to the American parent, we presume that it would be allowed to compete with its erstwhile affiliates in overseas markets, just as they would compete with their erstwhile parents in the domestic U.S. markets. In ordering the cross-licensing of critical patents and otherwise fashioning an effective remedy, the objective should always be to promote competition, not to emasculate one national firm or the other. Multinationals may thus derive competitive advantages over their domestic competition from their foreign operations, but those foreign operations may be a solution to, and not just a cause of, the problem of market power.[26]

In this same spirit it has been proposed that the foreign income of U.S. firms be taxed when earned rather than when remitted to the U.S. parent. The argument made is that U.S. international firms should be treated on the same basis as U.S. domestic firms. However, with reference to international competition, an alternative principle is that U.S. international firms be taxed on the same basis as the foreign-based international firms with which they compete throughout the world.

This brief overview of the world automobile industry suggests an important aspect of maintaining the international competitiveness of U.S. industry. U.S. auto firms do not appeal for special government sponsorship or aid to compete with the government assistance and subsidies provided in other countries. Rather the need is for an environment and policy in the United States less hostile in spirit and punitive in action. It would be helpful to have some assurance that efficiency and innovation that lead to improved products and cost competitiveness and thereby to improved market share and profitability, are not treated as a violation of U.S. antitrust laws under the structural theory of industrial organization.

The Heavy Electrical Equipment Industry

In the previous section on the automotive industry it was noted that government ownership is playing an increasingly important role. Government ownership is also a significant factor in influencing trade patterns in the heavy electrical equipment industry for reasons that will be developed.

Heavy electrical equipment is used primarily in the electricity industry. Every country has developed some degree of government control over its electricity supply system. Through government control and other influences the purchase of foreign equipment is highly restricted. The situation is summarized in Table 10.5, which shows that only in Canada and the United States is any extensive purchase of foreign equipment possible. The possibilities for the sale of foreign electrical equipment in other countries ranges from very limited to virtually impossible. The nature of the restrictions can be conveyed by brief summaries of patterns in individual countries.

The electricity supply industry in France was nationalized in 1946. The French national monopoly is a public enterprise, Electricité de France (EdF). In the effort to develop a strong French electrical equipment industry under the direction of the French government, EdF began to force mergers through its purchasing policy. In addition, French manufacturers receive loans for development of particular projects from a department under authority of the French prime minister.[27]

The British electrical supply industry was nationalized in 1948. It was reorganized under the Electricity Act of 1957, creating two administrative bodies, the General Electricity Generating Board (GEGB) and the Electricity Council (EC). The GEGB has encouraged mergers finally resulting in only two British producers of turbine-generators and power circuit breakers. In addition to GEGB policies which virtually exclude imports of heavy electrical equipment, bidding requirements create other barriers. British heavy electrical equipment manufacturers have benefited from technological research on generation and transmission conducted at the GEGB laboratories.[28]

While most electrical generation and distribution is privately owned in Japan, the barriers to imports of heavy electrical equipment are among the most formidable. "The Japanese maintain the most overt restrictions against imports of foreign heavy electrical equipment. The barriers include quota systems, import deposit schemes and licensing of domestic manufacturers as a prerequisite for selling in Japan."[29] Regulations set by MITI require import licenses in order to buy equipment from foreign firms. Cabinet Order No. 336 of September 1963 urges government agencies to show preference for domestic products

TABLE 10.5
National Electricity Supply Systems

Country	Number of Systems	Extent of Government Regulation	Purchases of Foreign Equipment
Austria	6	Government runs under one holding company	If domestic unavailable
Belgium	1	Nationalized system	If domestic unavailable
Canada	21	75% public ownership	Extensive
England & Wales	1	Nationalized system	None
France	1	Nationalized system	None
Italy	1	Nationalized system	None
Japan	10	One government owned	Prototypes only
Sweden	2	Over 50% of each, public ownership	Limited
Switzerland	28	Municipal control	None
United States	1,078	40% federal or municipal ownership	50% of market open
West Germany	12	70% government ownership (9 companies supply 75% power)	None

Source: Barbara Epstein, "Purchasing Policies in Industrial Nations," in Duncan Burn and Barbara Epstein, eds., Realities of Free Trade: Two Industry Studies (Toronto: University of Toronto Press, and London: George Allen & Unwin Ltd., 1972), Table 3, p. 9.

and asks private industry to do the same. In 1968 the Japanese government continued steam turbines on the list of 121 products Japan would not import except as prototypes. Even the imports of prototypes are subject to import deposit requirements, and standard methods of payments which exclude advance payments or progress payments generally common in the purchase of heavy electrical equipment and available to domestic Japanese producers. "These deposit and payment schemes could be important barriers if ever Japan lifts import embargoes."[30]

In the United States, because of the substantial number of individual private and public electrical utility companies, a common purchasing policy does not obtain. A survey demonstrated that companies accounting for 16 percent of installed steam generating capacity in 1968 indicated that they would not consider imports of transformers and circuit breakers. The procurement policies of the federally owned utilities are subject to provisions of the Buy American Acts. However, imports of power generation equipment in the United States have taken place. For example, in 1962 the Tennessee Valley Authority (TVA) took delivery of a 500 megawatt turbine-generator set produced by Parsons. When the set was tested in August 1965, it did not meet the efficiency rate guaranteed by Parsons. The poor operating experience of the Parsons set at TVA caused other prospective purchasers in the United States to become wary of foreign imports.

Steam turbine capacity in the EEC and EFTA countries in 1975 approximated 45,000 annual megawatts. Home demand was about 15,000 representing excess capacity of about 30,000 megawatts. The worldwide pattern is shown in Table 10.6.

Because of available capacity in each sector, competition for sales to developing countries is fierce. Western European countries, where excess capacity is greatest, developed very vigorous programs that combine development aid with commercial credit offered at low rates subsidized by the government. West Germany, Austria, France, Italy, and Japan have government programs to provide low-cost export credits. Among other things these export credit agencies provide funds for financing the difference between the market rate of interest and low rates for long-term export credits. American producers have not had comparable support from government financing programs. "The United States industry, although favoured with substantial tied-aid sales, has been hindered in bidding by lack of discretionary credit facilities. American manufacturers have no source of low-cost credit to use when they obtain export orders not tied to Aid or Export-Import Bank loans."[31]

TABLE 10.6
World Demand and Manufacturing Capacity for Steam Turbines
(Average annual megawatts, 1970s)

	EEC and EFTA	USA and Canada	Japan	Other Countries	Total
Home Demand	14,650	39,200	6,950	6,500	67,300
Capacity, 1975	44,600	44,000	10,000		98,600
Available Capacity	+29,950	+ 4,800	+ 3,050	(6,500)	+31,300

Source: Barbara Epstein, "Industry under Alternative Trade Conditions," in Duncan Burn and Barbara Epstein, eds., Realities of Free Trade: Two Industry Studies (Toronto: University of Toronto Press, and London: George Allen & Unwin Ltd., 1972), p. 98.

While numerous modifications were made in programs to provide exporters with financing, the main agencies in the United States have continued to be predominantly under private financing and on a self-supporting basis.[32] The U.S. government does not offer its producers subsidized export financing to match the programs of foreign governments for their manufacturers in aggressive sales efforts in developing countries.

The power equipment industry illustrates some important concepts with regard to the sources of cost of production differences. Economies of scale in manufacturing do not represent the critical source of differential efficiency. The major economies of scale are in product development. The nature of this influence is illustrated by British turbine development. Between 1959 and 1966 unit size was increased nine times, or more than one design change per year. Thus only a small fraction of research and development expenditures could be recovered by repeat orders. The rate of size progression was even faster in the United States. Thus to recover the cost of product development, the sales volume of a heavy electrical equipment company must be at least in the range of 10,000 to 20,000 megavolt-amperes per year.

While economies of scale do not exist in the traditional sense in heavy electrical equipment manufacturing, there are important size advantages in amortizing the costs of new product development. The economies of size are so substantial that world demand could most efficiently be supplied by a small number of firms. "Completely free trade could result in four to five large multi-product manufacturers operating worldwide."[33] The remaining firms might include transnational relationships. For example, Allis-Chalmers, a third manufacturer in the United States, ceased production of turbine generators in 1963 primarily because it could not afford the development work required "on 10 percent of the American market."[34] In 1970 Allis-Chalmers entered into a relationship with Kraftwerk-Union (KU) of West Germany which provided technology to Allis-Chalmers in the United States that would be required for marketing and servicing equipment manufactured by KU.

The U.S. market is relatively open to imports. Yet the potential for utilizing the efficiencies of size possessed by General Electric and Westinghouse in sales to the other developed countries is barred by the purchasing policies of electrical industries that are essentially government owned, or under tight government controls as in Japan. In the developing countries, competition is greatly affected by subsidized government export financing of foreign producers which may dominate price and performance characteristics on big ticket items such as electrical equipment. Thus the potentials for developing export surpluses in an industry where the United States has inherent structural advantages is offset by nontariff government exclusionary purchasing practices in countries that have producers and that provide subsidized export financing of sales in the developing countries. Generalized studies of price and productivity trends miss the significance of purchasing and financing practices that play a major role in this industry.

The Pharmaceutical Industry

Worldwide sales of the U.S. prescription pharmaceutical industry in 1978 are estimated at $16 billion.[35] The U.S. market represents about one-fourth of the world market.[36] A substantial body of literature has called attention to "the fact that innovation in the pharmaceutical industry has undergone some rather fundamental structural changes over recent years."[37]

One significant development is the decline in the annual number of new product introductions. One measure is the number of new chemical entities introduced each year. New chemical entities (NCEs) are the most important category of new products because they represent the most significant new therapeutic developments. The total number of new chemical entities introduced has declined very sharply. While average annual sales per NCE increased, the sales of NCEs as a percent of total ethical drug sales dropped from 20 percent during 1957-61 to slightly over 5 percent in 1967-71.[38] Another characterization of the trend has been made in the following terms: "The rate of innovation reached a maximum in the last half of the 1950s when the annual average of basic new agents reached almost 40. The rate was approximately halved during the 1961-65 period in comparison to the previous period. The rate further declined by almost half again, in the 1966-70 period, reaching a low of 12.[39]

A number of international comparisons have been made. In comparing the number of new products introduced during the period 1968-72 which reached sales of $1 million per year Clymer found that the number was twenty-six for the United States and forty-four for the United Kingdom.[40]

Grabowski comments on the "much lower absolute rates of introductions in the United States than abroad over the entire period. This is consistent with the notion that drug regulation, while increasing both here and abroad since the early 1960s has remained *relatively* more stringent in the United States."[41] One factor in the relative decline in the introduction of new drugs in the United States, particularly after the Drug Act of 1962, has been the increased cost of drug development. Before the Drug Act of 1962 the cost of bringing an NCE to market was under $1 million. By 1968 Clymer estimated that the cost had risen to $10.5 million.[42] More recent studies by Ronald Hansen, taking the time value of money into account, arrive at an estimate of $54 million.[43]

As a consequence of the increased costs of bringing a new drug to the market and the decline in the rate of drug innovation, various estimates of benefits and costs of the 1962 drug amendments have been made. One assessment quantifies the consequences in the following terms:

> Treated as a group, consumers seem clearly to have lost on balance from the amendments. Their annual gains and losses break down as follows:
> 1. missed benefits (consumer surplus) from the reduced flow of new drugs, producing a loss of $300-400 million;
> 2. reduced waste on purchases of ineffective new drugs, producing a gain of under $100 million; and
> 3. higher prices for existing drugs because of reduced competition from new drugs, producing a loss of $50 million.
> These measurable effects add up to a net loss of $250 to $350 million, or about 6 percent of total drug sales.[44]

However, the cost to American consumers has been only one narrow aspect of the consequences of slowing the rate of drug innovation. Other significant structural changes affecting the competitive position of the U.S. pharmaceutical industry have taken place. For example, Grabowski et al. observed that the ratio of foreign research and development to total research and development of U.S. pharmaceutical companies rose from 5 percent in 1961 to 15.4 percent in 1974. The more stringent regulation in the United States has caused a shift from domestic research and development in pharmaceuticals to foreign research and development.

Regulatory differences have not only caused R&D efforts to shift abroad but have appeared to cause a shift in investments in manufacturing plant capacity abroad as well. After commenting on a number of factors that influence multinational firms to substitute production abroad for exports, Grabowski et al. make the following observations:

> Foreign tariff barriers and tax and licensing measures are among the factors that provide incentives to substitute foreign production for exports.
>
> In the case of the drug industry, however, stringent regulatory conditions in the United States provide an additional inducement for firms to establish foreign manufacturing facilities, the more so because U.S. law prohibits the exporting of drugs not cleared by the FDA for marketing in the United States. In order to minimize the "spillover" effects of increased U.S. regulatory constraints and delays on the introductions of NCEs in foreign markets, U.S. firms have a strong incentive to develop and expand foreign production and other foreign operations.[45]

Thus not only are regulatory requirements more stringent in the United States, they are also restrictive in that drugs not yet cleared for U.S. use may not be manufactured in the United States and exported for sales overseas. However, the same drugs which have been approved in foreign countries can be produced and sold in foreign countries. Further structural shifts in innovation production have taken place since the drug amendments of 1962 in the United States.

The share of NCE sales to total sales which declined to 5.5 percent for the United States was relatively stable at about 13 percent between the two five-year periods for which data could be compiled for the United Kingdom (Table 10.7). The number of firms with an NCE was almost double in the United Kingdom compared with the United States. In addition, a significant structural shift took place. The largest four firms in the United States increased their share of innovation from 24 percent

TABLE 10.7
Structural Shifts in the Relation of Innovation to Firm Size
for U.S. and U.K. Pharmaceutical Industry

Period	Total NCEs[a] (1)	Share of NCE Sales to Total Sales (2)	Number of Firms with an NCE (3)	Largest Four Firms: Share of inno-vation (4)	Share of sales (5)	Ratio (6)
United States						
1957-61	233	20.0 %	51	24.0 %	26.5 %	0.91 %
1962-66	93	8.6	34	25.0	24.0	1.04
1967-71	76	5.5	23	48.7	26.1	1.87
United Kingdom						
1962-66	115	13.3	48	39.9	26.9	1.48
1967-71	95	12.9	44	14.5	29.5	0.49

Source: H.G. Grabowski, J.M. Vernon, and L.G. Thomas, "The
         Effects of Regulatory Policy on the Incentives to
         Innovate: An International Comparative Analysis,"
         in Impact of Public Policy on Drug Innovation and
         Pricing, eds. S.A. Mitchell and E.A. Link (Washington,
         D.C.: The American University, 1976), p. 57.

[a]New chemical entities.

to over 48 percent between 1957-61 and 1967-71. The share of the top four in the United Kingdom declined from about 40 percent in 1962-66 to 14.5 percent in 1967-71. The share of sales of the largest four firms in the United States remained stable at about 26 percent over the three time periods covered. The share of sales of the top four firms in the United Kingdom increased slightly from about 27 percent to somewhat over 29 percent. As a consequence, the ratio of the share of innovation to the share of sales increased from less than one to one for the United States to almost two while the ratio for firms in the United Kingdom declined from about one-and-a-half to less than one-half.

We thus have the paradox that while antitrust policy generally has sought to reduce the market share of the largest four firms in major industries, the behavior of other government agencies has run in the opposite direction. Considerable evidence establishes that the more stringent and extended review processes in the United States do not necessarily produce better results. It is more a matter of the rigidity of the nature of the review process in the United States. In foreign countries there has been much more reliance upon the use of outside experts to advise on drug safety and efficacy. In the United States much more emphasis has been placed on bureaucratic personnel, procedures, and processes. Careful students of the drug development process have commented as follows:

> The recent FDA trend to rely more on advisory committees is a hopeful sign; the curious belief, held until recently, that drug review could and should be an internal operation of the regulatory agency was an almost uniquely American phenomenon.
>
> There is a strong need for the FDA to establish its scientific expertise and credibility by using the best resources of talent in the nation. It is also desirable for scientific decisions to be separated from the regulatory function of the FDA. Advisory committees selected from the academic and professional communities are an obvious way to do this, and it is encouraging to observe the progress that is being made in this area.
>
> It is disturbing to note that this sensible trend within the FDA has been criticized by an overseeing committee of the House of Representatives. While excessive use of advisory committees is generally to be deplored in any branch of government, it should be clearly understood that in the area of drugs, advisory committees are needed on an increasingly large scale because of the exceptionally technical nature of the material and because of the difficulty of implementing law in a manner that makes sense both scientifically and medically.[46]

The use of advisory committees draws on professional expertise able and willing to make scientific judgments. This concept has been used with considerable success abroad.

A review of the data would lead to the conclusion that the United States appears to have been lagging in drug research and development efforts and in innovation since 1962. The data alone might suggest that the American pharmaceutical industry was becoming relatively inefficient in relation to its foreign competitors. This brief survey has outlined some of the basic forces at work. The root causes that explain the pattern of the data are found in U.S. government laws, regulations, and procedures. Unfortunately, the proposed Drug Regulation Reform Act of 1978 as expressed in Senate Bill 2755 and HR 12980 would further aggravate the regulatory conditions that have already produced adverse trends.

The International Steel Industry

In 1977 exports of iron and steel products from the United States were $1.7 billion. With imports of $5.8 billion, a balance of trade deficit of $4.1 billion was incurred. When indirect steel imports and exports are taken into account, probably another billion could be added to the trade deficit in steel. This raises questions as to the nature of the competitive position of the American steel industry in the international steel market. Detailed analyses of the American steel industry have been made.

The Issue of Technological Lag. One of the early charges by Adams and Dirlam was that the American steel industry fell behind because it lagged technologically.[47] This argument fails to recognize that one of the characteristics of the worldwide steel industry is that information on technology is rapidly and openly exchanged.

One of the central arguments made is that the steel industry lagged in installing the basic oxygen process. The data in Table 10.8 show that from 1960 to 1972 Japan added 74 million tons of capacity in the basic oxygen process; the United States added 71 million tons. During the same period of time the United States retired 51 million tons of open hearth capacity, while the Japanese retired only 13 million tons. The United States added about the same absolute amount of capacity in the basic oxygen process and retired much more open hearth capacity. Of course, the main difference came from the fact that Japan essentially built its steel industry during the 1960s and had a much smaller quantity of open hearth capacity to start with in 1960.

But why didn't the United States retire all of its open hearth capacity? The answer here would be found in financial analysis. From a capital budgeting standpoint, there was an open hearth capacity for which the ancillary processes and incremental cash flows required for rounding out an operation were less expensive than switching completely to the basic oxygen process. Technological considerations have to be translated into financial capital budgeting evaluations as well.

These findings are reinforced by the November 1977 FTC Study of the U.S. steel industry.[48] Data were assembled on the relative use of BOF capacity in relation to the change in total steelmaking capacity for two time periods. For both 1956-64 and 1964-74 the ratio of new BOF capacity to the change in total steelmaking capacity in the United States far outstripped the ratio for any other country of the world. For example, for the period 1956-64 the BOF adoption percentage for the United States

TABLE 10.8
Raw Steel Production by Process (Percent of Total)

	UNITED STATES					JAPAN			
	Bessemer	Open Hearth	Basic Oxygen	Electric Furnace	Bessemer	Open Hearth	Basic Oxygen	Electric Furnace	
1960	1.2%	87.0%	3.3%	8.5%	--	67.9%	11.8%	20.3%	
1965	0.4	71.7	17.4	10.5	--	24.8	54.8	20.4	
1966	0.2	63.4	25.3	11.1	--	18.0	62.7	19.3	
1967	--	55.6	32.6	11.8	--	14.5	67.2	18.3	
1968	--	50.1	37.1	12.8	--	8.1	73.7	18.2	
1969	--	43.1	42.6	14.3	--	6.3	77.0	16.7	
1970	--	36.5	48.2	15.3	--	4.2	79.1	16.7	
1971	--	29.5	53.1	17.4	--	2.4	80.0	17.6	
1972	--	26.2	56.0	17.8	--	2.0	79.5	18.5	
Tons (in millions) of Capacity added 1960-72		-51.5M	+71.3M	+15.3M		-12.9M	+74.4M	+13.4M	

Source: American Iron and Steel Institute; Japan Iron and Steel Federation; International Iron and Steel Institute (IISI)

was 131.8 as compared with 61.3 for Japan and 36.9 for West Germany. For the period 1964-74 the BOF adoption percentage was 356.1 for the United States as compared with 99.7 for Japan and 197.5 for West Germany. Clearly the U.S. steel industry did not lag in its utilization of the basic oxygen production method. Similar arguments were made about the adoption of continuous casting as an advanced method of production in the steel industry. Here again the record of the U.S. steel industry is outstanding. The continuous casting adoption percentage for the United States for the years 1969-74 was 109.2 as compared with 75.7 for Japan and 88.2 for West Germany.

Prior assertions that the American steel industry fell behind technologically have no basis in fact. Admittedly other countries benefited from building or rebuilding their steel industries during a period when modern technologies had become available. Thus even though the modern methods were used in the American steel industry to substitute for existing capacity that was being replaced, the American steel industry still remained with a substantial proportion of capacity with older technologies than was true for Japan and West Germany. So the date at which the steel industry in a country was put into place is undoubtedly a factor that influences relative costs. The major difference that most observers point to is in the level of labor costs.

Divergent Influences on Relative Labor Costs. A number of specific criticisms have been made of the steel industry to justify restrictive policies toward it. One of these is that the steel industry has been easy on wage increases because it had the monopoly power to pass wage increases on into price increases. Table 10.9 presents a comparison of the compound annual rate of change in employment costs per hour including fringe benefits for the steel industry in relation to all manufacturing since 1950. The increase in the employment costs in the steel industry had, in fact, been higher than for all manufacturing.

But even during the period of the 1950s there was strenuous and bitter bargaining. Table 10.10 lists the effective dates of new collective bargaining agreements with the United Steelworkers of America during the years 1946 through 1971. Beginning with the long strike in late 1949 during the following eleven-year period, of eight new agreements five were accompanied by a period of a general steel strike. This is certainly not consistent with the facile assumption that the steel industry was "easy in its wage negotiations."

The relatively high compensation increases in the steel industry in the 1950s have been extensively analyzed. A major influence was intervention of the federal government. The record of government

TABLE 10.9
Compound Annual Rate of Change in Employment Costs Per Hour Including Fringe Benefits, Steel Industry and All Manufacturing, 1950-1977

	Steel Industry	All Manufacturing Wage
1950-55	7.4%	5.3%
1955-60	7.0	4.0
1960-65	3.2	2.9
1965-70	4.9	2.6
1970-73	10.6	6.6
1973-77	14.1	8.5

Source: American Iron and Steel Institute, Annual Statistical Report, 1960 & 1973; U.S. Department of Labor, Handbook of Labor Statistics 1974, pp. 183, 297.

intervention is indicated in Table 10.11. During the eighteen-year period 1943-59 direct government intervention was absent only during the negotiations of 1947 and 1953-55. A major influence on the size of the compensation increases resulting from the negotiations was the politicization of the collective bargaining process. As Professors Harbison and Spencer observed:

> If, as we contend, intervention by the White House in an industry-wide steel dispute really cannot be "impartial," then the side which is likely to have the closest political alignment with the Administration may seek to increase its bargaining power by creating conditions which may call for the intervention of the government. At this point collective bargaining ceases to be a direct process of negotiation between unions and companies; it becomes a tripartite process of negotiation over public policy. In the steel strike of 1949, for example, the appointment of President Truman of a fact-finding board clearly improved the bargaining position of the Union. In a future steel controversy, a decision by another President to invoke the emergency dispute procedures of the Taft-Hartley Act might greatly strengthen the position of the companies. Our argument here is that if the parties know that the government will intervene to prevent an industry-wide strike, the side which has the closest alignment with the White House may favor such a strike.[49]

TABLE 10.10
Collective Bargaining Agreements with United Steelworkers Union

Year	Effective Date of New Agreement	Periods of General Steel Strikes	Length (Calendar Days)
1946	Feb. 15, 1946	Jan. 21-Feb. 17	28
1947	Apr. 22, 1947	. . .	. . .
1948	July 16, 1948	. . .	. . .
1949	Nov. 11, 1949	Oct. 1-Nov. 11	42
1950	Nov. 30, 1950	. . .	. . .
1952	July 26, 1952	⎰Apr. 29-May 2 ⎱June 2-July 26	3⎱ 55⎰
1953	June 12, 1953	. . .	. . .
1954	July 1, 1954	. . .	. . .
1955	June 30, 1955	July 1	A Few Hours
1956	Aug. 3, 1956	July 1-Aug. 3	34
1960	Jan. 4, 1960	July 15-Nov.7, 1959	116
1962	Apr. 6, 1962	. . .	. . .
1963	June 29, 1963	. . .	. . .
1965	Sept. 1, 1965	. . .	. . .
1968	Aug. 1, 1968	. . .	. . .
1971	Aug. 1, 1971	. . .	. . .

Source: American Iron and Steel Institute, Annual Statistical Report.

Note: Some companies have agreements with starting dates other than those listed above.

A different set of influences were operating in Japan. As a part of a broad government program to develop certain key industries the steel industry was one of those favored by a wide variety of programs.[50] As well as benefiting from a wide range of government subsidies, preferential treatments, and encouragements, financing was provided to put in place a steel industry representing the latest technologies. Japanese managers were able to draw upon a work force with a long tradition of education and a strong work ethic reinforced by a national drive to rebuild the strength of the economy after World War II. The Japanese economy at that time still had a high proportion of the

TABLE 10.11
Government Intervention in Steel Industry Wage Negotiations

	Years
Wage and Price Control	1942, 1944, 1946, 1952
Government Pressure Upon the Wage-Price Relationship	1941, 1948, 1950, 1956, 1959
Arbitration	1942, 1944
Mediation by Federal Mediation & Conciliation Service Officials	1949, 1952, 1956, 1959
Mediation by Other Government Officials	1946, 1952, 1956, 1959
Fact-Finding With Recommendations	1937, 1946, 1949, 1952
Fact-Finding Without Recommendations	1959
Seizure	1952
Injunction	1959

Source: U.S. Department of Labor, Collective Bargaining in the Basic Steel Industry, January 1961, p. 205.

population in agriculture. Thus as the Japanese steel industry expanded it was able to draw upon a population that could be relatively quickly developed into a skilled work force. Yet the level of wages remained low as compared with the United States.

In general, of course, it is argued that relative wage rates should not greatly influence a nation's competitive position. If wage rates are lower, generally this means that productivity is low so that a low-wage country should not have a basic advantage over a high-wage country. However, in a nation that has reached the stage of development where the work force can achieve high skills and utilize modern technology yet be drawn from a base of agriculture and low-wage manufacturing industries, productivity can be quite high while wage rates remain relatively low. Thus the productivity of Japanese steelworkers utilized in conjunction with modern plant quickly caught up with the productivity of American steelworkers. As a consequence, wages in the Japanese steel industry have risen faster than those in the United States. For example, during the period 1956-66 wages rose at a rate of 7.8 percent per annum in Japan and at only half that rate in the United States. During the subsequent decade wage rates in Japan rose at a 19.7 percent per annum rate while they rose at a 10.1 percent rate in the United States. Nevertheless, in 1976 the labor cost in the United States was $12.14 per hour as compared with $5.25 per hour in Japan.

The Japanese steel industry benefited from a program of determined government protection and encouragement. The emerging stage of economic development of the Japanese economy during the period when its steel industry was put in place also provided some advantages. The availability of modern technology as the bulk of the industry was created meant that on the average the modernity of the Japanese steel industry is more favorable than that of the United States. But when all the pluses and minuses are taken into account, there does not appear to be a fundamental difference in the economics of the Japanese steel industry as compared with the American steel industry. No absolute cost advantage of major magnitude appears to be involved. The pressing public policy issue from the standpoint of the United States is the formulation of a position with respect to Japanese imports.

Trade Policy Toward Steel Imports. The FTC study of the international steel industry concludes that since the Japanese steel industry no longer receives subsidies, the United States should follow free trade policies in steel. The study then goes through the standard demonstration that a tariff has undesirable effects and a quota has even worse ones. But the premises of the FTC study are wrong and their policy recommendations, therefore, invalid.

A substantial section of the FTC study describes in considerable detail a wide range of subsidies and benefits conferred by the Japanese government and administrative agencies on behalf of the Japanese steel industry. Even if all of these favorable policies had been discontinued at some date it is unrealistic to take the position that there are no longer any subsidies conferred. An example will illustrate the basic point involved here. Suppose the Japanese government had turned over to "private firms" a substantial portion of the facilities required for 100 million raw tons of steel-making capacity free of charge. Then suppose the Japanese government said it would provide no further grants. Could it be realistically stated under such circumstances that such an industry was operating independent of any continuing subsidy? But in fact, a number of the subsidies and benefits conferred on the Japanese steel industry by the Japanese government are continuing:

1. The Japanese steel industry continues to benefit from differentially low-cost, long-term debt financing representing a high percentage of total capitalization.
2. Fast depreciation writeoffs are provided for equipment generally and extremely fast writeoffs are provided for pollution control equipment.
3. Reserves deductible for tax purposes can be set aside when earnings are high and the entry reversed when earnings would otherwise be low. This helps the Japanese companies to avoid showing losses and to follow a relatively stable dividend policy.
4. The protection against imports of steel from the United States and other countries continues on a de facto basis. Strong evidence of this point is that the steel industries in Korea and Taiwan have been able to underprice the Japanese and make sales of steel in the California market in recent years, but in nearby Japan they have been unable to make any sales whatsoever.
5. Capacity growth is managed to facilitate large-scale capacity additions while at the same time controlling any tendency toward over-capacity within the broad planning framework of the government and the steel industry.
6. As a depressed industry during the period of current weakness in the level of international steel demand, subsidies are received to pay the wages of steelworkers who would otherwise be unemployed.

This list is not complete, but is representative of continued government policy of active promotion of one of the industries identified as a key export industry.

There is also considerable evidence that both the Japanese steel industry and steel industries in the European Economic Community during periods of weak demand follow the practice of dumping steel in the United States market.[51] Evidence developed mainly from the financial reports of the six leading Japanese steel companies is shown to satisfy two tests of dumping. One, foreign price levels are lower than domestic prices (this is facilitated by preventing reverse shipments by de facto import barriers). Second, foreign prices are below long-run marginal costs. While arguments may be made over technical details and with respect to the magnitude of dumping involved, my own independent investigations lead me to the judgment that the quantification developed by Putnam, Hayes, and Bartlett is of the correct order of magnitude.

Foreign government bounties and dumping are both in violation of free trade principles. Appropriate government responses to such practices are not in violation of free trade principles. It would call for the United States to impose appropriate countervailing duties. This reflects a well-established legal precedent in the United States. A more positive approach would be the negotiation of international agreements between governments which discouraged policies representing forms of long-term continuing subsidies to the industries of individual countries. It would be much better for the U.S. government to utilize its energies in dealing with other governments to eliminate subsidies and bounties so that countervailing actions would be unnecessary. But initial countervailing actions that are firm and realistic are necessary in order for such international negotiations to have any hope of progress.

Summary and Conclusions

The structural theory of industrial organization holds that when an industry is concentrated, the recognized interdependence between firms will result in some degree of monopoly behavior and performance. Systematic tests of this hypothesis have yielded, at best, mixed evidence. Generally when variables in addition to concentration are utilized in regressions to explain prices, profitability, or R&D effort, the results are not consistent with the structural theory.

Broad evidence that high concentration as measured in individual national markets is not a pathological condition is the existence of similar patterns of concentration among the same industries in the developed countries throughout the world. In addition, the most concentrated industries are characteristically worldwide in scope and subject to international competition. When the broader international markets are taken into account, concentration ratios constructed for domestic markets require substantial downward adjustment. The adjusted concentration ratios, under the structural theory itself, would lead to predictions of competitive behavior and performance rather than monopoly effects in major industries. Yet dominant U.S. government policy continues to be based on concentration ratios that lack economic meaningfulness because they are based on artificial markets.

Ideally, antitrust activities seeking to restructure firms and industries that have been stimulated by size and concentration data could be diminished through reliance on international competition. Even if some believe that small numbers and concentration when measured by reference to domestic industries leads to awareness and recognized interdependence, this is surely less plausible among a larger number of international rivals.

This paper has emphasized case studies of five major industries to describe how government policies in areas seemingly unrelated have had major impacts on competitiveness. Government policies in a number of areas have an important influence in defining the environment in which industries are either helped or hampered in international markets. The late Harry Johnson, commenting on the value of the case study approach, stated that "economic discussion, particularly of policy problems, is inclined to be far too aggregative in its approach and to treat both industrial and international trade problems as if production and competition were homogeneous activities undifferentiated by the facts of technology and the practices of governments."[52]

A weakness of the case-studies approach, of course, is that there is often a lack of a basis for generalization. In the present instance the central themes point to government subsidies abroad and/or U.S. government policies that reduce the international competitiveness of major U.S. industries. Yet the present study is also doubtless subject to another observation made by Professor Johnson. He stated that industrialists "are happy with and pleased by research that finds the mote in the neighbor's eye, but distressed and even angry with research that finds the beam in their own. More concretely, they are pleased with disclosure of discriminatory trade practices pursued by foreign firms and governments, but upset by disclosure of similar practices on their own parts which they would like to have regarded as entirely warranted defensive measures against foreign unfairness."[53]

Motes and beams may be abundant. For example, the United States experiences a substantially favorable balance of payments in aerospace products and computers. Complaints have been made that this results from the large expenditures by the U.S. government on research and development and in defense programs which have developed advanced capabilities in these areas by U.S. firms. A form of government assistance or subsidies may be argued to be present in these areas.

Thus further industry studies are required. In addition to the policy issues raised, the present paper has demonstrated that analyses of industry history, environment, and interactions with government policy are necessary for evaluation of the potentials for international performance. Such industry studies are necessary for a meaningful assessment of broader statistical surveys on directions or patterns of international trade.

Notes

1. W. Leontief, "Factor Proportions and the Structure of American Trade: Further Theoretical and Empirical Analysis," *Review of Economics and Statistics* 38 (November 1956):386-407; Robert E. Baldwin, "Determinants of the Commodity Structure of U.S. Trade," *The American Economic Review* 61 (March 1971):126-146; Roger W. Klein, "A Dynamic Theory of Comparative Advantage," *The American Economic Review* 63 (March 1973):184; Arye L. Hillman and Clark W. Bullard III, "Energy, the Heckscher-Ohlin Theorem, and U.S. International Trade," *The American Economic Review* 68 (March 1978):96-106.

2. This section summarizes J. Fred Weston, *Concentration and Efficiency: The Other Side of the Monopoly Issue*, Special Issues in the Public Interest No. 4 (New York: Hudson Institute, 1978).

3. J. S. Bain, "Relation of Profit Rate to Industrial Concentration: American Manufacturing 1936-1940," *Quarterly Journal of Economics* 65 (August 1951):293-324.

4. Lester G. Telser, *Competition, Collusion and Game Theory* (Chicago: Aldin Atherton, 1972), p. 353.

5. William S. Comanor and Thomas A. Wilson, "Advertising, Market Structure, and Performance," *Review of Economics and Statistics* 49 (November 1967):423-40.

6. S. I. Ornstein, "Concentration and Profits," *Journal of Business* 45 (October 1972):519-541.

7. H. Demsetz, "Industry Structure, Market Rivalry, and Public Policy," *The Journal of Law and Economics* 16 (April 1973):1-9.

8. S. I. Ornstein, "Empirical Uses of the Price-Cost Margin," *Journal of Industrial Economics* 24 (December 1975):105-117.

9. S. I. Ornstein, *Industrial Concentration and Advertising Intensity* (Washington, D.C.: American Enterprise Institute, 1977).

10. This section draws on the survey of the literature on innovation in Jesse W. Markham, "Concentration: A Stimulus or Retardant to Innovation?" in *Industrial Concentration: The New Learning*, eds. H. J. Goldschmid, H. M. Mann, and J. Fred Weston (Boston: Little, Brown and Company, 1974), pp. 246-277.

11. Ronald E. Shrieves, "Market Structure and Innovation: A New Perspective," *Journal of Industrial Economics* 26 (June 1978):329-347.

12. George J. Stigler, *The Organization of Industry* (Homewood, Ill.: R. D. Irwin, 1968), p. 244.

13. L. W. Weiss, "Business Pricing Policies and Inflation Reconsidered," *Journal of Political Economy* 74 (April 1966):177-187; J. F. Weston and S.

Lustgarten, "Concentration and Wage-Price Change," in *Industrial Concentration: The New Learning*, eds. H. J. Goldschmid, H. M. Mann, and J. F. Weston (Boston: Little, Brown and Company, 1974), pp. 307-331; S. Lustgarten, *Industrial Concentration and Inflation* (Washington, D.C.: American Enterprise Institute for Public Policy Research, 1975).

14. Louis Philips, "Business Pricing Policies and Inflation—Some Evidence from EEC," *Journal of Industrial Economics* 43 (November 1969):1-14.

15. J. S. Bain, *International Differences in Industrial Structure* (New Haven: Yale University Press, 1966).

16. F. L. Pryor, "An International Comparison of Concentration Ratios," *Review of Economics and Statistics* 54 (May 1972):138-39.

17. Such an argument is sketched out in Weston, *Concentration and Efficiency.*

18. This section is based on J. Fred Weston, "Do Multinational Corporations Have Market Power to Overprice?" in *The Case for the Multinational Corporation: Six Scholarly Views*, ed. Carl Madden (New York: Praeger Publishers, 1977), pp. 10-69.

19. These included the following studies by the Organization for Economic Co-operation and Development (OECD): *The Engineering Industries in OECD Member Countries: New Basic Statistics, 1963-1970* (Paris: Organization for Economic Co-operation and Development, 1972); *The Engineering Industries in North America, Europe, Japan 1966-1967 and 1967-1968* (Paris: Organization for Economic Co-operation and Development, Machinery Committee, 1967 and 1969); *The Iron and Steel Industry in 1964 and Trends in 1965* (Paris: Organization for Economic Co-operation and Development, Special Committee for Iron and Steel, 1965); *The Iron and Steel Industry in 1968 and Trends in 1969* (Paris: Organization for Economic Co-operation and Development, Special Committee for Iron and Steel, 1969); *The Chemical Industry 1964-65* (Paris: Organization for Economic Co-operation and Development, Chemical Products Special Committee, 1966); *The Chemical Industry 1967-1968* (Paris: Organization for Economic Co-operation and Development, Chemical Products Special Committee, 1969); and *Industrial Statistics 1900-1962*, OECD Statistical Bulletin (Paris: Organization for Economic Co-operation and Development, 1964). See also United Nations, *Statistical Yearbook 1971* (New York: Statistical Office of the United Nations, Department of Economic and Social Affairs, 1972).

20. "To a Global Car," *Business Week*, 20 November 1978, p. 102.

21. Lee Loevinger, "The Impacts of Government Regulation," manuscript, Hogan and Hartson, Washington, D.C., 25 October 1978, p. 18.

22. "Global Car," *Business Week*, p. 113.

23. Thomas Horst, "The American Multinationals and the U.S. Economy," *American Economic Review* 66 (May 1976):152.

24. Ibid., p. 153.

25. Ibid.

26. Ibid., p. 154.

27. Barbara Epstein, "Power Plant and Free Trade," in *Realities of Free*

Trade: Two Industry Studies (Toronto: University of Toronto Press, 1972), p. 62.

28. Ibid. p. 64.

29. Ibid. p. 20.

30. Ibid. p. 22.

31. Ibid. p. 34.

32. J. Fred Weston and Bart W. Sorge, "Export Insurance: Why the U.S. Lags," *Columbia Journal of World Business* 2 (September-October 1967):67-76.

33. Epstein, "Power Plant," p. 2.

34. Ibid. p. 51.

35. *PMA Newsletter,* Pharmaceutical Manufacturers Association, Washington, D.C., 8 January 1979, p. 5.

36. Harold A. Clymer, "The Economic and Regulatory Climate: U.S. and Overseas Trends," in *Drug Development and Marketing,* ed. Robert B. Helms (Washington, D.C.: American Enterprise Institute, 1975), p. 145.

37. H. G. Grabowski, J. M. Vernon, and L. G. Thomas, "The Effects of Regulatory Policy on the Incentives to Innovate: An International Comparative Analysis," in *Impact of Public Policy on Drug Innovation and Pricing,* eds. S. A. Mitchell and E. A. Link (Washington, D.C.: The American University, 1976), p. 49.

38. Grabowski et al., "Effects of Regulatory Policy," p. 51.

39. J. E. Schnee and E. Caglarcan, "The Changing Pharmaceutical Research and Development Environment," in *The Pharmaceutical Industry,* ed. C. M. Lindsay (New York: John Wiley & Sons, 1978), p. 101, quoting a study by Dr. Barry Bloom.

40. Clymer, "Regulatory Climate," p. 147.

41. Grabowski et al., "Effects of Regulatory Policy," p. 23.

42. Harold A. Clymer, "The Changing Costs and Risks of Pharmaceutical Innovation," in *The Economics of Drug Innovation,* ed. J. D. Cooper (Washington, D.C.: The American University, 1970), p. 124.

43. Ronald W. Hansen, "The Pharmaceutical Development Process: Estimates of Current Development Costs and Times and the Effects of Regulatory Changes," manuscript, Center for Government Policy and Business, Graduate School of Management, University of Rochester, August 1977, p. 51.

44. S. Peltzman, *Regulation of Pharmaceutical Innovation* (Washington, D.C.: American Enterprise Institute, 1974), p. 81.

45. Grabowski et al., "Effects of Regulatory Policy," p. 51.

46. W. M. Wardell and L. Lasagna, *Regulation and Drug Development* (Washington, D.C.: American Enterprise Institute, 1975), p. 157.

47. Walter Adams and Joel B. Dirlam, "Steel Imports and Vertical Oligopoly Power," *American Economic Review* 54 (September 1964):626-655.

48. Bureau of Economics of the Federal Trade Commission, *Staff Report on the United States Steel Industry and its International Rivals: Trends and Factors Determining International Competitiveness* (Washington, D.C.: U.S. Government Printing Office, 1977).

49. Frederick H. Harbison and Robert C. Spencer, "The Politics of Collective

Bargaining: The Postwar Record in Steel," *American Political Science Review* 68 (September 1954):719.

50. See, for example, Federal Trade Commission, *International Competitiveness*, at various pages and further detail in Hugh Patrick and Henry Rosovsky, *Asia's New Giant* (Washington, D.C.: The Brookings Institution, 1976).

51. Substantial data in support of this finding is presented in Putnam, Hayes and Bartlett, Inc., *The Economic Implications of Foreign Steel Pricing Practices in the United States Market* (Washington, D.C.: American Iron and Steel Institute, 1978).

52. *Realities of Free Trade*, p. xxiii.

53. *Realities of Free Trade*, p. xxii.

Commentary

H. Peter Gray

Professor J. Fred Weston has provided the conference with a thorough and broad overview of the interrelation between industrial concentration, international competition, and governmental economic policy. The paper is of high quality and compresses much erudition into a relatively short space. No one recognizes better than the author the limitations of the case-study approach and his conclusions are properly hedged in with warnings of this weakness.

In this discussion of Weston's paper, I want to agree briefly with his main argument that some antitrust policies are not dissimilar to witch hunts which fail to compute even a crude cost-benefit analysis; I want to offer some conflicting observations on a couple of his case studies; and I want to consider the implications of his argument for national domestic and international economic policies.

Antitrust Policies

Weston has summarized and supported the argument that high concentration ratios give misleading impressions of market power and the exercise of market power. The misleading quality of this impression is confirmed when concentration ratios are expanded from a domestic to an international base—as is analytically correct. The numerical values of concentration ratios are significantly reduced when an allowance for the role of foreign competition in the United States is incorporated in their computation. It is always possible that foreign sources of supply are controlled by or are in collusion with the market-dominating corporations in the United States through, respectively, multinational corporations or cartels. This possibility could restore the argument against highly concentrated industries but it suggests a very highly developed ability to collude and the burden of the proof should be placed on those wishing to argue in favor of the existence of collusion.[1]

Inflation

The idea that blame for inflation can be placed on concentrated industries is merely another symptom in the general feeling among liberals that business is inimical to social welfare. Of course, the best evidence for this comes not from the liberals but from miscreant corporate executives such as those jailed for collusive bidding on heavy electrical equipment and those who admitted guilt in gross interference in Chilean affairs. However, the idea that blame for inflation can be laid at the door of concentrated industries is somewhat ingenuous. It is true that the standard analysis of wage-push inflation requires not only a large and dominant labor union in a sector or industry but also a large and dominant price leader. But current inflation has a much broader base than aggressive wage-bargaining in and meek acceptance by concentrated industries.

Just as concentration ratios based solely on domestic firms are of little value, so too is analysis of the current inflation that neglects the international aspects. Certainly wages have increased quickly and these cost increases have been passed through to customers but it is arguable that the increased aggressiveness of bargaining is merely a response to a reduction in real wages in the manufacturing sectors of the U.S. economy. Rather, inflation can be seen as the result of an initial disturbance involving the depreciation of the U.S. dollar, the increase in the prices of primary products (including food), and the increased price of oil. These forces required a reduction in the real income of the United States and particularly of the manufacturing and tertiary sectors. Wage increases were aimed at reestablishing the real wage and caused induced secondary inflation. In turn, the prices of primary products went up again and in this way we can, unless we break the link, leapfrog our way to perpetual inflation. While the existence of real-wage resistance has been verified (albeit crudely) at an aggregate level, there has been no work done on disaggregated sectors and until that has been done, the inflation argument that concentration causes inflation must be regarded as a statement of a hypothesis roughly equivalent to those rebutted by Weston in his first two sections.

The Case Studies

I believe Weston's criticism of the controls on the pharmaceutical industry to be valid in that he requires not less stringent tests but rather more efficient testing. However, I thought he was at pains to whitewash the automobile industry. He complains of the cost of environmental controls but there is, it seems to me, a substantial argument that the U.S. automobile industry has been an abject failure in recent years. For all of its vaunted resources, the U.S. automotive industry has made little headway in solving the emissions problem—certainly it has nowhere near paralleled the success of the Japanese—MITI subsidization notwithstanding. It has designed cars which have been acknowledged as death traps. It has lost (or not increased) its market share despite large increases in competitiveness that derive from the fall in the value of the dollar in terms of yen and Deutschemarks. Whether these weaknesses are due to concentration is not clear, but to suggest that the poor performance of the automotive industry is due to governmental interference is to overlook a substantial amount of evidence that the corporations themselves seem to be doing their best to validate Galbraith's view of the world. Finally, there is the steel industry. Doubtless the government is responsible for some of the steel industry's problems with foreign competition but Weston paints too rosy a picture of the commercial virtues of steel executives. In the final analysis, it matters not whether the steel industry's wages have increased faster than productivity *relative to foreign steel* because of concentration in the industry, government interference, labor's aggressiveness, corporate passivity, or the costs of pollution controls. What matters is that U.S. steel is priced higher than foreign steel and the industry is by no means blameless.[2] Rather than argue for countervailing duties, Weston should argue for a complete freeze (indexed in terms of the price of manufactured goods) for steelworkers' wages in return for countervailing duties and with similar restrictions on dividend or profit rates of corporations.

Implications for National Policies

The main strength of Weston's paper is the argument that we cannot examine concentration without paying attention to international competition. Weston also lays the ground for an argument that the

United States cannot institute industrial policy without taking into account the existence or nonexistence of similar policies by the other large manufacturing nations. This is, perhaps, the most important aspect of the paper.

If industries in different nations have approximately equal basic costs (given exchange rates and absolute price levels), then government interference which is subsidizing or cost-enhancing can have drastic effects on the ability of an industry to export or to resist import competition. In general, this aspect of governmental policy has received explicit analysis only in terms of environmental protection and its international effects.[3] The "Polluter Pays" principle has been recognized (by OECD) as the fairest way of ensuring that environmental measures do not unduly affect the international competitiveness of different industries for equal concern with environmental protection. The most evident example here is in the steel industry. There the elimination of air pollution by government subsidy in one country will have a zero cost to the consumer and the application of the Polluter Pays principle in a second country will increase steel prices to the detriment of the competitiveness of the second country's industry. While this is intuitively obvious after a moment's thought, the implications of this interdependence have not been carefully observed by the executive and legislative branches of government or the spokesmen of industry.

If the competitiveness of industries in developed nations is extremely sensitive to differences in the net burden imposed upon industries in terms of cost-enhancing or subsidy measures, then governments do not have complete freedom of action. Moreover, they should not act as if they do. Here is a new dimension to the term 'interdependence' which has become so fashionable lately. Clearly, what have been viewed as domestic policy issues can no longer be analyzed and legislated in a purely domestic framework. Implications for economic policies for the international competitiveness of industries must also be analyzed. National governments are likely to need to ensure that their actions do not adversely affect the international competitiveness of their own industries. One possible scenario is that the first government to act will set the pattern for all other governments to follow. A second scenario is that the government which subsidizes most will set the standard by virtue of its being the equivalent of the "high-bidder" in terms of willingness to put the burden of support of an industry on general tax revenues. A third scenario is for there to be official and preagreed harmonization of policies toward major industries. A fourth scenario is that sketched in by Weston—a mass of countervailing duties and tariffs designed to achieve a complex, bureaucratically determined neutralizing effect. Of all of the four scenarios which I have sketched, I like the concept of a maze of countervailing duties and nontariff barriers least. If I had more faith in the ability of governments successfully and practically to negotiate harmonization policies, I would prefer that solution. For similar reasons, I consider harmonization of policies to be a better solution for the current chronic payments imbalances than competitive devaluations and refusals by surplus nations to allow their surpluses to be eliminated.[4]

Conclusion

The OECD nations will have to recognize in the future that their treatment of their major industries is no longer a matter to be decided purely on the basis of domestic considerations. Instead, the world must recognize that its interdependence now extends to differences in government policies toward major industries. The effects of tax structures, quality control regulations, pollution controls, and safety regulations on international competitiveness must be taken into account. Since the alternative to some sort of harmonization through imitation or preagreement and negotiation is a complex maze of commercial policy measures, the forum under which harmonization should take place is the GATT. Such a step would require a broadening of the task of the GATT as it is currently conceived but certainly that is to be preferred to an anarchic situation whereby nations strive with each other to penalize or subsidize their own industries in cutthroat competition for foreign exchange or voters' endorsement.

Notes

1. This suggests a commercial capability for cooperation that far exceeds any observed political capability in the so-called Western world.
2. A technical weakness in Weston's paper is that he compares growth rates of wages, not absolute increases. Japanese wages in money terms have decreased relative to those in the United States until recently.
3. See H. Peter Gray, "Commercial Policy Implications of Environmental Controls" in *Studies in International Environmental Economics,* ed. Ingo Walter (New York: John Wiley and Sons, 1976), pp. 159-176.
4. The concept of "reference rates of exchange" relies on some agreement among nations in the establishment of the reference rates. Unfortunately, most analyses of this proposal brush under the rug the difficult problem of negotiating the reference rate structure.

Commentary

Robert E. Baldwin

The first part of Professor Weston's paper is devoted to showing that most of the economic relationships predicted by structural theory when the number of firms in an industry is small is not supported by empirical research. He states that this casts serious doubts on the usefulness of this theory for public policy. In addition, he concludes that concentration is consistent with competition.

When I read statements about concentration being consistent with competition, I always wonder what is meant by competition. It certainly seems to me, from an analytical viewpoint, and from casual observation, that concentrated industries do not behave the same way as firms in the traditional model of perfect competition. For example, one does not observe in competitive markets the leadership role in price, output, and investment that one or two firms seem to play in many highly concentrated markets. This does not mean that these firms cannot perform well from an economy-wide point of view in terms of such variables as innovation, entry, and profits, but surely the mechanisms by which these results are reached are quite different. Adequate performance from an economic efficiency standpoint and the term "competition" seem often to be considered synonymous in this field. Yet I wonder if that is very helpful. I thought competition was a structural concept, a definition that yields certain criteria. These two concepts are frequently mixed up in this area.

Is it not possible to move beyond discussion of the conflicting views that concentration is per se bad and that concentration is not bad, to distinguish why, among cases where the degree of concentration is the same, the level of performance still varies? This would seem to be an avenue of research from which useful public policy guidelines could eventually result. But perhaps, and I think Weston feels this way, the structural theory is so entrenched and dominant in industrial organization that one has to keep responding to it on a simple and crude level—just answering the thesis on a very low level and showing that various predicted results do not always follow from the knowledge of an industry's structure.

The work on which Weston reports in the third section of his paper, concerning concentration measures when international competition is introduced, seems very interesting and very worthwhile. He first shows that, for the largest U.S. firms, their share of world production is considerably less than their share of U.S. production. Of course that obviously follows. Then he adds together the U.S. production of the largest four firms plus the output of their affiliates and computes this as a proportion of world production. This gives a picture of somewhat greater concentration, but it is still substantially less than if you look only at the United States. It would be preferable to compare the output of the largest four firms in the world, and their affiliates with world production. The figures probably will not change very much, however, and the data probably do not exist (which is probably why he did not do it), but it would be useful to mention it. Moreover, it would be useful to look at the concentration ratio not only for the largest four firms but also for the largest six and eight firms in the world.

The last section of the paper briefly reviews performance in some specific industries: petroleum, automobiles, heavy electrical equipment, pharmaceuticals, and steel. The generalization he draws from these case studies is that government subsidies abroad and our own U.S. government policies reduce the international competitiveness of major U.S. industries. I agree fully with Weston that we should try to reduce foreign nontariff trade barriers and in particular remove many of the trade-inhibiting effects of our own regulations to the extent that is feasible. That is, I hope, what we are doing in the Tokyo Round of the GATT negotiations, which are about to conclude.

But remember, barriers and regulations can cut both ways. I wonder if our pollution and safety regulations, for example on autos, have not actually had a more adverse effect on foreign producers in trying to get into this market than on domestic producers, as far as market shares are concerned. These are significant barriers; companies have to tool up to install pollution controls on just the cars they send to the United States, and that represents a considerable cost. At least I have heard the argument that these regulations are an unfair nontariff barrier on the part of the United States. It is not hurting American competition, but is giving the Americans a larger share of the domestic market than they otherwise would have. Maybe the health requirements in pharmaceuticals have had a similar effect, although I think Weston did present a very persuasive case in that instance. Certainly a lot of foreign producers seem to feel that many U.S. regulations are hurting them more than they are hurting our own firms. Indeed that is one of the reasons we have not had very much trouble in getting a standards code in the Tokyo Round. And of course, when you come to trade barriers, what about the quotas on specialty steel or quotas on oil that we have had on and off over the years? I am not so sure that all these regulations have hurt U.S. competitiveness. Maybe these are protective devices that are making the United States more competitive in the sense of getting more sales than otherwise, though perhaps less competitive in an efficiency sense.

It would be nice to have the kind of study that Anne Krueger did for imports. That is, how important are government regulations and import barriers in affecting some sort of measure of competitiveness? I feel that one would likely end up with the kind of conclusions that she did: that they have not been all that important; that competitiveness is basically determined by fundamental economic conditions related to comparative costs.

11

Industrial Policy and Firm Behavior in an International Context

*Emilio Pagoulatos
and Robert Sorensen*

Governments have intervened in private industrial affairs since the formation of the modern nation state. In recent years, however, there has been a marked increase and proliferation of the various forms of government involvement in the industrial sectors of OECD countries. This increased intervention, commonly termed "industrial policy" is fast becoming a source of concern and controversy.[1] This concern is due not only to the virtual absence of a coherent theoretical framework around which industrial policy can be designed, but also to a lack of information about the ultimate domestic and international effects of the various policies actually pursued. As such, industrial policy is now viewed by many as a potential threat to the existence of the mixed market economy, as well as a disguised form of new protectionism.

Any government action, of course, which affects the industrial pattern of resource allocation can be classified under the general rubric of industrial policy. It is customary, though, to classify industrial policies into the following general categories:

1. *Antitrust or Competition Policy*—whose goals usually are the promotion of competition and the control of restrictive business practices;
2. *Technological Policy*—whose purpose is to promote research and development activity in the nation;
3. *Regional Policy*—whose aim is to reduce regional imbalance in the allocation of economic activity;
4. *Adjustment Policy*—whose goal is to facilitate the adjustment of industrial structure to changes dictated by demand and technological forces or foreign competition;
5. *Commercial Policy*—whose objectives include the protection of domestic industries from foreign competition or the promotion of exports; and

6. *Environmental Policy*—whose goals are the preservation and improvement of the conditions of the environment of nature and the workplace.

This list is by no means exhaustive. Rather, it is indicative only of the broad range and diversity of industrial policy objectives pursued in recent years. Since these policies appear at first sight to have desirable objectives, one has to ask, why have they created so much controversy?

The reasons for this are many. First of all, some of many ways in which the state intervenes in the domestic industry cause, either by design or accident, distortions in international trade by assisting domestic firms in competing against foreign suppliers or by aiding them to increase their exports. Some industrial policies designed with purely domestic goals in mind, such as the facilitation of adjustment to structural changes or an improvement in the mobility of resources, are also likely indirectly to affect comparative advantage and international trade flows. The public financing of research and development, the granting of tax and payroll relief, and the provision of low interest loans and other subsidies to prevent the decline of particular firms, industries, or regions are all examples of policies which could have spillover effects into international trade.

Other measures of industrial policy affect international trade directly. These include the use of discriminatory procurement practices, the promotion of national and international export cartels, the existence of state trading, the imposition of countervailing duties, and the provision of favorable export credits and guarantees. These types of practices represent examples of nontariff barriers to trade.

Because industrial policies lack transparency in terms of their effects on international trade, it is widely feared that the increased use of these measures represents a disguised form of "new protectionism." Moreover, this trend of increased intervention in industrial affairs is seen by many as a threat to the gains from trade (tariff) liberalization achieved among advanced economies since the end of World War II.[2]

A second reason for the controversial nature of industrial policies is the lack of coherence in both their conception and their application. At times they constitute a sequence of ad hoc measures introduced as a response to problems faced by individual firms, branches of industry, or depressed regions without much design or evidence as to the need for such policies or their effectiveness in achieving the desired objectives. This lack of design may be symptomatic of the symbolic nature of many of the measures of industrial policy when their adoption serves the purpose of showing that the government is in control of actual or perceived situations. But more seriously, the lack of coherence in industrial policies may lead to potential conflicts among the various goals of government intervention.

An example of such a conflict can be found in cases where policies have been pursued with the objective of promoting competition in the domestic market, while at the same time other policies have encouraged mergers and industry concentration for the purpose of increasing the power of domestic firms in international markets. Another example involves the use of subsidies and other forms of government aid to industry. The result of such practices is to reduce the uncertainties inherent in the competitive process. Since uncertainty is the spur of innovation, the ultimate effect of many industrial policies could very well be a slowdown in the rate of creation of new ideas, products, and processes. This result will cancel to a large extent the results of those industrial policies that aim to promote technological progress and innovation.

In general, industrial policies in advanced countries are bound to alter the operation of firms and markets by delaying the contraction of industries (defensive policies) or promoting the emergence of others (positive policies). Indeed, their stated objectives often advocate the promotion of industries with good prospects (like high technology sectors) or the rescue of industries and firms in financial trouble. If a firm or industry has good prospects, however, why does it need government assistance? One would think that under such circumstances, private capital would be attracted. If, on the other hand, a firm or industry is incapable of self-survival, why should we use public funds to save it? There could, of course, exist some cases of marginal firms and industries capable of growth and survival, but for a variety of reasons are unable to attract support from private investors. Government assistance in these cases might well be justified. Is it possible, though, in such a complex industrial world to determine which firms and industries these marginal cases really are?

A large number of industrial policy measures have been adopted as a defensive reaction to structural changes which are perceived as being caused by shifts in comparative advantage and international trade flows. While the dynamics of international trade and the shifting of comparative advantage have had painfully adverse effects upon certain industries such as textiles, the evidence on the adjustment problems faced by manufacturing industries as a result of trade liberalization does not justify massive intervention through industrial policy. This is because trade among advanced countries has expanded according to intraindustry rather than interindustry specialization. As a result factors have moved into new and expanding product lines within the same industry rather than into new industries.[3]

In summary, industrial policies have become a major source of controversy in the relations among advanced economies because of both their potential international trade effects and their lack of internal consistency. At the same time, there exists very little economic research to make possible an evaluation of the coherence of industrial policy objectives, and an empirical assessment of its impact on domestic structure and international trade flows.

To provide such a comprehensive evaluation of industrial policies is a task beyond the scope of this paper. Instead, in the remainder of this paper we focus our attention on three specific issues. First, we analyze the role of commercial policy in affecting the conditions of competition in domestic markets. In particular, we examine the effects of international trade and investment on domestic industry structure and performance. The purpose here is to evaluate the interrelationship between commercial policy and competition policy. Second, we analyze the potential conflicts between domestic competition policy goals and international trade goals. Here we are interested in whether or not competition in the domestic market is consistent with the ability of firms to meet import competition or to expand their exports. Finally, we close by reviewing the limited quantitative evidence on the international trade effects of some measures of industrial policy.

International Trade and Competition Policy

Governments in market economies are generally committed to promoting effective competition among firms or, where technological or other conditions make competition impossible, to insuring that firms behave in ways that maximize the social benefits from their productive efforts. A policy of openness towards international trade is one of the many ways of facilitating the achievement of these goals. Indeed, as we shall discuss in this section, both the existing theoretical literature and empirical evidence suggest that import competition does improve the pricing and allocative performance of firms in domestic markets. In contrast, protective commercial policies, or other industrial policies which have as an effect the restriction of international trade flows, are in conflict with the promotion of effective competition in domestic markets.

Promoting effective competition, of course, does not imply that government should act to establish industrial structures which conform to some theoretical norm. Rather, policies should be aimed towards limiting the degree to which firms are able to secure market power. In the real world firms may display differing degrees of market power depending upon the number of rival sellers and other elements of industry structure. Market power constitutes a long run problem only to the extent that entry barriers deter the elimination of monopoly prices and profits through the entry of new firms into the market. In situations where barriers to entry exist, the most likely entrants may well be foreign rather than domestic firms. If foreign firms can more easily scale the various barriers to entry than domestic ones, then international trade will provide a constraining force on the market power of firms in the domestic market.

Industries in which entry is difficult are usually characterized by the existence of substantial economies of scale, high capital cost of entry, or significant product differentiation. Both potential foreign and domestic entrants must overcome these barriers, but the foreign entrant faces some additional barriers in the form of transportation costs, tariffs, and other artifical impediments to trade. The existence of these additional barriers need not imply that the overall height of barriers is greater for foreign firms than domestic ones. This is because foreign firms with established markets elsewhere in the world can potentially avoid the disadvantages associated with scale economies and high capital costs.[4] Therefore, in industries where scale economies or capital costs are the main barriers to entry, a liberal trade policy could provide an important constraint upon the pricing and output decisions of domestic firms.

This same result may not always hold for industries in which product differentiation is the important barrier to entry. It depends upon the form in which differentiation occurs. When differentiation is based upon significant physical differences in style and design, or where customizing the product to the buyers' specifications is important, foreign firms may not find themselves at substantial disadvantage relative to potential domestic entrants. When differentiation is based upon direct efforts to persuade consumers through advertising or brand image creation, foreign entrants may face severe disadvantages. In the first place, this type of differentiated product could be specific to a national market, so that foreign products may not be close substitutes for goods produced by domestic firms. Second, the necessity of undertaking national sales promotion may make it difficult for foreign firms to penetrate the domestic market because of the substantial economies of scale in marketing that usually characterize promotion efforts; import competition may not be an effective force in eliminating monopolistic distortions in the domestic market. We shall argue in more detail later, however, that it is these industries which are likely to experience entry via foreign investment.

In recent years a number of empirical studies have investigated the degree to which import competition might act as a restraining force upon pricing decisions of domestic firms. These studies have included both cross-section multi-variate as well as detailed industry studies. The cross-section studies have generally examined industry rates of return on equity or industry price-cost margins (as proxies for the exercise of monopoly pricing) in relation to elements of domestic structure and measures of the industry's exposure to international forces, such as the share of the market accounted for by imports, or the height of tariff protection afforded domestic producers.

The results of these studies are interesting and merit some detailed description. Before reviewing some of the results of these studies, however, mention should be made of the difficulty of modeling the degree of import competition facing a domestic industry. Theoretically, one would wish to have information on the elasticity of foreign supply with respect to the domestic market price. This type of information is not generally available. Therefore, most studies have relied upon measures of either the share of the domestic market accounted for by imports, or proxies for the height of tariff and nontariff protection afforded domestic producers.

Both of these measures are subject to qualification. For example, it might be reasonable to expect that a high import share would reflect substantial import competition and thus measures of profitability should be inversely related to the share of the market taken by imports. Nonetheless, it is conceivable that a small import share, ex post, could in fact be associated with a high elasticity of foreign supply which yielded pricing decisions in domestic markets that resulted in relatively low profits. In other words, potential, rather than actual, import competition may affect the pricing decisions of domestic firms. One might also surmise that the higher the degree of tariff and nontariff protection given to firms, the greater would be the barriers to foreign firms, and hence, ceteris paribus, the higher could be the profits of domestic firms. In practice, however, tariffs and other forms of protection are often sought and obtained by industries which are troubled either by chronic excess capacity and/or high unit cost relative to the rest of the world, and hence protection may be associated with industries experiencing low rather than high profitability.

The problems above notwithstanding, the available cross-section evidence for a variety of countries as well as industry studies suggests that import competition does act as a restraining force upon domestic pricing. For example, results by Pagoulatos and Sorensen and by Esposito and Esposito indicate that even for the large relatively closed economy of the United States, the profitability of domestic producers was inversely related to the share of the market accounted for by imports.[5]

With such results for the U.S. economy, one might expect perhaps even more definitive results for the economies of smaller and more internationally open nations. While the results for other countries tend to parallel those for the United States, some significant differences do arise. In the United Kingdom, for example, Hart and Morgan found no significant relationship between import shares and profitability. Khalilzadeh-Shirazi found import shares to be negatively related to profits in his analysis of U.K. data, but the variable was only marginally significant. Hitiris, on the other hand, found that effective protection rates were strikingly significant in explaining industry profitability in his study of the United Kingdom. Results presented by Pagoulatos and Sorensen for five Common Market countries (France, Italy, Germany, Netherlands, and Belgium-Luxembourg) indicated that in all of the countries except Italy price-cost margins were negatively influenced by the degree of import competition as measured by the share of output accounted for by imports.[6]

Studies for Canada present different conclusions. An analysis by Jones, Laudadio, and Percy found no systematic relationship between import competition (as measured by dummy variables) and profitability of Canadian industry. Likewise McFertridge could not detect any significant relationship between rates of effective protection and industry price-cost margins in Canada. Finally, Bloch found that differentials in profits between Canadian and U.S. firms were similar in both highly protected Canadian industries and in those with low tariffs.[7] Since he did find, however, that the prices in heavily protected industries were higher in Canada than in the United States, his results suggest that the effect of tariff protection may have been on efficiency rather than profitability. Indeed there is growing evidence that the tariff levels in Canada have resulted in inefficient industrial structures in which too many suboptimum-sized firms have crowded into markets yielding fragmentation and an elevation of cost and prices.

Two reasons may explain some of these disparate results. The first is that import competition should only affect industry profits when market power in an industry is high enough that excess profits could in fact be achieved if foreign rivals were kept out of the market. The second is the problem that neither the import share nor the level of protection variables may accurately represent the unobserved elasticity of foreign supply.

In regard to the first argument it is interesting to note the work of Caves and others for the Canadian economy. These authors find that an interaction variable between seller concentration and the import share does have a significant effect upon industry profits, but that neither has an effect independently. Thus they conclude that concentration appears only to significantly affect profits when in fact import competition is low.[8] In regard to the second problem, some interesting results have recently been reported by Turner in his study of the United Kingdom.[9] He looked at the effects of the change in imports on industry profits in the United Kingdom after the 1967 devaluation. Since the devaluation should have raised world prices relative to those in the United Kingdom, the change in imports in the years following the devaluation should provide a fair indication of the elasticity of foreign supply. Turner finds that changes in imports are significantly related to industry price cost margins.

The results obtained from individual industry studies tend to confirm those obtained from the cross-section results. Frederiksen has studied several highly concentrated U.S. industries and found that import competition had resulted in stimulating price competition in three industries (flat glass, portable typewriters, and aluminum), but had less salutary effects in two more differentiated industries (electric typewriters and wheel tractors).[10] In the latter two industries, however, it is interesting to note that a good deal of foreign production was in fact controlled by U.S. companies. Sichel's survey of large manufacturing firms also indicates the importance of import competition.[11] When the firms were asked about rivals in their principle industry, the respondents indicated that in forty-two of the sixty-nine industries a foreign company was among their chief competitors. Finally, in a study of the U.S. automobile industry, Toder finds that the prices of "quality equivalent" domestically produced automobiles were significantly affected by the share of foreign automobile imports.[12]

Taken as a whole the existing evidence suggests that import competition can improve the pricing and allocative performance in domestic markets. In contrast, impediments to trade, such as tariffs, quotas, voluntary export restrictions, and other barriers to trade associated with industrial policy, appear to amplify the possibilities for monopolistic distortions. Moreover, barriers to international trade, particularly in countries with small markets, may lead to inefficient industry organization and fragmentation.

Foreign Investment and Competition Policy

A second international force which may influence market structure and the conditions of competition in the domestic market is the multinational enterprise. The analysis presented in this section suggests that the multinational firm is another force which may improve the pricing performance of firms in domestic markets. This conclusion is based upon the proposition that entry by multinational firms adds a degree of rivalry and competition to domestic markets that could not be forthcoming from other domestic or international sources. Thus, the formulation of policies for the regulation of direct foreign investment should take the goals of domestic competition policy into consideration.

Firms which establish production facilities abroad are, at least initially, at a disadvantage in terms of knowlege of laws, language, customs, and so forth, relative to national firms in the markets they enter. It is therefore difficult to explain exactly why such investment occurs. Early analyses of the causes of foreign investment concentrated upon macroeconomic explanations of the phenomenon. The observation, however, that differences arise among industries and firms in regard to the volume of foreign direct investment undertaken has led to more sectoral-specific explanations of the process, with greater emphasis placed upon aspects of industrial organization and market imperfections.[13]

If, for example, a foreign firm is to overcome inherent disadvantages relative to national firms in entering markets, it appears that two conditions must be present. First, the firm must possess some unique asset which enables it to enter the foreign market and earn rents in spite of its disadvantages relative to national firms. Second, the asset must possess some characteristics of a public good such that it can easily be transferred and utilized in other markets without impairing its value in the home market. The set of assets which satisfy the above criterion, however, is limited. In particular, it would seem to consist of intangible assets in the form of firm-specific advantages embodied in the firm's possession of patents, trademarks, specialized products in technology or design, and/or managerial knowledge and expertise in the adaptation, modification, and marketing of products to specific markets. In the parlance of industrial organization, this suggests that the types of industries in which substantial foreign investment is likely to emerge are those characterized by product differentiation.

Another characteristic of foreign investment activity is that it appears to be dominated by firms that are relatively large and possess substantial market shares in the parent country.[14] It is not difficult to see why this should be the case. Besides having to undertake the potentially substantial cost of search and information, required before entry, the firm must in addition be able and prepared to make the necessary investment in plant and equipment as well as the expenditures associated with the establishment of marketing and distribution channels. Therefore, the firms that have already established a substantial position in the parent market and, hence, can more easily generate funds through either external or internal financing constitute the more likely foreign investors. For these reasons multinational activity is bound to be most pronounced in industries characterized by both oligopoly and product differentiation in the parent country.

Even recognizing that foreign investment tends to be associated with large firms selling differentiated products, the question still remains as to why firms invest rather than export or license local production.[15] In many cases the nature of the firm's unique intangible assets may be such that investment is the only alternative. For example, if the firm's advantage lies in managerial expertise in adapting its products to local market conditions and/or providing specialized services to buyers, this may predispose the firm toward foreign investment. In other cases, however, foreign direct investment may have simply been induced by restriction to international trade imposed by the host country. The evidence from historical accounts and surveys of multinational firms is replete with examples of this so-called "defensive" investment.[16] That is, subsidiary production is established in order to protect markets which are threatened by tariffs, other import restrictions, or a depreciation of the host country's currency.

One conclusion to be drawn from the analysis thus far is that foreign direct investment tends to move into areas and industries where international trade cannot. First, the fact that foreign investment takes place (for whatever resons) suggests that it is a preferred alternative to exporting. Moreover, foreign investment is most concentrated in industries characterized by product differentiation. But it is precisely these industries in which national marketing and advertising are an important source of differentiation that are less susceptible to effective import competition.

The implication, therefore, is that the multinational company may be a source of rivalry and competition in domestic markets that could not come from international trade. Moreover, its ability to scale major barriers to entry (ample supply of funds, ability to market and differentiate its product) may render it the most favored entrant into industries in which barriers to entry are high.

The multinational firm is not only a new market participant and rival that could come from few other sources, but is also likely to represent a more disruptive influence than a domestic entrant. It may, for example, utilize different technology and be importing more of its components from the parent firm and thus have a different cost structure than that of its national rivals. Ita alien status may also render it less respectful of established modes of behavior and pricing. Finally, being geographically diversified, it is likely to be less dependent upon the host country market than its national rivals and thus may be more disposed to undertake risk associated with price cutting. Potentially then, the multinational entrant can be given high marks in increasing the competitive pressures in the markets it enters.

The analysis thus far has cast a favorable light upon the multinational enterprise as a potential competitive force. Before accepting this conclusion a number of caveats must be considered. In the first place since multinational entry is likely to occur in industries in which product differentiation is an important element, the conduct of the multinational firm may result in the industry being directed away from price competition towards forms of nonprice competition such as model and style changes, proliferation of brands and product lines, and excessive advertising. These activities may not only be socially wasteful, but may also tend to ultimately heighten barriers to entry and result in increased prices.

Second, the entry of a multinational firm may provoke defensive mergers among national firms in the host market. In cases where genuine economies of scale exist the result may be an improved rationalization of the domestic industry. In other cases, however, the result may simply be an increased level of concentration and a tightening of oligopoly interdependence. Which way the sword will cut is difficult to generalize.

Finally, the entry of a single multinational firm may bring about "follow the leader" tactics by other firms in the investing country, if they feel they can only protect their market by following the leader in investing abroad.[17] The results of this, particularly in smaller countries and in industries where economies of scale are important, may be a fragmentation of industry with too many firms crowding into the market for any to achieve optimum output levels. This problem is likely to be most acute in circumstances in which investment was induced for defensive purposes in order to overcome a tariff or other protective devices.

The caveats mentoned above, however, are practices which can be controlled through domestic competition policy, or even avoided through appropriate commercial policy. Thus, on balance, given the potential competitive effects of the multinational firm, a liberal policy towards direct investment is warranted.

Competition Policy and International Trade

Thus far we have argued that a policy of openness towards both international trade and investment enhances competition in domestic markets. The observations that much of international trade is dominated by large firms, and that large firms, at least up to some point, tend to export a larger percentage of their output than do their smaller rivals,[18] have led some to conclude that the enforcement of domestic competition may conflict with the goals of commercial policy. Indeed, in recent years policies aimed at relaxing antitrust enforcement and encouraging or promoting mergers have been advocated both in Europe and in the United States in order to improve export performance or to enable industries to better confront import competition.[19]

Most economists would probably argue that a policy of flexible exchange rates is a more appropriate response to trade imbalances than changes in antitrust. Because the relaxation of antitrust for the achievement of international trade objectives is receiving enough support from politicians and some economists, a more careful examination of the desirability of this policy is required. In this section we evaluate the effectiveness of such a policy by analyzing the role of changes in the degree of domestic competition in altering international trade performance.[20] Our examination of the limited available evidence leads us to conclude that a relaxation of competition policy is an uncertain means of improving an industry's export or import competing performance.

Perhaps the most thorough theoretical analysis of the issue is a recent paper by Lawrence White.[21] Under a variety of alternative assumptions he compares the performance of a domestic monopoly versus a competitive industry in export and import competing situations. His analysis shows that a domestic monopolist in virtually all cases (homogeneous products, differentiated products, differing cost conditions) is likely to yield a higher level of imports than would a competitive industry. This result can occur even in cases where a monopoly structure would result in lower costs than a competitive one. This conclusion follows from the fact that in the monopoly case, imports will be reduced only to the extent that the most cost efficient monopolist is willing to produce a larger output (i.e., charge a lower price) than would have the competitive industry.

The important implication of White's results is that the potential efficiency gains from a monopoly structure are not sufficient in and of themselves to guarantee a reduction in the level of imports. Rather, the efficiency gains must be large enough to offset the increase in market power that results from the transformation of the competitive industry into a monopoly. Without such assurances, a policy aimed at increasing domestic market power may result in a rise rather than a decline in the level of imports.

The scant empirical evidence for the United States seems at least indirectly to support White's conclusions concerning the role of industry structure in import-competing situations. Pagoulatos and Sorensen, for example, found that for import-competing manufacturing industries (after allowing for differentials in plant scale economies, research and development effort, product differentiation, and transport cost) a positive and statistically significant relationship existed between imports as a percentage of domestic value of shipments and the level of industry concentration.[22] This evidence is also supported by results presented by Caves and Khalilzadeh-Shirazi.[23] Utilizing rather detailed individual firm data, they found that the level of industry concentration was significantly higher in U.S. industries in which imports as a percentage of domestic disappearance (shipments minus exports plus imports) was large compared to industries in which the import share was small.

White's analysis for export-competing situations leads to ambiguous conclusions. Assuming costs are identical under the monopoly and competitive industry structures (and assuming homogeneous products and the absence of dumping), then the monopoly structure yields lower levels of exports than the competitive one. If, however, international price discrimination (dumping) is allowed, then a monopoly industry is likely to export more than a competitive one. Under conditions in which the foreign and domestic products are imperfect substitutes (product differentiation) or the monopoly structure results in cost savings, almost anything can happen depending upon the conditions of demand in the two markets and the size of the efficiency gain resulting from monopolization.

While White's analysis leads to inconclusive results in predicting the impact of domestic monopoly on export activity, empirical evidence as well as less formal analysis suggest that firm size and a limited degree of market power may be conducive to the enhancement of exporting even beyond the achievement of economies of scale or the use of price discrimination. Conceptually, this conclusion is based upon the existence of market imperfections which render the securing of sales in foreign markets more difficult than in domestic markets.

For example, fluctuations in foreign exchange rates as well as the possibility of political developments affecting markets abroad make export sales relatively risky, especially if new capacity may be needed to serve foreign demand.[24] In addition, the fixed cost of information is likely to be higher in foreign than domestic markets owing to differences in language, customs, habits, and increased distance of the foreign markets from the firm's home base. Finally, the ability of a firm to simply compete on the basis of price may not be sufficient for it to secure foreign sales. It is reported, for example, that nonprice factors such as the ability of firms to supply credit to foreign buyers and the speed and certainty with which a firm can deliver its product often take precedence over price in determining foreign sales.[25]

Given the existence of these imperfections it is arguable that the firms which are best equipped to handle the problems and difficulties of exporting are those which are relatively large and possess some degree of market power in their domestic markets. It is these firms which are likely to have the sources of internal profits, the access to capital, and the volume of domestic sales necessary to overcome the inherent difficulties of penetrating foreign markets.

The available empirical evidence seems to support the conclusion that a limited degree of market power may aid export performance. Pagoulatos and Sorensen, for example, found that in U.S. export-competing manufacturing industries a statistically significant and positive relationship between the level of industry concentration and the proportion of industry output exported even after accounting for other industry characteristics such as the degree of plant scale economies, the amount of product differentiation, and the intensity of industry research and development activity.[26] Similar results have been reported by Caves and Khalilazdeh-Shirazi for their sample of U.S. firms.[27] In a study of trade among France, West Germany, and Italy, Owen found that industry concentration contributed a positive effect upon bilateral trade flows, but only up to a threshold level of concentration (between 45 and 60 percent) for the top eight firms.[28] For levels of concentration beyond the threshold, bilateral trade flows declined. The implication of Owen's result is that increases in firm size and market shares may aid export performance up to a point, but once the threshold is reached, oligopolistic interdependence may impede trade. Finally, Goodman and Ceyhun found in their study of U.S. international trade in manufactures that for industries which they classified as "new" (those with research and development expenditures as a percentage of sales greater than the overall manufacturing average), industry concentration exerted a positive influence upon export performance, but for industries classified as "old" (those with research and development expenditures below the average), the concentration-export relationship turned negative.[29]

Additional evidence on this matter can be drawn from the recent analyses of the effects of the Webb-Pomerene Act on U.S. export trade. Under the provisions of this act, firms are effectively exempted from U.S. antitrust laws and permitted to collude for purposes of export sales. Indeed, the original intent of the act was to increase the participation of small firms in export trade by providing them opportunities to overcome the difficulties of entering foreign markets mentioned earlier by the pooling of risk, information, and marketing costs, through export associations authorized by the act.

Perhaps the most interesting result obtained from the empirical studies of Webb associations is how little they have actually contributed to export promotion. Not only has the number of successful associations formed been small, but also the amount of exports which have been assisted through these associations has been limited. The U.S. Federal Trade Commission, for example, has estimated that only about 2.4 percent of annual aggregate U.S. exports receive Webb association assistance, and that even within individual industries Webb assistance seldom applied to as much as 10 percent of industry exports.[30] Some of the more successful Webb associations have been studied by Larson.[31] He finds that the successful associations were usually those formed by firms in industries already highly concentrated in the domestic market and producing relatively homogenous products. This result is not surprising, since these conditions are favorable to cartel formation. The activities of these associations, however, were such that they frequently choose to cooperate and seek "peaceful coexistence" with their overseas rivals rather than compete with them.

In conclusion, the existing evidence suggests that relaxation of antitrust enforcement and the promotion of mergers and cartels is a highly uncertain method of improving an industry's export or import competing performance. In many instances such policies may be counterproductive in that imports may actually increase and exports decline. Competition policies should rather be based upon their domestic merit. Mergers essential to the achievement of genuine economies of scale or to the rationalization of fragmented industries should rightfully be encouraged. At the same time, authorities should not fear to promote and preserve competitively structured industries where possible.

Measuring the Protective Effect of Industrial Policies

Many industrial policies have been adopted in recent years without the benefit of economic studies or data supporting their effectiveness in achieving the desired objective. Indeed, very few quantitative measurements have been made of the ex ante or ex post impact of these policies on domestic industry structures and international trade flows. One reason for this can be found in the lack of design in the adoption of industrial policy as a response to actual or presumed needs to facilitate industrial adjustment and structural change. Furthermore, only part of this increased government intervention has been motivated by the domestic and international effects of trade liberalization, and only some of the adopted measures have an intentional protective effect. It is thus very difficult to assess what the pattern of domestic production and international trade would be in the absence of such measures. Finally, few governments compile the necessary information for emprical evaluation, nor is it always very clear what the meaning and exact content of industrial policy is. For these reasons, the domestic structure and protective effects of such forms of government intervention are difficult to quantify.

A modest amount of research has now begun to fill the need for a quantitative measurement of the domestic and trade effects of industrial policies. This research has focused on two types of industrial policy: public procurement and government assistance to domestic and export industries. But these two policies represent only a small fraction of the wide range and variety of industrial policies implemented in recent years. The broad spectrum of such policies has simply not been studied. In the remaining part of this section we review the scant empirical evidence available up to now on the protective effect of a few industrial policy instruments.

One of the most widespread forms of discrimination against imports in industrialized countries is the public procurement of merchandise under various "buy domestic" regulations and procedures. This discrimination against foreign firms may manifest itself in the terms for soliciting bids, the various bidding requirements, and the criteria for selecting bids and awarding government contracts. There is little doubt that this form of government intervention, with the possible exception of cases involving public health of national security, represents a deliberate import restriction.

Two recent studies by Baldwin[32] and by Lowinger[33] have provided a quantitative assessment of the extent and impact of government discrimination as a nontariff barrier in the United States and EEC countries. Both studies utilize input-output information in the calculation of a hypothetical import figure under the assumption that the government has an import propensity similar to that of the private sector. The difference between this hypothetical figure and actual government imports provides an estimate of the degree of discrimination against foreign suppliers. The estimates obtained by Baldwin and Lowinger for the mid-1960s suggest that discriminatory procurement practices had a significant impact in curtailing imports in the United States and to a lesser extent in France and England.[34] Under the assumption of no government discrimination, U.S. government imports would have been more than six times their actual value. In contrast, these authors found no significant evidence of government discrimination against imports in the case of Belgium, Germany, Italy, and the Netherlands.

The above estimates refer mainly to the trade-diverting effects of public procurement. Government discrimination may also affect international trade flows indirectly, through the impact of this policy on domestic industry structure. This structural effect could result from reduced foreign competition, from the subsidy granted to the research and development activity of a company (as is often the case with aerospace), or through the strengthening and stabilization of leading-firm positions in particular industries. How significant is the domestic structural impact of discriminatory government procurement practices? More research is needed before any conclusive answer can be provided. Furthermore, while quantitative estimates are not available for Japan and other OECD countries, the general conclusion from the Baldwin and Lowinger results is that reduction in government discrimination will result in greater trade liberalization for U.S. industries as compared to the EEC.

A second type of industrial policy for which some tentative quantitative estimates exist in regard to its impact on trade is government assistance to industry. A wide variety of instruments have been utilized by OECD governments as aids to manufacturing industry. These range from direct grants to companies, to low interest rate loans, wage and social security subsidies, research and development support, preferential tax and credit treatment, retraining and technical assistance subsidies, and various export promotion subsidies. The scope and magnitude of these government aids varies from country to country as does the explicit objective for their adoption. This increased state involvement in the private sector has at times been part of a concerted effort to facilitate regional development or to promote certain technologically advanced industries. It has also been an attempt to facilitate structural changes imposed on domestic industry by technological factors and increased foreign competition. Whatever the announced goal of such policies, however, there is growing agreement that such industrial assistance policies have indirect, and sometimes direct, distorting effects on international trade flows.

One of the first attempts to capture the effect of domestic subsidies on changes in the pattern of trade is made by Denton, O'Cleirecain, and Ash with reference to the United Kingdom.[35] Their method consists of relating the pattern of British trade to a number of determinants of international trade flows including the role of U.K. subsidies to private enterprise. They found no hard evidence that trade flows or other indicators of domestic performance were correlated with the industrial pattern of U.K. government subsidies. Denton has subsequently provided further quantitative estimates of the extent of subsidization of British industry through assistance direct to specific industries as well as various general incentives, such as investment grants and the selective employment tax.[36] His study concludes that wide variations exist in the degree of subsidization among industries and between firms of the same industry. Denton further concludes that some types of subsidy, especially that given to save a firm from liquidation, had a considerable effect on the pattern of trade in the short run. On the other hand, public assistance granted for the purpose of industry modernization, may distort trade only in the long run if firms succeed in competing in world markets. Denton's general conclusion is that British industrial policy has been incoherent in terms of its objectives and the validity and effectiveness of its means in securing these objectives.

Melvyn Krauss has recently attempted to separate that portion of government subsidies that is more directed toward export promotion from domestic purposes.[37] His conclusion on the basis of U.K. input-output information is that the rate of subsidy to exported value, added in manufacturing, ranged from 0.91 percent to 3.59 percent. These figures impy a relatively low impact of subsidy payments on U.K. trade. His reliance, however, on input-output sources limits the validity of his results, since subsidy practices such as interest rate concessions, loan guarantees, and procurement policies are not included in input-output tables.

The public assistance given to West German industry has been recently evaluated by Gerhard Fels.[38] This author has surveyed German assistance policies and supplemented effective protection rates with the effective rate of direct industrial assistance. His results indicate that agriculture, food processing, and consumer goods industries were the sectors more highly protected as a result of direct government assistance.

Finally, the preferential tax treatment of exporters in U.S. industries has received considerable attention in recent years. This means of government export promotion is the Domestic International Sales Corporation (DISC), authorized in the United States by the Revenue Act of 1971. The procedure of the DISC consists of the establishment of special tax shelters that provide tax advantages to U.S. exporters for the purpose of inducing them to expand exports. Recent quantitative estimates by Horst and Pugel[39] and the U.S. Congressional Research Service[40] indicate that in 1974 U.S. exports were increased by about $1.4 to $2.1 billion and that 100,000 additional jobs were created as a result of the stimulative effect of DISC. This constitutes an approximate increase in the value of exports of only 2-3 percent. In general, the available evidence suggests that the adoption of the DISC as a means of improving U.S. export performance was more instrumental in increasing corporate profitability than in expanding exports.

Conclusions

Both domestic and international forces over the last few years have brought about pressures for structural transformation within the industrial sectors of OECD countries. Faced with the need to respond to these forces, governments in industrial countries have been divided between two courses of action: let the automatic forces, operating through the decentralized market process, guide the direction of structural transformation, or intervene with government action any time a firm, industry, or region feels threatened by either home or foreign developments. The recent proliferation of various instruments of industrial policy exemplifies the second, more interventionist, course of action.

In this paper, we argue on the basis of available theory and empirical evidence that the first course of action, reliance on market processes, is the preferable alternative. In the first place, we simply do not have a theory of structural change which allows us to determine what optimal industrial structures are, let alone their optimal rate of transformation. An industrial policy, designed to accommodate structural changes, presupposes the knowledge of precisely such a theory. Moreover, the ad hoc nature of many industrial policies is bound to result in conflicts between their various goals, which may cause them to become counterproductive.

If we accept the market alternative, our analysis suggests several policy implications. The available evidence indicates that free trade can lead not only to a more efficient utilization of the world's resources but also to greater competition in domestic markets. From the point of promoting effective competition, our analysis generally supports a policy of openness toward entry via international trade or multinational investment. In contrast, tariffs and other government-imposed impediments to trade reduce the scope for the elimination of monopoly distortions through foreign entry. On the other hand, the promotion of merger activity or the relaxation of antitrust as a means of improving export or import competing performance is an uncertain policy instrument both in terms of achieving the desired results and in terms of its conflict with competition policy. Competition policy is thus best undertaken in terms of its domestic merits.

Finally, the limited quantitative evidence on the international trade effects of two types of industrial policies, public procurement and subsidies, indicates that they do have a distorting effect upon international trade flows. Moreover, the available evidence suggests that their effects are more pronounced in restricting imports rather than promoting exports. This quantitative evidence is too limited and covers only a few of the many instruments of industrial policy to be of real help to policymakers. More studies of the broad spectrum of industrial policies and their domestic and international effects are necessary to achieve this goal.

Clearly industrial policies in advanced countries are becoming a topic of concern in the eyes of both private businesses and national governments. Their lack of transparency creates uncertainty and concern, not justified at times, about their protectionist effects. Moreover, the wide variety of measures applied and the specificity of industrial policies in terms of individual firms and industries makes a comprehensive study of their effects on domestic and international markets extremely difficult. Even if further research were to disentangle their effects on international trade and domestic structure, by their very nature, industrial policies are bound to be politically difficult to negotiate.

Notes

1. Among the various writings on industrial policy, the following are worth noting: *The Industrial Policies of 14 Member Countries* (Paris: Organization for Economic Co-operation and Development, 1971); G. Ohlin, "Trade in a Non-Laissez-Faire World," in *International Economic Relations*, ed., P. A. Samuelson (London: Macmillan, 1969); G. Ohlin, "National Industrial Policies and International Trade," in *Toward a New World Trade Policy*, ed. C. F. Bergsten (Lexington, Mass.: Lexington Books, 1975); S. J. Warnecke and E. N. Suleiman, eds., *Industrial Policies in Western Europe* (New York: Praeger, 1975); P. Uri, "Industrial Policy: Location, Technology, Multinational Firms, Competition, and Integration of Product Markets," in *Economic Integration: Worldwide, Regional, Sectoral*, ed. F. Machlup (London: Macmillan, 1976); S. J. Warnecke, ed., *International Trade and Industrial Policies* (New York: Holmes and Meier, 1978).

2. For more discussion on the needs and implications of the "new protectionism" see: B. Balassa, "The 'New Protectionism' and the International Economy," *Journal of World Trade Law* 12 (September/October 1978):409-36.

3. See, for example: B. Balassa, "Tariff Reductions and Trade in Manufactures Among the Industrial Countries," *American Economic Review* 56 (June 1966):466-73; H. P. Gray, *A Generalized Theory of International Trade* (New York: Holmes and Meier Publishers, 1976); H. G. Grubel and P. J. Lloyd, *Intra-Industry Trade* (London: Macmillan Press, 1975); G. C. Hufbauer, and J. G. Chilas, "Specialization by Industrial Countries: Extent and Consequences" in *The International Division of Labour: Problems and Perspectives*, ed. Herbert Giersch (Tubingen: J. C. B. Mohr, Paul Siebeck, 1974); Emilio Pagoulatos, and Robert Sorensen, "Two-Way International Trade: An Econometric Analysis," *Weltwirtschaftliches Archiv*, no. 3 (1975):454-65.

4. A more complete discussion of the advantages of foreign entrants as compared to domestic entrants is provided by: L. Esposito and F. Esposito, "Foreign Competition and Domestic Industry Profitability," *Review of Economics and Statistics* 53 (November 1971):343-53.

5. Emilio Pagoulatos and Robert Sorensen, "International Trade and Investment and Industrial Profitability of U.S. Manufacturing," *Southern Economic Journal* 42 (January 1976):425-34; and Esposito and Esposito, "Foreign Competition."

6. The relevant studies cited are: P. Hart and E. Morgan, "Market Structure and Economic Performance in the United Kingdom," *Journal of Industrial Economics* 25 (March 1977):177-93; J. Khalilzadeh-Shirazi, "Market Structure and Price-Cost Margins in United Kingdom Manufacturing Industries," *Review of Economics and Statistics* 56 (February 1974):67-76; T. Hitiris, "Effective Protection and Economic Performance in U.K. Manufacturing Industry, 1963 and 1968," *The Economic Journal* 88 (March 1978):107-20; E. Toder, *Trade Policy and the U.S. Automobile Industry* (New York: Praeger Publishers, 1978); Emilio Pagoulatos and Robert Sorensen, "Foreign Trade, Concentration and Profitability in Open Economies," *European Economic Review* (October 1976).

7. The relevant studies cited are: J. Jones, L. Laudadio, and M. Percy, "Market Structure and Profitability in Canadian Manufacturing Industry: Some Cross Section Results," *Canadian Journal of Economies* 6 (August 1973):356-68; D. McFertridge, "Market Structure and Price-Cost Margins: An Analysis of the Canadian Manufacturing Sector," *Canadian Journal of Economics* 6 (August 1973):344-55; H. Bloch, "Prices, Costs, and Profits in Canadian Manufacturing: The Influence of Tariffs and Concentration," *Canadian Journal of Economics* 7 (November 1974):594-610.

8. R. Caves et al., *Studies in Canadian Industrial Organization* (Ottawa: Information Canada, 1977).

9. P. Turner, "Some Effects of Devaluation: A Study Based on the U.K.'s Trade in Manufactured Goods" (Ph.D. dissertation, Harvard University, 1976).

10. P. Frederiksen, "Prospects of Competition from Abroad in Major Manufacturing Oligopolies," *Antitrust Bulletin* 20 (Summer 1975):339-76.

11. W. Sichel, "The Foreign Competition Omission in Census Concentration Ratios: An Empirical Evaluation," *Antitrust Bulletin* 20 (Spring 1975):89-105.

12. Toder, *Trade Policy.*

13. The most systematic treatment of this approach can be found in R. Caves, "International Corporations: The Industrial Economics of Foreign Investment," *Economica* 38 (February 1971):1-27; and R. Caves, "Industrial Organization" in *Economic Analysis and the Multinational Enterprise*, ed. J. Dunning (London: Allen and Unwin, 1974).

14. Indeed, Horst finds that within individual industries the only consistent difference between those firms that become multinational and those that do not is their relative size. See T. Horst, "The Firm and Industry Determinants of the Decision to Invest Abroad: An Empirical Study," *Review of Economics and Statistics* 54 (August 1972):258-66.

15. An excellent summary of these is provided in J. Baranson, "Technology Transfer Through the International Firm," *American Economic Review, Papers and Proceedings* 60 (May 1970):435-40.

16. See, for example, the surveys in C. Bergsten et al., *American Multinationals and American Interests* (Washington, D.C.: Brookings Institution, 1978); and G. Hufbauer, "The Multinational Corporation and Direct Investment" in *International Trade and Finance*, ed. P. Kenen (Cambridge: Cambridge University Press, 1975).

17. Evidence of this type of behavior has been found by F. Knickerbocker, *Oligopolistic Reaction and the Multinational Enterprise* (Cambridge: Harvard University Graduate School of Business Administration, 1973).

18. See, for example, S. Hirsch, *The Export Performance of Six Manufacturing Industries: A Comparative Study of Denmark, Holland, and Israel* (New York: Praeger Publishers, 1971).

19. See, for example, U.S. Department of State, Bureau of Public Affairs, Office of Media Services, *News Release,* 11 April 1973; *New York Times,* 9 January 1972 and 12 November 1972; and *Washington Post,* 13 April 1973.

20. While many differences still exist, there appears to be a convergence of thinking between the United States and Western European nations regarding the importance of antitrust and the maintenance of competitive market structures. See: Wilburn L. Fugate, "Antitrust Aspects of Transatlantic Investment," *Law and Contemporary Problems* 34 (Winter 1969):135-45.

21. L. White, "Industrial Organization and International Trade: Some Theoretical Considerations," *American Economic Review* (December 1974).

22. Emilio Pagoulatos and Robert Sorensen, "Domestic Market Structure and International Trade: An Empirical Analysis," *Quarterly Review of Economics and Business* 16 (Spring 1976):45-59.

23. R. Caves and J. Khalizadeh-Shirazi, "International Trade and Industrial Organization: Some Statistical Evidence," in *Welfare Aspects of Industrial Markets*, eds. A. P. Jacquemin and H. W. deJong (Leiden: Martinus Nijhoff, 1977).

24. This does not necessarily imply that an exporting firm is exposed to more overall risk than a nonexporting firm. A firm may in fact be able to reduce total

risk by diversifying sales over several geographically distinct export markets.

25. A detailed account of the importance of nonprice factors in affecting international trade is provided by I. Kravis and R. Lipsey, *Price Competitiveness in World Trade* (New York: National Bureau of Economic Research, 1971).

26. Pagoulatos and Sorensen, "Domestic Market Structure."

27. Caves and Khalilzadeh-Shirazi, "International Trade."

28. N. Owen, *Intra EEC Trade and Industry Structure*, mimeographed (London: Department of Trade and Industry, 1973).

29. B. Goodman and F. Ceyhun, "U.S. Export Performance in Manufacturing Industries: An Empirical Investigation," *Weltwirtschaftliches Archiv*, no. 3 (1976).

30. *Webb-Pomerene Association: A 50 Year Review* (Washington, D.C.: Federal Trade Commission, 1967).

31. D. Larson, "An Economic Analysis of the Webb-Pomerene Act," *Journal of Law and Economics* 13 (October 1970):461-500.

32. R. E. Baldwin, *Nontariff Distortions of International Trade* (Washington, D.C.: The Brookings Institution, 1970), pp. 58-83.

33. T. C. Lowinger, "Discrimination in Government Procurement of Foreign Goods in the U.S. and Western Europe," *Southern Economic Journal* 42 (January 1976):451-60.

34. The crudeness of the data utilized, and the possibility that some of the products purchased by the government are not directly comparable to those utilized by the private sector impose limitations on the interpretation and validity of these results. For further discussion of these estimates see, W. R. Cline et al., *Trade Negotiations in the Tokyo Round: A Quantitative Assessment* (Washington, D.C.: The Brookings Institution, 1978), pp. 189-194.

35. G. Denton, S. O'Cleireacain, and S. Ash, *Trade Effects of Public Subsidies to Private Enterprise* (London: Macmillan, 1975).

36. G. Denton, "Financial Assistance to British Industry" in *Public Assistance to Industry*, eds. W. M. Corden and G. Fels (London: Macmillan, 1976), pp. 120-164.

37. M. Krauss, "Export-Promoting Subsidies in the United Kingdom: Theoretical and Empirical Aspects," paper cited in S. O'Cleireacain, "Measuring the International Effect of Subsidies," in *Industrial Trade and Industrial Policies*, ed. S. J. Warnecke (New York: Holmes and Meier, 1978), p. 209.

38. G. Fels, "Overall Assistance to German Industry," in *Public Assistance to Industry*, eds., W. M. Corden and G. Fels (London: Macmillan, 1976), pp. 91-119.

39. For a more detailed account of the DISC legislation, its subsequent modifications, and an estimate of its effect on U.S. exports, see: T. Horst and T. Pugel, "The Impact of DISC on the Prices and Profitability of U.S. Exports," *Journal of Public Economics* 7 (February 1977):73-87.

40. J. Gravelle et al., "The Domestic International Sales Corporation (DISC) and Its Effect on U.S. Foreign Trade and Unemployment" (Washington, D.C.: Congressional Research Service, Library of Congress, May 4, 1976).

Commentary

Robert G. Hawkins

The Pagoulatos-Sorensen paper deals with the economic literature on three aspects of the relationships between domestic industrial (and competitive) structure and international trade. The first involves the linkages running from import competition (and inward investment from foreign multinational firms) to domestic competitive performance and industry structure. The second concerns the reverse linkage; i.e., the linkage from domestic competition/monopoly policy to international trade and export competitiveness. And the third examines the effects on international trade of certain types of industrial policies to aid export- or import-competing industries in the OECD countries.

In general the paper is readable and informative. The paper is largely a survey of research already published by themselves and others on the topics mentioned. I have few comments concerned with errors of commission; my real quarrel involves some significant omissions.

In examining the literature on the linkage between international trade and domestic competition, Pagoulatos and Sorensen find that the bulk of the evidence, although in some cases somewhat ambiguous, is that import competition restrains price behavior in domestic industry and thus represents a force to lessen monopoly in domestic industry. Although with more qualification and less evidence, their conclusion on the role of market entry by multinational firms is also favorable—that competition is likely to be increased in the host country, and indeed that inward foreign direct investment may substitute for imports.

In general, my reading of the empirical evidence on these relationships jibes with theirs. Competition from foreign firms, in the import markets and from foreign firms operating affiliates in the local market, is a substitute for domestic competition. There are obviously instances in which this need not be beneficial—as when there are collusive arrangements between foreign exporters or investors and local firms, or when foreign firms which used to serve the local market via imports merge with one of the local competitors. This *may* increase monopoly in the local market, but need not if the local merger candidate would have disappeared anyway. Despite the ambiguity of outcome on a priori grounds, the empirical evidence points overwhelmingly toward a salutory effect on the competitive nature of local markets from import and foreign investment penetration.

While Pagoulatos and Sorensen are thorough in their treatment of domestic competitive effects of imports, they largely neglect the second step in the linkage, which is of major concern. Do these competitive effects from imports or foreign investment significantly affect domestic industrial structure? And if so, favorably or unfavorably? This question leads to the crux of the debate over structural adjustment policies to changing international competitiveness. Should domestic policies facilitate the adjustment? Should they block the adjustment (or at least slow it down)? Or are they irrelevant in any event? In short, the paper does not relate the findings of the literature surveyed to the more important policy issues.

The second area of literature examined is that relating to the reverse of the above linkage—the effects of domestic competition (or antimonopoly) policy on export- or import-competitive performance of the nation. The evidence offered here is more meager, and more ambiguous. The authors end with a pro-competition and pro-free trade policy point of view, by interpreting various empirical studies and studies of U.S. Webb-Pomerene associations showing that monopolies (or exclusion from antitrust restrictions) and concentrated industries do not have better export performance than "competitive" industries (or those with low concentration ratios). Nor does high concentration improve an industry's ability to compete with imports. In short, a "competitive" or unconcentrated industry is about the best bet to achieve good relative export- and import-competitive performance.

Again, I do not seriously question this interpretation of the evidence. But the implications are not drawn from this evidence for the extent of structural change in the industrial countries, or their capacity to make structural adjustments, and how the competitive structure of domestic industry, working through international competitiveness, affects such magnitudes.

The third area covered in the paper deals with the protective effects of industrial policies, but focuses almost exclusively on two types of policies—discriminatory government procurement policies and aids to export industries. It is this part of the paper which I find least satisfying.

First, the authors' unquestioned acceptance of the conclusions of two studies, heavily qualified by Baldwin and Lowinger, the authors of the original research, that government procurement policies in the United

States have been *more restrictive* than those in Europe (France, the United Kingdom, Italy, Belgium) is rather incredible. Perhaps the only area where this interpretation may be correct is in defense procurement. For nondefense items, the United States has buy-American preferences, but most of the countries mentioned do not even announce most government procurement contracts for foreign, or even domestic, public bidding. Indeed, the U.S. trade negotiators have been the strongest advocate of liberalization of government procurement nontariff barriers—hardly a posture to be expected from a country whose government procurement restrictiveness was highest.

That minor point of interpretation aside, a more fundamental issue of governmental "protection" through industrial policies is not discussed at all. This involves direct government involvement in decision making and ownership of industry. In some major industries this may involve either nonmarket decisions or public ownership of major enterprises. Public ownership, or even public (governmental) representation on the board of directors of a major firm may influence company decisions with respect to exports, imports, foreign investment, and the like which, either with or without explicit subsidies, may dramatically influence industrial adjustment and international competitiveness.

There are many major examples of governmental effects on industrial structure and international trade and competitiveness: the European decision to build the Concorde and Airbus jetliners, with substantial governmental involvement in each; direct governmental financing of steel, chemicals, and other industries in Europe and the United States; direct and indirect governmental participation in the computer industry in Japan, and the security accorded to Fujitsu in that industry. All of these are industrial policies—discrete and direct—which have affected international competition in major, observable ways. But they are examples which fall beyond the scope of the paper.

As many of the papers in this volume emphasize, government intervention in the economic process, both to bring about structural change and to avoid structural change, has increased dramatically in the postwar period, and perhaps has quickened in the 1970s. This has caused shifts in comparative advantages in many instances, and has blocked or slowed such shifts in other instances. But, as Anne Krueger's paper argues, there has been relatively little disruption in U.S. industrial structure arising from import competition—especially imports from LDCs. And international trade and investment has continued to grow apace, in spite of (or perhaps because of) growing government interventon and the new protectionism.

How can these seemingly incompatible trends exist side-by-side? One reason may be, as suggested by Mr. Nukazawa, that many governmental interferences in the trade and industrial process are ineffective. If we restrict imports of rice, rice crackers are imported instead. However, this cannot be the whole story.

If the growing restrictionism is effective in retarding structural change, then some nations must lose—the gains from trade or the gains from growth are reduced. But this raises an anomaly as well. Japan, which has been most directly activist among the industrial countries in pursuing an interventionist industrial policy, apparently has not suffered greatly in lower gains from trade or loss of economic growth.

A final interpretation of the anomaly of growing government intervention with growing world trade and investment is that the impact of the intervention occurs with a lag that it has not yet been fully felt. Are we, then, in for a period of slower growth in world trade and slower growth in production and productivity as a result of the inefficiencies of interventionist industrial policies? Victoria Curzon Price's paper argues that we are, and so have others in this volume. Time will tell, but that interpretation of the anomaly should make some policymakers uneasy.

Commentary

Victoria Curzon Price

I enjoyed reading this paper. What I got out of it was the proposition that government industrial policy tends to be self-defeating and contradictory. For anybody who has gone into this area a bit, this rings absolutely true. Governments cross wires all the time when they indulge in industrial policy.

The paper starts with a very long list of industrial policies and then focuses on three of them in detail—trade policy, competition policy, and public procurement. Only the last few pages are devoted to industrial policy in its narrower sense—public assistance to industry. If I had to criticize this paper, which is very difficult to do, I would say that the authors did not put enough emphasis on this last section.

Industrial policy in its narrow sense is any microeconomic or discretionary measure to prevent or to promote structural change. This differs radically from old-fashioned industrial policies, which set a general framework through tariffs, tax systems and the like, and let the market get on with the business of allocating resources within that framework. The new microeconomic industrial policy brings the government right down into the nitty-gritty of deciding which sector, indeed, which *firm,* is eligible for access to investment funds, and how those funds should be spent. This introduces a new discretionary element into government economic policy which was not there in the 1960s.

Pagoulatos and Sorensen rightly point out that it is very difficult to measure the importance of the "new" industrial policy. I would agree with this. For instance, even when a government converts a company's debt into state equity, as France did in 1978 for its troubled steel industry, it is difficult to determine the extent of the subsidy element. How much more difficult it is to measure the subsidy element contained in a cartel!

In Europe we have one official cartel for steel, permitted under the terms of the Treaty of Paris establishing the European Coal and Steel Community, and a more controversial one for man-made fibers agreed to in 1978 between the eleven large chemical/fiber producers in Europe under the auspices of the Industrial Policy Directorate of the EEC Commission. After a while, the director in charge of competition policy said, "Ah, but this is illegal," and the director of the industrial policy division replied, "Yes, but it's necessary. Can't you find a way out?"—a good example, incidentally, of a public body at war with itself. The matter remains undecided: the Competition Directorate continues to say that the fiber cartel is illegal, but has not prosecuted it. How do you measure the value to the industry of that form of protection? It is huge because it allows firms to get together, fix prices, share markets, plan reductions in capacity, and so forth. And it is very much part of the "new" industrial policy.

Now Pagoulatos and Sorensen are quite kind to industrial policy, saying that it is not always protectionist in intent or effect. Perhaps. But I have the feeling that most of the time it *is* protectionist both in intent and in effect. Take the much vaunted adjustment assistance which is often cited as a positive facet of industrial policy. The argument goes: "If we can give our stricken industries adjustment assistance we shall be able to reduce tariffs and to increase trade." This is not always how it works out. Give a firm or an industry adjustment assistance and you very quickly obscure market signals for it. Soon, neither labor nor management will see the need to make more than marginal adjustments. Adjustment assistance then tends to become adjustment resistance, even when the original intention is simply to give firms a "breathing space." After a while, if the sector is really faced with large structural change, it will ask for a permanent nontariff barrier. This has happened in textiles and it is happening with steel.

In Europe we have another kind of industrial policy which is called industrial strategy. This is a much grander name. Here, the government has a long-term vision, extending at least beyond the next twelve months, about where it thinks the economy should go, and how it should get there. This means that the government gets together with industry and labor to talk things over on a sector by sector basis, to swap plans, spot potential floods and bottlenecks, and direct investment accordingly. This huddling together would be called concerted action and would be illegal in terms of most antitrust laws if government officials were not present, but under their benign chairmanship, it becomes known as industrial strategy.

Well, you might think that if this is how a country like the United Kingdom wants to run its economy, that is its own business. But this system has international repercussions. Suppose we get an open-ended "indicative" plan for a sector and everyone goes back and tries to do his bit, but there is one market participant who was not invited to participate in the planning process and who is capable of upsetting the apple cart completely: the foreign producer. Since he is the disturbing element, there is a terrific incentive to exclude him. So industrial strategy goes hand in hand with an increase in protection. You can see this happening very clearly in textiles and steel in Europe.

I agree wholeheartedly with the thesis of the paper that free trade is the world's best antitrust policy. The authors, however, add to this the fact that we also have free investment, which brings with it competition in the form of multinational corporations. They point out that, by extraordinary good fortune, this foreign investment goes right where it is most needed—into markets where oligopolistic structures and product differentiation are rife. They then draw the conclusion that free trade and free investment together are potent factors favoring competition and efficiency. I do not dispute this general thesis, but I worry about the assumption that the foreign multinational entering an oligopolistic market will necessarily compete strongly with the resident oligarchs; he may do so to begin with, in order to establish his position, but since he presumably shares many of their features, as likely as not he will in due course settle down to "not rocking the boat" like the others. The number of firms may have risen, the concentration ratio may have declined, but has the quality of competition been improved? I prefer to remain agnostic on this point—it surely depends on the circumstances. If one views trade, direct investment, and licensing as three alternative methods of reaching foreign markets, all one can say is that it is undoubtedly better to have all three possibilities open, instead of just one or two. The one chosen will then reflect the least-cost avenue and will offset attempts by government to distort market signals in one or another of them. However, if one had to choose between them, one would presumably put free trade well ahead of free investment as a guarantee of effective competition.

The authors cite studies by Baldwin and Lowinger to the effect that "discriminatory procurement practices had a significant impact in curtailing imports in the United States and to a lesser extent in France and England" but that they found "no significant evidence of government discrimination against imports in the case of Belgium, Germany, Italy, and the Netherlands." These absolutely stunning findings need urgent comment. First, if the figures do not show Italy as supporting its industry through public procurement, then the correct inference is not that Italy does not support its industry, but that it does so some other way. There are more ways to skin this particular cat than one has even dreamed of in this innocent country. Or the figures themselves may be misleading: when the City of Rome awarded a contract to Siemens for a couple of generators in 1971, there was a virtual revolution and the decision had to be revoked. I have no reason to believe that the situation has changed since. Secondly, governments have very different consumption patterns compared to households. They buy armaments, aircraft, computers, satellites, and nuclear power plants as well as shoes and socks for the military, and paper clips and red tape for the civil service. It is therefore unwarranted to assume that the government's average propensity to import (GAPM) is the same as the nation's (APM). In Europe, the GAPM is probably much higher than the APM because many costly high technology items have to be imported. In the United States on the other hand, the government's undistorted marginal propensity to import is probably lower than the nation's because these costly high technology items are produced locally. I would suggest that this might be another reason why the United States shows up comparatively poorly, and Europe comparatively well, in the reported calculations.

The principal contribution of this paper is, I believe, to have reviewed the extensive literature on the subject of industrial policy most conscientiously, to have emphasized the lack of coherence in these policies, and to have reported on the as yet scanty quantitative evidence that has been brought in by the research hounds. My only fear is that as the latter are trained to go after figures, they may, in this supremely unquantified field, miss the main point—the fact that the state is not only in the marketplace (which is quantifiable) but that it also increasingly uses its power to manipulate private market participants (which is not).

12

The New Protectionism

Sidney Golt

On two successive days in November 1977, the United Kingdom secretaries of state for trade and for industry answered questions in the House of Commons about:

- the figures of the index of competitiveness for British export prices;
- the movement in the terms of trade for machinery and transport equipment;
- the fourth directive of the European Commission on aids to shipbuilding;
- how many applications had been received for government support under the clothing industry scheme, and what total amount of assistance had been given (the answers were 482 and £ 3.9 million);
- the total amount given out under the ferrous foundry scheme (£ 65 million);
- whether to confer full development area status on the whole county of Clwyd;
- how much of the shipbuilding fund had been committed (£ 50 million);
- what discussions had taken place with European Community ministers and commissioners about the future of the steel industry;
- how representatives from trade unions were to be included in the membership of the Regional National Enterprise Boards;
- the corporate plan for the future strategy of British Leyland;
- a list of bodies concerned with industrial organization to which the government appointed members (there were 106);
- limitation of steel imports from Comecon countries;

- a study commissioned by the government on how industries might be attracted to Merseyside; and
- the state of discussions between the government and a Japanese manufacturing company about its proposals to establish a television set–making factory in Britain (it eventually withdrew because of opposition from existing domestic firms and the trade unions).

The number and range of questions is illustrative, and by no means exceptional; the issue of *Trade and Industry* from which they come was picked at random. They begin to indicate that extent of the involvement of government, at any rate in the United Kingdom, in industrial affairs, though not perhaps the depth and the degree of detail into which that involvement has gone in relation to the day-to-day affairs of the many individual firms (such as the 482 clothing manufacturers) who are affected by those government activities.

Britain was in some respects a rather late arrival in this kind of government interventionism; in its present manifestations it has perhaps gone further and faster than many other countries. Perhaps, also, the process of daily parliamentary questioning of ministers makes the position in Britain somewhat more transparent than elsewhere. It is generally accepted, however, that in one way or another most of the OECD countries—including, increasingly, the United States—are now set on similar paths. The methods used vary substantially from country to country, depending on the inherited institutional pattern, especially, perhaps, the pattern of traditional methods of financing of industry.

The tendencies illustrated above are, of course, not new. It is, however, the growth and intensity of their manifestations during the last decade, and especially since 1973, which has prompted the present degree of interest—an interest symbolized most importantly, perhaps, by the OECD decision that its industry committee should prepare a report on "Positive Adjustment Policies" for submission to the council in March 1979.

Goran Ohlin has summarized the basic considerations as follows:

> For some decades now, programs and agencies to aid industry in different ways have proliferated in industrial countries, pari passu with the liberalisation of international trade. This is a source of concern to those who see in such practices the demise of the mixed economy, a new and covert protectionism, a source of international conflict, and an issue on which negotiated agreement may be difficult to come by.
>
> Concern has focussed on the extent to which increased state involvement in the private sector and the concomitant multiplication of

direct and indirect forms of subsidization have contributed to the erosion of the validity and viability of the liberal economic concepts and assumptions upon which much of contemporary commercial diplomacy, such as takes place in the GATT, has been based. The changed relationship between governments and their private sectors has affected both the operation of firms and markets. The minimization of risk through subsidies has influenced the conditions under which international competition takes place. And active government industrial policies have challenged traditional notions of comparative advantage, thereby affecting the processes and rates at which the global distribution of industry advances.[1]

In considering these developments, I once drew attention to a lighthearted contribution to the discussion which was made by the British delegation to the negotiations which produced the Stockholm Convention which established the European Free Trade Association in 1959. This was the draft of a parallel "Convention for the Frustration of Trade," under which there would be set up an "Association for the Frustration of Trade," trade being defined as "the benefits which it is feared may be conferred by the Convention." Article 3 reads:

The objectives of the Association shall be
  a. to frustrate the normal tendency of trade to increase and to ensure its diminution
  b. to frustrate all measures that any Member States might attempt to introduce in pursuit of its first objective; and
  c. to ensure, by use of subsidies, by the encouragement of dumping, and by discrimination on all possible grounds, that the following provisions of the Convention, in so far as they may apply, shall be circumvented.

What was quite an amusing joke in 1959 has, by 1979, got rather uncomfortably close to reality, at any rate in a few areas of trade. It is, perhaps, particularly interesting to note the implication that subsidies might be used to prevent imports, rather than—as would have been the more prevalent accusation at the time—as illegitimate means of promoting exports.

It must, of course, be accepted that the practices of government referred to are not presented primarily, and often not at all, as instruments of protectionism. They are seen as the mechanisms by which governments intervene in, or try to influence, the market so as to produce a variety of results desired by the concerns of government policies. These policies are very varied in their origins and objectives.

They may be concerned with matters quite remote from, or only very indirectly concerned with, international trade. They are, indeed, part of the very large and not yet sufficiently analyzed growth of the power and the role of the state over the whole postwar period. The philosophic basis of this development might well lie in the way in which, almost without noticing it, the countries which fought a great war against the centralized, all powerful, Fascist states, found it necessary, in order to intensify their own war-waging machine and the mechanisms of recovery from war, to exercise similar central and dictatorial authority; and that the habit of authority so assumed has never been shed.

Meanwhile, an attitude of mind which accepts a very much larger and more pervasive role for central authority has become the general atmosphere of the whole society. Certainly, there are now very few who would seriously contest the proposition that it is part of the proper function of government to act as the agent for all of us in remedying obvious social evils, relieving poverty, improving the environment, and, in general, to protect and promote the welfare of people, and especially of the least powerful sections of the population—the young, the old, and the sick. These are functions which have been in the past, and to a certain extent still are, the concern of private charity and private endeavor, but—even though it is arguable that the innovative impulses in these fields still flow from private efforts—there is at least a century of development of the role of the state. (It should, however, be noted that what the state gives away for these purposes is what it has taken in taxation; and this on the one hand leaves less room for the exercise of the still valuable virtue of private charity, and on the other hand opens up a considerable debate on whether the right balance is struck between equity and efficiency.)[2]

But alongside this concept of the role of the state in humanitarian affairs, the growth of government intervention stems also from the belief of some sections of our societies that there should be a very considerable measure of central direction and control of economic activity for two main reasons—first, to ensure the fulfillment of social ends more certainly than would result from private action, and, secondly, because the central authority, it is said, can and will make "better" decisions about the organization and planning of industry and investment than would be made by the uncontrolled and undirected decisions of the myriad of individuals, companies, and private institutions which constitute the market.

At this stage, without attempting to argue on this issue, it seems to me important to draw the distinction between these two separate sets of causes. It is certainly not proven that the attainment of welfare objectives requires a high degree of involvement by the state in the control and direction of industry. On the contrary, it is increasingly clear that the more governments intervene in the operations of the market, especially by detailed incursions into the activities of individual firms, the greater the likelihood of international friction and tension, and the greater the probability of dislocation and disturbance of international trade, for the adoption of these lines of policy both exposes government to the greatest pressures towards protectionism and offers it the easiest and most insidious means of practicing it.

This is why the question of new forms of protectionism is so much absorbed into the more general question of what is now called either "industrial policy" or "adjustment assistance." The connection was put clearly by Professor H. Johnson in his presidential address to Section F of the British Association in 1973:

> The new techniques of mercantilist policy, for their part, reflect recognition of two facts. One is that the protective tariff of traditional mercantilist philosophy is a very crude and blunt instrument for favoring domestic industry, by comparison with the techniques now available. In a modern economy, the government both imposes heavy taxation that can be remitted, or converted into a subsidy, conditionally on the beneficiary behaving in ways specified by the government—the tariff by contrast rests only on the hope of desired performance—and is itself the largest or one of the largest customers of private industry, and, because it is subject neither to the test of profit maximization or to its own restrictive practice legislation, can use its spending power to discriminate in favor of domestic over foreign industry. It can even be argued—and has been seriously suggested[3]—that the inferiority of the tariff as a protective device, rather than enthusiasm for the principle of free trade as such, has been largely responsible for the postwar movement towards trade liberalization by multilateral tariff reducing negotiations under the General Agreement on Tariffs and Trade.
>
> The second fact is that in the modern world of industries based on high technology and hence subject to important economies of scale and diminishing cost, as overhead research-and-development investment is spread over a larger volume of output, protection of domestic producers in the domestic national market is no longer adequate or efficient. To be efficient, production must extend to the export market. But since the rules of GATT frown on export subsidization, protection in the export market must be at least semi-disguised in acceptable form. Techniques for achieving this include subsidization of export credit rather than of the exports themselves; tying of foreign development assistance and overseas military expenditure to purchases from domestic suppliers; and subsidization of research and development costs for potentially export-

winning industries (on this last technique, consider the justification commonly advanced for the investment of over £900 million of public money in the development of the Concorde).[4]

All this said, it would be mistaken to suppose that protectionism in the 1970s is confined to the range of policies pursued by governments, either through their own ideological predilections, or—as often—under pressure from sectional interests, as part of industrial policy or adjustment assistance programs. Other forms of action, and other arguments of various kinds, have also been deployed, and should be described before we return to a fuller discussion of the "adjustment" theme.

Among these other devices, what were once thought of as monstrous efforts to circumvent the disciplines and rules of the GATT, the so-called voluntary restraint arrangements, have by now almost acquired a patina of respectable normality. This is, no doubt, merely one aspect of the continuous weakening of respect for the fabric, and especially the procedures, of the GATT, which has characterized the current decade. But perhaps even more ominously for the future, the negotiation of some, at least, of the "voluntary" export restraints has been the clearest instance of a return to the kind of exercise of commercial, political, or sometimes, financial power in imposing the protective policies of the strong on the weak, which was a characteristic of the 1930s. In form, the arrangements have usually avoided direct contravention of GATT articles. In substance they have been among the most obvious departures from the principles on which the GATT was based. Moreover, the lack of internal constraints on their use by the government of the importing country, the absence of consultation with other domestic interests who might be adversely affected, and the extralegal character of their operation are among the characteristics which make them habit-forming and infectious.[5] Nor is the character of these arrangements fundamentally changed if they result from negotiations between groups of traders on each side instead of from pressure by one government or another. There is almost always in the background a common knowledge that governmental pressure, and power, is in reserve.

Nonetheless, arrangements of this kind, and more formal "orderly marketing arrangements"—more openly negotiated by governments—have been, to a considerable extent, condoned and even encouraged by some sections of liberal opinion, both in the United States and in Europe. The general line of argument has been that in a world where governments cannot resist the volume of pressure on them to provide some protection against loss of jobs resulting from imports, it is less damaging to make some concession to these pressures in a limited, controlled way, than to create a situation in which much more full-blooded protectionist legislation and action will be irresistible. It is ostensibly on this basis that the U.S. and Japanese governments have condoned interindustry arrangements that might well be a contravention of their domestic legislation, as well as repugnant to the spirit, if not the letter, of the GATT; that the U.S. government has negotiated orderly marketing agreements for television sets and shoes; that the United Kingdom government has encouraged talk between the industries in the U.K. and Japan in pursuit of arrangements on bicycles, automobiles, television receivers, and other products; that most other European governments have acted similarly; and that there has been resistance to the idea that such private arrangements should be subject to scrutiny in the GATT through notification and consultation procedures.

It was in the context of developments of this kind that French leaders floated the concept which was variously labelled "organized liberalization," "organized free trade," and "managed trade expansion." The concept has never been spelled out in any detail; but its ancestry can readily be traced to the French philosophy of "organized markets" which underlay the bitterest conflicts between French and (at that time) Anglo-American trade philosophies in the early 1960s, and especially during the first United Nations Conference on Trade and Development. It is both a powerful symptom of the transformation of international attitudes in the intervening period, and a somewhat frightening example of the debasement of language. (Compare the British usage "industrial action" to describe a stoppage of work by strikes.)

To a substantial extent, the Multifibres Arrangement, and its predecessor, the Long Term Cotton Textiles Agreement, might be taken as models of the kind of system which could be brought within the "organized liberalization" concept. Certainly, in its original form the LTA could be defended, with some degree of conviction, as seeking to provide an orderly and progressive mechanism for abolishing existing import restictions, and as a way of buying time during which a new equilibrium of the world's industrial pattern could establish itself. There could then be a restoration of normal competitive conditions, without recourse to intervention by governments in the trading process. This is not how things turned out, however. In the event, at the end of sixteen years of the system, it is still restrictive—indeed, more so than before, since its latest renegotiation; it has apparently proved to be a weapon at hand for retaining and solidifying protection, and in some respects for extending it. It is no doubt true that during the period of the currency of the LTA and MFA, changes have been carried through in some of the older manufacturing countries which have both slimmed down their textile industries and left the surviving sections stronger and more competitive. But it is at least arguable that these changes have been brought about to a far greater extent by changes in technology and fashion than because of the effect of the arrangements, and it would be difficult to substantiate a claim that the restrictions, as they have operated, have made a significant contribution to the total well-being of the restricting countries, and probably equally difficult to demonstrate more than a marginal effect on the geographical pattern of development of textile industries throughout the world over the period.

More detailed discussion of potential developments of the concept of "organization" would bring us back into the field of industrial policy; before doing this there should at least be some mention of the very substantial increase in the use of various administrative and judicial procedures to harass, and sometimes positively obstruct, imports. This frequently manifests itself in emphasizing the concept of "fairness" in international trade. Certainly "fairness" is an important element which the GATT has always recognized. But the slogan of "free but fair" trade easily lends itself to the exploitation of legal provisions against "unfair" trade, which are particularly characteristic of U.S. trade law. Indeed, it is in the United States, with its more elaborate system of trade jurisdiction and procedure, that the use, to some limited extent by government but much more vigorously by domestic industry and the trade unions (now firmly revising their long tradition of support for free trade), is seen most openly. It is in the United States, too, that there has been an outbreak of new pressures for legislation for government to buy nationally instead of making procurement more accessible internationally. The pressure here is in state legislation, not on the federal government directly; and during the last year or so five states have in fact enacted new "buy American" requirements.[6] But similar developments, both in the use of administrative procedures—the much readier resort by governments to anti-dumping duties; more vigorous pressures on the subsidiaries of foreign firms to increase the "local content" of their products; and less perceptible, but more insidious, a good deal of arbitrariness in the administrative handling of what are regarded as sensitive imports—and in the emergence in some countries of "buy national" campaigns, can be observed in Europe also.

Nothing in the present state of political or industrial affairs in most OECD countries suggests that there is any likelihood of an early change in attitudes, or in the pressures producing these protectionist tendencies. Certainly, the official pronouncements of both governments and of the official representative bodies of industry still support the objective of open world trade. Indeed, the wording of the communiques following the London Summit meeting of 1977 and the Bonn Summit of 1978 rejected protectionist policies in the most forthright terms; they would "foster unemployment, increase inflation and undermine the welfare of our people," and the governments were therefore determined "on the need to maintain our political commitment to an open and non-discriminatory world trading system." The OECD communiques after the ministerial meetings in both 1977 and 1978 echoed and reinforced this. In 1977, it was emphasized that "recourse to protectionist policies would foster unemployment, increase inflation and reduce economic welfare" and that increasing interdependence reinforced the need for a "renewed political commitment to avoid restrictive unilateral trade and current account measures" which "tended to carry the risk of proliferation with self defeating implications." In the 1978 communique, the ministers congratulated themselves in noting that "despite the difficult circumstances . . . an open trading system has been maintained" and they reiterated their "commitment to an open multilateral trading system." But in spite of these protestations, no serious observer would now question the growth of protectionist action. Indeed, the 1978 OECD communique could not altogether resist a touch of realism breaking through—perhaps more than a touch, with the recognition by ministers of:

the costs and dangers inherent in the continuation of present-day trends:
    There are growing pressures for protection against foreign competition and for export subsidies, and a growing risk that unilateral trade and other current account measures could touch off chain reactions. There has been a tendency for sectoral, regional and manpower policies to shift from action to foster adjustment to structural change to measures of a defensive character that tend to preserve the status quo, which thus in important respects have the same effects as protectionist trade measures. Under conditions of high unemployment some domestic measures to maintain existing employment in sectors or companies in financial difficulty may in certain circumstances be justified in the short run. But their continuation on a large scale would, over time, undermine the dynamic process which underlies rising productivity and would inhibit sustained non-inflationary growth.[7]

It was, one must suppose, with this in mind that the ministers also agreed on the "general orientations for policies to facilitate the structural adjustments needed to sustain faster economic growth" which were contained in an annex to the communique. I shall return to discussion of this annex later; at this stage I would simply comment that one must suppose that not all the ministers who endorsed it can have read it, given the policies that their governments are following.

To try to assess the direction in which OECD government policies might move, it seems worth examining two particular statements which illustrate underlying philosophies—deeply opposed to each other—and then to consider whether the trends of the Geneva multilateral trade negotiations, so far as they are known at the time of writing, are likely to affect policies fundamentally.

The first document is a United Kingdom government paper, prepared by the Department of Industry and notified to Parliament in January 1976. It was published in July 1976 as an appendix to that year's Annual Report on the Industry Act, 1972.[8] This aims to set out the conclusions reached by the government on the criteria for assistance to industry. It defines the objective as being that "British industry should compete more successfully in meeting the requirements of home and overseas markets" (so the objective is clearly set in the context of international trade). To produce this result, the state has to establish the broad social and economic framework within which industry operates and, within this framework, to be "concerned with the allocation of resources to industries, public or private . . . operating in a market economy."

Generally speaking, it says, profitability and return on capital are the best prima facie indicators of where available resources should go. But "the process of price allocation through the price mechanism does not ensure an adequate level of aggregate demand and employment, nor produce an acceptable distribution of income, or cause resources to be set aside for the public services. All these are mainly functions of government, not the market." Moreover, company profits and losses are not, in all cases, a "wholly accurate" measure of resource costs and benefits. The "community" may strike a cost and benefit account different from that of the individual enterprise. In such cases, the divergence may be redressed by "taxation, planning controls or subsidies." One essential and clear-cut criterion for such action is "the creation, maintenance and safeguarding of employment" in particular, disadvantaged localities. But there is more difficulty in defining any other general class of case where "there is a presupposition that resources costs and benefits will diverge from money costs and benefits." Apart from the employment criterion, "the balance of payments has provided the most clearly identifiable reason for believing this to be the case in certain situtations, and has been the most common reason for assistance" on the grounds of "benefit to the economy and the national interest."

The paper then goes on to study in considerable detail the factors to be taken into account in assessing the viability of candidates for assistance, on the one hand, and social costs and benefits, on the other. The cost of achieving viability has to be set against the value of these benefits, and the public expenditure implications must be an "important element in the total valuation" (though clearly not a decisive one). Job security is important, but "if we are to break through the balance of payments constraint and thus achieve more room for maneuver . . . more and not less emphasis will be required on competitiveness in home and export markets."

There is thus a good deal of balanced discussion in what, as government papers go, is an exceptionally closely argued and well-presented one. Its most interesting feature, in our present context, is the way in which it takes for granted that there is a recognizable and measurable scale of social costs and benefits, and that central intervention will both be capable of quantifying these satisfactorily (as well as being able to make appropriate commercial judgments about the viability, in the long term, of firms) and know how to operate—whether through "taxation, planning controls or subsidy"—so as to produce a "better" result than the market. Once these assumptions are made, the paper presents a very plausible rationalization of the mechanics of an adjustment assistance system.

The second document is a so far unpublished memorandum on the European Community's structural policy for industry which was presented by the government of the Federal Republic of Germany to a council meeting of the European Community in May 1978. (Although the document itself has not been published, the remarks made by the German minister have been widely reported.)

This paper puts the emphasis in almost precisely the opposite direction. It recognizes at the outset that there are many factors operating in the world which call for extensive structural adjustments in large sections of the community's economy, and that these structural changes must make for the maintenance and strengthening of competitiveness on the international front and long-term employment guarantees. But confronting and coming to terms with structural changes is primarily a task for the enterprises concerned. The community and governments should support market-induced processes by providing a suitable framework of general policy; but they should not suppose that they can, or should even try to, foresee the directions of change, much less any detailed manifestations. The pressure should be to maintain market competition—the biggest incentive to the adaptation of outdated structures.

This does not rule out regional and social assistance measures (including also, however, some assistance "in accordance with banking criteria . . . for financing projects involving modernization and reorganization of industry"). The paper also accepts that it may, in very limited and exceptional cases, prove necessary to slow down the process of adjustment to the market through temporary arrangements for a fixed period of time, and, indeed, is not opposed to some "emergency structural cartels." Nor does it rule out the possibility of "sectoral measures" in the case of "certain justified exceptions, like the steel and textiles sector." But its emphasis is on the condemnation of measures to "protect structures," particularly as it argues that "sectors for which such measures are taken are rarely subsequently re-exposed to a normal competitive situation." Accordingly, it criticizes agreements, whether formal or informal, on capacity and production and planning and on the division of markets, interventions in price formation, and "adjustment aids," which it regards as self-perpetuating, liable to maintain outdated and unprofitable production, and to lead to expensive international subsidy competition. It goes so far, indeed, as to discourage the establishment of institutionalized discussion arrangements—"joint sectoral committees"—for particular sectors, since "the mere fact of such committees being set up leads the parties concerned to expect that structures can basically be left unchanged. They then act with reference to their sectoral interests and make demands for resolving their specific problems which it is then difficult for the Community to resist." Overall, the Community and the Member States must avoid damaging the efficiency of the economy as a whole by the aggregation of intervention measures.

It was clear from the published accounts of the council debate which followed the German minister's statement that it did not carry the wholehearted consent of his colleagues (and not only the British). Had it done so, the course of discussion in Geneva in the second half of 1978 might have been significantly different.

Meanwhile, multilateral trade negotiations went ahead, if not at a headlong pace, and on a bilateral, or at most trilateral, rather than multilateral, basis, at least with some degree of momentum among the principal participants.

Much international time and effort were absorbed in the Tokyo Round, both in keeping it tenuously alive during the doldrum years from the end of 1973 to 1977, and after the resumption of active negotiation in mid-1977. A considerable weight of hope for the future course of international trade rests on the supposition that the outcome of the negotiations will signify a new beginning both for the GATT as an institution and for international commercial policy in general.

Writing at the beginning of 1979, it has to be assumed that by the time of publication, the United States and the European Community will have reached some agreement. Failure to do so would be a signal for the beginning of a period of quite intense trade conflict among the major trading countries, and of a growth in protectionism and economic nationalism on the scale of the 1930s. It would also mean the virtual collapse of the General Agreement on Tariffs and Trade as an instrument of trade cooperation in the world. The consequences would be grave, particularly for the small and poor trading countries, since in spite of all their complaints against the GATT, and of the protectionist developments of the last decade the agreement remains a still substantial safeguard for them. The political consequences for the Western Alliance would also be substantial.

However, assuming the conclusion of an agreement by the publication of this paper the continuing question is whether the delay and frustrations which have taken place, and the evident differences of views, principally between the United States and the European Community, which these indicate, may in the event mean an outcome which may be insubstantial and unconvincing.

We are not concerned, for this purpose, with the tariff content of the agreement. The principal sections which are relevant are those dealing with subsidies, with "safeguards," and to a rather lesser extent, with public procurement. The declared objective of the negotiations has been to produce codes of conduct, which would consist partly of rules with a status virtually equivalent to that of the existing articles of the GATT, partly of annotations on existing articles which would serve as interpretations and clarifications of some present obscurities, and partly of provisions for new forms of procedure, consultation, resolution of disputes, and operation of surveillance.

On subsidies, the division of view between the United States and the European Community throughout has been—to oversimplify rather drastically—that the United States wanted a maximal, and the European Community a minimal, result. (The European position—as may be inferred from the previous discussion—has no doubt been influenced by the desire of some member states to retain a high degree of freedom of action for themselves within the community, as well as for the community as a whole vis-à-vis the outside world.) The debate has also turned on what sort of government action constituted a subsidy, as well as on whether it was feasible to classify subsidies into categories, so as to identify what forms of subsidy were, respectively, noxious and specifically to be prohibited, innocuous and unequivocally permissible, or indeterminate and therefore to be subject to ad hoc consideration. The right to countervail, and the basis of justification for countervailing, is clearly closely bound up with the whole question; and the negotiating situation—though not the real substance of the issue—was, of course, complicated by the special position of the United States on counter-vailing and the U.S. legislation.

There was certainly never any likelihood that there might emerge from the negotiations a definition of subsidies going at all near to Harald Malmgren's complete definition: "any government action which causes a firm's, or a particular industry's, total net private costs of production to be below the level of costs that would have been incurred in the course of producing the same level of output in the absence of the government action."[9] Had this been so, it would have brought within the GATT scope much of the governmental practice described above as significant. On the contrary, the measure of agreement achieved contains no definition. What it does do—at any rate as foreshadowed in the "framework of understanding" agreed by the delegations of some of the major industrial countries in July 1978, and in the documents accompanying the framework—is to modify substantially the attitude and emphasis of the text of the general agreement itself. The text of the GATT is studiously neutral. It neither approves nor condemns the use of subsidies, but confines itself to prescribing that, if a country operates a subsidy which directly or indirectly affects its international trade—whether its exports or its imports—it should provide information and justification. The MTN agreements are much more elaborate. Certainly, they aim at establishing rather stronger machinery of consultation and, perhaps, of surveillance. At the same time, however, they go much further than does the GATT towards explictly accepting the legitimacy and appropriateness of the use of subsidies. They "recognize" that subsidies in general are used by governments "to promote important objectives of national policy," and that subsidies other than export subsidies are "widely used as important instruments for the promotion of social and economic objectives of national policy"; and they say specifically that it is not intended "to restrict the right of signatories to use such subsidies." The only commitment would be a general one to "seek to avoid causing serious prejudice through the use of subsidies."

It would be distinctly bold, in the light of an outcome on these lines to the kind of debate which is known to have taken place, both inside the European Community and in Geneva, to suppose that the Tokyo Round will bring about an early or a dramatic shift in conduct. It may well be, on the contrary, that those governments who have consistently negotiated with the objective of securing as small a limitation as possible on their freedom of action in this area will see the outcome as a specific condonation, within the GATT system, of actions which, under the general agreement itself, might have been more questionable. The positive assertion that no restriction on national policy is intended is a somewhat surprising intrusion in the context of agreements whose normal intention would be precisely to impose such restrictions in the common interest.

The test of the new provisions will come when an effort is made to operate the consultation arrangements, and to see whether the schemes of one country which can be demonstrated to have adverse trade effects on other countries, can be brought under control—specifically, whether governments can be influenced, through the GATT consultative machinery, to abandon or modify their internal policies. The processes involved—which include the creation, over time, of a willingness of the countries concerned to cooperate in good faith in the procedures, the creation of a high degree of consensus and acceptance of their fairness and validity, and the building up of a body of case law and interpretative guidelines—are similar in some ways to the way in which GATT worked in the first decade of its existence. It is a matter for speculation how far the 1980s will match the 1950s in this regard.

With respect to safeguards, the issue is still how, and under what circumstances and conditions, safeguard measures can "legitimately" be applied discriminatorily, and what forms of redress may be available to those against whom such discrimination is exercised. Here again, it remains to be tested in practice whether the outcome will significantly limit the range and extent of the variety of protectionist practices of this kind—which include voluntary export restraints and orderly marketing arrangements. The smaller exporting countries, including some of the more advanced developing countries—South Korea, Singapore, Brazil, the Crown Colony of Hong Kong, and so on—who see themselves as most at risk in this regard may well feel that, by sanctioning "selectivity," the new agreement may simply make resort to safeguard measures the normal and natural response to any sizeable increase in competition from imports, especially from new entrants into a particular sector, and to any sustained domestic pressure for protection.

So the negotiations leave in the hands of governments most of the weapons which they are currently using; and the likelihood seems to be that they will not, at any rate for some time to come, significantly hamper the use of them, and that in some cases they may indeed appear to legitimize actions which have hitherto been regarded as doubtfully compatible with the GATT. The one area where there may emerge the outline of a more liberal outcome than this is public procurement. Here the Tokyo Round looks like providing a new approach which could, from the beginning, increase the openness of international trade, and which offers the opportunity for progressive enlargement of its scope. One difficult question remains, however; if, as seems to be envisaged, the benefits of access to the government purchase market (in those sections of it which are, or may in the future be, within the coverage of the agreement) are confined to signatories of the codes, can the code itself be regarded as complying with the nondiscriminatory requirements? Would not every signatory of the general agreement—all the contracting parties—have the right to claim that the "advantage, favor, privilege or immunity" which resulted from the application of the code by "any contracting party to any product originating in or destined for any other country" should be "accorded immediately and unconditionally to the like product originating in or destined for the territories of all other contracting parties"? And if this proposition were dismissed as unduly legalistic, would it not be the case that some limited advance in liberal trade among a number of countries—the signatories of the code—was being bought at the cost of a significant undermining of the basic fabric of the general agreement? It might indeed be argued that what was created would be equivalent to a new area of mutually granted preferences—precisely what it was a principal objective of U.S. commercial policy to eradicate in its sponsorship of the GATT and the liberal international trading system generally. Nonetheless, it is to be expected that the developing countries, in spite of the minor part they were able to play in framing the total package, will in the last analysis, acquiesce in the bargains struck by the major negotiating countries.

It is against this background that we can come back to the OECD "general orientations," and consider whether the lines of policy it foreshadows suggest that the type of protectionism we have been looking at may be expected to wane. (It is interesting, by the way, to identify, quite early in its career, the appearance of another new euphemism in the international vocabulary—"defensive action." Who, after all, can have the effrontery to suggest that "defensive action" can be reprehensible?)

So far as it has gone, however, the general orientation paper offers considerable support for the view that government intervention in the adjustment process, at any rate in much of its current manifestation, is frequently damaging rather than helpful, especially over time; that it will tend to make the economy "less productive and more inflation prone"; and that, like other forms of protection, it may enable "inefficient producers to compete with foreign suppliers and so delay necessary structural adjustments" (so it might have been stimulating if the description of such policies had not been "defensive action" but say, "adjustment resistance").

It also argues against direct and detailed intervention and in favor of general measures affecting the economy as a whole. "Even where the difficulties are deep-seated, special intervention will normally only be justified if the economic or social costs of the necessary adjustments are likely to be unacceptably high in the short run." It then sets out a series of fairly onerous criteria which should be taken into account in the exceptional cases where governments find it "necessary" to intervene.

A particularly refreshing passage, in an official document approved by the ministers of some twenty countries, is the proposition that "in order to increase the ability of the economy to adjust to new conditions, governments could do more to reduce the uncertainties and the additional costs caused by their own policy actions. This implies efforts to avoid unnecessary regulation and reporting requirements, and to maintain better coordination, clarity and continuity in government regulations, including those regarding safety, health and the environment."

On these bases, the paper calls for a more constructive approach, described as being "to further adjustment to new conditions, relying as much as possible on market forces to encourage mobility of labor and capital to their most productive uses." Additionally governments are admonished that their other social and political objectives should be sought through policies "which minimize any resulting costs in terms of reduced economic efficiency."

All this would imply a very substantial change in both emphasis and direction in the policies of a number of OECD governments, and a considerable change of attitude for many sections of industry, and especially for the trade unions, in most OECD countries. A modicum of skepticism about the political possibility of these developments is unavoidable, particularly, perhaps, at this stage of the electoral cycle in some major countries. Moreoever, the paper itself, while its general philosophy is not dissimilar to that of the German paper referred to above, still seems to envisage a substantial residuum of government intervention in and direction of the adjustment process. But there is not inconsiderable danger that the phrase "more positive adjustment policies" itself, to which the authors of the OECD paper have sought to give content based heavily on general measures designed to reduce rigidities, increase factor mobility, and put emphasis on long-term objectives reflecting market considerations, may lend itself only too easily to those who wish for more government intervention rather than less, more specific and more detailed measures rather than more general ones, and activity calculated to produce more visible and quicker short-term results rather than quieter, slower, more fundamental but less politically advantageous action. Nor is it particularly fanciful to see, growing out of this kind of positive activity, the concept that what is really needed is activity not on the national, but on the international scale—agreement on an international division of labor and of markets.

If this were indeed to be the end product of present tendencies—as in a few sectors it very nearly begins to be—a real and desirable return to prosperity and growth, which in the last resort can be achieved only through enterprise and innovation, may be very long delayed. It is, perhaps, part of the troubles of our policies in the major industrialized countries that so much of the energies of our administrators and politicians is devoted to considering the problems of sectors of industry already in an advanced state of hemorrhage, and of generalizing policies based on keeping a life machine going for those sectors, without any very clear conception of how and in what circumstances it can be switched off. If they were more aware of, and were prepared to give more weight and more opportunity to the factors within firms and industries which create the power to adapt and adjust, the factors which make it possible for industry to help and to renew itself, rather than to be forced into a client relationship with government, those energies might, in the long run, be more fruitful.

Notes

1. Goran Ohlin, "Subsidies and Other Industrial Aids," in S. J. Warnecke et al., *International Trade and Industrial Policies* (London: Macmillan Press, 1978).

2. For an illuminating discussion on equity and efficiency, see two papers by Theodore Geiger: "On Not Pushing a Good Thing Too Far" (Washington, D.C.: National Planning Association, July 1975); and "Welfare and Efficiency," the main findings of a study by the National Planning Committee on the Changing International Realities (Washington, D.C.: National Planning Committee, 1978).

3. By Goran Ohlin in a paper to the 1968 World Congress of the International Economic Association: G. Ohlin, "Trade in a Non-Laissez-Faire World," in *International Economic Relations*, ed. P. A. Samuelson (London: Macmillan, 1969).

4. H. G. Johnson, "Mercantilism: Past, Present & Future," in *The New Mercantilism*, ed. H. G. Johnson (Oxford: Basil Blackwell, 1974).

5. See C. Fred Bergsten, "On the Equivalence of Import Quotas and Voluntary Export Restrictions," in *Toward a New World Trade Policy: The Maidenhead Papers*, ed. C. F. Bergsten (Lexington: Lexington Books, 1975).

6. For fuller accounts, see Harald Malmgren, "Protectionist Tendencies in the World Economy," a paper for the World Outlook Conference (Washington,

D.C.: SR1/Wharton Economic Forecasting Associates, June 1978); and Matthew J. Marks, "New Directions in U.S. Trade Policy" (New York: Belgian-American Chamber of Commerce, October 1977).

7. Organization for Economic Co-operation and Development, *Press Release* (Press/A (78) 23), 15 June 1978.

8. Great Britain, "Report of the Secretaries of State for Industry, Scotland and Wales on Operations under the Industry Act, 1972" (London: H.M.S.O., July 1976).

9. H. Malmgren, *International Order for Public Subsidies*, Thames Essay (London: Trade Policy Research Centre, 1977). See also Caroline Pestieau, "Revising the GATT Approach to Subsidies," in S. J. Warnecke et al., *International Trade and Industrial Policies* (London: Macmillan Press, 1978).

Commentary

Kazuo Nukazawa

I do not have any disagreement with Golt's description of the Tokyo Round. The Tokyo Round has a basic asymmetry in that its success will not bring us much further in liberalizing international trade, while its failure would be a disaster for world trade. The greatest merit of the Tokyo Round has been that each government could tell its domestic protectionist forces: "I understand your problem, but we cannot rock the boat while the Multilateral Trade Negotiations (MTN) are going on." If the MTN were to drag on for half a century or more, it would prove to be a boon for international trade.

Compared with past GATT rounds, the Tokyo Round was hard hit by the oil crisis. And the inroads made by the newly industrializing LDCs also loomed large on the international trade horizon. The negotiations soon became more bilateral (contrary to the original spirit of the GATT) and reciprocal than multilateral. The tariff reductions looked minimal compared with the dramatic exchange rate changes during the MTN period. Since the main focus of the Tokyo Round—non-tariff barriers (NTB)—are inextricably connected with the bureaucratic way of life, pressures to maintain the status quo have been strong among the regulatory agencies of the industrialized countries. Environmentalists and consumer groups in Japan and similar groups in the United States call for more safety regulations, longer drug testing, perfectionistic anti-insecticide/anti-fungicide testing, and so on, instead of pushing for wider access for imports. I endorse Mr. Golt's skepticism about the effectiveness of government subsidies for industries. Their protective impact is not very great. Yukio Noguchi, assistant professor of Hitotsubashi University, claims that Japan's past pattern of subsidization has been to shift resources from efficient sectors to inefficient sectors, such as agriculture.[1] He argues that they have proved to be a waste of money. Very few subsidies have actually been effective in either infant industries or declining industries. In the case of Japan, computers may be the only exception. This is true of many countries. The Concorde, a fine technological achievement, is a miserable economic failure, despite heavy government subsidization. As an alternative to import restriction or blatant export incentives, subsidization is a condonable vice. It has to seek a budgetary allocation every year and therefore has to prove its case to administrative and legislative branches, a process which import restrictions or orderly marketing arrangements do not have to go through. Moreover, if a country heavily and generally subsidizes its export industries, its currency will float up, and that automatically neutralizes these efforts.

Products of the planned economies are heavily subsidized, but these economies suffer huge trade deficits vis-à-vis free enterprise economies. The R&D efforts of the Russian and the Eastern bloc are carried out by government agencies, but these countries are heavy importers of technology.

Shukan Toyo Keizai of November 25, 1978, carried an interesting list showing how Japanese agricultural import restrictions are circumvented:

a. Rice imports are restricted and the government encourages rice consumption. But the importation of rice crackers is liberalized. Major domestic manufacturers of these crackers are starting to defend themselves by investing abroad (Thailand, Korea, and Taiwan). As a result domestic rice consumption by industrial users is reduced.

b. Similar results occur in the candy and confectionary industry. Major candy makers have become importers of Spanish, Brazilian, Danish, and even Cuban products.

Prices of raw materials (wheat, butter, milk, sugar, etc.) are far higher in Japan than in the countries where their competitors are located. (If you can't beat them, you simply join them.) Macaroni, spaghetti, and unbaked bread are other examples. Also red beans are import restricted but "anko" (boiled, mashed, and, sugar-added products) imports are not, and Taiwan is expanding "anko" exports to Japan. When beef imports are restricted, the importation of live animals by air soared.

c. The interests of the agricultural sector and industrial consumers are sharply divergent for many other products (processed cocoa products and beer malt, for example). Although agriculture is the most protected sector in Japan, the self-sufficiency ratio is steadily declining; traditional food consumption (rice, sake) is waning, and the agricultural population is rapidly dwindling. Economic forces are so strong that, in the long run, they will circumvent or overcome any administrative and political resistance. Perhaps unintentionally, governments frustrate protectionist moves all over the world.

One of the most important reasons for protectionism is a "vulnerability mentality." Concern about military and economic security is mounting in Japan, while concern about food shortages is ebbing. Economic security depends essentially on diversification of supply sources, export markets, and interdependence among nations. A stable interdependence relationship requires division of labor based upon mutual confidence. If this cannot be assured, resistance within Japan against depending on other countries for stable foods and other important strategic goods will not diminish.

Many governments use diplomatic and political means to promote the export of heavy equipment and weapons by private domestic firms. Geopolitical factors and diplomatic considerations therefore play an important role in world trade in capital goods related to natural resources development, major industrialization programs, and the construction of infrastructure.

I use the term "sovereignty goods" to refer to items (such as weapons, wheat, and oil) whose trade is affected by governmental decisions as to when, to whom, how much and/or at what price to sell. These goods represent an increasingly important share of international trade. Following many years of efforts to liberalize international trade, one-fourth of the international trade is cartelized; this includes petroleum exports.

Cartelization and bureaucratic controls over trade are obvious threats to international free trade and to economic freedom within trading nations.

The paper by Mr. Golt discusses the problem of free trade versus protectionism from a purely economic standpoint, focusing his analysis on the effects of these policies on real income. But it is important to understand that free trade also can play an important role in bringing more economic and political democracy to many countries. I welcome the OECD communique of June 1978, but it should have emphasized the importance of separating the machinery of protectionism from the political process as much as possible. The U.S. International Trade Commission is an example.

Mr. Golt's discussion of German and British policy and practice is interesting. The sad truth is that domestic full employment policy buys more votes than free trade policy in any country. As for "selective safeguards" and government procurement, I expect that the industrialized countries will seek more reciprocity from LDCs in the future.

GATT may become divided de facto into two groups. One group would consist of industrialized nations that permit completely free access to imports among themselves, and the second group those not participating in this arrangement. Such a situation might have the beneficial effect of inducing countries like Brazil and Korea and other countries to liberalize their trade policies. Nevertheless, it is a very dangerous strategy.

I share the author's concern over the strong bias in Europe and Japan in favor of welfare rather than efficiency through competition. I feel that this phenomenon is the essential philosophical background for the new protectionism which will emerge in the 1980s.

Note

1. Yukio Noguchi, *Ekonomisuto*, 19 December 1978.

Commentary

Robert Sorensen

Sidney Golt's paper seems to contain three basic themes. First, it suggests that within the OECD countries protectionist sentiment is on the rise; and that this is so even among groups which had heretofore supported liberal policies towards international trade. Second, the forms of protection being applied are different, more sophisticated, and less transparent than traditional instruments such as tariffs. Third, despite government protestations to the contrary, it is unlikely that this protectionist sentiment is likely to wane in the near future. While we might have hoped that the moves toward more flexible exchange rates in the 1970s would have mitigated protectionist pressures, this has not been the case. Thus, I basically agree with Sidney Golt's analysis.

It should be mentioned, however, that most of the increase in overt restrictions to trade, such as imposition of voluntary export agreements, countervailing duties, and antidumping duties has occurred subsequent to the oil crisis of 1974.[1] As such, we might hope that this new protectionism represents only temporary measures in response to structural changes and balance-of-payments adjustments necessitated by the energy problem. Under such a scenario we might expect a return towards normalcy as the OECD economies complete adjustment to the changed energy situation. I believe such an assessment would be overly optimistic. When we witness such spectacles as governments justifying protective measures with the argument that without them even more restrictive measures would be legislatively enacted, it becomes obvious how strong the lean toward protectionism has become.

If we believe in the principle of free international trade, then we ought to consider why protectionist sentiment has so much appeal. The decline in the rate of productivity growth coupled with higher than historical rates of unemployment in the OECD countries has certainly been a main contributor to the current pressures. Perhaps we are observing a demonstration of the oft-cited notion that governments view free trade as a luxury that can only be afforded during periods of rapid economic growth. Rather than simply accept this conclusion, I would like to look at some other factors which may be important in explaining the recent resort to protectionism.

In the first place, there is a marked tendency to overestimate costs of trade and underestimate its benefits. Benefits of lower cost goods from abroad tend to be dispersed among large numbers of buyers of intermediate and final goods. Moreover, many of the benefits are relatively hidden as the lower cost goods work their way through the input-output structure of the economy. On the contrary, the perceived cost of increased imports tends to be highly concentrated and highly visible. For example, the loss of jobs and employment, often associated with increased imports, is an isolated and visible cost. Foreign producers thus become likely targets for retaliation even in circumstances where firms or industries had been suffering from a variety of ailments, and import penetration was simply a reflection of the disease rather than its cause. The immediateness and visibility of the perceived costs of trade as compared to its distant and disperse benefits thus create political pressure for greater protection.

Second, it seems to me that modern governments are in the awkward position of being big, but at the same time relatively weak. The sheer size of governments and the degree to which they have become involved in the private economy has created expectations that they can, and should, act to remedy more and more economic and social problems. At the same time dismemberment of traditional political coalitions and the rise of more "one issue" political groups (especially in the United States) works at eroding the political strength of governments. Under these circumstances it becomes easy for governments to behave in ways which conform to what Max Corden has termed the "conservative welfare function."[2] In essence this implies that governments feel obligated to undertake whatever actions may be necessary to protect the real income of any segment of society. Thus, if imports are perceived to threaten some group's real income, protection may be granted even though it reduces the real income of society as a whole.

Finally, the lack of both transparency and estimates of the actual effects of the various industrial policies undertaken by governments in recent years has led to suspicions of unfair trade practices. For example, even in cases where an industrial policy has a minimal effect upon international trade, an American businessman is likely to be outraged upon hearing that a subsidy or tax relief has been given to a French or German firm which may be his rival. Such suspicions of unfair trade practices are likely to lead to demands for government action and protection. But an action by one government may set off chain reactions by others resulting in what Richard Cooper has termed "policy competition" and increased protectionism all around.[3] I am afraid we are coming dangerously close to just such a situation. Witness, for example, the notion currently being circulated that regulation of oil prices below the world price in the United States constitutes a subsidy to U.S. energy-intensive exporters and thus countervailing duties against these exporters is justified. Can this proposal not be viewed as simply a competitive policy response to U.S. allegations of unfair subsidy practices used by governments of its trading partners?

While disseminating better information concerning the net benefits of freer international trade and the effects of government policies on trade might help to reduce some protectionist pressures, I doubt that this constitutes a solution. I believe that the fundamental problem revolves around the degree of reliance to be placed upon markets as opposed to governments as the major allocator of goods and services. Until this question is resolved (and I hope in favor of the former) protectionist pressures are bound to persist.

Notes

1. See, for instance, B. Balassa, "The New Protectionism and the International Economy," *Journal of World Trade Law* 12 (September/October 1978):409-36.
2. M. Corden, *Trade Policy and Economic Welfare* (Oxford: Clarendon Press, 1974).
3. See Balassa, "New Protectionism."

13

Structural Consequences of Changing International Trade Patterns and Possible Alternative Policies

H. Peter Gray

The word "interdependence" has become fashionable recently in international matters. It has superseded "integration." But, in an economic sense, the distinction between the two is quite small. During the past thirty years the world has integrated its economies and, by a substantial margin, increased its interdependence. Many forces have contributed to that trend but persistent reduction in barriers to international trade and the growth of multinational corporations must be accounted as two of the primary forces. This paper analyzes the implications of this trend and of its continuation on the performance of the economies of developed (OECD) nations and on the adjustment strains that must inevitably occur. While the paper is couched mainly in terms of the United States, its argument may be expected to apply to other OECD nations in greater or lesser degree.

In a recent paper, Diaz-Alejandro assessed the global economy from the point of view of a visiting Martian economist. The Martian's conclusion was that resources of this planet were very badly distributed in a geographic sense since the bulk of the capital goods appeared to be located in places where labor was relatively scarce. The solution was to transfer much physical capital from the developed world to the poor nations where labor was in plentiful supply, or to facilitate the migration of workers from the poorer developing nations to those nations in which capital was relatively abundant. In essence, the Martian was arguing for a complete integration of the global economy. In practice, the ostensibly inefficient global allocation of labor and capital is gradually being eliminated by international investment (largely through multinational corporations), by immigration of people into the developed world, and by international trade. Thus, the Martian would approve of the reduction of barriers to trade, investment, and migration.[1]

However, the arguments in favor of a liberal world economic system with no artificial impediment to the international movement of goods and factors are based on a simplified theory using comparative statics. Some of the assumptions of that theory are not valid in the real world even when mature economies are performing at satisfactory rates of capacity utilization. Any comparative static analysis will neglect costs of adjustment.

The focus of this paper is the market for low-skilled labor in developed nations and its potential vulnerability to continued increases in imports from the developing nations. Probably the United States and Canada are likely to be most affected by increases in imports from developing nations, but European members of OECD are also likely to prove vulnerable. Given the high rates of teenage unemployment in many OECD countries, concern with the rate of increase of imports from developing nations may for some be a temporary, demographic-bulge type of problem. For others with reserve armies of low-skilled unemployed, the problem will last longer. It should be noted at the outset that the tenor of the argument is not opposed to reductions in barriers to international trade either among OECD nations or between the blocs of developed and developing nations provided that the costs of adjustments are reduced to tolerable levels. Because some of the argument will imply less free access to the markets of developed nations for the products of developing nations, it is important to note that the final section addresses itself to this problem with a view to eliminating any adverse effect the conclusions of this paper may have on hard currency earnings of developing nations.[2]

The first section of the paper considers the problem of the market for low-skilled workers and the need for a realistic time dimension if the concept of nonclearance is to be operational. The second section develops an analysis of the linkage between the composition of international trade and the demand for low-skilled labor. The third section provides a variant of the traditional approach to international trade theory that better addresses the problem of low-skilled labor. And the fourth section lists the feasible options for protection and analyses their implications for the achievement of generally accepted national economic goals. The final section considers the impact of such policies on the interests of the developing countries and outlines a proposal which will negate the impact of any protectionist measures.

The Market for Low-skilled Labor

In traditional international economic theory, on which the argument for free or freer trade rests, all markets are assumed to clear at a price equal to the marginal value of the factor or good. Factors of production are assumed to be fully employed at their marginal value product. When these assumptions hold, the displacement or disemployment of a factor of production from the international sector (as a result of a change in the composition of goods traded internationally) would have income-distributional effects only. The factor of production put into excess supply at the going price would suffer a reduction in that price (relative to other factors). If the effects were considered socially undesirable, they could be countered by an appropriate set of transfers and there would be no need for a change in national commercial policy or in the long-range target of free trade.[3] This paper denies the assumption that all markets clear themselves automatically. It assumes that the market for low-skilled labor does not clear itself automatically and that there exists a long-lasting excess supply of low-skilled labor at the going wage. Consequently, any displacement of low-skilled workers from the international goods sector will generate a net addition to the pool of unemployed.[4] Therfore the assumption that the low-skilled labor market does not clear itself means that the analysis conducted here is essentially an exercise in the theory of the second best.

Several strands of evidence can be presented in support of the fundamental premise of this paper that the market for low-skilled labor in the United States in particular and in some other OECD nations, will not clear itself even when satisfactory rates of capacity utilization are being achieved.

Johnson asserts that: "Even when the aggregate employment rate (in the United States) is around 5 percent, given the current composition of the labor force, the unskilled unemployment rate is usually between 12 and 20 percent depending on how skill is defined. And this rate is much higher if the potential rather than the measured labor force is used in calculating the unemployment rate."[5] Cain also provides a general acceptance of the premise that "low-skilled labor suffers inordinately high unemployment rates."[6]

Additional evidence can be found in the significantly higher than average rates of unemployment reported in those sex, age, and ethnic categories of workers which may be expected to be heavily populated by low-skilled workers. A recent review of some of these categories is to be found in Williams.[7] As Johnson notes, the exclusion from unemployment data of those deemed not to be seeking employment must reinforce the premise since the 'drop-outs' will be disproportionately biased by large numbers of low-skilled workers who are discouraged by the perceived lack of employment opportunities.[8]

The role of the international sector in this problem can be gauged from the fact that the three industries in the United States most seriously besieged by foreign competition—apparel, including knitting mills; footwear; and textiles—are those characterized by very high ratios of low-skilled to total workers. Keesing reports the following ratios: apparel, including knitting mills, 80.76 percent; footwear, 79.62 percent; and textiles, 73.4 percent.[9] Further supportive evidence is given by Hawkins in a study of the employment effects of multinational corporations.[10] Hawkins found no aggregate change in the demand for labor as a result of multinationals' creation of manufacturing capacity abroad but he was able to identify a change in skill-mix requirements as professional and skilled workers gained in employment at the expense of low-skilled workers.

The final strand of support for the premise derives from Mincer.[11] This study of the effects of minimum wages on employment shows that minimum wages are an important cause of the failure of the market for low-skilled labor to clear. At the theoretical level, Mincer recognizes only equilibrium (search) and voluntary unemployment.[12] Since the availability of alternative sources of funds, such as welfare, are considered to affect the supply curve of labor and therefore voluntary unemployment, the theoretical analysis is relevant to the present paper only insofar as it shows how a change in the mix of output in the covered sector might affect the amount of low-skilled labor to be absorbed by the uncovered sector. If there is a net reduction in the demand for low-skilled labor in the covered sector because of the effects of a changing mix in international trade, the demand curve for labor will shift to the left (in the relevant range) and impose a greater burden on the uncovered sector. Mincer's empirical analysis shows clearly how minimum wage increases (or increases in coverage) adversely affect the subsectors of the labor force in which low-skilled workers are likely to predominate. All subsectors of the labor force suffered from reduced employment as a result of an increase in the minimum wage and the burden fell most heavily on teenagers and young males (age 20-24) and, within these two categories, most heavily on non-whites. The smallest effects were felt by white males (age 25-64) and non-white women (age 20+). The latter result may be due to the fact that few non-white women had employment in the covered sector. Further, labor force participation rates were very much more adversely affected for teenagers and young male adults, suggesting that "low-wage workers who are not employed in the covered sector perceive the minimum wage hike as a deterioration of their wage prospects."[13]

Define "market failure" to mean that excess demand or supply in a market continues to persist through time. The meaning of the term here is different from the way the term is used in Bator.[14] Bator's concern is with the failure of a system of markets to achieve specified goals. In the present context, "market failure" must either involve some rigidity in the market in a static sense or in differential rates of growth of supply and demand for a protracted period of time in a dynamic sense.

It is necessary to develop a working definition of low-skilled labor. Distinguish three qualities which an individual can bring to the job market: vocational skills, work discipline, and general skills. Vocational skills are skills which apply directly to a trade or profession. They can be both general and industry-specific skills. General vocational skills might be mechanical training, and industry-specific vocational skills those concerned with experience as a production worker in a particular industry. General vocational skills are clearly applicable to a wide range of jobs but industry specific skills can be rendered valueless if the industry to which they are specific ceases to exist. Thus an unemployed worker's employability depends upon his or her general vocational skills and this in turn depends upon the level of overall skill attained including any transferability to another industry of industry-specific skills. Second, work discipline involves an experience with working conditions and the ability to adjust to them. This quality is possessed by anyone with a history of satisfactory work but lack of it may be a cause of low productivity for inexperienced and socially maladjusted workers. Individual workers' efficiency loss due to alcoholism might be considered as a reduction in work discipline.[15] General skills can best be summarized as the product of the educational system—the ability to think, write, and verbalize clearly as well as to manipulate figures: in brief, the three R's.

The separation of the work force into so-called low-skilled and skilled labor is necessarily an arbitrary act. For present purposes we propose that the term "low-skilled workers" will comprise the usual categories of unskilled and semi-skilled workers. The argument of the paper requires only that the market for this category of labor not clear itself completely when either total demand is reduced or total supply increases. In this context, market failure exists when a decrease in the demand for low-skilled labor in tradeable goods industries is not matched by increased absorption of workers of this category by the domestic sector either through growth or through a response to changes in relative costs of factors of production.

The time-dimension by which the existence of market failure can be judged depends directly upon society's standards as to what constitutes an efficient market. The standards of society are likely to be determined by noneconomic as well as economic considerations. Presumably, the market mechanism will work more efficiently, the greater the geographic mobility of low-skilled workers, the better the job vacancy information network, and the greater the degree to which government is prepared to facilitate these two qualities of the market by deliberate expenditure of funds. In an operational sense, market failure will be taken to occur when 25 percent of new entrants into the labor force cannot find employment within fifteen weeks. In December 1976, these categories could have amounted to two and a half million workers. Moreover, official data will tend to underestimate the seriousness of the problem simply because of the tendency for low-skilled people to drop out of the official labor force by ceasing to seek employment. It is clearly not practicable to expect that all people who would like to work at the going wage can find employment. For some families, the location of the main source of income may preclude mobility on the part of some unemployed persons.

Departures from existing policies are only warranted if the problem can be shown to be intractable to orthodox policies. But the time dimension is as crucial to this aspect as it is to the definition of market failure. For market failure to exist it is only necessary to show that unemployment will last for a socially unacceptable period of time. The problem could be permanent if continuous substitutability of factors of production does not prevail or if the marginal physical product of the marginal low-skilled worker is below subsistence. It is also possible that the problem could be caused by dynamic factors whereby the rate of increase in the supply of low-skilled workers exceeded the ability of the economy to adapt to employ them. It is possible that excessively high rates of unemployment among low-skilled workers are due to inappropriate aggregate demand policies. The expansion of aggregate demand will reduce unemployment of low-skilled workers when cooperating factors are also unemployed. (In this respect it is worth noting that low-skilled workers do seem to have larger cyclical variations in employment rates than do skilled workers.)

Another possible cause of excessive unemployment of low-skilled workers is the (quite rapid) change in composition of the labor force.[16] If changes in the composition of the labor force are a contributing factor to observed high rates of unemployment of low-skilled workers, the problem could be eventually self-curing. But, this would not eliminate the unemployment and the argument for special policies to reduce the social hardship caused by a population bulge is a function of the time needed for its cure.

It is not possible to consider the problem of market failure without some mention of price rigidities. Minimum wage legislation could bring about unemployment of low-skilled workers when the marginal product of that labor is less than the stipulated minimum wage. However, the fact that minimum wage legislation exists is not a necessary cause of market failure since that circumstance could occur when the marginal revenue product of low-skilled labor was less than subsistence.[17] Moreover, the fact that market failure exists in an institutional setting that includes a minimum wage does not condone the market failure. If society, through its elected representatives, deems minimum wage legislation to be socially desirable, it should not at the same time neglect any repercussions of that legislation. Market failure attributable to minimum wage legislation requires elimination in a rich nation equally as much as market failure due to a subsistence floor to money wages. The poor unfortunates who are rendered unemployed by market failure are not to be neglected. This is particularly true if those who will be penalized by the existence of minimum wage legislation are new entrants to the labor force, and those who are displaced from tradeable goods industries by foreign competition.

Since the argument for long-term unemployment hinges on a wage rigidity, it has clear ties to Milton Friedman's concept of "the natural rate of unemployment."[18] While this concept provides a convenient analytic device for incorporating unemployment as an ongoing phenomenon into economic analysis, Friedman's argument does not distinguish among workers by skills and therefore is not directly applicable to the problem at hand: nor do his positions associated with the phenomenon of a natural rate necessarily apply. There are many reasons for the less-than-perfect functioning of the labor market in the short or medium run and Tobin conceives of labor (and product) markets being in some sort of "perpetual disequilibrium" in his rebuttal of the natural rate argument.[19] Unemployment that is sustained because of structural conditions within the system constitutes inefficiency and its reduction must be considered a valid goal of economic policy.

International Trade and the Excess Supply of Low-skilled Labor

Figure 13.1 shows how unemployment of medium-term duration can be analyzed in a static framework. The terminology relies upon the natural rate argument. Labor is considered to be homogenous input. The number of employed persons, n, is determined by the intersection between the marginal review product of labor schedule (MRP_L) and the legislated minimum wage, w. The position and shape of the MRP_L schedule derives from the stock of available capital, the technology embodied in that capital, and the mix of goods produced. Let the total

Figure 13-1

THE RATE OF EXCESS UNEMPLOYMENT

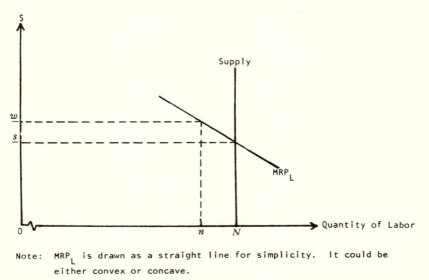

Note: MRP$_L$ is drawn as a straight line for simplicity. It could be either convex or concave.

supply of labor (N) be inelastic to the wage over the relevant range so that the market clearing wage would be s, determined by the intersection of the supply schedule and MRP_L. Excess unemployment (the natural rate in Friedman's analysis) (U) is $(N - n)/N$. U is a function of the difference between s and w and the average slope of the MRP_L schedule between n and N. Any change in the position and slope of MRP_L will alter the relationship between s and w and will change U.

Now introduce labor skills into the analysis. The MRP_L schedule must now be drawn for a composite input of pure labor and embodied human capital. The human capital component is measured by the market process and can be conceived as being computed from the difference between the wage of the individual worker and the wage earned by a completely unskilled laborer. The position of MRP_L will be higher for the composite input but Figure 13.1 can still be used to describe the rate of excess unemployment of the composite input. For any given output mix of goods that use human capital and pure labor in different proportions, the slope and position of MRP_L will be given by the amount and distribution of the skill content embodied in the labor force.

Similarly, for any given level and distribution of skill content, the slope and position of MRP_L will change with a change in the output mix demanded. If labor were considered a homogeneous input, the MRP_L schedule would be constructed independently of the way in which individual workers were included in the labor force. Once human capital is embodied in the individual worker, individual workers are no longer homogeneous and MRP_L must be computed with workers ranked in decreasing order of the amount of their human capital. This ranking is necessary if the marginal revenue product schedule is to have a negative slope. The schedule is drawn on the assumption that the mix of skilled workers who are employed is efficiently allocated among the various tasks. If human capital is distributed unequally in the labor force, the MRP_L schedule slopes downward because of the combination of the diminishing skill owned by marginal workers. Excepting short-run incompatibilities between specific skills demanded and available— the equivalent in a market for skilled workers of frictional unemployment in neoclassical theory—*excess unemployment will always consist of those workers with the least amount of embodied human capital.*[20] A proportionate increase in the skills of all workers will cause the MRP_L schedule to shift upwards. A change in the distribution of skills in the work force will cause the slope of the schedule to change. Both phenomena will change s and therefore U. When the human capital of the work force increases over time, both effects can be expected to take place—this presupposes a gradual improvement in educational efficiency and greater awareness of the need to apply oneself to education. Changes on the supply side will therefore tend to be secular changes. The rate of excess unemployment can also be affected by changes in the output mix—by forces working on the (derived) demand for labor. An increase in the output of goods requiring relatively high proportions of low-skilled labor at the expense of goods using relatively little low-skilled labor, will flatten the MRP_L schedule throughout its length, increase the marginal revenue product of the low-skilled workers, and thereby reduce U.

At any time, the skill composition of the work force depends upon inherited traits, upon the institutions of the economy, the effectiveness of the educational system (in the broadest sense), and upon recent changes in the pattern of output.

The skill potential of the work force is not distributed evenly across all workers. Two factors, inherited or genetic intelligence and the opportunity to acquire human capital, determine the skill potential for an individual. Genetic intelligence is positively related to the ability to acquire large amounts of human capital. The opportunity to avail oneself of educational opportunity is not equal. The inequality derives, in turn, from two sources: the inequalities in the educational system and the emphasis placed upon and the support given to the educational attainment in the home environment. These factors may be considered to be haphazardly distributed across the population so that at any moment of time there exists a distribution of human capital that is combined with individual units of labor. If the educational system were perfect and home factors were not correlated with genetic intelligence, then the distribution of human capital would reflect the ability of individuals to absorb human capital. This (efficient) distribution is shown by the solid line in Figure 13.2. The distribution is shown as a truncated normal distribution—truncated because the distribution must be bounded at zero and normal since the distribution of inherited intelligence is most likely to approximate a normal distribution.

Any inefficiency in the educational system will imply inequality of opportunity, whether the inefficiency be neutral with respect to sex and ethnic group or not. For a given expenditure of inputs, the stock of human capital will be both smaller and its distribution asymmetric.

Figure 13-2

FREQUENCY DISTRIBUTIONS OF HUMAN CAPITAL

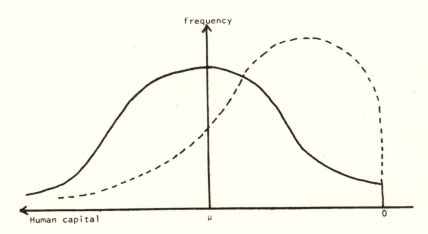

Note: Nothing precludes a bimodal distribution of the inefficient
         (dotted) frequency distribution.

human capital will be both smaller and its distribution asymmetric.

Finally, the amount and distribution of skills in the work force is not independent of the recent achievements of total employment in the country. If total employment has dropped from previous highs, some of the work force will have work experience. Some of these workers with work experience may be low-skilled workers laid off because of change in output mix. These workers will be more skilled than new entrants to the labor force who will not have the work discipline. In this sense, work discipline is a transferable or general skill acquired through work experience.[21]

Characteristics of the work force will affect the position and slope of MRP_L in Figure 13.1. It is now necessary to identify the interrelationship between changes in the distribution and total quantity of skills available and the shape and height of MRP_L. Assume that there is a given stock of skills and a given distribution. Shortcomings of the home environments and the educational system are taken as given, as is the distribution of genetic intelligence. There is no basis for presuming any correlation between the distribution of genetic intelligence and either home environment or weakness in the available educational facilities. But there is likely to be a positive correlation between a lack of support for educational achievement in the home environment and the quality of the available educational facilities. Both of these are likely to be negatively correlated with household income. MRP_L slopes downward and to the right as shown in Figure 13.1. The greater the total skills available to the labor force (with given distribution), the higher is MRP_L and the smaller is U for any given w and output mix. If the distribution of skills becomes less equal (a shift away from the solid distribution in Figure 13.2 toward the dotted, less efficient distribution), then the stock of human capital decreases. The effect of such a change on the slope of MRP_L is indeterminate. If all unemployed workers are completely unskilled (shown by the vertical or truncated part of the frequency curve), then the MRP_L schedule will be less steeply sloped than if some of the unemployed have positive skills—because to diminishing marginal returns must be added diminishing human capital. However, if the distribution is inefficient then the stock of human capital or skills is presumably smaller and therefore the whole MRP_L schedule is lower. The disparity between s and a given w is that much greater and this effect must be expected to outweigh any effect caused by changes in the slope of MRP_L. Thus, for any given output mix, the rate of excess unemployment can be reduced by improving the skills of the marginal workers or by improving the efficiency of the educational system (coupled with the generation of any required increase in aggregate demand).

As described, the labor market will always concentrate any excess unemployment in the low-skilled segment of the work force. In the real world, this relationship can still be expected to hold but not as "tidily" as in the model just developed.

The next question is to examine the interrelationship between trends in the composition of international trade and the skill mix employed in the tradeable goods industries. Keesing has provided empirical evidence (but not absolute proof) in support of the proposition that human capital is used more intensively in exports than in import-substitutes in the manufacturing industries in the United States.[22] Using 1960 census data, Keesing generated the skill composition in the United States of forty-six exports and imports. Using the 1962 pattern of international trade as weights, he computed the amount of skill embodied in the labor utilized in internationally traded manufactures. The net result was that only 45 percent of workers in export industries were "unskilled or semi-skilled" while 57 percent of workers in import-competing industries were "unskilled or semi-skilled." Thus, an increase in the volume of exports made possible by an increase in the value of imports would lead to a net reduction in the demand for low-skilled labor. A general reduction in protection of U.S. import-competing industries either through a relative increase in the cost competitiveness of nations that export to the United States or as a result of negotiated changes in commercial policy will increase imports of goods whose domestic producers use relatively large amounts of low-skilled labor by the norms of the United States. The argument can be expected to hold for virtually all manufacturing nations with respect to imports from developing nations. Aho and Orr have demonstrated this empirically for the United States by applying weights reflecting trade volume to the demographic and skill characteristics of different industries.[23] Their results would have been more pronounced had they utilized the change in employment or the change in trade volume in different industries between 1964 and 1975.

Assume an increase in the volume of imported goods competitive with domestic production matched by a corresponding increase in the value of exports. The increase in the volume of imports will lower MRP_L over the relevant range.[24] When the price of import substitutes is forced down by the greater volume of imports, the marginal product of low-skilled workers will be reduced. Unless the displaced workers are absorbed by the domestic sector, an increase in the excess supply of low-skilled workers will result.

Increases in imports of goods competitive with domestic production have occurred and such increases are likely to continue in the future. There are several reasons to expect that import substitute production will decrease in the United States in the future.

1. In an industry with constant returns to scale, all domestic production of import substitutes will ultimately be eliminated as foreign suppliers expand capacity if the domestic industry is not competitive in the international market. While a complete two-digit industry may not be eliminated because of the differing types of product that may be included in an "industry," a substantial portion of an industry can be eliminated in this way.[25]

2. The urgency of the need for foreign exchange by developing nations causes them to encourage export industries to the fullest extent possible and developing nations have a large comparative advantage in all goods using low-skilled labor intensively because of the very low cost (subsistence) of that labor.

3. The political pressures exerted by developing nations for special treatment by rich nations will lead to a reduction in the degree of protection to manufacturers in developed nations.

4. The Tokyo Round could lead to across-the-board reductions of tariffs by developed nations which will benefit exporters of manufactures with high proportions of unskilled labor.

5. The United States relies on "voluntary export restraints" and "orderly market arrangements." These types of commercial policy are usually designed to provide some protection to a domestic industry for a finite period of time. The rationale for the protection may be to allow time for the senile industry to waste away at a socially-tolerable rate[26] or it may be an Article XIX–type reason according to which the industry merely needs a breathing space to recover its international competitiveness. Because of the temporary nature of this type of commercial policy arrangement, the degree of protection afforded the domestic industry is likely to decline over its life. The reason for the decrease could be "built in" as when quotas are scheduled to increase annually at some predetermined rate. Equally, orderly market arrangements are frequently subject to being bypassed or exploited by the exporting nations. The so-called Multifibres Arrangement is an example of both sources of decrease in protectiveness.

6. Multinational corporations reacting to market pressures from foreign concerns as well as in a search to increase their profits have resorted to "production sharing."[27] Production sharing occurs when multinational corporations combine domestic and foreign production facilities to manufacture goods for the U.S. market. The integration of production facilities involves the production of complex parts in the United States and their shipment to a developing nation for assembly and finishing before being returned to the United States for marketing and distribution. The essence of the operation is the utilization of

foreign workers in those processes which require relatively important amounts of low-skilled labor. While this has obvious advantages for the developing nation that is host to the MNC factory, the cost to the United States can be significant if market failure exists in the market for low-skilled labor. Drucker admits that the data on the volume of production sharing are unreliable but he cites estimates that indicate a doubling of this type of production worldwide between 1974 and 1977. A variant on production sharing occurs when MNCs, aware of domestic and foreign costs, contract abroad for production of goods designed exclusively for the market in the United States. These goods are likely to use low-skilled labor intensively.[28]

The purpose of this paper is to present a theoretical analysis of the impact of the international sector on the market for low-skilled labor when market failure exists in that market. One thing must be noted about the problems inherent in empirical studies of this problem. If an international sector industry declines and lays off workers, one method of studying the effect of the decline is to trace the employment history of those laid off. This is usually referred to as a longitudinal study and it casts light upon the ability of persons to find alternative employment, the amount of search time needed, the change in income, the need to relocate, and the rate of withdrawal from the labor force. Workers laid off from an industry in the international sector, even those with relatively few transferable skills, will, in all likelihood, be able to find a job in another industry. The impact of the decline in the international sector industry is more far-reaching than the problem of adjustment of displaced workers. When a low-skilled worker finds another occupation (presumably in the domestic sector), that worker uses up one of the jobs available to the set of low-skilled workers. Displaced workers have the asset of work discipline as well as some general skills that are inevitably acquired during employment. The main impact of a decline in jobs in the international sector is felt by low-skilled new entrants to the labor force who find one less vacancy for which they can realistically compete. The already unemployed are supplanted.

A Model Derived from Factor Prices

The orthodox theory of international trade is set in an equilibrium framework so that the composition and the direction of trade, the relative costs of goods and the returns to factors of production are all determined simultaneously. The emphasis is on the real causes of comparative advantage and on the direction of trade of individual goods. In practice goods are traded because of differences in money costs and prices and these derive directly from input prices and variations in factor intensities in different goods. Factor prices will reflect factor endowments and opportunity costs if all markets are perfect. Determination of the direction of trade can usefully be traced to the cost functions of individual goods. This will permit direct observation of variation in the level of factor prices on the competitiveness of different goods. This approach will more clearly delineate the problems inherent in market failure in an importing nation and allow some deductions about policy implications to be drawn in the following section.

A good will be imported when its money cost of domestic production exceeds the landed (duty-paid) costs of imports. Similarly a good will be exported if the money cost of domestic production (plus transport costs and tariffs) is less than foreign production costs (computed in some common numéraire). Identifying marginal costs of production as the sum of the money cost of marginal inputs will allow the theory to use factor prices that are determined in perfect markets *or* to use factor prices that reflect varying degrees of market imperfection. In the present context, low-skilled labor can be costed at its going price. Assuming firms are efficient in a domestic context,[29] and utilizing a least-cost input mix, the marginal cost of the ith good can be expressed as the sum of the cost of the needed inputs. Using a four-input cost function, the cost of one unit of the ith good in country A, $(C_i{}^A)$ is:

$$C_i{}^A = a_{ik} \cdot p_k{}^A + a_{in} \cdot p_n{}^A + a_{ih} \cdot p_h{}^A + a_{il} \cdot p_l{}^A$$

where the a_{ij} are the technical coefficients showing how many units of the jth factor are needed to produce one unit of the ith good. The per-unit prices of capital (k), natural resources (n), human capital (h), and low-skilled labor (l), are given to the firm. Production functions are assumed to be the same in all nations in order to keep the argument simple. If need be, a fifth factor of production (proprietary knowledge or technology) can be added explicitly.[30] Factor prices include any fringe benefits or taxes levied on a firm (such as FICA and state unemployment taxes in the United States). The a_{ij} are the inverse of the marginal physical products. With a least-cost combination of inputs, each factor will be utilized until the ratio of marginal physical products to factor price is equal for all factors of production used.

Foreign costs can be set down in the same way except that an exchange rate (r) between foreign and domestic currencies must be added to allow a direct comparison of the money costs in the two countries. Foreign firms face different factor prices and will, therefore, have a different factor mix in each good. The a_{ij}'s will not be the same in the two nations and those in country B are primed to distinguish them. In a two-country model the foreign industry must represent the internationally efficient producer nation in the rest of the world—transport costs and preferential tariffs excepted. What determines the direction of trade of the ith good is the difference between the money costs of production.[31] This difference is shown in the following equation.

$$C_i^A - C_i^B \cdot r = (a_{ik} \cdot P_k^A - a_{ik}' \cdot P_k^B \cdot r) + (a_{in} \cdot P_n^A - a_{in}' \cdot P_n)$$

$$+ (a_{ih} \cdot P_h^A - a_{ih}' \cdot P_h^B \cdot r) + (a_{i1} \cdot P_1^A - a_{i1}' \cdot P_1^B \cdot r)$$

To the extent that factor prices represent opportunity costs or real costs (that is except when market failure exists), the more a factor is in demand in other industries, the higher its price will be. Trade patterns are determined by the differences in input costs weighted by the intensity of use of the factor (the a_{ij}). The international competitiveness of a single good depends upon three things: the relative prices of the individual factors used in the good in the two countries, the intensity of use of the different factors used in the good in the two countries, and the degree to which one factor can be substituted for another. Provided that diminishing marginal rates of substitution exist in all dimensions of the production function which allow substitution, a change in the relative weights can never completely offset international differences in the cost of factors. Thus, the question of export or import for a particular good depends directly upon factor intensities and on the output mix that determines factor prices when factors are in inelastic or given supply.

If a particular factor is more costly in country A, then any good using that factor with greater than average intensity is likely to be imported. Using the first and last terms of the right-hand side of the second equation only, the simple two-factor model is re-created. But if the particular factor is a generally applicable factor (such as labor or human or physical capital), there can be no assurance that a good which uses an expensive generic factor relatively intensively will be imported. The contributions to cost of generic factors can be overwhelmed by differences in the costs of industry-specific factors of production. Manufactured goods tend to be produced with generally applicable factors of production and proprietary knowledge. The direction of trade of manufactures is likely to reflect the relative intensities and relative costs of factors of production.[32] A good which uses a high-priced input intensively will be imported because the nation will have a comparative disadvantage in that good. The greater the disparity in the cost of the factor not offset by differences in productivity (or factor intensity), the greater is the comparative disadvantage of the country in that good. This applies irrespective of the existence of market failure. If market failure exists and the relatively costly factor is not able to adjust its price, any good which uses that factor intensively is more likely to be imported. In context, any good in which low-skilled labor is used intensively will be imported. Domestic production, if it exists, will be acutely vulnerable to reductions in the degree of protection or to changes in the terms of trade between the United States and supplier nations. Any increase in imports of such goods will, under conditions of market failure, generate equivalent increases in unemployment for a substantial period of time.

The return to a factor of production is specified in local currency and the real rate of return is determined by the local prices of goods on which the money return is spent. Given complete international purchasing power parity, there will be no difference between relative money and relative real returns in different countries. However, when the factor is low-skilled labor, there is good reason to assume that purchasing power parity does not exist. The difference lies in the cost of nontradeable or domestic goods in the two countries as well as in differences in the "market basket" of the low-skilled workers. If low-skilled workers in foreign countries spend a great deal of their incomes on domestic goods which are cheap relative to goods consumed in the home country, the real income of low-skilled workers abroad could exceed that of domestic workers despite the higher money incomes of the latter. Usher[33] shows that comparisons of money incomes at the prevailing rate of exchange vastly exaggerate the real incomes of workers in rich countries relative to those in poor countries.[34] The distinction applies particularly to those at the lower end of the income scale. The wage or cost of low-skilled labor in a developing nation can be significantly less (when measured in an international numéraire) than that required for a comparable standard of living in a rich or developed nation. When adjusted for social norms, the difference will be even more stark.

It is quite possible that wages in the United States merely reflect differences in living costs. For poor workers this is especially likely to be true. Payroll taxes are regressive and the cost of food is high because of price supports given to agriculture (only partially offset by food stamps for those on welfare and probably not offset for the actual or potential working poor). Sheer subsistence may require a money wage-rate for low-skilled labor in the United States significantly in excess of that required in poor countries. Goods using low-skilled labor intensively will be imported (unless protected) and the inferences of orthodox theory are supported by the factor-price model derived here. Any reduction in protection or other disturbance that increases the vulnerability of import substitute industries to foreign competition is likely to increase the excess supply of low-skilled labor that must be absorbed by the domestic goods sector. Manufacturing industries are particularly vulnerable because of their highly elastic supply schedules and their reliance upon generally applicable factors.[35]

Options in Commercial Policy

When market failure exists and excess supply of a factor is aggravated by international trade, there is an argument for protection of the vulnerable industries. The decision as to whether to institute protection of some sort is not independent of the means by which that protection would be achieved and of the domestic repercussions of such policies.

Any policy which seeks to protect an industry from foreign competition must enable domestic firms to cover their costs of production. This requires limiting the admission of imports (a quota) so that a part of the domestic market is immune to foreign competition, raising the price of imports sold in the country (a tariff), or reducing the cost of inputs to domestic firms by some kind of subsidy. The apparent option of inaction avoids interference by tolerating the excess supply of labor at the cost of the transfer payments and nonpecuniary social costs needed to keep the disemployed at a level of subsistence compatible with the conscience of the nation.

A tariff or a quota will raise the price of the good in question and will have inflationary effects. To the extent that real-wage resistance exists, any such inflation could have multiplicative effects.[36] If the domestic costs of the tariff or quota are deemed less than the social costs of unemployment (both monetary and human), a tariff may be an acceptable policy option.[37] But a subsidy of costs to domestic producers has several advantages. First, the subsidy could be applied directly to the use of the factor in excess supply.[38] In the present context, the use of low-skilled labor by a firm could be rewarded by payment of a flat subsidy per unit of low-skilled labor used. It would not, of course, be necessary or even desirable to subsidize low-skilled labor inputs to the point that $p_1{}^A = p_1{}^B \cdot r$ since the wealth of cooperating factors in the richer country would give low-skilled labor higher productivity. Nor would it necessarily be desirable to subsidize low-skilled labor in all industries in the international sector. Import-substitute industries which use relatively small amounts of low-skilled labor would not be subsidized.

Only those industries in which the payment of a subsidy would have a marked effect would warrant having the subsidy paid to them. Such a requirement might be that the value added by low-skilled labor should equal some predetermined proportion of total value added. An analysis of the industries excluded from those for which generalized preferences were granted could also provide the necessary benchmark.

The inflationary effect of a subsidy would be negligible and the subsidy may even contribute to a lower price level. This will provide less cause for resistance to the policy by consumer groups. Another advantage of the subsidy is that it is likely to lead to less severe distortions of the world trading pattern although this is an argument in "second best" and therefore not substantiable.[39] A disadvantage of a subsidy is that it might lead to a greater than desirable expansion of protected industries and will bring about a transfer of low-skilled workers from the domestic sector to the international sector. Such an outcome seems unlikely.[40]

The subsidy (or the tariff) should not be seen as a temporary phenomenon: the protection will be needed for as long as market failure constitutes a serious problem. The causes of market failure are intractable social conditions and are not likely to disappear quickly even if the federal government instigates steps to improve the skill levels of the work force. The U.S. government has not been able to effect significant improvements in this area. It is possible that the actual disbursing of the subsidy might prove to be a catalyst in improving this kind of program but such a reaction is improbable. In any consideration of programs of this kind, it is important to distinguish between giving already displaced workers new skills to replace the industry-specific skills lost when their industry declined and providing workers with greater skills. A requirement for the retraining of displaced workers has been included in the Trade Reform Act of 1974. Such arrangements will attempt merely to replace one industry-specific skill with another of approximately equal difficulty. These arrangements will not increase the human capital in the labor force, they would merely prevent its reduction. As such, they will not increase the number of jobs available to low-skilled workers, they will merely train the displaced worker to supplant one of the pool of low-skilled employed. If market failure exists, what is needed is job creation and this involves either increasing the demand for low-skilled workers or raising the skill levels of the unemployed.[41]

The argument for protection of the import-substitute industries in the event of failure in a factor market is quite different from the protection authorized under Article XIX of the GATT. This is the so-called "escape clause" whereby industries that have become noncompetitive may receive temporary protection. The concept here is of an industry that has become domestically inefficient through the use of outworn managerial techniques or worn, outdated capital goods. The country has a comparative advantage if its industry can achieve domestic efficiency and protection is warranted to afford the industry time to achieve that minimum-cost position. Even under Article XIX there is a good argument for a subsidy rather than a tariff. The key difference between the need for protection in the case of market failure and the escape-clause argument is the potential duration of the need for protection. Industries are not being protected for their own sake under the market-failure argument, only for the derived demand for low-skilled labor that they produce.

The factor-cost approach provides a strong argument for the preferability of a subsidy over a tariff and, at the same time, indicates that present U.S. policies toward the textile and shoe industries, at least, are inappropriate if market failure exists. When an industry is afforded protection through a tariff or a quota, firms in the industry have every incentive to achieve as much domestic efficiency as they can.[42] The tariff allows the firms in the industry to achieve some return over costs. The less the costs, the greater will be the net profit achieved. To the extent that it is low-skilled labor that is excessively overpriced in international terms relative to its marginal productivity, there will be every incentive for firms in protected industries to substitute other factors of production for low-skilled labor. A reduction in foreign competitive pressure brought about by protection will encourage the use of labor-saving capital goods. This will tend to offset the gains in the demand for low-skilled labor that derive from the imposition of the tariff. The problem has been further compounded by recent federal policies. Investment tax credits reduce the cost of capital and tend to lead to even greater substitution of capital for (low-skilled) labor in both the international and domestic sectors of the economy. Increases in payroll tax rates also favor the substitution of capital for labor in both sectors. These measures suggest that the domestic sector will be even less likely to absorb low-skilled workers displaced from the international sector. Under conditions of market failure, the mechanism used must directly relate the form of protection chosen to the specific reason for the protection.

Any system of subsidy will require safeguards to prevent abuse of the program. It is possible that workers could attempt to increase their wage rates by the amount of the subsidy through aggressive bargaining. Such action would prevent the desired expansion of jobs for the low skilled. This problem could be prevented by linking the payment of the subsidy to the number of person-hours worked for a firm by workers earning within some specified percentage of the minimum wage or less than some absolute amount. The workers would receive wages in the usual way and the employer would be reimbursed. Returns would be audited in the same way as corporate tax returns.

None of the foregoing allows for any additional total costs of adjustment that may be incurred as a result of the diminution of the speed of adjustment by the cushioning impact of a subsidy. Certainly, the adjustment process may last longer because of the subsidy but that does not necessarily entail higher social cost since the shorter adjustment period may well be accompanied by deeper reductions in resource utilization. But the point is that existing measures (subsidized loans and orderly marketing arrangements) have equal if not greater costs. It is arguable that overt recognition of the problem of the employment of low-skilled labor could lead to greater realism in overall economic policy and greater emphasis being placed on mechanisms that promote the mobility of low-skilled labor both geographically and among different industries.

International Complications

In the jargon of commercial policy, a subsidy to a factor of production amounts to a nontariff barrier. As such it is recognized as being conceptually equivalent to a tariff and its introduction would constitute a measure of commercial policy that is subject to retaliation by trading partners. Given that the main brunt of the protection is directed against imports from developing nations, the introduction of the subsidy would affect mainly members of UNCTAD. The subsidy would directly reduce the foreign exchange earnings of the developing nations. Such a measure is clearly undesirable on economic, moral, and political grounds. For the right to subsidize import-competing industries, the importing nation will pay compensation equal in principle to the net value of foreign exchange lost by the frustrated exporter. Compensation is paid for a refusal on the part of developed nations to allow the free market to work in an unhindered fashion because of their own internal problems and rigidities. Compensation is defined as "payment for economic harm experienced by a nation whether or not the paying nation is the cause of the harm or merely an actor in a system which inflicts harm because of its inherent, essentially development-retarding character." Compensation will be different from foreign aid in the sense that it is not charity. Moreover, compensation will be predetermined by formula and not annually subjected to the budgetary caprices of legislatures. Exact measurement of the foreign-exchange lost by frustrated exporters is not feasible and therefore a rule of thumb would have to be adopted. This would probably specify compensation in terms of some percentage of the value added by the protected industry. As domestic labor market improvements allow, the protection and therefore the compensation would be reduced. The amount of compensation paid will vary from nation to nation according to the degree to which each nation chooses to protect its own unskilled labor. The format can also be applied to such thorny problems as protecting domestic agriculture against imports of tropical agricultural products.

A second international consideration relates to the introduction of predetermined rates of reduction of protective devices following an international agreement. Any reduction in protection would be likely, according to the theory presented here, to exacerbate the problem of the excess supply of low-skilled workers. Whatever chance a displaced worker has of finding a job in the domestic economy in a period of prosperity is greatly reduced during a period of recession. There is, then, a strong argument to be made in favor of interrupting any agreed-to reduction in protection when the level of unemployment in the tariff-reducing nation exceeds some predetermined norm. The historical records of the individual nations' employment rates would be used to define the norm. This procedure is advisable under ordinary assumptions but becomes even more desirable if market failure exists.

Conclusion

The paper has asserted that market failure exists in the market for low-skilled labor so that low-skilled labor is in excess supply and will remain so for a protracted period of time. This problem is aggravated to the extent that external phenomena, natural developments, or trade agreements lead to increased imports of goods using large amounts of low-skilled labor. While this effect can be discerned from traditional theory, its causes and implications stand out more strongly when the factor-price model of international trade is developed. This model allows the market-failure price of the factor to be inserted for the competitive solution (a wage rate of w rather than s in terms of Figure 13.1). The clear implication of the factor-price model is that a subsidy of the factor in excess supply is the most efficient means of countering the market failure and of reestablishing high rates of employment of low-skilled workers. In addition, the paper shows that normal protective devices used in the United States to shield vulnerable industries are not appropriate to the problem of market failure. The institution of protection, whether through a tariff or subsidy, has serious implications for the well-being of our allies and trading partners. Any damage done to the economies of frustrated exporting nations can be offset by the payment of "compensation." There are obvious difficulties in computing the appropriate amount of compensation to be paid and there is some danger that the compensation would tend to be deducted from the normal foreign aid request contained in the annual budget. But the impact of international trade on the demand for low-skilled labor in developed nations may slow the rate of approach to perfectly free trade and is likely to require a departure from simple laissez-faire.

Notes

1. He would subscribe to the views expressed on trade in the Communique issued after the June 23-24 OECD Ministerial Conference, 1977; Carlos D. Diaz-Alejandro, "International Markets for the LDCs—The Old and the New," *American Economic Association Papers and Proceedings* 68 (May 1978):264-69.

2. This section summarizes H. Peter Gray, "The New International Economic Order: A Constructive Alternative," mimeographed (1978).

3. Except as a means of slowing the speed of reallocation of factors in adjusting to changes in foreign supply; see H. Peter Gray, "Senile Industry Protection: A Proposal," *Southern Economic Journal* 39 (1973):569-74; Geoffrey E. Wood, "Senile Industry Protection: Comment," *Southern Economic Journal* 41 (1975):535-37; and H. Peter Gray, "Senile Industry Protection: Reply," *Southern Economic Journal* 41 (1975):538-41.

4. It is useful to distinguish here among definitions of unemployment. Modern theory distinguishes among equilibrium or search-employment, involuntary unemployment because of a shortage of aggregate demand, and voluntary unemployment where the worker chooses to remain unemployed because, for example, the wage is less than the welfare payment. This definition of voluntary unemployment, however appropriate to analyses of labor markets is not appropriate to analyses of national policy. National policy must also take into account the cost of welfare payments (pecuniary and social) so that national employment policy must be concerned with minimizing the number of people supported by welfare payments with given coverage and rates, and therefore with maximizing employment opportunities.

5. George E. Johnson, "Structural Unemployment Consequences of Job Creation Policies," in *Creating Jobs*, ed. John L. Palmer (Washington, D.C.: The Brookings Institution, 1978), p. 125.

6. Glen Cain, "The Challenge of Segmented Labor Market Theories to Orthodox Theory: A Survey," *Journal of Economic Literature* 14 (December 1976):1939-41.

7. Walter E. Williams, "Youth and Minority Unemployment," *Committee Print* (Washington D.C.: Joint Economic Committee, 1977).

8. Jacob Mincer, "Unemployment Effects of Minimum Wages," *Journal of Political Economy* 84, part 2 (August 1976):104.

9. D. B. Kessing, "Labor Skills and the Structure of Trade in Manufacturing," in *The Open Economy*, eds. Peter B. Kenen and Roger Lawrence (New York: Columbia University Press, 1968), pp. 3-18.

10. Robert G. Hawkins, "Jobs, Skills and U.S. Multinationals," in *Hearings* (Washington, D.C.: U.S. Congress, House of Representatives, Committee on International Relations, Subcommittee on International Economic Policy, U.S. Government Printing Office, 1976).

11. Mincer, "Unemployment Effects."

12. See note 4 above.

13. Mincer, "Unemployment Effects," p. 104.

14. F. M. Bator, "The Anatomy of Market Failure," *Quarterly Journal of Economics* 72 (1958):351-79.

15. "Work discipline" is used here as a catch-all for social, cultural, and psychological problems afflicting some workers. For a summary of the literature on this problem, see Cain, "Challenge Segmented Labor," pp. 1222-23.

16. It is assumed that the increase in the supply of low-skilled workers is disproportionately large. For a review of this problem see Sharon P. Smith, "The Changing Composition of the Labor Force," Federal Reserve Bank of New York *Quarterly Review* (Winter 1976):24-30.

17. G. Ranis and J. C. Fei, "A Theory of Economic Development," *American Economic Review* 51, no. 5 (1961):533-65.

18. Milton Friedman, "The Role of Monetary Policy," *American Economic Review* 58, no. 1 (1968):1-17.

19. Tobin cites market imperfections, stochastic variability in conditions, costs of gathering information, and costs of search and mobility. He does not analyze the possibility of a protracted excess supply of low-skilled labor. James Tobin, *The New Economics One Decade Older* (Princeton: Princeton University Press, 1972), pp. 93-96.

20. The pure labor content is still considered homogeneous. The quantity of human capital is determined in part by any difference between the present and historic mix of output because of the acquisition of industry-specific skills.

21. See note 15 above.

22. Keesing, "Labor Skills," pp. 3-18.

23. Michael C. Aho and James A. Orr, "International Trade's Impact on U.S. Workers: Demographic and Occupational Characteristics of Workers in Trade-Sensitive Industries," mimeographed, International Labor Affairs Bureau (Washington, D.C.: U.S. Department of Commerce, 25 January 1979).

24. Say from N to $[N-2(N-n)]$.

25. Note that the growth-enhancing effects of the elimination of inefficient industries do not apply when some of the released factors are not utilized in the economy.

26. Gray, "Senile Industry: Proposal," pp. 569-74.

27. Peter F. Drucker, "The Rise of Production Sharing," *The Wall Street Journal*, 15 March 1977.

28. Note that there is the added problem that the workers disemployed from the international sector must be employed by the domestic sector; this reemployment is made more difficult when labor-saving technology supplanting low-skilled workers is the more usual form of innovation.

29. There is a tendency to stigmatize firms as "inefficient" when a firm is competing (unsuccessfully) with import competition from a country which has a comparative cost advantage. When discussing the real world it is useful to distinguish between "domestic efficiency" and "international efficiency." The latter refers to a firm that can compete in the world markets and will nearly always apply to a firm in a nation with a comparative advantage in the good being produced. "Domestic efficiency" exists when a firm is minimizing costs of production given the set of factor prices which it faces. If an industry is under severe pressure from import competition, surviving firms in that industry are almost necessarily domestically efficient if their capital goods are up-to-date. Interestingly enough, a firm that is internationally efficient will also be domestically efficient only if there is an effective degree of competition in its own country.

30. For a model of international trade of this kind, see H. Peter Gray, *A Generalized Theory of International Trade* (London: Macmillan Press, 1976), chapter 5.

31. There is always the possibility that marginal costs will be equal in both countries. This comparison should therefore be made using the value of r that balances trade or payments, the value of factor prices that would exist in a world of free trade and the quantity of output of the ith good that would be required in both nations if international trade in i were blocked by a pair of prohibitive tariffs.

32. This is particularly true for the United States when runaway plants are created by MNCs to transfer proprietary knowledge whenever that will reduce total costs. This is at the root of production sharing.

33. Dan Usher, "The Transportation Bias in Comparisons of National Income," *Economica* 30 (1963):140-58, idem, "The Thai National Income at U.K. Prices," *Bulletin of the Oxford Institute of Economics and Statistics* 25 (1963):199-214.

34. As an example of the difference the following excerpt is invaluable: "The conventional comparisons show that *per capita* national income of the United Kingdom is about fourteen times that of Thailand. Recomputations by the author to allow for various biases in the comparison suggest that the effective ratio of living standards is about three to one." Usher, "Transportation Bias," p. 140.

35. While manufactures do use proprietary know-how, for most manufactures these inputs are cost-reducing rather than absolutely essential so that generally applicable factors can be used to make the same goods even if the firm or nation has no proprietary know-how.

36. Real-wage resistance exists when union bargaining stances become more

than usually aggressive when inflation has brought about a decrease in real wage rates.

37. International repercussions are considered in the following section.

38. See Daniel S. Hamermesh, "Subsidies for Jobs in the Private Sector," in *Creating Jobs*, ed. John L. Palmer (Washington, D.C.: The Brookings Institution, 1978), pp. 87-114 for an analysis of the effect of subsidies on employment levels. In Hammermesh's terms, payment of a subsidy to low-skilled labor would be a categorical subsidy, and payment to low-skilled labor in particular industries would be doubly categorical. Note that Hammermesh's analysis considers the effectiveness of subsidies independently of any induced change in product mix.

39. Jagdish Bhagwati and V. K. S. Ramaswami, "Domestic Distortions, Tariffs and the Theory of the Optimum Subsidy," *Journal of Political Economy* 71 (1963):48-50.

40. This problem is analyzed in Gray, "Senile Industry: Proposal," pp. 569-74.

41. Note that the history of nonsuccess should make increases in demand for low-skilled workers the more effective policy.

42. See note 29 above.

Commentary

Sidney Golt

I approach proposals of the kind made in Professor Gray's paper from the experience of an administrator, not as an economist, so I cannot even attempt to consider the economic infrastructure but will confine myself to the general analysis and policy judgments. The whole argument of the paper rests very heavily on what Professor Gray has frankly put forward as an assumption. This is that the "market for low-skilled labor does not clear itself automatically, and that there exists a long-lasting excess supply of low-skilled labor at the going wage" (a phrase which in itself conceals a whole Fort Knox full of assumptions). Consequently— this time an assertion, not an assumption—"any displacement of low-skilled workers from the international goods sector will generate a net addition to the pool of unemployed." As he himself implies, the strands of evidence for both the assumption and the assertion do seem to be stretched pretty thin. However, I would not, for my part, wish to question the general propositions—which indeed have emerged in some of the other papers—that in industrially advanced countries (1) it is the least skilled workers who are most susceptible to unemployment, and (2) the tendency for this to be the case is aggravated (if indeed it is not caused) by a legislated minimum wage. Neither of those propositions seems to me at all a cause for surprise. Indeed one might perhaps define an industrially advanced society as one in which, increasingly, the demand for labor (outside and perhaps even inside the field of personal service, at any rate) moves up the scale of skills. What I do not understand is how a market is supposed to operate if an arbitrary price is inserted to prevent it from doing so. On this section of the paper I therefore have a number of questions. The passages which cause me trouble are, first, the two sentences that I have already referred to, and then the passage which reads:

> Minimum wage legislation could bring about unemployment of low-skilled workers when the marginal product of that labor is less than the stipulated minimum wage. However, the fact that minimum wage legislation exists is not a necessary cause of market failure since that circumstance could occur when the marginal revenue product of low-skilled labor was less than subsistence. [In either case,] the fact that market failure exists in an institutional setting that includes a minimum wage does not condone the market failure. If society, through its elected representatives, deems minimum wage legislation to be socially desirable, it should not at the same time neglect any repercussions of that legislation. Market failure attributable to minimum wage legislation requires elimination in a rich nation equally as much as market failure due to a subsistence floor to money wages. The poor unfortunates who are rendered unemployed by market failure are not to be neglected. This is particularly true if those who will be penalized by the minimum wage legislation are new entrants to the labor force, and those who are displaced from tradeable goods industries industries by foreign competition (pp. 364-365).

It seems to me that the substance of almost every one of those sentences, and the logical connection between them, are extremely tenuous. First, what is meant by the proposition about not "condoning" the market failure—apparently an ethical judgment? Does the whole sentence mean anything more than to say that something which is priced too highly for the buyer to afford will not be bought? If it does mean more than that, are there any limits to the proposition? What impediments do you have to put in the way of market operation before it is permissible to suggest that it may be the impediments and not the market which is to be blamed for the failure? Nor do I see that if there are "poor unfortunates," who are not to be neglected, that the proposition applies with more force either to the young or to people who are displaced by imports rather than to those displaced by any other event. And certainly the elected representatives of society, if they choose to pass legislation, must not neglect the repercussions of the legislation they have passed. But the implication of that is not necessarily that anything then has to be done about the price system of the goods or protection of the manufacturers concerned; this is, as I understand it, the purpose of social security legislation and unemployment pay. On the face of it, if "market failure attributable to minimum wage legislation requires elimination," the logic seems to require elimination of the legislation. But that clearly is not what's intended here.

I turn now to the later section of the paper—the policy prescriptions, with the suggestions about subsidies (of two kinds). Professor Gray begins this analysis by saying: "The apparent option of inaction avoids interference by tolerating the excess supply of labor at the cost of transfer payments and nonpecuniary social costs needed to keep the disemployed at a level of subsistence compatible with the conscience of the nation" (p. 376). That seems to be a perfectly viable option, not only an apparent one. But having stated it, Professor Gray has not gone on to discuss it at all. The tariff or quota option is, at this stage, equally summarily dismissed, on the grounds that tariffs or quotas will raise the price of the goods in question and will have an inflationary effect. Later in the paper, there is a distinctly novel and sophisticated argument on this subject. This is that tariffs or quotas would provide an incentive to firms to become more efficient; and since this runs counter to the objective of employing more low-skilled labor, it becomes anathema. One might call this Gray's Law of the Social Value of Diminishing Efficiency. So we are brought to the proposal for a payroll subsidy, specifically related to low-skilled labor. The proposition is, as he puts it, that, "The use of low-skilled labor by a firm could be rewarded by payment of a flat subsidy per unit of low-skilled labor used" (p. 376). Some of the problems of implementing such a scheme are touched on in the paper; Professor Gray recognizes that it would not be an easy one to devise. But again the paper does slide over this ice rather lightly. The only definition or qualification suggested is that "low-skilled labor should equal some predetermined proportion of total value added" (p. 377). I have had some acquaintance with the problems of administering very much simpler payroll subsidy schemes than this in the United Kingdom, and I am bound to say that the problems which arise in any such operation are very, very substantial indeed. You have to define the classes of employees covered, the activities covered, the problems arising in the firms and establishments which are engaged partly in activities which are covered and partly in those that are not, the whole range of equity problems in the treatment of competing firms, and of different individuals in the same firm (some of whom may and some of whom may not be involved in the scheme)—a really immensely complex piece of administration.

Undeterred, and with the merit of honesty, the paper makes it explicit that the proposition is not put forward as a temporary measure to give breathing space for adaptation or adjustment; on the contrary, it will be needed "for as long as market failure constitutes a serious problem" (p. 377). But, as will be recalled, the hypothesis of the paper is that this is a permanent condition, and that there is a continuing and presumably self-generating reserve of new entrants into the pool. If there is not already, the subsidy will ensure that there is in the future. So the scheme is, clearly, to be a permanent feature of the structure of industry.

In its closing passage, the paper takes up the question of the countries whose exports are kept out by the protection provided. It would be wicked, Professor Gray says, to deprive the developing countries of what would have been earned by these exports. The remedy is a simple one. The government of the protecting country will pay compensation—not, of course, to the firms and workers in the countries who would have produced and sold the goods, but to the governments of the countries concerned, to make up for the loss of foreign exchange. I am, indeed, very much in favor of improving the balance of payments position of developing countries; but not, I think, in this way. The amount involved is to be given, not as "charity" but under some "contractual" arrangement—presumably as part of a nontrade agreement. It would be fascinating indeed to sit at the table in Geneva at the negotiations about what might have been the respective nonshares of frustrated exporting countries in the nonexistent market, and how much foreign exchange each of them has failed to earn. And is this to set a precedent for similar contractual compensation for all other forms of protection?

I conclude by noting how astonishingly aptly Professor Gray's proposals bring out nearly all the points which have been made in many of the papers of the conference: adjustment resistance in extreme form; the destructive logical conclusion of the welfare/efficiency dilemma; the recourse to direct intervention to deal with symptoms; the belief in the competence of governments to cure mischiefs which, at least in part, are the consequence of their own actions; and finally, the establishment of open-ended financial commitments in a way which will create their own perpetuation.

I am tempted, and I would very much like to believe, that Professor Gray has put forward this paper with the specific dead-pan, tongue-in-cheek intention of illustrating the difficulties and contradictions which governments are led to by the pursuit of this kind of policy. Two things persuade me against this hypothesis. The first is that if he had, he would surely have given his compensation scheme for the nonexporting countries another turn of the screw, and made the compensation payments tied to purchases of U.S. goods and services. The second is the sheer horrible plausibility of the proposals in the trend of what is already happening in some countries. I am quite fearful that if the Hudson Institute publishes this volume of our conference papers before the next British general election, the main outcome of our deliberations might be the eager espousal of a scheme like this by the U.K. government, and its absorption into the OECD exercise on positive adjustment policy, before we know where we are.

In a 1973 paper, a member of the present U.S. administration, Dr. Richard Cooper, then of Yale, wrote: "Liberal trade may hurt less-skilled labor in the short run. The long run answer to this problem, of course, is to upgrade further the education and skills of American labor, and to move unskilled labor into non-tradable services where wages will be pulled up by the growth of the economy."[1] Professor Gray himself has, in fact, seen this truth, but put it aside as too difficult to achieve. No doubt, if his assumptions are correct, it would be a very long haul indeed; but it does seem to offer the only positive answer, and the only viable one in the long term. For my part, speaking as a non-American with a considerable sense of privilege at having been able to participate in this American occasion, I cannot believe it to be beyond the capacity of the United States to achieve.

Note

1. Richard N. Cooper, "The Economic Assumptions of the Case for Liberal Trade," in *Toward a New World Trade Policy* ed. C. S. Bergstrum (Lexington: Lexington Books, 1975).

Commentary

James H. Cassing

Professor Gray gives us an interesting theoretical paper on an important topic. In the spirit of this conference, the paper is concerned not only with projecting the future industrial structural composition of the OECD countries but also with addressing implications of the dynamic adjustment process itself. In particular, the paper suggests that private and social optimal adjustment paths diverge in response to altered trade patterns and that direct policy intervention is therefore appropriate. The source of this divergence resides in some downward rigidity in the wage rate—especially, a minimum legal wage—which effectively concentrates unemployment in the low-skilled segment of the work force. Since the rising imports of OECD countries use low-skilled labor relatively intensively, the pool of unemployed low-skilled job searchers is bound to grow. The paper recommends on "second-best" grounds some protection of the vulnerable industries.

Although the conclusions may be suspect, two general aspects of the analysis deserve praise. First, Gray emphasizes that the *indirect* effects of an industry's decline can be substantial. For example, workers displaced in the international sector will undoubtedly find employment in another industry. This temporary job dislocation is part of the direct effect of an industry's decline and the focus of many longitudinal studies of "worker adjustment costs." But with a minimum legal wage the main impact of the import-competing sector's release of labor to the economy falls upon low-skilled new labor force entrants who now find less vacancies in covered sectors for which they can compete. Structural adjustment necessarily occurs economy-wide and a policymaker must be wary of being led astray by various partial equilibrium studies and conclusions.

Second, Gray reminds us that structural change is a dynamic process which requires dynamic models of adjustment for theoretical research. A policymaker must know in what way the private and social optimum adjustment paths diverge. But empirical investigations for guidance require theoretical structures and, unfortunately, the choice-theoretic underpinnngs of disequilibrium factor market adjustment are not developed. Gray's rather impressionistic discussion of frictions in the human capital market serves to highlight the need for more research in this important area.

Despite these insights, however, the paper probably goes too far in recommending a subsidy-cum-compensation scheme for impacted domestic industries and exporting nations. Surely a better policy response to the increasing unemployment among low-skilled workers entails a looser minimum legal wage or direct (lump-sum) income maintenance. A subsidy to labor in a declining industry discourages efficient accumulation of both nonhuman and human capital. Also, the determination of which industries qualify for the subsidy and which nations qualify for compensation, based on *potential* exports, must be costly, political, and only roughly accurate at best.

But perhaps the "market failure" is only illusory in the first place. Gray recognizes but seems not to appreciate the existence and extent of a sector not covered by minimum-wage laws. This sector always exists for many reasons. Some important industries are not legally bound to the federal minimum wage. Anyway, many covered firms may illegally ignore the floor or, more commonly, trade a higher money wage off against lower non-wage payments such as quality of the working environment. In any case, self-employment as in the household sector is never covered by a legal minimum wage.

A job searcher's choice, then, is between certain employment at a lower wage in the uncovered sector or a probabilistic chance at higher wage employment in the covered sector. Labor market equilibrium obtains when the uncovered sector wage equals the probability of finding a minimum wage job times the covered sector wage rate plus the probability of not finding a higher wage job times the replacement wage (e.g., unemployment insurance). The relevant probability depends upon turnover rates and job search patterns in the covered sector. Naturally there exists "unemployment." But there is no market failure in any meaningful sense.

Increased low-skilled intensive imports will, as Gray says, increase measured unemployment. There are no efficiency grounds, however, for retarding the flow of labor into the market. Of course, if society is not happy with the income maintenance implied by higher unemployment, the appropriate policy is to lower the minimum wage. A wage subsidy to import-competing firms only very indirectly mops up some of the minimum legal wage which is the unemployment's source in the first place. Compensation to impacted exporters abroad makes a country pay the wage subsidy twice.

Nonetheless, Gray's paper is provocative and focuses our attention on dynamic structural adjustment problems. He is certainly correct to caution us that a competitive world—even with static efficiency properties—may not be dynamically efficient during the transition from one "steady-state" to another.

14

Alternatives to Protectionism

James H. Cassing

Introduction

Economic conditions within and between nations depend upon a myriad of continually changing factors: population growth rates, taste patterns, technology, capital accumulation, resource base, and more. But this continual change alters society's opportunity set and presents a challenge. The ability of society to maintain and improve its living standard depends crucially upon its ability to readily exploit new opportunities as they appear. And this ability, from an economist's perspective, turns upon the facility with which productive resources may be reallocated from lower return to higher return occupations.

In this same sense, international trade presents such a challenge. On the one hand, the opportunity to trade along lines of international comparative advantage offers a source of growth and prosperity. The relatively more efficient industries of each nation can expand while the relatively less efficient industries contract. Real national income of every country rises as nations trade that which they produce comparatively most efficiently for that which they produce comparatively least efficiently. The exponential growth in technical progress, the divergence in population growth rates between developed and developing countries, and the emergence of developing nations as more important trading partners suggest that international trade and increasing national specialization in certain industries will continue as a source of potential real income gains. Surely any policy against the attendant continual structural adjustment to the national advantage is a policy for economic stagnation.

On the other hand, however, adjustment in the industrial composi-

The author acknowledges the helpful comments of Jack Ochs, Norman Miller, Andrew Blair, and the graduate students in the International Economics Workshop at the University of Pittsburgh.

tion is not costless in two senses. First, there is a cost associated with collecting information on where returns to a particular resource are highest and with physically moving the resource from one location or endeavor to another. These are explicit costs of resource reallocation. Second, almost any economic change—no matter how large the net national gain—imposes a pure capital loss on some individuals. The unanticipated opportunity to import cheaply, for example, is on balance a boon. Nonetheless, a loss is imposed on productive factors specific to the import-competing industries wherein capital values—including human capital values—are written down.

Some vocal opposition to changing comparative advantage therefore might well be expected. Recently this reluctance to adjust has been partially validated through the commercial policies of some OECD countries. As a result, the spectre of increasing levels of industrial "protection"—that is, "protectionism"—has arisen. In 1977, the secretariat of the GATT estimated that 3 to 5 percent of world trade was being adversely affected by import restriction policies of industrially advanced countries.[1] And the array of protectionist's tools is growing.

This paper is an inquiry into the ability of industrial democracies to defuse protectionism at the policy level. The paper proceeds as follows. First, we discuss the concept of "optimal adjustment" and the nature of obstacles (resistance) to efficient adjustment. In particular, we identify the natural allies for protection and discuss the failure of market institutions to defuse protectionism. Second, we generally propose *desiderata* of a policy tool intended to reduce protectionist pressure and to facilitate efficient structural adjustment. Finally, we use this criteria to evaluate explicitly a range of suggested options for improving the adjustment capability of industrial countries without permanently increasing the level of protection. Our focus is international trade-related change. In principle, however, the issue is one of mobilizing efficient domestic factor reallocation in response to any change—no matter how induced—in the economic environment.

The Optimal Adjustment Path and
Obstacles of Efficient Adjustment—
Why Policy Intervention?

When terms of trade change, productivity gains may be secured with a proper reallocation of the domestic resource base. Over time, the relatively favored (higher-return) industries should expand and absorb resources from the relatively unfavored (lower-return) industries which must contract and release resources. The speed at which this process unfolds depends upon the atomistic decision making of resource owners who respond to newly structured incentives. Optimally the factor reallocation would proceed at a pace which maximizes the discounted present value of real national income. (Note that this does not ordinarily entail maximizing real national income at each point in time.) Since national income is just the sum of individuals' incomes, we would expect individual-income-maximizing behavior to ensure that the optimal rate of resource redeployment obtains. Two types of considerations, however, might qualify this argument and mitigate a noninterventionist policy. These qualifications are market distortions and political considerations. Below, we dismiss market distortions as grounds for policy intervention and focus upon the economics of special interest politics.

Market Distortions

When terms of trade change, the economy's incentive structure is revised. Individuals weigh new costs and benefits and act appropriately. In particular, productive factors leave (are forced out of) lower-return industries and are enticed into higher-return industries. Adjustment will proceed optimally and real national income will be maximized so long as there is no divergence between private and social costs or benefits. But what if private and social incentives do diverge as in the presence of monopoly or monopsony power. Can we still rest assured that free market incentives direct resource adjustment in the right direction as comparative advantage shifts?

The answer is, on balance, yes. While it is theoretically possible that certain market distortions may disrupt the *static* efficiency of free trade, the appropriate static remedies are well-aimed particular taxes or subsidies. Anyway, the static inefficiencies are not widespread. Over time, the optimal *dynamic* policy is one of barrier-free trade which itself works against the static inefficiencies to increase market size, promote competition, and stimulate innovation. Considerable empirical evidence supports this view.

This explains why the bulk of disinterested economists favor free trade as a policy which promotes economic efficiency.[2] Any government receptive to protectionist arguments in the name of market efficiency is missing the mark.[3]

Political Considerations

A more serious obstacle to efficient structural adjustment concerns the nature of policy intervention itself. Even if markets are efficient when allowed to operate, the political process may prevent their full operation. This might occur for two reasons which appear somewhat similar but are conceptually very different.

First, citizens might collectively have a preference for "equity" and opt for nonneutral schemes to prevent the market mechanism working undo hardship on some subset of society. For example, the removal of a solitary import tax is well known to carry widespread benefit and limited, but concentrated, hardship. In order to ensure that everyone shares fairly in the benefits of freer trade, some income redistribution (compensation) is mandated. If there are no effective income redistribution policies, then society might prefer an import tax to free trade. The source of any inefficient adjustment is presumably a bad choice of redistribution schemes—for example, tariff protection. In general, if society desires to socialize the risk of market vagaries and chooses to proceed even if there does not exist a neutral insurance scheme, then there really is no inefficiency in any meaningful sense. Optimization is properly over real national income and if society's preference function contains equity as an argument, then national income and real national income diverge in the absence of a costless, neutral compensation mechanism. Pleas for economic justice generally can rally considerable public sentiment and cannot be ignored.

Second, a subset of factor owners might devise and seek to enact Pareto-inefficient schemes to resist certain factor adjustments attendant to a shift in comparative advantage. This is straightforward protectionism and is the focus of this paper. The incentive for such schemes is clear and eloquently put by Wicksteed in 1910:

> every man who lives by supplying any want, dreads anything which tends either to dry up that want or to supply it more easily and abundantly. It is to his interest that scarcity should reign in the very thing which it is his function to make abundant, and that abundance should reign everywhere else. . . . The desire for relative scarcity in his own skill, or his own commodity, is, therefore, only too natural and intelligible in any man. It is the desire for the conditions that will secure to him what every one desires. Only these conditions must, by their nature, tend to exclude others from the privileges they secure to him.[4]

There is certainly incentive to increase or, at least, to protect both human and nonhuman capital values and perhaps to avoid adjustment or relocation costs. But, on balance, policies which prevent domestic price changes consistent with true comparative advantage will lower real national income. This suggests two lines of investigation. In order to understand who would support such a Pareto-inefficient resource allocation, we first need to identify the net losers from import competition and the extent of their losses. Then, in order to assess genuine alternatives to protectionism, we need to explain how vested interests can secure and maintain policies which underwrite a suboptimal distribution of resources.

Natural Allies for Protection. In general, four groups are adversely affected by a decline in an industry's real trading terms and might be expected to support protection. First, some owners of truly mobile factors—e.g., unskilled labor—might incur a real wage loss to the extent that imports embody relatively much of this input. This group should only weakly support protection, however. The consumption gains and increased returns to acquiring specific job skills in expanding sectors are likely to more than offset this group's loss. Also, these factor owners gain if imports use this factor relatively less intensively. The immediate concern of this group involves the temporary income loss, job search, and training costs of industry and place relocation. Mobile factors are receptive to traditional unemployment insurance and adjustment assistance programs.[5]

Second, some individuals own factors which are specific to the particular industry—e.g., specific plant and equipment or job skills. To the extent that these factors become less valued but cannot migrate to higher return sectors, this group absorbs a pure capital loss. For marginal firms and facilities, the discounted present value will fall below zero and "shut-down" will be an optimal response. Similarly, marginal owners of specific human capital must completely write off the value of training or skills acquired over time. This marginal group must also find new employment and thus absorbs a capital loss *and* adjustment costs.

For inframarginal firms and facilities, the capital values are simply written down and the owners absorb a loss of pure Ricardian rent.[6] Inframarginal owners of specific job skills similarly must write down capital values. Paradoxically, the inframarginal firms, which need not adjust, lose more rent and are likely to mount a more intense lobby for protection than the marginal factors which must actually adjust. Since Magee finds American labor and capital to be quite sector specific, we might expect this "nonadjusting" group to be both large and vocal.[7] Furthermore, even relatively mobile labor may share in the rents of specific capital through a collective-bargaining agreement. Consequently, the mobile factor may also have an interest in preserving an inframarginal firm's capital value.

Some casual evidence suggests the extent of the inframarginal factors' ambitions to preserve capital values. For example, empirical studies typically find that growth factors would eliminate unemployment problems caused by tariff reductions in most import-sensitive industries.[8] Nonetheless, leaders in these industries remain vocal opponents of tariff cuts. Also, if only physical adjustment is the primary concern of firms and labor, then industries with higher supply elasticities should be more vigorous opponents of tariff cuts. In fact, in most countries, it is the lower supply elasticity industries—agriculture and certain mineral products—that enjoy more effective protection than do the higher supply elasticity industries such as manufacturing. (Of course, different income elasticities of demand might explain this.) To the extent that union bargaining provides a mechanism for sharing in capital's rents, more unionized sectors should be more protectionist and, other things equal, enjoy higher tariff walls. This appears to be the case. The rank correlation coefficient between labor union participation rates and effective protection rates by industry is +0.64.[9]

Third, to the extent that impacted firms or facilities represent a substantial portion of certain local economies, communities in general oppose adverse terms of trade changes. This is particularly true of local land and homeowners whose assets are entirely place specific. Similarly, local merchants may justifiably fear a decline in regional income.

Finally, if the industry is largely unionized, then in the absence of protection union leadership may see its constituency contract. To the extent that the leaders maximize membership, unions may support protection. (Unions may also support protection on income grounds alone, of course.)

There is motivation for these four groups to oppose the restructured market incentives which must accompany structural change. To the extent that changing patterns of comparative advantage can inflict adjustment costs and capital loss, there is ample opportunity to protect values through commercial policy. But such protection is Pareto inefficient. That is, simply accepting terms of trade shifts and adjusting to exploit true comparative advantage increases real national income. The gains accrue to consumers, productive factors specific to the favored industries, and relatively mobile factors. In principle, the gains from adjusting to comparative advantage shifts can many times offset the losses inflicted on a few.

But since protection is Pareto inefficient, a natural question arises: How can protectionism persist if by unanimous agreement an alternative resource allocation dominates? In other words, why have market institutions not arisen which will effect compensating transfers in order to secure Pareto-efficient resource allocation?

At the heart of the answer is the source of protectionism. And, it is impossible to evaluate alternatives to protectionism without the answer. After all, if the market fails here, can we expect policy intervention to successfully compensate?

A significant source of factor owners' resistance to adjustment resides in the apparent failure of "insurance" markets to operate. In a world of fluctuating prices, individuals may avoid risk or capital loss through portfolio diversification and preserve capital values by diversifying their ownership portfolios. If a landowner, for example, would rather not bear the entire risk of owning land, then he may sell some portion of the land and acquire ownership of an asset for which the price moves countercyclically with land prices. In general, the existence of stock (equity) markets allows owners of nonhuman wealth to spread the risk of capital loss through portfolio diversification. Many firms even spread risk internally by diversifying product lines. The principal asset of most individuals, however, resides in their human labor potential and in the skills acquired over time. But diversification or divestiture in human capital across humans is not legal. And, for an individual, diversification of skills is not practical. Consequently, the burden of structural change is apt to fall more heavily on a group that really has little opportunity to spread risk. It may therefore be entirely fitting that government policy socialize the risk of human capital loss even at the expense of opportunity. To some extent, the same argument applies to trade-impacted communities as a whole. Policy intervention, however, is justifiable only if private insurance markets have indeed failed *and* if government policy can succeed where private actions cannot.

Private programs to spread the trade-related risk of capital loss may fail for reasons other than legal constraints regarding human capital. Private insurance companies may themselves be unable to spread the risk of a general depression during which they would go bankrupt. Hence, private enterprise does not sell "income insurance." Also, sufficient actuarial data are difficult to collect. Furthermore, the "moral hazard" involved in underwriting a worker's or firm's income stream might be significant.

In sum, structural change, although net beneficial, inflicts adjustment costs and capital losses for which market institutions do not compensate. The incentive for protection remains. Next, we suggest how this incentive for a suboptimal resource allocation is translated into policy.

Securing Protection. There are three links in securing protection. Schematically, they are shown in Figure 14.1.[10] Alternatives to protectionism must break this chain of causality.

The first link involves individuals assessing their net gains or losses incurred upon enactment of some policy measure. This entails one's perception of his stake in a complicated general equilibrium system. Presumably the individual is somewhat myopic and reacts to such things as magnitude, proximity, and certainty of the impact. Thus, for example, individuals widely oppose a blanket closing of all tax

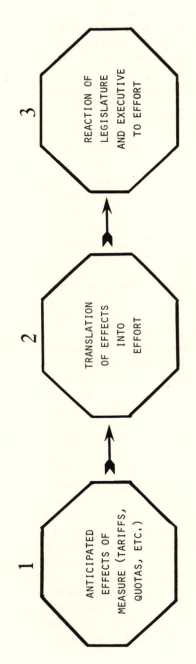

FIGURE 14.1
Three Links in Securing Protection

"loopholes" including their own even though they might be net beneficiaries from such a policy. Obvious and certain effects dominate.

The second link in the protectionist chain entails translating perceived effects into effort. Roughly, this involves the formation of pressure groups for and against a policy. The cohesion of and effort expended by a group depends upon the cost of coalition formation and of transmitting a signal. Probably the group is more cohesive and vocal as the effect is more concentrated in terms of numbers of people impacted and geography. Thus, in tariff matters, producer coalitions are more vocal than consumer coalitions. (This is the mechanism emphasized by Downs.)[11]

The final link depends upon the legislature's reaction to its constituency—that is, the political process. This process, in turn, entails a complicated institution of bargaining, log-rolling, and so forth. Where protection is concerned, greater consideration is given to the proximate causes and effects of alleged market disruption.

Apparently protectionism may be defused at any of these three levels. At level three, protectionist pressure could fall on the deaf ears of statesmen more mindful of the widespread gain of undistorted trading than the real but relatively insignificant plight of a few. But this seems unlikely once we consider the political process. Initially, economic power confers political power. But, a shift in comparative advantage and the erosion of economic power implies not that political power will be relinquished but that it will be used to preserve the initial power base. Can a legislator ignore so broad a group as "labor" if it takes a protectionist stand?

At level two, more intense effort by those on balance harmed due to protection might counterbalance the few beneficiaries. This group consists largely of consumers and exporters. But consumer coalitions are notoriously unstable. And, the production gains from exploiting comparative advantage are frequently difficult to calculate, seemingly distant, and fall largely upon unrepresented future generations. The smaller good of protection, to paraphrase Bastiat, concentrates on one point and is visible to the naked eye; the greater evils it inflicts are spread over masses and visible only to the eye of the mind.

It is therefore entirely appropriate that alternatives to protectionism work at level one and that they obviously and certainly ameliorate the losses incurred as a result of the market's unfettered operation. That is, it must be made more attractive to adjust than not to adjust. Economic theory and many empirical studies ensure us that in principle any losses incurred in lieu of protection may be more than offset by the resulting gains.[12] The task, of course, lies in designing the mechanism whereby relative unanimity for structural adjustment and against protection is secured.

It should be clearly understood that compensation to "adjusting" factors alone will not eliminate protectionist pressure. This is because some of the "adjustment" to a terms-of-trade change involves diminution of pure Ricardian rents. Inframarginal firms write down capital values but never need to physically adjust. To the extent that labor possesses industry-specific skills or shares in firms' rents through a union contract, human capital values are likewise written down. Thus, for industries with a great deal of specific capital, the extension of generous trade adjustment assistance to "adjusting" factors means little and cannot be expected to relieve protectionist pressure.

We should furthermore emphasize that we are now in a "second best" world of sorts. Philosophically, one may or may not agree with a policy which ameliorates market-induced losses connected with international competition and ever-changing comparative advantage. The alternative to a compensation policy, however, is *not* "free trade": it is protectionism. The objective becomes not unconstrained maximization of real national income, but rather enactment of a coherent adjustment policy for which the real cost is less than that of protectionism (no adjustment) through international commercial policy.

In the next section we suggest the *desiderata* of a policy instrument which facilitates adjustment. We are then in a position to critically assess options for improving the adjustment capabilities of industrial countries.

Desiderata of an Adjustment
Policy Instrument

A policy to enhance the adjustment capability of an economy combines some subset of available policy instruments. The policy should aim at motivating acceptance of efficient structural change and compensating for market failure. But which instruments are appropriate? In this section we suggest the standard of a good policy instrument. In particular we identify four reasonable requirements and then use these as a framework for evaluating specific options.

1. *Adjustment.* An appropriate policy instrument should encourage factor reallocation in the right direction over a finite time horizon. Ideally, society's optimal time-path for structural adjustment would obtain. That is, free trade is dynamically efficient. In the presence of strong protectionist pressure, however, explicit policy intervention may be appropriate. In particular, the policy must undermine resistance to adjustment by ameliorating the perceived capital losses, risks, and

adjustment costs imposed upon factor owners and communities.

A bit of a dilemma arises here. Above all, an adjustment policy must be clear, certain, and expeditious. A flexible, obviously negotiable policy forestalls efficient adjustment as import-competing producers appeal to more protectionist measures and divert energy into seeking political influence and away from adjusting to reality. Indeed, the deadweight loss from lobbying may itself be substantial. Kravis cites this as the most important single lesson of the relatively painless liberalization of European trade in the 1950s.[13] Yet, it is difficult to design inflexible, blanket adjustment tools since different industries and firms adjust over different time paths. A policy appropriate to one firm may be inappropriate to another.[14]

Since protectionism is rooted in the perceived losses of four distinct groups, an array of policy tools may be required to break down resistance to structural change. Mobile factors are receptive to policies which defray the cost of job search and relocation—e.g., unemployment preserve capital values—e.g., direct subsidies, reequipment aid, and retraining assistance. Sufficiently high severance pay appeals to workers of both groups. Communities' interests lie in policies that preserve property and local business values—e.g., assistance in attracting new firms. Finally, union leaders may desire policies which preserve union membership.

2. *Efficiency.* The policy instrument should be efficient in two senses. First, among instruments which impart equivalent impact, the appropriate choice is the least real cost instrument. This entails, among other things, that the tool be suitably monitored, enforced, and administered. Second, the overall adjustment-enhancing policy should spread the burdens of adjustment—in particular, the costs of migration—so that all factors' marginal costs of relocating are equal. Roughly, not only should labor move to new firms, but new firms should move to impacted communities.

3. *Focus.* Recent literature in policy modeling emphasizes the importance of a narrowly focused instrument. The policy mechanism should achieve desired goals with minimal side effects. In the present case, these side effects are both national and international. It does little good to defuse protectionism at home if the enacted policy fosters protection abroad. As the Tokyo Round makes clear, a suitable international agreement concerning industry subsidies and regional develoment policies is needed. Similarly, a policy which ameliorates losses of trade-impacted individuals at the expense of imposing great loss on another group of individuals is not acceptable.

4. *Viability.* The policy mechanism must be politically palatable. This suggests that the policy must both appeal to the electorate—

perhaps achieving some norm of equity—and effectively defuse protectionist pressure. It is at least on this score that a noninterventionist policy fails.

Nonintervention and Export Restraint Agreements

By way of illustration, it is useful to assess briefly two options popularly offered as alternatives to protectionism: nonintervention and bilateral export restraint agreements.

The efficacy of noninterventionist policy lies in the coincidence of the private and social optimal adjustment paths. Since economic theory is wanting for a choice theoretical model of disequilibrium factor market adjustment, it is fair to say that the social optimality of private adjustment decisions is somewhat an article of faith. Nonetheless, the nonintervention policy undoubtedly restructures the economy in the right direction within a finite time if allowed to proceed.

But here is its failing. The costs of adjustment fall heavily and obviously on contracting sectors and this, in turn, brings the viability of the policy into question. Some factor owners may have not been able to insure against this loss and so may be quite vocal. The politics of protectionism coupled with a constituency's concern for "fairness" make reluctance to adjust politically difficult to resist. Political power, once accumulated, is used to resist change.

This reluctance to adjust will undoubtedly increase with demographic and macroeconomic changes in the OECD countries. When an economy's labor force growth rate is high, structural adjustment can be effected through attrition in contracting sectors and new entrants in expanding sectors. Few individuals actually change jobs or locations as the economy adjusts to new opportunities. As labor force growth rates decline, however, structural adjustment entails individuals actually moving geographically or occupationally and writing down the capital values of skills acquired over time. Western Europe's labor force has been growing very slowly since the early 1960s. Demographic trends indicate that the United States and Japan will soon experience similar declines. Hence, contraction in some sectors—e.g., unskilled-labor-intensive industries—is inevitable. Recently, sluggish economic growth rates and high inflation rates worldwide have compounded the resistance to adjustment. The potential force of this reluctance to adjust is evidenced by recent government aid in some industrial countries to industries such as shipbuilding, textiles, and steel. Nonintervention is apparently not a real choice.

Increasingly governments have abandoned nonintervention and appealed to bilaterally negotiated export restraint agreements as an alternative to blanket protection. For example, the United States limits the growth of nonrubber footwear exports from the Republic of China and the Republic of Korea. There are similar arrangements in other industries. Euphemistically called "voluntary," such agreements are typically negotiated in response to a domestic industry's "deteriorating market share" or increased "import penetration." Far from being an alternative to protectionism, such an agreement offers an example of a policy that incorporates virtually none of the *desiderata* of a good adjustment policy. Nonetheless, many of the "safeguard" mechanisms proposed involve elements of such quotas and a brief review of the deficiencies is warranted.

Foremost, export restraint agreements are intended to prevent, not to encourage, optimal adjustment. If enacted, they freeze factors in less productive sectors. From an efficiency standpoint, the ratio of imports to domestic production or consumption is meaningless. Furthermore, the actual enactment and implementation is always uncertain and unclear. By their nature, such agreements emerge from negotiations between industry, domestic government, and foreign governments. Each agreement is a bit different and the terms are often varied even after enactment. Therefore, harm is done even if no export restraint agreement is enacted since firms and workers may nonetheless seek to salvage politically a lost position rather than to adjust. Considerable effort is frequently expended in lobbying for a favorable agreement. Finally, if enacted, export restraint agreements tend to proliferate across industries and across nations.

Even if the preservation of market shares or lower import penetration ratios were a coherent national goal, the export restraining agreements fail the efficiency criteria as a tool to achieve the goal. Generally, direct subsidies to marginal firms dominate quotas as a policy tool for preserving domestic industry size. Quotas entail larger deadweight losses, pure rent bestowed upon inframarginal firms—which accounts for the industry-wide popularity—and an arbitrary distribution over consumers of financing the costs of not adjusting. Furthermore, to the extent that restraint agreements are bilateral, they induce the deadweight inefficiency of trade diversion internationally. (This, of course, is why such agreements tend to multiply. Witness, for example, the U.S. "trigger price" mechanism in steel.)

Finally, the focus of export-restraint agreements is hardly narrow. In order to protect the economic security of one sector, widespread harm is done. Domestically, export industries are adversely impacted, consumers are taxed arbitrarily, and future generations are deprived of higher-paying jobs. Typically, the programs grow and spread.

Internationally, trade diversion may be widespread and some nations—
especially developing ones—are severely impacted. In any case, the
agreements are always ammunition for protectionists both at home
where industries want equal treatment and abroad where retaliation
becomes politically difficult to resist.

Alternatives to Protectionism: An Assessment

Finally, we are in a position to assess various policy options intended
to facilitate structural adjustment and defuse protectionism. In
particular, we shall address various safeguards: adjustment assistance
to workers, firms, and communities; certain measures to ensure
economic security; and encouragement to R&D. We make mention of
antidumping charges and countervailing duties. We should reiterate
our perspective. The extent to which governments should intervene in
the adjustment process for positive economic reasons is probably limited. This depends upon some divergence between the social and private
adjustment response to changing incentives; but this divergence is not
adequately articulated at the theory level. Perhaps there is a case for
socializing risk or reducing factor market congestion. We take the view,
however, that even if markets are efficient, the political process affords
an effective opportunity for some sectors to resist structural change and
maintain a Pareto-inefficient domestic resource allocation. Thus, the
problem has a "second best" flavor—that is, a search for relatively
efficient adjustment policies which are, above all, politically viable
alternatives to protectionism. Our focus is structural change induced by
changing patterns of international comparative advantage. If there are
grounds for intervention, however, there is no reason to tie efficient
policy to international trade issues alone.

Safeguards

"Safeguards" broadly encompass actions which governments might
take to prevent disruption of domestic production in a particular
industry as a result of a rapid rise in imports. Provision for such actions
is made in Article XIX of the GATT wherein the measures are also
required to be temporary. The measures may take various forms.

In the United States, "import relief" may include any combination of:

1. increases in, or imposition of, duties
2. tariff-rate quotas
3. quantitative restrictions
4. orderly marketing agreements; voluntary export restraint agreements

TABLE 14.1
U.S. Actions to Restrict Imports Under Safeguard Provisions of GATT, 1971-77

	1971	1972	1973	1974	1975	1976	1977
Ceramic Tableware	--	1	--	--	--	--	--
Ball Bearings	--	--	1	--	--	--	--
Certain dried milk	--	--	--	--	--	1	--
Stainless and alloy tool steel	--	--	--	--	--	10	--
Footwear	--	--	--	--	--	--	1

Source: General Agreement on Tariffs and Trade Secretariat.

Table 14.1 indicates the extent to which the United States has recently appealed to Article XIX. (Countervailing duties and antidumping duties are considered separately.) All safeguard actions are not reported to the secretariat of the GATT, however.

The safeguard provisions may be enacted in two very different ways. First, and in the spirit of the GATT, the safeguards may be "self-liquidating." That is, the measures terminate on schedule and perhaps provide for gradual diminution of the restrictions and so permit adjustment eventually. For example, in November 1973 Canada imposed a three-month declining surtax on live cattle and fresh beef imports. More recently, however, safeguards have been tied to some measure of market penetration and, if the import penetration persists, then so do the safeguards. This is the spirit of the French concept of "organized free trade." The former genre of safeguards have something to recommend them: the latter have little.

Self-liquidating Safeguards. Presumably the imposition of safeguards requires a prima facie case for import relief. In the United States, the International Trade Commission (ITC) considers relevant such factors as idling of productive facilities, significant unemployment, decline in sales, and import penetration. If enacted, the measures are by law to terminate within five years and to be phased down after not later than three years. The safeguards may be extended at existing levels for not more than three years. Table 14.2 itemizes recent safeguard actions worldwide.

In terms of the *desiderata* of an adjustment-facilitating tool, self-liquidating safeguards have some merit. Factor adjustment obtains and does so in a relatively brief time period. The self-liquidating feature

TABLE 14.2
Actions Taken Under Safeguard Provisions of GATT, 1971-77

Country	Product	Measure[a]	Year Introduced
Australia	Footwear	QR	1974
	Motor vehicles	QR	1975
	Certain apparel items	T	1975
	Sheets and plates of iron and steel	QR	1975
	Ophthalmic frames, sunglasses	QR	1975
	Files and rasps	QR	1976
	Knitted and woven dresses	T	1976
	Electric freezer chests	QR	1976
	Passenger motor vehicles	QR	1977
	Brandy	T and TQ	1977
	Fired resistors	QR	1977
Canada	Strawberries	T	1971
	Men's and boys' shirts, woven or knitted	QR	1971
	Fresh cherries	T	1973
	Live cattle and beef	T	1973
	Cattle, beef, veal	QR	1974
	Worsted spun acrylic yarns	QR	1976
	Work gloves	QR	1976
	Certain textured polyester yarns	T	1976
	Fresh and frozen beef and veal	QR	1976
	Double-knit fabrics	QR	1976
	A range of clothing items	QR	1976
	Certain footwear	QR	1976
EEC	Tomato concentrates	QR	1971
	Timber (Germany only)	QR	1973

	Measure	Year
Magnetophones (Italy only)	QR	1973
Bovine meat and live cattle	QR/E	1974
Peaches	E	1974
Preserved mushrooms	QR	1974
Frozen hake fillets (France only)	E	1975
Tunny (France only)	E	1975
Portable TV sets from Korea	QR	1977
Squids (Italy only)	QR	1977
Finland Women's pantyhose	T	1976
Israel Radio equipment	T	1971
Japan Bovine meat	QR	1974
New Zealand Fabrics	QR	1975
Switzerland Bottled white wines	QR	1975
Bottled red wines	TQ	1976
United States Ceramic tableware	T	1972
Ball bearings	T	1974
Certain dried milk	E	1976
Stainless and alloy tool steel	QR(OMA)	1976
Footwear	BRA	1977

Source: General Agreement on Tariffs and Trade Secretariat.

[a] Letters indicate the following: BRA = bilateral restraint agreement;
E = embargo;
OMA = orderly marketing agreement;
QR = quantitative restriction
T = tariff
TQ = tariff quota

promotes factor adjustment in two senses. First, some adjustment occurs immediately. Labor tends to drift away in anticipation of the safeguard's phaseout. Similarly, plant and equipment are depreciated and investment is diverted to higher return industries. Paradoxically, employment may temporarily expand in the contracting sector as physical plant is depreciated more rapidly.

Second, if the safeguard is clearly posed as temporary, then opposition to necessary structural adjustment may be substantially lessened. The advance notice of pending cutbacks is one way of spreading adjustment costs over all factors and the lead time may substantially reduce individuals' adjustment costs. Marginal plants and equipment can be depreciated optimally. Workers can begin smoothing income and consumption plans. Also, part-time job search can begin. To an extent, market institutions have already incorporated this feature. Workers' preference for advance notice of layoffs is evidenced by particular clauses in many labor contracts. Many industries are not covered by such contracts, however, and no advance notice of a structural change is afforded owners of specific capital.

Also, to the extent that factor markets are characterized by congestion, optimal adjustment requires a policy which retards but does not obviate adjustment. A gradual phasing out of a safeguard allows attrition and prevents congestion. This is particularly important when a specific region or community is especially impacted. Of course, in a high growth economy layoffs are not necessary anyway and so the merit of advanced notice is diminished. For example, with a generalized 50 percent tariff cut in the United States, Baldwin and Lewis estimate that unemployment would result in only twenty-one of fifty-four import-sensitive industries.[15] This, however, may be of little consolation to particular depressed communities or regions.

Unfortunately, the termination date for safeguards has tended to be too negotiable. The uncertainty with respect to policy and the hope for prolonged protection then delay adjustment which might otherwise occur. Also, the mere threat of "escape clause" action creates uncertainties among trading partners and may have significant trade-retarding effects.[16] Finally, what begin as temporary safeguards sometimes proliferate and become permanent. For example, the *Short-Term* Arrangement on Cotton Textiles in 1961 soon became the *Long-Term* Arrangement Regarding International Trade in Cotton Textiles and, in 1973, simply the Arrangement Regarding International Trade in Textiles. The Multifibres Arrangement has now been extended to at least 1981. Thus, what began as a temporary quota on Japanese cotton textile imports into the United States has led to eighteen years of restrictions which have expanded in terms of product coverage and members adhering to the arrangements.

In terms of economic efficiency, traditional safeguards are generally inferior to other policy options. Quotas, tariffs, tariff-rate quotas, and so forth entail the usual deadweight losses and are welfare-dominated by direct subsidies and taxes. Also, traditional safeguards confer pure rent on inframarginal firms and inputs which need not adjust even in the long-run. And, the program's financing falls somewhat arbitrarily upon individuals in proportion to their consumption of the protected commodity.

The focus of most safeguards is not narrow. Domestically, the effects are widespread and impact not only marginal firms but also consumers, export industries, and inframarginal firms in the protected sector. (The latter impact undoubtedly contributes to safeguards' industry-wide popularity). Internationally, the trade barriers—no matter how temporary they are announced to be—harm foreign exporters, create uncertainty, and foster retaliation. The U.S. trigger price mechanism in steel, for example, has strengthened the position of protectionist forces in Japan and the EEC.

Finally, safeguards are indeed politically viable. The self-liquidating aspects, however, are what distinguish safeguards from protection and the real danger is that the safeguards may become permanent protection. Historically, for example, export-restraint agreements have undergone steady expansion in both geographic and product coverage.

Triggered Safeguards. Recently enacted safeguards have incorporated an element of automaticity. Thus, when import penetration ratios rise, certain safeguards are triggered. For example, the U.S. Meat Import Act of 1964 established import quotas which were to go into effect if imports exceeded trigger amounts. In fact, whenever imports have exceeded the key amounts, voluntary restraint agreements have been negotiated. The United States maintained agreements with thirteen meat exporting countries in 1977. The EEC policy of *jumelage* is similar in spirit, as is the U.S. trigger price mechanism to control steel imports. The EEC members are proceeding with a similar "rationalization" of the steel industry's structure and may extend the concept to shipbuilding and synthetic fibers. (This is the so-called Davignon plan.)

These triggered mechanisms clearly prevent beneficial structural adjustment. Depending upon the particular scheme, more or less factor redeployment occurs as the pattern of comparative advantage shifts. The triggered safeguard, however, ensures that complete adjustment never obtains and effectively underwrites suboptimal resource allocation.

Unlike self-liquidating safeguards, there can be no "smoothing the adjustment" defense here. Trigger mechanisms are straightforward policies to preserve particular capital values by preventing net beneficial adjustment. The costs of these mechanisms, as in the case of the steel trigger price system and other orderly marketing arrangements, are likely to be relatively large in terms of both standard deadweight costs and trade diversion. The criticisms of export-restraint agreements cited earlier apply and so we dispense with a prolonged discussion. The point is that these devices are protection and not alternatives.

Adjustment Assistance

A more promising approach to mitigating the isolated adverse consequences of evolving comparative advantage while securing the benefits of freer trade involves direct reallocation assistance to impacted workers, firms, and communities. The rationale for such a policy is principally one of risk socialization. If resource holders—especially, owners of labor skills—have a substantial portion of their wealth tied to a particular resource, then powerful and vocal resistance to structural adjustment can be anticipated. And, to the extent that legal barriers prevent some resource ownership diversification in the first place, such resistance is widely supported as justifiable and equitable. An appropriate policy response therefore is that society assume some portion of the adjustment costs. This may properly be viewed as a "bribe" aimed at breaking down resistance to structural adjustment. It is a "second best" optimal strategy. We consider separately policies directed toward workers, firms, and communities.

Compensation to Workers. Adjustment assistance cannot guarantee a worker his particular job. After all, structural change diverts resources to new uses. Adjustment assistance does, however, aim at insuring a worker an income and a standard of living as good as or better than he had before the structural change. The concentrated cost of economic change is thus borne by society in general and the public is more likely to support liberal trade policies which are net beneficial.

Adjustment assistance aims not at inframarginal (nonadjusting) firms and labor but at marginal firms and dislocated labor. The numbers of workers actually dislocated by increased imports has not been large. The loss of job potential in import-competing industries due to foreign trade has been estimated to be as low as 44,000 per year and as high as 170,000 per year.[17] Even the high estimate is only 0.2 percent of the U.S. labor force and the growth of domestic demand alone had a favorable impact of twice this amount. The average period of unemployment for workers who became involuntarily unemployed because of increased imports was thirty weeks during the 1975-76 recession. Typically it is less. In any case, studies invariably indicate that the adjustment costs to labor from liberalizing trade fall short of the benefits. Magee and Baldwin and Mutti find that the gains range from two to five times the costs of associated unemployment.[18] The same must be true of adjustment to changing patterns of comparative advantage. There is no doubt that the loss to trade-impacted workers can be many times offset by the resulting social gains. Efficiently effecting the compensating transfer can be difficult, however, and market institutions have not responded sufficiently well. Several policy options are open and there is some preliminary evidence concerning adjustment assistance programs. Here we assess both direct payment and retraining programs.

1. *Trade-related income maintenance programs.* Most industrial countries reduce the risk to current income of being temporarily unemployed and thus reduce somewhat resistance to structural change. The programs range from liberal severance pay as in Britain and Sweden to small relocation allowances as in West Germany. Only the United States and Canada link income maintenance to workers specifically affected by increased imports. (Of course, these countries also have comprehensive unemployment insurance.) In the United States, adjustment assistance benefits may range up to 100 percent of the average weekly wage in manufacturing or 70 percent of the worker's weekly wage. Relocation allowances up to $500 are available. The United States experience has been with provisions of the 1962 Trade Expansion Act and the Trade Act of 1974.

Income maintenance probably encourages overall structural adjustment. It clearly moves labor out of lower return sectors for two reasons. First, the supplementary income underwrites job search and so pulls labor out of the lower-return sectors. Second, even if layoffs are associated with a comparative advantage shift, the income maintenance reduces protectionist pressure from dislocated workers and from a general public demanding equity for the unemployed. Less clear is the effect of compensation in facilitating the reabsorption of labor into the higher-return industries. Some studies suggest that unemployment insurance in the United States reduces search intensity and work effort. Neumann, however, finds a beneficial impact of Trade Adjustment Assistance (TAA) on search effort.[19] Still, TAA payments may initially increase flows of new searchers into the labor market and indirectly affect adversely those already unemployed who must now compete for employment with the TAA supplemented searchers.

The effectiveness of TAA depends upon reducing the *perceived* costs of adjustment. Therefore, in order to socialize adjustment costs through income maintenance, the program must be certain, clear, and expeditious. Otherwise, resistance to change will not be broken. Presumably, clearcut standards can be devised. Historically, however, failure on this count has led to the failure of TAA. In the United States, the TAA program of the 1962 Trade Expansion Act was a complete failure. The criteria for worker certification was inflexible and stringent. Furthermore, the time interval between injury and delivery of benefits was too long. (The average was twenty-two months.) The 1974 act was a great improvement. Benefits were increased and the criteria for adjustment assistance liberalized. Still, substantial uncertainty with respect to certification persists and so even relatively mobile labor groups have preferred other "escape clause" remedies. This is true even though TAA benefits must be determined within sixty days whereas escape clause relief may be reviewed for up to six months.

The program is efficient in the sense that compensation is directed only at physically adjusting resource holders and not at inframarginal workers and firms. Yet, in a sense, the focus of the programs has been too narrow. The United States and Canada have enfranchised only directly trade-impacted firms and workers. Clearly, however, much of the adjustment cost is borne by indirectly impacted job searchers and workers in firms which service the contracting sectors. Again, the certification problem arises. In any case, this narrow focus has cost political support. No relief is offered firms and workers indirectly harmed. And, inframarginal firms prefer industry-wide escape-clause relief and thus access to some pure rent. Indeed, Frank cites broader coverage as the difference between the relatively successful Canadian-American Automotive Agreement and the woefully deficient 1962 Trade Expansion Act.

An important policy implication emerges. Generous income maintenance programs will relieve protectionist pressure from "physically adjusting" workers. These programs do not protect capital values of firm-specific factors, however. Since the quantity of factors physically relocating is positively related to the industry supply elasticity, generous TAA programs will probably succeed in industries characterized by higher supply elasticities. This is significant because protection does more allocative harm in these industries. For industries characterized by lower supply elasticities, TAA will not significantly reduce protectionist pressure because few factors actually relocate. In these industries, specific factors' capital values are simply written down. On the one hand, protectionist pressure is harder to break down in these industries. On the other hand, however, the allocative harm of protection is smaller in these sectors. A coherent policy to facilitate adjustment therefore might extend generous TAA benefits and accept as unavoidable protectionist pressure from low supply elasticity industries.

Overall, direct unemployment and relocation compensation can be a success. If the payments are easily obtained, certain, and generous, then protectionist sentiment is effectively dissipated in important sectors. Politically, these programs give the legislature a genuine alternative to protection and secure compliance with the market incentives directing structural change. To date, however, a substantial commitment to a viable program has not been made in the United States.

2. *Manpower and counseling.* As the industrial structure of an economy changes, the pattern of skills demanded also changes. Workers in contracting sectors find that the capital value of their labor skills may be decreased substantially. Statistically, this may show up as structural unemployment. In order to lessen resistance to structural change and to guarantee trade-impacted workers access to new, higher-paying jobs, a government policy of manpower training and job counseling is warranted. Again, the rationale is one of socializing adjustment costs and implicitly allowing workers to diversify their labor skills portfolio. Most countries provide such assistance. In the United States, the important programs have been the Area Redevelopment Act (ARA), the Manpower Development and Training Act (MDTA), and now the Comprehensive Employment and Training Act of 1973 (CETA). The 1974 Trade Act includes some manpower provisions specifically for trade-impacted workers. These programs aim at relieving pressure from both mobile and industry-specific labor.

It is not clear that the programs per se facilitate adjustment, however. At first face, studies have found very high rates of return to MDTA programs—the range is 12.2 percent to 138.0 percent.[20] Some studies indicate that the return to on-the-job training is particularly high which may recommend a program of training subsidies for firms in expanding sectors.

There is, however, an important but unsettled issue concerning these studies. From the standpoint of the economy as a whole, training programs may just rearrange the order in which individuals are hired. In particular, if "trade-related" unemployed workers' training is subsidized, then other unemployed workers may be bumped down in the hiring queue. There is no a priori reason to believe that social and private investment in human capital should diverge.

Yet, as an alternative to protectionism, it is the perceived diminution of trade-related adjustment that is important. Thus, manpower training programs geared to import competition may be attractive "bribes" to potentially displaced workers and may be politically acceptable as an alternative to no adjustment. Since widening wage differentials across industries is apparently unacceptable, retraining programs may be an effective alternative to import-related job dislocations. (Of course, there is also a danger that the public sector may expand disproportionately as with the CETA program.)

3. *Comprehensive programs for economic security.* Besides direct income maintenance related to unemployment, three provisions are repeatedly shown to be important in reducing the resistance to economy-wide adjustment: advance notice, severance pay, and pension vesting. Sweden and Britain, in particular, have made a substantial commitment in these areas.

First, financial and psychological burdens of job displacement are considerably reduced by advanced notice of plant closings, wage freezes, or terminations. In general, whenever necessary adjustment is forthcoming, more information and a longer planning horizon are important and can lower adjustment costs.

In any case, the principle of spreading adjustment costs over all factors mandates that workers as well as firms be privy to plant closing information. To some extent, the market has responded to this preference. In 1973, over one million U.S. workers out of 6.5 million sampled were covered by collective bargaining agreements providing advance notice of plant closure or relocation. And this represented an increase from a 1969 survey.[21] Such provisions could be extended to other sectors.

Second, severance pay may be an important aspect of an adjustment assistance policy. A lump-sum payment conditional upon job displacement smooths the workers' income during job search yet does not distort the adjustment process. Market institutions have responded to this need in a limited way. In 1973, nearly one-half of 6.7 million workers sampled in the United States had severance pay provisions in their collective bargaining agreements. Again, such agreements may spread the perceived risk of necessary adjustment between firms and workers. Also, severance pay benefit levels and advance notice provisions can be used in conjunction to prevent workers in closing plants from drifting off early and disrupting the production process.

Finally, a suitable adjustment assistance policy should provide for pension vesting and funding. A considerable amount of a worker's wealth may consist of pension rights. If structural change involves losing or curtailing these rights, then strong resistance to change is predictable. These rights may be lost if either pension funds cannot be transferred or a failing firm has underfunded the plan. In the United States, the Employee Retirement Income Security Act of 1974 (ERISA) guarantees vesting of at least a portion of employee pension rights. Complete funding, however, is not guaranteed.

In a sense, severance pay and pension vesting are the types of economic security programs that the private market has not made fully available. Several reasons for the failure of private markets to exist here were mentioned earlier. A principal reason that this "income insurance" market does not function well resides in the problem of moral hazard common to most insurance markets. In particular, if workers lose nothing when laid off, then someone might encourage layoffs or even contribute to a firm's failure. So, there is a dilemma. Governments can socialize the insurance of income streams and thereby reduce protectionist pressure. Yet, if governments cannot overcome the moral hazard problem, then new inefficiencies are introduced.

The United Kingdom relies heavily on advance notice provisions and severance pay. Specific provision is made in the Contracts of Employment Act of 1963 and the Redundancy Act of 1965. Advance notice ranges from one to eight weeks. Severance pay ranges from a week's pay to a week and a half's pay for each year of service. The program is financed by mandatory employer contributions. The net effects of these programs are not clear. The British worker is certainly afforded a great deal of economic security. Yet, the overall effect has not been to facilitate rapid economic change. Whether or not the moral hazard issue is the problem is not clear.

Compensation to Firms. Resistance to structural change is often mounted at the firm level. It may, therefore, be necessary to compensate owners of firm-specific resources since these capital values can be lowered due to changing comparative advantage. Also, to the extent that labor's and communities' fates are tied to firms, policies for smoothing adjustment might be administered at the firm level. Assistance to firms may consist of financial (especially tax and loan incentives) and technical aid. In the United States, the Trade Act of 1974 includes such provisions. Table 14.3 itemizes the outlays. Sweden and Britain emphasize adjustment aid to firms.

On any positive economic criteria, compensation to firms is hard to justify. It is difficult to see why the private and social optimal adjustment paths would diverge. There is no reason to expect an analogue of labor market congestion in capital markets. (Of course, as a second best policy to smooth labor adjustment, temporary subsidies to failing firms retain some merit.) And, there can be no argument concerning risk spreading. Owners of capital stock may freely and inexpensively diversify their portfolios through equity markets. There is

TABLE 14.3
Department of Commerce Action on Adjustment Assistance to Firms, December 1969 to April 2, 1975

Item	Petition Approved by Tariff Commission	Eligibility Certified by Commerce	Proposal Submitted and Certified
Industry			
Shoes	11	11	6
Pianos	6	5	2
Textiles	5	5	3
Granite and marble	4	4	0
Consumer electronics	2	2	1
Electronic components	2	2	2
Stainless steel flatware	2	2	1
Glass	2	2	2
Ball bearings	1	1	0
Data processing	1	1	1
Barber chairs	1	1	1
Earthenware	1	0	0
Total	38	36	19
Year			
1969	8	0	0
1970	4	7	2
1971	11	9	4
1972	7	6	5
1973	4	9	4
1974	3	3	4
1975	1	2	0

Source: U.S. Department of Commerce, Office of Trade Adjustment Assistance, "Case Summary" (July 10, 1975; processed).

no case for governments socializing the risk of bankruptcy. Private markets exist and are efficient.

Furthermore, financial assistance geared to a failing firm's operation retards efficient adjustment. Unanticipated changes in the terms of trade inflict capital loss. The value of plant, equipment, inventory, and so forth is written down. No amount of payment will add real net value to existing plant and equipment. (Tariff or quota protection, of course, will restore capital values in the protected sector. This is why protection prevents adjustment.) The firms or marginal facilities for which the discounted present value drops below zero are best retired.

Experience with compensation to firms supports this view. Most private banks are not willing to lend to failing firms. Under the Trade Expansion Act of 1962, arrangements with private lending institutions were hard to make. The few firms in the United States receiving government adjustment assistance have frequently failed anyway.

Direct technical assistance is also difficult to justify on any positive grounds. One argument runs that if a trade-impacted firm can update its technology, then in the long run the firm will again be profitable and so dislocations are minimized. Yet, it is not clear why private decision making would fail here. If updating technology is profitable, then the firm has an incentive to update with or without government assistance. Of course, there is a case for the government disseminating any superior technical information it might have.

The British experience has been a bad one. Through a series of acts, the government has used mergers, reequipment loans, management consulting, and so forth to rationalize contracting industries— shipbuilding and cotton textiles, for example. The approach has not halted the decline of Britain's competitive position in these sectors, although it has fostered some outright protection. In general, a 1975 OECD study suggests that governments have too often used adjustment assistance resources as complicated income-support schemes which have made little contribution to underlying problems of adjustment for ailing industries.[22]

If financial assistance is to be given to firms, then it should probably be directed toward updating skills for workers entering the expanding sectors. The return to on-the-job training might be high and at least this moves resources in the desired direction.

As compensation to gain marginal and inframarginal firms' support of structural change, financial assistance should be in the form of a direct subsidy. This subsidy is the nonhuman capital analogue of severance pay. Such a policy is difficult to support, however. Equity markets provide a mechanism for diversification across firms. If the amount of industry-specific capital is really so great, then temporary operating subsidies could be extended to key sectors. Self-liquidating safeguards would be a second-best alternative. Simultaneously, however, if capital values are artificially preserved, then future investment in this sector must be discouraged. For example, existing investment tax credits to these industries should be withheld. Also, new labor force entrants should be discouraged from acquiring skills specific to the temporarily protected sector.

Compensation to Communities. Adjustment assistance programs in some industrial countries—again, notably Sweden and Britain—have a distinctly regional focus. The justification for community-oriented adjustment assistance is twofold. First, there may be a genuine divergence between the private and social optimum adjustment paths where heavily trade-impacted communities are concerned. A particular firm or industry might be a substantial employer of local citizens. If the firm or industry contracts, the local labor force must absorb the entire cost of adjusting. Furthermore, with the dispersal of the labor force, a certain quality of life—a sense of community—is lost. To some extent, however, the community and workers may have had no opportunity to diversify the portfolio of employers. A risk socialization policy therefore may be appropriate. Second, land values and home values represent a substantial portion of many individuals' wealth positions and the attendant decline in these capital values invariably rallies concentrated political pressure for protection. If political representation is by geographic district and if certain industries are regionally important, then powerful political coalitions will form along industry lines. The "steel communities coalition" in the U.S. legislature provides an example. An adjustment policy aimed at preserving community viability is not only politically palatable, but politically popular as well. A good adjustment policy should encourage expanding sectors to locate in trade impacted areas. To the extent that many OECD countries' comparative advantage lies in "footloose" industries, a policy of regional development is viable.

The U.S. experience with adjustment aid to communities and regions is limited but well documented. The Department of Defense has operated a program of adjustment assistance for communities harmed by military base closings and cutbacks in defense contracts. Between 1967 and 1973, the Office of Economic Adjustment assisted seventy-one communities across the nation. There are also some more specific cases such as the 1963 Studebaker adjustment program in South Bend, Indiana. And, there is experience with some continuing programs in broadly depressed regions such as Appalachia. The 1974 Trade Act contains provisions for community adjustment assistance.

The common successful features of these programs have been assistance in drafting a community plan of action and underwriting loans and grants aimed at attracting industry. Also, assistance in applying for aid from existing government agencies—HUD, Labor, etc.—has been helpful. Following a sharp cutback of defense contracts in Wichita, Kansas, for example, the unemployment rate jumped to 11.6 percent in June 1971. Concentrated government effort at utility improvement for an industrial park and other projects—and the unemployed labor pool itself—attracted industry and by April 1972 the unemployment rate had dropped to 4.7 percent.[23] Similar defense-related rapid structural change and adjustment were experienced in Rockford, Illinois, Sherman, Texas, and Denison, Texas.

Such adjustment assistance administered at the community level may be justified as a way of socializing otherwise unavoidable risk to the community. From an efficiency standpoint, it is reasonable that firms move to labor as well as labor migrate to firms. That is, the cost of factor relocation should be equated at the margin.

As an alternative to protectionism, community-directed assistance for structural change is attractive. It is politically acceptable and focuses community attention on the need to adjust. The emphasis on place permits legislators to protect the population base and economic viability of their areas without protecting the specific industrial composition. Indeed, to the extent that programs like the ARA failed, it was because they were too broadly based.

Encouragement of Research and Development and Industrial Innovation

Productivity changes by industry influence relative costs and prices. This, in turn, affects the international competitiveness of those industries for which foreign trade is important. If productivity increases for a domestic industry are less than for that same industry abroad, then the domestic industry must contract, or at least expand more slowly. If the industry is in the import-competing sector, then import penetration will rise and pressure for domestic protection thus builds. It is consequently sometimes posed as an alternative to protectionism that productivity gains be encouraged at the policy level. But such a policy is not obviously desirable and four unresolved issues emerge.

First, the case for policy intervention is loose. As a best policy, such intervention requires that the time paths of private and social optimum investment in productivity advances diverge. Since private enterprises seek to maximize their individual discounted present values, any divergence must reside in some gain to investment in productivity that the individual firm cannot wholly capture. Of course, it is true that such external benefits are frequently apparent. For example, education and training may not be firm specific; new processes may be accessible to other firms and industries; health services may lower communicable diseases; and high technology might contribute to national defense. Governments may justifiably underwrite such sources of productivity gains. But there is no justification here for concentrating any effort in trade-related sectors and, in particular, import-competing sectors. Any nonredundant assistance in increasing productivity in import-competing sectors, however, will reduce the extent of comparative advantage internationally and so reduce international trade.

Second, even if government policy is directed toward increasing domestic industry's competitiveness in international markets, just how to proceed is not clear. Despite casual statements to the contrary, very little is known about the link between R&D and economic growth and development. Until this link is made clear, specific subsidies for R&D seem ill-advised.[24]

Third, even if government subsidies to encourage R&D and industrial innovation are justified, a policy issue arises: To what extent are such subsidies grounds for countervailing duties? (The same might be asked of manpower training and public education.) Government policy which invokes protectionism abroad is counterproductive. Unfortunately, the Tokyo Round seems to have offered little guidance.

Finally, all other issues aside, it must be remembered that comparative advantage is after all *comparative*. Higher productivity in export sectors will increase exports *and* imports. Productivity changes are a source of structural change. Government policy to defuse protectionism must be wary of working at cross-purposes.

Antidumping Charges and Domestic Response to Foreign Commercial Policy

An important source of protection resides in certain laws intended to underwrite international economic efficiency. To the extent that these laws are abused and used to underwrite suboptimal resource allocation, the laws themselves reflect bad economics and bad legislation. A brief discussion serves to highlight the well-known deficiencies of anti-dumping charges and countervailing duties. In principle, however, these remedies are not protection per se.

Antidumping charges are common to most OECD countries. In theory, dumping signals the possibility of a static market imperfection—discriminating monopoly—and warrants an investigation of efficiency grounds. The correct signal is pricing below average return presently earned in all markets. Since predatory monopoly is uncommon and preclusive dumping is net beneficial, the investigation might be expected to yield little support for protectionists. In any case, penalties should require that competition is being reduced or, at least, domestic injury incurred.

Unfortunately, the United States Antidumping Act is entirely too ambiguous. The investigation is triggered by the pricing of exports below the producer's home market price or a constructed measure of cost. This is the wrong signal of predation. Then, the act directs the ITC to determine whether "an industry in the United States is being or is likely to be injured, or prevented from being established" because of foreign dumping. But the act does not define "injury." Dumping therefore may be prohibited when it is neither anticompetitive nor temporary in duration.

Because of these deficiencies, the act is somewhat of a tool for protectionists. The proper alternative involves rewriting the code. Wares, for example, provides a useful proposal.[25]

Another important source of protection resides in the application of countervailing duties. In the United States, the Treasury determines whether imported products are receiving government subsidies in the country of production. The ITC then determines whether a domestic industry is being or is likely to be injured. If the determination is in the affirmative, a duty equal to the estimated amount of the subsidy is assessed. Other countries have similar procedures.

This is a growing area of confrontation among industrial countries. It is a complex problem and this is not the place to review the issues. Guidelines for the application of countervailing duties must emerge from a multilateral negotiation process. Again, the Tokyo Round has been a disappointment in this respect.

Conclusions

If they have not been able to diversify their ownership portfolio, then some individuals will oppose any change which restructures capital values. Protectionism arises precisely because international trade restructures capital values and some owners of human capital or other resources cannot find an "insurance" market to spread the risk of capital loss. Private markets fail to exist for reasons of legal constraint, data deficiency, and "moral hazard." Thus some factor owners turn to the political process for protection.

Alternatives to protectionism must diffuse protectionist pressure by spreading the risks and gains associated with structural change. This strongly recommends a government policy of generous severance pay and regional development aid. Self-liquidating safeguards are a second-best alternative. Temporary protection, however, artificially underwrites capital values and so must be supplemented with a policy which discourages future investment in human or nonhuman capital in the protected sector.

Still, many questions remain. In the absence of further research, manpower training and encouragement of R&D cannot be recommended. Perhaps more important is the issue of moral hazard surrounding generous severance pay schemes. It is not obvious that government intervention can succeed where private institutions fail.

Notes

1. Press Release No. 1199 (Geneva: General Agreement on Tariffs and Trade, 9 November 1977).

2. This point is made, for example, by Rachel McCulloch, "United States Foreign Trade Policy: Emerging Choices," in *Trade, Inflation and Ethics* (Lexington: Lexington Books, 1976).

3. The possibility of a *dynamic* adjustment distortion is introduced when there is "congestion" in a factor market. For example, Lapan suggests a theoretical model wherein the labor market is subject to congestion in the sense that each job searcher's probability of finding employment is inversely related to the total number of job searchers. But individuals disregard the effect of their presence on other searchers' employment prospects. Optimal adjustment to a terms-of-trade shift therefore necessitates a subsidy to the contracting sector in order to retard the influx into the labor market. Temporary tariff protection is a second-best alternative. See Harvey E. Lapan, "International Trade, Factor Market Distortions, and the Optimal Dynamic Subsidy," *American Economic Review* 66 (June 1976):335-46.

4. P. Wicksteed, *The Common Sense of Political Economy and Selected Papers and Reviews of Economic Theory* (London: G. Routledge, 1933).

5. See, for example, G. Neumann, "The Direct Labor Market Effects of the Trade Adjustment Program: The Evidence from the TAA Survey," in *The Impact of International Trade and Investment on Employment*, Bureau of International Labor Affairs (Washington, D.C.: U.S. Department of Labor, 1978). Note that "unskilled" here entails skills particular to no specific industry.

6. To the extent that rents can be bid away in the long run, owners of industry-specific assets naturally press for increased levels of protection.

7. S. Magee, "Three Simple Tests of the Stolper-Samuelson Theorem," working paper No. 77-28 (Austin: University of Texas, February 1977).

8. See Baldwin and Lewis, "U.S. Tariff Effects on Trade and Employment in Detailed SIC Industries," in *The Impact of International Trade*, Bureau of International Labor Affairs.

9. See Baldwin and Lewis, "U.S. Tariff Effects." Supply elasticity data are available in A. A. Walters, "Production and Cost Functions: An Econometric Survey," *Econometrica* 31 (January/April 1963):1-66; and in J. David Richardson, "Estimating Demand and Supply Parameters Without Important Prices: Methodology and Empirical Results," 1973 Proceedings of the Business and Economics Section of the Allied Social Science Associations.

Labor union participation rates may be found in *Labor Union Membership in 1966*, Bureau of the Census (Washington, D.C.: U.S. Department of Commerce, 1966); and in *Directory of National Unions and Employee Associations*, Bureau of Labor Statistics (Washington, D.C.: U.S. Department of Labor, 1975).

10. A similar "political model" has been tested in J. J. Pincus, "Pressure

Groups and the Pattern of Tariffs," *Journal of Political Economy* 83 (August 1975): 757-78.

11. A. Downs, *An Economic Theory of Democracy* (New York: Harper & Row, 1975).

12. For example, see R. Baldwin and J. Mutti, "Policy Problem in the Adjustment Process (U.S.)," World Bank Seminar on Industrialization and Trade Policies in the 1970s (Washington, D.C.: World Bank, 1972); or Stephen P. Magee, "The Welfare Effects of Restrictions on U.S. Trade," *Brookings Papers on Economic Activity* 3 (1972):645-701.

13. I. Kravis, Hearing before a subcommittee on the Joint Economic Committee, in *Foreign Economic Policy* (Washington, D.C.: Government Printing Office, 1962).

14. Malmgren in particular has made this point in "Trade Policies of the Developed Countries for the Next Decade," in *The New International Economic Order: The North-South Debate* (Cambridge: The MIT Press, 1977). There is a clear need for more research concerning the dynamics of disequilibrium factor market adjustment.

15. Baldwin and Lewis, "U.S. Tariff Effects."

16. J. Bhagwati, "Market Disruption, Export Market Disruption, Compensation, and GATT Reform," in *The New International Economic Order: The North-South Debate* (Cambridge: The MIT Press, 1977), provides an analysis of this effect.

17. The lower estimate is by C. Frank, *Foreign Trade and Domestic Aid* (Washington, D.C.: Brookings Institution, 1977). The higher estimate is by the AFL-CIO, "Needed: A Constructive Foreign Trade Policy," mimeographed (Washington, D.C.: S. H. Ruttenberg and Associates, 1971).

18. R. Baldwin and J. Mutti, "Policy Problem," and S. Magee, "Welfare Effects."

19. G. Neumann, "The Direct Labor Market Effects of the Trade Adjustment Assistance Program: The Evidence from the TAA Survey," in *The Impact of International Trade*, Bureau of International Labor Affairs.

20. See J. Goldstein, *The Effectiveness of Manpower Training Programs: A Review of Research on the Impact on the Poor* (Washington, D.C.: Government Printing Office, 1972).

21. See *Characteristics of Agreements Covering 1,000 Workers or More: July 1, 1973*, Bureau of Labor Statistics (Washington, D.C.: Government Printing Office, 1974).

22. OECD, *Adjustment for Trade: Studies on Industrial Adjustment Problems and Policies*, 1975.

23. These figures are compiled and reported in Frank, C., op. cit.

24. This is noted, for example, in R. Nelson and S. Winter, "In Search of Useful Theory of Innovation," *Research Policy*, January 1977. They state:

The current dialogue regarding policy toward innovation rests on two premises. The first is that technological advance has been a powerful instrument of human progress in the past. The second is that we have the knowledge to guide that instrument toward high priority objectives in the future. The first premise is unquestionable; the second may be presumptuous. While all the attention recently given by politicians to scholars is flattering, we believe that the scholarly community has much less to say about appropriate policy toward innovation than many scholars like to believe. Prevailing theory of innovation has neither the breadth nor the strength to provide much guidance regarding the variables that are plausible to change, or to predict with much confidence the effect of significant changes.

25. Wares, W., *The Theory of Dumping and American Commercial Policy*, Lexington, 1977.

Commentary

Kazuo Nukazawa

The Cassing paper is such a solid evaluation of adjustment assistance that I can only confess my jealousy. Most of my general comments on the Golt paper are relevant here.

Basically, industries hit by imports should be treated the same as those hit by domestic competition. Adjustment assistance should be seen for what it is: a bribe, a vice condoned among consenting adults. For example, U.S. restrictions over textile imports began in late 1950, and have been expanded and extended for two decades. Must we continue to pay for the adjustment yet to take place? I really wonder. Domestic textile producers have been amply forewarned. If they don't read newspapers, they don't deserve to be helped.

There are various types of protectionism. The Cassing paper discusses alternatives to the usual protection against merchandise imports, which is the main stream of protectionism. In addition, the following list groups forms of protectionism according to types of economic activities which are protected:

1. Trade in services has its own protectionism; banking and transportation (air and maritime) are examples.
2. Tied-aid is also a form of protectionism. It distorts the effects of comparative advantage on trade flows.
3. Restraint on the transfer of technology is another form of

protectionism. Industrialized countries have become increasingly wary of technology exports to LDCs, the East bloc, and OPEC members because they fear boomerang effects. Yet, why don't American electronics manufacturers buy technology from Japan and use it to compete with imports from Japan?

4. For similar reasons, labor unions tend to call for restraint of capital exports to protect jobs.
5. International labor mobility is strictly restricted and represents a serious barrier to resource flows among nations. But this probably should not be included as a form of protectionism for our present purposes.

The Cassing paper applies to some of these alternate cases. Other pertinent classifications include those listed below:

When protection involves export or import of goods, options include:

1. Relaxation of anti-trust laws on mergers and joint R&D efforts, and
2. Relaxation of environmental standards.

When protection involves export or import of services,

3. A variety of institution improvements might be pertinent.[1]
4. Regarding overseas investment and technology exports, those directly affected by further liberalization of international trade probably do not need adjustment assistance beyond correction of tax advantages given to these exports.

Protectionism can be classified in several ways. One is a macro-micro differentiation.

1. Excessive devaluation is a form of protectionism. Import surcharges, import deposits, and other devices are also used as a general tool of macro-protectionism to defend domestic industry as a whole.
2. Micro-protectionism involves protection for a specific industry or segments thereof.

Another classification of protection follows:

1. The extension of a breathing period for a graceful exit or mercy death for a declining industry.

2. The imposition of high taxes against imports until an infant industry takes off.

Cassing's analysis applies to the first case, but it may not fit the second.

I believe that the alternative policies presented by Cassing should include middle-term and long-term suggestions in addition to the immediate palliatives he discusses, but I have no disagreement with his discussion. A stratified strategy for coping with protectionism is called for. It should differentiate along the following lines: a perception level (facts and figures), a value level (cultural and priority differences), and an interest level (who benefits?).

The paper suggests that unions tend to be protectionistic forces. It is interesting that unions in one sector favor the liberalization of imports for other sectors. For example, in January 1979, Mr. Miyata, Chairman of the Steelworkers Union in Japan, submitted his views on the new economic plan (1979-85) being formulated by the government. He urged that agricultural imports be liberalized to increase the real income of workers. I would add to Cassing's description of the process of securing protection by pointing out that the process is effective only because inefficient and protection-prone industries tend to employ more workers than other industries and, therefore, represent a larger voting bloc. If an efficient industrial sector gains from free trade and represents a larger voting bloc, the government might not have to "bribe" the inefficient sector.

Concerning export restraint arrangements. When Japan had to restrain its exports to the United States, the Japanese government and business community in general perceived this as a sort of tax paid to keep the U.S. market relatively open. Compared with the imposition of a quota (specific or general) on Japan's exports by the United States, export restraints gave Japanese exporters a degree of maneuverability. Moreover, if the United States legally restricts imports of any item, this tends to perpetuate itself and may spread to other items. If the United States establishes administrative machinery to restrict imports, this creates a constituency to perpetuate the restriction.

The sluggishness of technological innovation and the maldistribution of international liquidity have caused a global gap between supply and demand. This is at the root of worldwide unemployment and protectionism. Fundamentally, the only cure is a global Keynesian policy. Excess international liquidity should be used for long-term productive investments. To accomplish this and to expand worldwide employment, a "Global New Deal" is needed—a combination of the Marshall Plan and the New Deal. Monetary discipline could be compatible with global expansion of employment if, in the long run, international outlays lead to increased harnessing of new resources, such as dams, solar energy, canals, weather control, desert reforestation, and so on, or they are accompanied by technological breakthroughs.

Note

1. See Kazuo Nukazawa, "Japan's Emerging Service Economy and the International Economic Implications" (New York: The Rockefeller Foundation, 1979).

Commentary

Anne O. Krueger

Professor Cassing has very ably summarized the current state of professional thinking about adjustment assistance and analyzed the issues very competently. There is not much point in reiterating what he has said, so instead I want to try to analyze why it is that economists have had such a difficult time formulating useful proposals for adjustment assistance.

The basic difficulty is that economic growth calls for change, and import competition is often symptomatic of the difficulties in adjusting to change. The cry for protection is, therefore, a political reaction to the pressures which lead to adjustment. If I have any disagreement with Professor Cassing, it is that I am not convinced that we understand the reasons why there are cries for protection, as distinct from political pressures to offset the impact of change. A fundamental problem, therefore, is to establish a model where, on the one hand, the pressures leading to protection can be evaluated, and on the other hand, the tradeoffs between the efficiency (and growth) losses emanating from protection or adjustment assistance and the increase in political welfare by reducing pressures on the afflicted groups can be evaluated.

Professor Cassing's paper essentially assumes that demands for protection are based on rational behavior. A fundamental weakness of economists' models is that all political events are assumed to be exogenous, while individuals are assumed to be rationally maximizing and economic behavior explained thereby. Because of our lack of ability to model the economic components of the political process, we do not know what leads to cries for protection. It is quite possible to argue, as I have done in my paper, that much of the protectionist pressure is really misplaced. If so, can adjustment assistance with respect to imports allay that pressure?

The minute economists begin discussing the political process, difficulties arise, as assumptions about what is feasible politically are implicit and never laid forth. What is needed is an explicit framework for modelling political behavior, with some kind of positive model of the political system and a positive model of the economic system. Then one could analyze the rationality and optimality of both systems and their interaction. One could start by sorting out at least two levels of rationality. There would be political rationality at the level at which the individual who was advocating an action would find that his own objective was not met if that action were undertaken. This is an extreme form of irrationality and many government policies may perhaps be characterized in that way. Sidney Golt pointed to some earlier today. When this happens, the politicians deciding upon a measure have a particular set of objectives in mind and the measure achieves the precise opposite.

A first level of rationality might be one where each actor advocated policies which would in fact benefit the group he represented, but where there existed opportunities for a superior bargain for the body politic as a whole. It is this "special interest" politics which appears to be behind much of the present tendency to advocate regulation and political measures covering all aspects of economic activity. It is evident that an alternative political mechanism, perhaps not yet invented, might enable bargains in which individuals could all be better off than when each looked after his narrow self-interest. This would represent a second level of rationality as all actors achieved outcomes superior to that of "special interest" politics. Ironically, in the marketplace economists tend to believe in the "invisible hand," and that each individual acting in his self-interest may nonetheless promote the group interest. And yet, if the first level of rationality is the one in which the political process would suggest the absence of any desirable "invisible hand" mechanism.

The implications of all this for adjustment assistance and for protection are fairly straightforward. There are real questions as to whether advocacy of protection is rational, even in the narrow self-interest of the advocates. However, even if it is, Professor Cassing believes that protection is not rational from the viewpoint of society as a whole and that, in other words, the political process can somehow design a superior solution. This represents something of a difference between us in terms of where we think protectionism originates, but we both agree that there are political alternatives superior to protection in any event.

Until we begin delving into models of the political process, I am not sure that economists can proceed further with analysis of issues such as adjustment assistance. Until we do, I prefer to remain an economist and believe that economists' knowledge can be of some assistance in issues such as protection. Since protectionism is not going to accomplish anything resembling what its advocates expect, our own contribution to the political discussion has to be a demonstration that protectionism often does not make much sense.

Index